THE ORDEAL OF PHILIP YALE DREW

Richard Whittington-Egan was born in Liverpool and has written widely on his native city: *Liverpool Colonnade* (1955), *Liverpool Roundabout* (1957), *Liverpool Soundings* (1969) and *Liverpool: This is My City* (1972). He is co-author, with Geoffrey Smerdon, of *The Quest of the Golden Boy* (1960), the standard biography of the nineties poet and man of letters Richard Le Gallienne. He has an extensive interest in psychical research and, between 1975 and 1985, edited five volumes of *The Weekend Book of Ghosts and Horror*. His other criminological writings include: *A Casebook on Jack the Ripper* (1975), a subject on which he is an acknowledged expert, and *The Riddle of Birdhurst Rise* (1975, Penguin 1988). He co-edited *The Story of Mr. George Edalji* with his lawyer-wife, Molly, and together they wrote *The Bedside Book of Murder* (1988). His forthcoming publications are: a study of the Scottish criminologist William Roughead and his cases; a monograph on the Oscar Slater Murder Mystery; and a literary critical biography of the poet and dramatist Stephen Phillips. The great-grandson of Ireland's Crown pathologist, he originally read medicine and is now a member of the Medico-Legal Society, the Crime Writers' Association and the very respected Our Society – sometimes called the Crimes Club. He is also on the board of directors of *Contemporary Review*.

THE ORDEAL OF PHILIP YALE DREW

*A Real Life Murder
Melodrama in Three Acts*

by
RICHARD WHITTINGTON-EGAN

PENGUIN BOOKS

PENGUIN BOOKS

Published by the Penguin Group
27 Wrights Lane, London w8 5TZ, England
Viking Penguin Inc., 40 West 23rd Street, New York, New York 10010, USA
Penguin Books Australia Ltd, Ringwood, Victoria, Australia
Penguin Books Canada Ltd, 2801 John Street, Markham, Ontario, Canada L3R 1B4
Penguin Books (NZ) Ltd, 182–190 Wairau Road, Auckland 10, New Zealand

Penguin Books Ltd, Registered Offices: Harmondsworth, Middlesex, England

First published by George G. Harrap & Co. 1972
Published in Penguin Books 1989
1 3 5 7 9 10 8 6 4 2

Printed and bound in Great Britain by
Richard Clay Ltd, Bungay, Suffolk

FOR
M. and B.,
"The Four-footed Feller"
Fiat Justitia

"Fate plays tricks with coincidence
that fiction would never dare."

The Monster

PROGRAMME NOTE

THERE must be a reason for producing any play . . . writing any book . . . and it seems to me that a programme note is called for to explain why I have chosen to revive the forty-year-old drama of Philip Yale Drew.

This is a long book. It could have been much longer. Can it justify the detail into which it has gone?

I believe that, for a number of reasons, it can.

In the first place, this is not just the story of a crime—the murder of an obscure little Reading tobacconist.

It is the very terrible story of a human being under stress.

It is the story of how a series of incredible coincidences reduced a celebrated actor to selling newspapers outside those same theatres where once he had stood top of the bill.

It is the unique story of an inquest which, because of the circumstances surrounding it, became historically important, for it aroused widespread dissatisfaction, and caused a public outcry leading to Parliamentary action to restrict the powers of coroners' courts.

It is a study in legal fallibility . . . and human frailty.

In order to do the theme justice it has been necessary to encompass many atmospheres—the richly nostalgic ambience which swaddles the world of the old-time theatre; the sleepy New England villages, and sage and brushwood prairies of the American wild west of the turn of the century; the English country town of the 1920's; the grey London of down-and-outs and doss-houses of the thirties.

So large and varied a tapestry could not, without suffering, be crammed into a narrower frame.

A word now as to the manner in which I have mounted the production. . . .

It seemed appropriate to the subject-matter to choose a theatrical format—with Acts and Scenes instead of parts and chapters, and with Intermissions in which background material could be presented.

Act One tells the story of the crime and the police investigation.

It establishes what manner of man the victim was, gives human depth to the hunter who sought his killer, and introduces the Number One suspect.

In the first intermission we humanize the hunted, Philip Yale Drew, examine his life and background, follow his trail from the day of his birth in 1880 to the very eve of his 'trial' at Reading in 1929.

Act Two reconstructs that trial, presents the Chaucerian tales of the Theatrical Landlady, the Men of Law, the Actor, the Butcher, and two score other witnesses, and places all the official evidence before us. The curtain descends upon a fantastic balcony scene in Reading, the like of which had never taken place at any inquest before or since.

The second intermission explains how that which seemed to be a happy ending was in reality a tragic beginning, for on the day that Philip Yale Drew walked free and unfettered out of that coroner's court his real and personal tragedy began.

Act Three follows Drew through the shadowed remainder of his ordeal—the aftermath, the unique focal-point of the whole story. Here is disintegration, despair, deliverance, and death. A final act in which triumph and tragedy are most curiously yoked.

The objective account completed, the production closes with a subjective codicil.

In 'Curtain-Call' I summon the survivors of the original cast back to the stage, talk with men and women who knew Philip Yale Drew —family, friends, acquaintances—and those who were called to play parts in his tragedy, and put my brief to the audience-become-jury as I argue for a definite posthumous verdict.

RICHARD WHITTINGTON-EGAN

ACKNOWLEDGMENTS

A production of this kind necessarily involves an immense supporting cast of helpers. To them is due a large measure of credit for any success it may achieve. Any defects are mine alone.

Top of the bill are:

Mr Joseph Hatchell Hogarth Gaute, valued friend, publisher and unfailing mentor in all matters criminous.

Mr Jonathan Goodman, who was always at hand to give me the benefit of his wide criminological knowledge and broad theatrical experience.

Mr Angus Hall, who helped me enormously with fieldwork on location in Boston and Marshfield Hills, Massachusetts.

Then there were Philip Yale Drew's family and friends. Had it not been for the very considerable assistance that I have received from them, this book, at least in its present form, would not have been possible. I am, therefore, very happy to express my warmest thanks to Mrs Dorothy Drew Damon; Miss Eleanor Magoon; Miss Gertrude Adams Lynd; the late Harry T. Drew; and to Mr Robert P. Oakman.

In gathering the facts of Drew's life in America, I have incurred debts of gratitude to Mrs William Krusell, of Marshfield Hills; Miss Helen D. Willard, Curator of the Theatre Collection, Harvard College Library, Cambridge, Massachusetts; Mr Paul Myers, Curator of the Theatre Collection, New York Public Library; Mr Edwin G. Sanford, Reference Librarian, Boston Public Library; and Mr Thomas M. McDade, of New York.

Personal friends and acquaintances of Drew's in this country have been at great pains to help me. My sincere gratitude for all that they have done to: Mr Andrew Melville; the late Bernard O'Donnell; Mrs Betty Wigley; the late Henry Oscar; Mrs Minnie Green; Mr Sidney Spring; Mr Ewart Wheeler; Mr Reginald J. Sackville-West; and Mr W. Wilson.

And I am especially grateful to those who were actually involved in the case, and who were good enough to tell me the story in their own words. They are: Mr John Lancelot Martin, Reading Borough

Coroner; Mr John Maurice Harris; Mr Percy Richard Cross-Ellington; Mrs Nellie Taylor; Mr Alfred John Wells; Mr George Charles Jefferies; and Mrs Nancy Fearnley-Whittingstall.

I would also wish to thank:

Mr Barry Duncan; Mr Douglas Blake, of the *Stage* Information Department; Miss Brenda Davies, of the National Film Archive; Mr Gordon Harbord, Mr Raymond Mander and Mr Joe Mitchenson, for their help in elucidating a number of theatrical problems.

Professor Francis Camps and Professor C. Keith Simpson, for guiding me through sundry pathological thickets.

Mr Stanley Pryor, for making available to me a mass of invaluable documentation.

Mr John M. Hall, for placing his specialized knowledge of the history of the Wild West at my disposal.

Mrs Roxana Stinson, for filling in so many gaps concerning the life and times of her grandmother, Mrs Kitty Magnus.

Mr Eric Tyler; Mr Nigel Morland; and Mr Ronald Camp, for many excellent suggestions and much good advice.

My friends Mr Fenton Bresler and Mr Arnold de Montmorency, Barristers-at-Law, for sound counsel.

Mr David Ward, whose long-time friendship and unfailing interest in what I had found out helped me to weather the bleaker phases in the voyage of discovery.

Miss Marie B. Woodman and Mr Basil Donne-Smith, for helping me to secure elusive reference books.

Mr John Carnac, whose artistic contribution has added visual clarity to this book.

Dr H. F. Goldring, who attended Drew in his terminal illness, and provided me with clinical notes.

His Honour Judge H. C. Leon.

Dr John Joyce, of Newbury, Berkshire.

Mr W. J. McGinty, of Louis Tussaud's Waxworks, Blackpool.

Mr R. Binks, The Registrar, West London County Court.

Mr David Drummond, of Pleasures of Past Times.

Mr John Bush, of Victor Gollancz Ltd.

Mrs Eileen Young, of Reading.

And Mrs Beryl M. Tibbs, of Nottingham.

Mr J. A. Robertson, C.B.E., B.L., Chief Constable of Glasgow, was exceedingly kind and helpful. So too were the Hertfordshire Constabulary, St Albans, and the Lancashire Constabulary, Bolton.

Unfortunately, their contrasting conduct does not warrant my extending the same gratitude to the Thames Valley Constabulary.

I want to place on record, too, my appreciation of the trouble that so many people took to write to me in answer to my requests for information. In particular: Mrs J. Amor; Miss Vera M. Chard; Mr W. Hamblin; Mr and Mrs Christopher Hodge—Miss Elsie Arnold; Mr Leslie Hogben; Mr Geoffrey C. Kingham; Mr Herbert S. Lambert; Mr Robert T. Rivington; Mr G. Tomlins; and Mr Jack M. Young, of Reading.

My thanks also to Mr C. A. Webb, of the Bibliographical Research Section of the National Central Library; The Superintendent of the Department of Printed Books, the British Museum; the staff of the British Museum Newspaper Library, Colindale; and the staff of the Map Room of the Royal Geographical Society.

In the old days of the theatre, the bottom of the bill was considered almost as important a position to occupy as the top, and so, bottom of the bill, I want to place the name of the late Edgar Martlew. It is a matter of great sadness to me that he did not live to see the completion of this book, for it was he who was truly responsible for the inception of *The Ordeal of Philip Yale Drew*.

RICHARD WHITTINGTON-EGAN

CONTENTS

ILLUSTRATIONS

DRAMATIS PERSONAE

The principal characters in order of appearance

Alfred Oliver, tobacconist and murder victim.

Annie Elizabeth Oliver, his wife.

Thomas Alfred Burrows, Chief Constable of Reading.

Chief Inspector James Berrett, Scotland Yard officer in charge of the murder hunt.

Detective Sergeant John Harris, his assistant.

John Lancelot Martin, Reading Borough Coroner.

George Charles Jefferies, a dilatory errand-boy.

William George Loxton, butcher for the prosecution.

Alice James, the caretaker who saw.

Philip Yale Drew, actor and murder suspect.

Frank Lindo, actor-manager and staunch supporter.

Marion Lindo, alias Marion Wakeford, his wife. Actress and mother-surrogate.

Mary Eleanor Goodall, the solicitous landlady.

William Arthur Fearnley-Whittingstall, counsel for the defence.

Dorothy Gladys Irene Shepherd—she saw the running man.

Bernard O'Donnell, newspaperman and saviour.

Alfred John Wells, butcher for the defence and eleventh-hour witness.

Dolores, the woman in the case. Model and wife-surrogate.

Albert Magnus, friend in need.

Kitty Clover, his wife. Friend in deed.

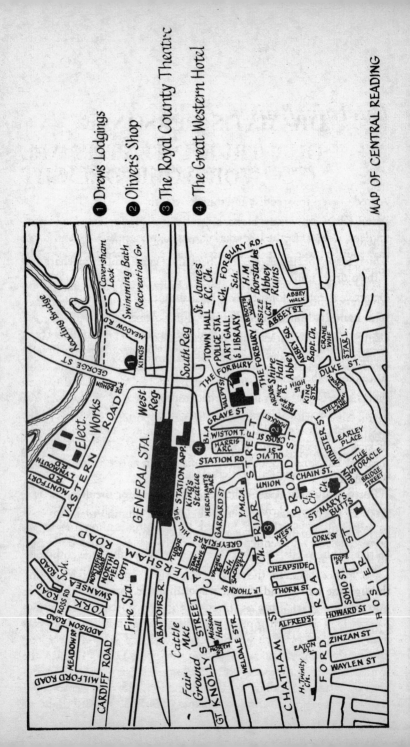

● 1 Drew's Lodgings

● 2 Oliver's Shop

● 3 The Royal County Theatre

● 4 The Great Western Hotel

MAP OF CENTRAL READING

Curtain-Raiser

OUR TRUE INTENT IS ALL
FOR YOUR DELIGHT

FORLORN on windy corners, gently mouldering in the winter-gardens, skeletal in the lace-market, in towns and cities up and down the country, the lost playhouses, the vanquished Empires, the ruined Palaces of Britain, droop in quiet decay.

The gilt on the plaster cherubim loses its glister, peels and drops. The proscenium arch sags. Cobwebs shroud its sculpted earnest of intention—"Our True Intent is All For Your Delight".

Gone the delight. Only a threadbare reality where make-believe tears and laughter, instant joy and sorrow, dwelt; old dreams dreamt in imitation marble halls. Sparrows nest in the rafters. The floats are snuffed out. In the corridored maze of No Man's Land beyond the blackened desert of the stage, the sweet and fusty smell of mice. A cold wind blows through passages where velvet swept the dust, scabbards scraped the walls, and cockades nodded in the high flickering shadows. And with the disappearance of these forgotten theatres, has vanished, or almost vanished, an entire world, a whole way of life.

Forty years ago, dozens of brave little bands of strolling players were taking to the road, the iron road of the railway, restlessly measuring the length and breadth of Britain, leading the harsh, peripatetic life of twentieth-century troubadours—their true intent, all for your delight.

To glance back to their barn-storming heyday is like looking through the wrong end of a telescope. England shrinks. Time clicks into another gear. Curtains rise at Darlington, Derby and Notting-ham; fall at Wolverhampton, Hull and Stoke-on-Trent. Hampers litter the station platforms of Birmingham, Bradford and Liverpool, Shrewsbury, Manchester and Newcastle-upon-Tyne. This is the world, so near in time and yet so immeasurably far away in atmos-phere, of theatrical digs; of Crewe Station, the still centre of a revolving score of touring companies, in the last gold light of

Sunday evenings; of the old puffing trains lumbering through the smoky countryside with their cargoes of mummers: and in a hundred dark brick houses, a hundred 'Mas'—the theatrical landladies —setting the kippers by the stove, or cold mutton on the supper table, smoothing open the brass beds, filling the water-jugs on the marble tops of ricket-legged wash-stands.

It is the booming world of Thespian declaimers . . . "It can't be sin, Sybil, so long as we are sensible and sincere", with wealth of sibilance, dramatic r-rolling, florid gesture and gesticulation. The world of one-week stands and grubby-white tiled dressing-rooms, with the stale taint of last week's occupant's gin or Guinness still lingering on the breath of the place. The second, third, fourth rate world of the B, C, D grade touring companies, where the Theatre Royal is in Hanley, the Lyric is in Blackburn, the Lyceum in Folkestone—or Bury, or Buxton, or Sheffield. It is the dusty, dear, departed world from which comes the strange story with which this book is concerned.

The particular corner which must engage our attention is the Royal County Theatre, Reading. Today that theatre is no more. The parcel of space in Friar Street which it once enclosed is now prosperously divided between thriving branches of Woolworth's and Littlewood's stores. But on the evening of Monday, June 17th, 1929, the Royal County Theatre was very much alive. At 6.45 P.M., five minutes before curtain-rise, the house, well papered, is agog and eager for the spinal delights of *The Monster*, a murder melodrama in three acts by Crane Wilbur. It is a simple story to be enacted for simple folk. The mechanism may creak a little to the sophisticated ear, but all the ingredients are here—a remote country house, a dark and stormy night, a mad scientist, Dr Ziska, a distressed damsel, and the peerless dénouement of an electric chair (guaranteed "an *exact* replica" of the real thing "in Sing Sing prison, New York").

The star part of "Red" Mackenzie, the tramp-detective, is to be played by a 49-year-old actor named Philip Yale Drew. Drew has seen better days. Now, he is not so much a star in the theatrical firmament as a planet, a wanderer, moving in a lowly orbit of seedy provincial circuits. As the curtains rustle open he is on-stage, hiding behind his bogus thicket of red whiskers, masking his true identity beneath a camouflage of rags. And now the advertised "thrills and chills" come thick and fast.

Ninety minutes later, the first-house curtain falls.

Nine performances later, the curtain will rise upon an unrehearsed drama of real life.

This time it will not be counterfeit murder. Beyond the footlights, out in the workaday, unromantic streets, a monster who is not make-believe will strike. Events are moving briskly towards that climax.

Philip Yale Drew will once again be the star. He is about to play out his greatest rôle.

Chance has laid an ambush.

Fate is the call-boy.

Mr Drew, please.

Stage waits . . .

Act One

The action takes place in the shop of Mr Alfred Oliver, tobacconist, in Cross Street, Reading.

The time: Black Saturday,
        June 22nd, 1929

Scene 1

DEATH OVER THE COUNTER

IT was tea-time in Reading. The hour when the afternoon streets were emptying and the teacups filling. Some stalls were being stripped and packed away in the market. The shutters were going up on the shops.

Saturday, June 22nd, 1929—Black Saturday the locals called it, because it was the day each year that their town was invaded by the race gangs, the flotsam of louts and touts, the jetsam of roughs and toughs, attracted by the annual Ascot and Windsor meetings.

Now, this year's race week was over, and the publicans were polishing their glasses and checking the change in their tills, making everything ready for the great wash-in of visiting punters and riff-raff from the courses, all set to celebrate their winnings, or console themselves for their losses.

The trams rattled along Broad Street. Shoppers and shop-assistants trekked homeward to high tea through mellow, red-gold sunlight, that gilded the old streets of the town.

In Friar Street, the Royal County Theatre, as yet still empty, was preparing for the influx of first-house patrons.

This was the brief interval of quiet before the Saturday night bustle of pleasure began. The lull. The in-between time. When lovers hesitated on the brink of meetings, when blue serge suits and frilly dance frocks were being taken out from wardrobes where they had hung in waiting all the week.

But at six o'clock on this bright June evening, a small enclave of shops in Cross Street still remained open—among them, the superior tobacconist's at No. 15.

Sedately, unmindful of the advancing evening, its sixty-year-old proprietor, Mr Alfred Oliver, sat behind his fine mahogany counter deep in his book. He and his wife were off on their holidays on Monday. They were going to Teignmouth, and the book which he was reading, *Through the Window: Paddington to Penzance*,[1] told of all the interesting sights that they would be able to see from the train.

There were few customers at this time to interrupt Mr Oliver's anticipatory pleasures.

The shuffle of approaching footsteps.

Mr Oliver blinked absent-mindedly up through his glasses as the man came into the shop.

"A packet of cigarettes, please."

A half-crown tendered.

Suddenly the world within the little tobacconist's skull exploded in a numbing crimson burst. . . .

As Mr Oliver sank in a warm and salty sea of blood, the man reached across the counter, scrabbled in the wooden till-drawer, and snatched its thin treasure of pound and ten-shilling notes.

Then, in a flurry of draughty speed, was gone.

Silence.

The irreversible process of murder had been initiated.

(2)

Put the clock back thirty-five minutes. Let the hands stand at 5.25 P.M.

An early tea is just finishing in the cosy dining-room behind the shop. Mr Oliver rises from the table and begins to collect the plates, the cups and saucers, into a neat pile. He will, he says, wash up the tea things. He usually does. He likes to help his wife.

"It won't take me a jiffy, dear."

His wife, Annie, goes into the shop while, up in the first-floor kitchen, he splashes and tinkles his way through his self-appointed chore.

By 5.50 P.M. all is dried and tidied away. Mr Oliver comes down into the shop, and Mrs Oliver goes upstairs and busies herself briefly in her bedroom.

Ten, twelve minutes later, she comes down again. Now Mr Oliver is sitting in the shop, reading his Great Western Railway

[1] *Through the Window. Number One: Paddington to Penzance (Cornish Riviera Route) 300 Miles of English Country As Seen From the G.W.R. Trains.* Issued by The Great Western Railway, 1924. Price: One Shilling.

holiday handbook. Or so she thinks. She does not actually see him, does not disturb him, but slips quietly out to take her little Pekingese for a run. She exercises the dog and chats for a while with a neighbour, a Mr Matthews, whom she encounters in Percy Place, a small court at the rear of the shop.

(3)

The hands of the clock creep round.

It is a quarter past six when Mrs Oliver returns. She looks into the shop, and is surprised to find it apparently empty, unattended. Where is Alfred? She calls his name—the pet name she always uses . . . "Olly!"

No answer.

Then she sees him, a frail, pathetic figure, huddled—half-lying, half-sitting—propped against the wall on the floor behind the counter. He holds a scarlet, saturated handkerchief to his mouth. Blood oozes from his head and trickles in fat, slow drops down his face.

There is no thought of murder in Annie Oliver's mind as she kneels down beside him and gathers her husband in her arms. If in those first shocked seconds she thinks of anything at all, it is that he has had a seizure.

"My darling, what is the matter?"

And in a voice so faint that his wife can barely distinguish the words, the stricken man answers, "My dear, I don't know. I don't know." His head slumps forward. He gives a tiny sigh—and drifts away from her into fitful unconsciousness.

Momentarily, Mrs Oliver remains there, stock-still on her knees, immobilized with horror. Then, moving with the strength and speed of overwhelming panic, she rushes out into the street and dashes distractedly into the Welcome Café, a few doors away. Its proprietors, George and Nellie Taylor, are her friends.

"Come quickly. Something's happened to Olly."

Mrs Taylor listens with dismay as Mrs Oliver gasps out her story in a tumble of words. Then runs with her into Hieatt's butcher's shop at No. 19, where George Taylor is making some purchases.

Mr Taylor immediately goes off with Mrs Oliver to the shop. Between them, they help Mr Oliver to his feet, get him into the dining-room, and sit him down in an armchair.

"Who are you?" asks the dazed Mr Oliver.

"George," says Mr Taylor.

And Mr Oliver mumbles something.

Meanwhile, Mrs Taylor asks the manager at Hieatt's, Mr William George Loxton, to telephone for Dr Stansfield, of 120 Oxford Road, and also for the police.

Quite by chance, P.C.43, Frank Chandler, happens to be in Hieatt's. He is off duty, in plain clothes, doing a bit of week-end shopping, but Mrs Taylor recognizes him and asks him if he will come round to the Olivers'.

When Mrs Taylor and P.C. Chandler reach the tobacconist's they find Mr Taylor and Mrs Oliver bending over the bewildered Alfred Oliver, bathing his wounds.

A few minutes later, Dr Stansfield arrives. He dresses Mr Oliver's injuries and says that they will have to get him to hospital as soon as possible.

P.C. Chandler telephones for an ambulance, and also sends a message to the police-station.

Mr Oliver starts to mumble. His wife bends close to him to catch the incoherent drift of what he is trying to say. It is that he does not want to go to hospital. But he is in no fit state to argue.

It is not long before, supported by two stalwart constables, he stumbles blindly into the police ambulance, and is driven swiftly and smoothly to the Royal Berkshire Hospital.

He has precisely twenty-four hours left to live.

(4)

The killing of Alfred Oliver was not in itself a particularly interesting murder. It was crude, messy, haphazard, lacking in subtlety. There was about it none of the finesse that one finds in the majority of classic murder cases. A Seddon, an Armstrong, a Crippen—these were a kind of artist. Adepts of venenation. Cruelly refined planners. Magi. But the destroyer of Mr Oliver was a mere pole-axing butcher—as a *Feldscher* was to a doctor, or a barber to a surgeon, a vulgar imitation.

The Olivers were a very ordinary couple. That was part of the horror. They were good, honest, respectable, but colourless folk. Alfred Oliver's life had had its moment of Greek tragedy, the death, ten years before, of an only child, followed by the suicide of a wife. Yet even this had somehow been absorbed by the inviolable wax coat of mediocrity in which he was encased. His violent griefs, like his quiet pleasures, manifested well below the smooth-flowing surface. He seems to have been an involuntary stoic. A character in a minor key. A man who wore his indifference on his sleeve.

Alfred was kind, decent, and charitable—in an uninvolved sort of way. Although, latterly, he had played no part in public life, there was a time, a decade before, when he had served as a sidesman at St Laurence's Church, in Friar Street, and he had also sat on the St Laurence's Church Board, before the Parochial Church Council came into existence. A keen churchman, he had for the last few years attended All Saints', in Downshire Square, and had a large circle of friends, despite the fact that he was of a retiring disposition and his interests outside his business were few.

High on that limited list of interests was music. The possessor of a fine tenor voice, he loved to sing, and was a member of the University Choral Society. Another enthusiasm was walking, and his familiar striding figure was frequently to be encountered in the country lanes around Reading. He enjoyed a good book and a superior cigar, but his demands of life were moderate. He had long ago achieved a truce with his own mediocrity, and now, in his sixty-first year, the compromise was no longer painful. He may not have been entirely happy, but he was completely content.

Certainly he was fortunate in his second wife, 55-year-old Annie. Their autumnal coming together, originally rooted in loneliness, the need each had had for the other, blossomed into the kind of mutual satisfaction and affection that outlasts all the more violent lists of youthful passion. Framed, hanging on the wall of the little dining-room behind the shop, were two coach tickets. They were the sentimental souvenirs of the char-à-banc trip on which Annie and Olly had first met. Their relationship was, above all else, that of what they themselves described as 'good pals'. There were no children, and this very fact bonded the ageing pair the closer.

The Olivers' position in the hierarchy of the small community in which they lived was clearly defined and cheerfully accepted. Alfred was a tradesman, a shopkeeper, but of a rather higher order than the proverbial butcher, baker, and candlestick-maker. He dealt in cigars. There was a certain mystique surrounding these slightly exotic commodities. He was an acknowledged connoisseur of them, sound on the relative merits of coronas and aromas, Cuban, Jamaican, and Sumatran.

"Our cigar trade," Mrs Oliver was to say later—and the way she said "cigar trade" lent to it a distinct echo of 'carriage trade'— "was really the mainstay of our business. Even our window display was not one that would induce anyone who wanted to buy a cheap packet of cigarettes to enter for that purpose."

This little shop, where he had been in business for close on thirty-six years, was almost a club. His customers, well-heeled professional men, pursy businessmen, town councillors, respected his expertise. They played down to him as assiduously as he played up to them. It was perhaps something of a mutual admiration society, bedded on a nexus of esoteric, quasi-mystical cultism; a certain snobbishness, even. He administered, as he was expected to administer, to their self-esteem, and, in so doing, won their esteem. His function was somewhat that of a mirror, reflecting back precisely the flattering image that the user, paying for the privilege, requires to see. And so well did he fulfil this harmless obligation, this politic piece of social wheel-greasing, that he had not an enemy in the world—and many friends who admired his perceptive acumen. Mr Oliver surely knew that the sovereign way to earn a man's respect is to proclaim, tacitly, your own inferiority to him.

Meticulously courteous, speaking with an unexpectedly cultured voice, Mr Oliver was witty in his quiet way, always ready with a droll tale or joke, but never smutty. A 'perfect gentleman', by instinct and comportment, if not by breeding.

Mrs Oliver, besides helping out in the shop, conducted her own small business in the private region of the house. She was a *corsetière*, an agent of the Spirella Company.

The Olivers were the most unlikely couple to tangle with violence. Financially sound, their troubles behind them, by all the rules they should have lived out the last days of their years in peace and comfort, going down to old age in, as it were, the gentle fragrance of fine quality cigar-smoke. It was the shock of the unexpected, undeserved, and undignified violence that suddenly disrupted their well-ordered existence—and extinguished Mr Oliver —that horrified and outraged their illustrious patrons. Alfred and Annie Oliver were the very last people in all that neat little Reading world to whom such a thing should have happened.

But it *had* happened. And once the smoke-haze of initial incredulity had evaporated, what remained was a glowing determination, fierce and partisan, that the town would not rest until "the blooded hand that wrought this appalling unwonted havoc is well and truly circled by a manacle".

In the words of Mr John Lancelot Martin, the Reading Borough Coroner, "We all hope that the police will trace the villain who was responsible for the death of our old friend".

And to a man, the jury, and all Reading, echoed, "Hear, hear!"

Scene 2
AN INSPECTOR IS CALLED

(1)

AS the 4.35 train pulled out of Paddington station on the afternoon of Sunday, June 23rd, 1929, two bulky men sat opposite each other in the window seats of an otherwise empty first-class compartment. Soberly dressed in neat, dark suits, they looked for all the world like a brace of giant-sized commercial travellers. The elder of the two, tall, portly, and bearded, puffed away quietly at his pipe. The other, equally stout, round-faced, heavy-browed, and clean-shaven, gazed out of the carriage window with an abstracted air of deceptive innocence. Mild, inoffensive travellers, gentle giants—who should have guessed that the business that these two travelled in was murder? But indeed it was. For the bearded man was Chief Inspector James Berrett of Scotland Yard; his companion, Detective Sergeant John Harris.

A formidable team, their reputation matched their stature—a stature so immense that when they were working together on a case in the provinces landlords had a legendarily anxious time providing a couple of suitably outsized beds to accommodate them. Between them, just thirteen months before, Jim Berrett and Jack Harris had put the noose around the bull necks of Browne and Kennedy, the pair of thugs who, in September 1927, had callously shot down Police Constable Gutteridge in an Essex lane, and had then as the constable lay there, helpless, put a bullet through each of his eyes.

Four hours ago on this June Sunday, Berrett and Harris had been instructed to "proceed forthwith" to Reading to "render assistance" to the Reading Borough Police in their search for the unknown assailant of Mr Alfred Oliver.

The train gathered speed.

(2)

As yet, the picture was still hazy. Events had not shaped themselves into clear perspective.

The first message dispatched to Scotland Yard had been couched in unsatisfactorily vague terms.

At 7.30 on the previous evening—Saturday, June 22nd—a Reading constable named Mogford had telephoned an item to Whitehall 1212. The duty officer at the Yard had duly recorded it on an official message-form:

> Attack at 6.15 p.m. on tobacconist in Cross Street, Reading. Seriously injured by man who entered shop and stole contents of till. At 6 p.m. two musquash coats and small brown attaché-case, containing women's clothes and toilet-set, stolen from motor-car in Broad Street, adjacent Cross Street, by man aged 30 to 40 years, blue suit, clean-shaven, very red face, speaks with Scotch accent. Suspect this man may be assailant of tobacconist. Please circulate description and message.

At 11.55 the following morning, however, a second and much more urgent message buzzed along the thirty-nine miles of telephone wire:

> Re. robbery with violence in Cross Street, Reading. Injured tobacconist now in a very critical state. Not expected to live. Please send officer to aid me as soon as possible.
>
> T. A. BURROWS,
> Chief Constable

The standard procedure had moved into smooth, routine action. The duty officer told the Inspector. The Inspector told the Superintendent. The Superintendent told the Chief Constable. And Berrett and Harris had been detailed off to go to Reading.

So it was that, at 4.56 P.M. that day, the two C.I.D. officers from the Yard stepped out on to the platform of Reading General Station to play their part in what was to prove one of the most difficult cases in all Jim Berrett's thirty-eight years of service.

(3)

Two detective sergeants—Pope and Knight—of the local Force were there to meet them. A police-car whisked the quartet off the short distance to Reading Central Police Station, in Valpy Street, and just after five o'clock Berrett and Harris were being introduced to Chief Constable Thomas Alfred Burrows.

The plain recital of such few facts as were available did not take long, and, after a quick cup of tea, Berrett, Harris, Burrows, Pope and Knight set off for the scene of the crime.

The acreage of central Reading is small, the disposition of the main streets simple, and the chief landmarks obvious. All the principal streets are close to the railway station. Friar Street runs parallel to the railway, and is situated scarcely more than a hundred yards from it. At one end is the Town Hall, with its fine clock, and towards the other end is the Royal County Theatre. It is intersected by a thoroughfare divided into two sections—Station Road, and its continuation, Queen Victoria Street—which runs directly from the railway station to Broad Street, the chief street of the town. Near the Town Hall is the General Post Office, opposite which is Cross Street, a short, normally busy thoroughfare of shops and offices, running parallel with Queen Victoria Street, and linking Friar and Broad streets, the two main shopping streets of the town. Anyone moving about the centre of Reading would be likely to find himself continually traversing and retraversing this circumscribed plexus of mainly non-residential business and shopping streets.

Mr Oliver's shop, No. 15 Cross Street, was situated about half-way up on the left-hand side, going from Friar Street towards Broad Street.

That Sunday evening the yellow and black striped blinds were drawn at the locked shop in Cross Street. A uniformed constable was standing guard at the door. He saluted smartly as the investigation team arrived.

They were greeted by Mrs Oliver with the news that her husband had just died at the hospital.

It was now a case of murder.

Before going into the shop Berrett took care to spy out the lie of the land.

The premises, he noted, consisted of the shop itself, with a self-contained dining-room behind it, and three storeys of living accommodation overhead.

The shop-door was set slightly back from the street in a shallow

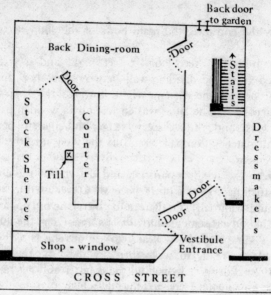

Plan of Oliver's Shop

vestibule, and was placed on the left-hand side. Beside it, also set back in this small alcove, about five feet from the line of the shop-window but facing directly on to the street, was a second door. This gave access to a long passage, from which a flight of stairs led up to the private regions of the house.

If you were in the shop's back dining-room, those stairs could be reached in two ways. Either you went through the shop to the front, and then retraced your steps back along the length of the passage, or else you could pass through a side-door, leading from the dining-room directly into the passage, and opening close to the foot of the stairs.

Beyond the stairs, the passage continued for several feet before ending at another door. This led out into a small garden, from which a gate opened on to a back courtyard, known as Percy Place. From the right-hand extremity of Percy Place, a narrow, covered public passageway ran through into Broad Street.

Having established this general geography, Berrett went into the shop itself.

There, his practised eye automatically registered the minutiae. Notebook and tape-measure in hand, he recorded a careful description of the place. Tedious but essential data.

From the entrance, the main body of the shop stretched to the right.

A counter—9½ feet long, 3 feet high, and 2½ feet wide—extended from the dividing-wall between the shop and the back dining-room, at the extreme right, towards the shop-window, at the extreme left. The latter was enclosed by a wooden partition with frosted glass, and a high display of cigar and cigarette boxes, tobacco tins and matches, completely cut off the view into the inside from the pavement.

Between the window-partition and the end of the counter there was a small gap. In this open space Mr Oliver used to keep a chair. He would habitually sit there and, by glancing up to his left at a set of advertisement mirrors hanging on the shop/dining-room dividing-wall, he was able to see anyone entering the shop, and could be ready to serve them by the time they reached the counter. In order to pass behind the counter and get to the dining-room door you would have to move this chair.

Behind the counter, and separated from it by a space of 2½ feet, was the back wall of the shop, covered with shelves which ran along the entire length of the premises, and upon which was ranged the stock.

Standing upon the counter itself were two low glass show-cases. There was a space of 2½ feet between them, and it was here, in this 'trade gap', that sales were conducted.

On the public side of the counter, placed on the floor immediately in front of the 'trade gap', was a rubber mat.

The show-case on the right contained sweetmeats, in which Mr Oliver did a small trade. The one on the left was filled with tobacco and various smoking accessories.

Immediately behind the right-hand show-case stood a pair of tobacconist's scales. Below the scales, and underneath the counter, was the till-drawer. In this were two wooden bowls—one for silver and one for copper—and a piece of thick cardboard on which, secured by a rubber band, Mr Oliver kept his bank-notes—pound-notes on one side, ten-shilling notes on the other. This piece of cardboard, empty of notes, the elastic band broken, was found lying on top of the counter, and underneath it was a half-crown. Close by was a crushed packet of Player's cigarettes. The silver and copper coins in the till-drawer appeared to have been left untouched.

Before Berrett's arrival Sergeant Pope had cleaned all the blood up from the shop floor, and removed a broken arm of the scales, Mr Oliver's splintered glasses, and his shattered false teeth, all of which he had found lying there, but he pointed out to Berrett the exact positions in which he had discovered them. Mr Oliver's chair had had to be moved, too, when assistance was brought to him, but Pope assured Berrett that there had been no bloodstains on the floor on the public side of the counter, and none actually on the counter either.

Berrett noticed that the packets of cigarettes on the stock shelves behind the counter, and in particular those immediately behind the trading space between the show-cases, were spattered with blood for a width of 4 feet 2 inches, and to a height of 5½ feet from the ground. From these facts he concluded that Mr Oliver had been attacked while in the act of serving at the centre of the counter, and had been struck down before he had had a chance to get to grips with his assailant.

Sergeant Harris called his chief over to inspect what appeared to be a bloodstained thumbprint which he had spotted on the glass of the right-hand show-case. And that seemed to be the one and only possible clue that the murderer had left behind.

After ordering the shop premises to be locked up again for the night, Berrett had a short interview with Mrs Oliver, listening attentively as she recounted the story of how she had discovered her mortally injured husband. It told him little that he did not already know.

From Cross Street Berrett returned to the police-station in Valpy Street, where he had set up his murder-hunt headquarters. There, after a further conference with Chief Constable Burrows, he telephoned Superintendent Percy Savage at the Yard, and asked him to send a fingerprint expert and an official photographer to Reading the following morning.

The local officers had told Berrett of the inquiries which they had made on the evening of the crime, and of the various people whom they had interviewed.

Information had been received that a woman had been bumped into by a man outside Oliver's shop at the time of the attack. Sergeant Pope had succeeded in tracing this woman—a Mrs Jackson, who lived at 35 Curzon Street, Reading—on the Sunday morning, but she had refused to make any written statement.

Hearing this, Berrett decided that Mrs Jackson must be seen

again, and accordingly at 10.15 that Sunday evening he, Pope and Harris paid her a visit.

Mrs Jackson admitted leaving her home at about 5.30 P.M. on the Saturday, and confirmed that she was in Cross Street at the time of the murder—but she still refused to put anything in writing.

"I'll have to talk to my husband first. If he says it's all right, I'll make a written statement tomorrow," she promised.

And nothing that Berrett could say would induce her to change her mind.

Temporarily defeated, the three officers went back to the police-station, where Berrett spent several hours going through the sizeable sheaf of voluntary statements that the police had already collected.

It was late that night when he finally left the station and walked the few hundred yards along the silent, moonlit length of Valpy Street to the hotel in Blagrave Street where he and Sergeant Harris were putting up. And it was later still when the light in his room at the Blagrave Arms went out.

While Berrett snatches those few hours of sleep, let us briefly consider what manner of man he is.

(4)

Jim Berrett looked, and was, a character.

Physically, he was enormous; one of the biggest men in the C.I.D. So big that he had to have his ties specially made for him, and they were all of a yard long.

Berrett in full sail was a majestic sight. With his splendid, grey-tinged beard—he was, incidentally, London's only bearded detective—he was frequently mistaken for a Frenchman, and his picturesque appearance has been aptly described as a cross between that of King Edward VII and Augustus John, the resemblance to the latter being emphasized by the broad-brimmed black hat and thick, dark, double-breasted overcoat which he wore.

Despite this dapper, metropolitan exterior, however, Berrett was really a countryman at heart. Not even thirty-eight years of crime-hunting through the greyer streets of London could atrophy the rural roots of the lad who, back in 1893, had arrived in the capital raw from his native Gloucestershire.

Atavistically, he had created his own small pale of English countryside in the modest but magnificent garden of his little house in Balham. Here, only slugs and aphids challenged his detective powers. Roses were his passion, and he raised them to a splendour that was the wonder, the envy and despair, of his less green-fingered neighbours in Pentney Road. He constantly flaunted the evidence of his rosaceous superiority in his lapel, and, each morning during the season, regularly carried great bunches of it to adorn his room at the Yard. There, dilating upon this or that superlative quality of his choicest blooms, he would preach his rosy doctrine to his colleagues, urging them to go forth and grow likewise—and, indeed, his was the leading spirit in the founding of the annual police flower-show. Of no-one could it be more truly said that it was, in a literal sense, roses, roses all the way.

His other great hobby was reading. He had an insatiable appetite for criminological books, and would pore happily hour after hour over the reports of the great criminal trials of the past.

By 1929, at the age of fifty-eight, Berrett was nearing retirement. He was among the last of that old school of policeman who had come into the Force in the tough days of the eighteen-nineties, and survived into the tamer 'twenties.

He had joined the Metropolitan Police almost by chance, when, after days of fruitless searching, he had been unable to find a job. He started off as a constable in the East End, but P.C. Berrett was very soon transferred from the uniformed branch to the C.I.D., for he had two natural gifts which stood him in good stead in his chosen career—he never forgot a face, or a voice. Faculties which, years later, were to prove of considerable value when he was rounding up members of an armed race-gang which had been creating a reign of terror at Epsom.

From detective constable he was promoted detective sergeant, and then inspector. For many years he served as Divisional Inspector in charge of W Division—Brixton—one of the largest areas in the whole Metropolitan district. While there, he investigated, in 1923, the Brixton taxicab murder, and, within a few days, working on only the slenderest of clues, succeeded in arresting Alexander Campbell Mason, the killer of Jacob Dickey. Finally, in August 1927, he was transferred, with the rank of Chief Inspector, to become one of the top men at the Yard.

Berrett had come up the hard way—through the ranks. His formal schooling had been limited. He was widely rather than deeply educated. An old dog who had learned all the tricks, and knew the book. Not that he always acted by it. True, he had an enormous respect for the law which he was sworn to represent and administer, but he was a kindly as well as a just man, and he realized—none better—that there were times when turning a blind eye could achieve far more towards upholding the spirit of justice than any rigid enforcement of the letter of the law. Make no mistake, he hated crime and despised criminals, yet he had also a rough and ready compassion for those whom he felt that life had dealt short. To these he could be as good a friend as he was implacable enemy to the dyed-in-the-wool villains. "There's good in every man, but often men don't get a chance," was one of his maxims, and the record of his service is starred with many unexpectedly touching little acts of kindness. Not that he nurtured any sentimental illusions. He saw criminals for the fools they were, but, generally, with a wry humour, a bewildered sadness, rather than any retributory vindictiveness. "The habitual criminal is a sick animal," he would say, shaking his head sadly.

One of the most polite and urbane officers in the Force, Berrett was never a bully. He held that rough methods demeaned the man who used them. He rarely lost his temper; seldom raised his voice. But he was a bad man to have on your trail. He was not afraid to work long hours, and nothing was too much trouble once the hunt was on. His exemplary patience was a byword, and he had a deadly facility for probing statements and for attention to detail. To James Berrett, police work was not a job, but a vocation—and he was utterly dedicated.

He had a ripe sense of humour, he liked his drink, doted on his pipe, was fanatical about his garden, and as devoted to his home and family as the next man, but all these things went by the board when he got his teeth into an investigation. Then, eating, drinking, even sleeping, became mere incidentals. Everything was subjugated to the discipline of the hunt. And once he had taken a notion into that broad, round head of his, it took an almighty amount of shifting. He could be devious and cunning, too, when the circumstances called for it. Like all really first-rate detectives, Jim Berrett worked by instinct and possessed that odd sort of sixth sense—that tendency to develop hunches which have a way of proving absolutely right. He and Sergeant Jack Harris made one of the most famous teams that ever worked at the Yard. Now that team was mobilized once again. All set for action. So far, the killer of

Alfred Oliver had been lucky. From now on he was going to need every last ounce of that luck if he was to escape the menace that slumbered in that upstairs room at Mrs Nellie Forrest's hotel.

(5)

Eight A.M. Monday, June 24th.

Chief Inspector Harry Battley, head of the Yard's fingerprint bureau, and photographic expert, Inspector William McBride, arrived at Reading. They, Berrett, Harris and Pope all trooped off to Cross Street.

Chief Inspector Battley made a careful and systematic examination of the shop, but found nothing significant, other than the blood-stained impression which Sergeant Harris had already noticed on the show-case. It was, he thought, possible that George Taylor had made the mark. He accordingly saw Mr Taylor, took his finger-prints, and was able to establish that the impression was not his.

Inspector McBride clicked busily away with his camera, manu-facturing what Berrett was afterwards to describe as "photographs that are, in my opinion, perfect specimens of the photographer's art".

The company then adjourned to the Royal Berkshire Hospital, where they viewed Mr Oliver's corpse in the mortuary. McBride took three photographs of the head, and Battley took the deceased's fingerprints. These gruesome duties performed, the officers were glad to escape and make their way back to the police-station.

Berrett saw Mrs Jackson's husband and, later in the evening, Mrs Jackson herself called at the police-station. She was still refusing to make any statement, and now wanted to alter the time that she had previously given of her leaving home on the Saturday, from 5.30 to 6.30 P.M. His patience stretched, Berrett decided that she was a gossiping type of woman whose evidence, even if she had wished to give it (which she did not), would be of scant value. He allowed himself the luxury of giving her a sharp little lecture, and some advice as to her civic duty.

There was some excitement at half-past four that afternoon, when a message was received from the Pangbourne police that they were holding a man who had given himself up for the murder. Berrett and Harris immediately drove out to Pangbourne, where they found a sixty-one-year-old tailor of no fixed abode, Owen

Roberts, awaiting them. The man had obviously been drinking, and told so confused and circumstantially inaccurate a story of his alleged crime that Berrett knew in a matter of minutes that it was a completely bogus confession.

The disappointed detectives returned to Reading to find that Sergeant Knight had arrested the man responsible for the theft of the musquash coats from the car in Broad Street, and that inquiries had definitely eliminated him from the murder.[1]

And on that abortive note the day ended.

(6)

The inquest on Alfred Oliver was opened at 2.45 on the following afternoon, Tuesday, June 25th.

The tiny coroner's court in Duke Street was crowded.

The first to arrive was Berrett, closely followed by Harris and Chief Constable Burrows, and behind them came Mrs Oliver, a pathetic figure in black, leaning on the arm of her brother, Mr Arthur Crouch.

The coroner, Mr John Lancelot Martin, sat with a jury, and there was quite an unusual atmosphere about the proceedings, for not only was the dead man a personal friend of the coroner's, but he was also well known to several of the jury.

Immediately after the jury had elected Mr S. Terry as their foreman, the coroner told them that, although there was no necessity for them to do so, they might view the body if they so desired. They said that they would like to, and went off, accompanied by the chief medical witness, Dr James Leonard Joyce.

When they returned to the court, the coroner, speaking with some emotion, said, "It needs very few words from me to tell you the reason why you are here this afternoon. I suppose you were all horrified to hear that there had been a brutal attack on one of our citizens in the heart of our town on a busy Saturday afternoon. Speaking for myself, I can only say I feel it intensely, because the

---

[1] On Tuesday, June 25th, 1929, a 36-year-old Reading labourer was charged with the theft. With him in the dock was his 35-year-old wife.

After being remanded for a week, he was sentenced to two months' hard labour, and his wife to one month. "I was worried over the Reading murder case. It was my description that was published, and I didn't know what to do," he said.

late Mr Oliver was not only my tobacconist, but my friend—for, I think, nearly thirty years. I knew his family. I helped him to tide over his troubles, and he helped me to tide over mine. So you can imagine my feelings."

After a brief consultation with Inspector Berrett and Chief Constable Burrows, Mr Martin told the court that he had decided to take that day merely evidence of identity and a careful record of the post-mortem report from Dr Joyce. After that he proposed to adjourn.

The first witness to be called was Arthur William Crouch, of 34 Coventry Road, Reading.

Speaking in little more than a whisper, Mr Crouch said that he had identified the body as that of his brother-in-law, Alfred Oliver, who was sixty on February 24th last. So far as he knew him, he was a very healthy man for his age, and he lived very happily with his wife, who was witness's sister.

The coroner said that he would put no further questions to Mr Crouch, as he did not wish to enter into the facts of the case at all at this stage.

Dr James Leonard Joyce, of 10 Bath Road, Reading, was then called.

Dr Joyce told the court that Mr Oliver was admitted to the Royal Berkshire Hospital at about 6 P.M. on Saturday, June 22nd. He was suffering from severe head injuries, but was conscious when brought in. Witness said that it was three hours later, at 9 P.M., that he took over the case and first saw Mr Oliver.

He had then asked him if he could remember how he came by his injuries, and he said, "The last thing I remember is reading a book in my shop". He had no memory of any strange person's coming in.

The doctor went on to say that at 9.30 that night he took the patient into the operating room, cleaned up his wounds, and operated to explore beneath the wounds for damage. "He got through that all right, and was conscious again on Sunday morning. He was, however, unable at any time to give any account of what had happened."

At about 5.50 P.M. on Sunday he died, and on the following afternoon Dr Joyce made a post-mortem examination.

The doctor then gave a detailed description of the dead man's injuries—a recital which shocked everyone in court.

There were, he said, thirteen lacerated wounds on the scalp, varying in length between one and two inches. Some of them were in the front, over the forehead; others were at the back of the scalp. There were also six lacerated wounds in the region of the left ear.

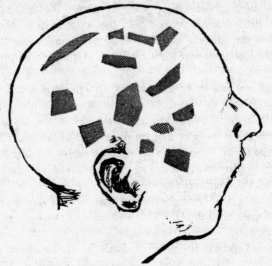

The Head Injuries of Alfred Oliver

There was a wound under the left jaw, and another on the right side of the face, immediately above the lip. The right eye and eyelids were very severely bruised. So was the left side of the neck, and there was a small bruise on the back of the right hand. There were three large depressed fractures of the vault of the skull, and a complete fracture right across the base. Both the upper and lower jaws were fractured on the right side, and the right wing of the hyoid bone, at the root of the tongue, was also broken.

It was a truly appalling catalogue of injuries.

"What, in your opinion," asked the coroner, "was the cause of death?"

"Multiple fractures of the skull, associated with severe cerebral contusion," replied the doctor. "The brain showed evidence of extensive bruising all over."

"Having seen those injuries, and examined them, have you formed any opinion as to what weapon might have caused them?"

"The only thing I can say is that the blows must have been inflicted with a very heavy instrument."

"Blunt?"

"I should say so. But", the doctor added, "there were several curious features about the injuries, and I think it is possible that two instruments were used—or at least one instrument with two edges. Something very heavy was used to give not only the depressed fractures but a fracture at the base of the skull, and yet at the same time the smaller injuries could hardly have been produced by a large blunt instrument. Very considerable violence was used."

The coroner asked, "The fracture was not such as to have been caused by a fall—a fall to the floor, for instance?"

"No," replied Dr Joyce. "That would have been quite impossible with this type of fracture."

"It seems to me," said the coroner, "that it must have been a rain of blows, each wound representing a blow."

The doctor agreed.

At this point the foreman of the jury asked, "Do you think from the nature of the thirteen scalp wounds that they might have been brought about by the use of a knuckle-duster?"

"It is possible," said Dr Joyce, "the wounds on the scalp might have been, but not the fractures."

The coroner came up with a suggestion: "Would a tyre-lever do it?"

"It might, although I should not have expected a tyre-lever to give rise to that type of fracture of the skull. The kind of thing that might do it would be a large hammer brought down on the top of a man's head. It was a kind of bursting effect. I am not clear about the six lacerated wounds under the ear. They might easily have been produced by multiple blows, or by something flat hitting the man there and giving rise to bursting wounds of the skin."

A heavy coal-hammer or a spanner—one or other of those seemed to Dr Joyce the most probable weapon.

But Inspector Berrett had ideas of his own on the subject.

"Do you know what a jemmy is, Doctor?"

"Yes—although I've never seen one."

"Well, it's a very heavy weapon. Some are straight and some are curved. It has a sharp point to it. They vary in length, and run from an inch to two inches in thickness. Do you think the injuries could be caused by that?"

The doctor nodded. "Yes," he said, "they could have been."

One of the jury suggested that a jemmy was similar to an

instrument known as a tommy-bar, used to open packing-cases, and the coroner interjected that although he did not know if there was such a case-opener in Mr Oliver's shop, he did know that he used to open packing-cases there.

A tyre-lever, a coal-hammer, a spanner, a jemmy, or a packing-case opener—with that vague and unsatisfactory series of guesses the doctor's evidence ended.

As Dr Joyce turned to leave the court, the coroner remarked that he hoped that they would require him again.

"I hope you will," said the doctor.

Mr Martin then addressed the jury.

"We shall now leave the matter in the very capable hands of Chief Inspector Berrett and his assistant and the local police. I know we all hope that the police will trace the villain who was responsible for the death of our old friend."

From the jury came a sympathetic, "Hear, hear!"

The coroner then announced that he would adjourn the court *sine die*. "It may be necessary to call you again—or it may not," he added.

The foreman of the jury stood up and said that the members wished to express their deep sympathy with the widow, and Mr Martin said that he associated himself most deeply with that expression. He had, in fact, already written to Mrs Oliver privately.

This concluded the proceedings.

(7)

Apart from attending the inquest, Berrett had two new aspects of the case to keep him busy that Tuesday.

The first was information he received from a Mr Percy T. Taylor, of 160 Friar Street, who came forward to state that he had handed an open-order cheque for one pound to Mr Oliver at 1.45 P.M. on the day of the attack. This cheque was missing from Mr Oliver's till. Berrett was impaled on the horns of a small dilemma. Ought he to publicize the fact that the cheque had vanished—thus effectively giving the assailant the tip-off to destroy it? Or should he keep quiet about it—thus risking the loss of the chance of getting a first-hand description of any man who might try to pass it? He decided to publish the details in the newspapers—and hope for the best.

The second piece of information seemed very important indeed. It came to Berrett's ears that a youth had actually been in Oliver's shop about the time the murder was committed. The name of this youth was George Charles Jefferies, and, at seven o'clock on the evening of June 25th, he, together with two friends of his, Frank Hart and Walter Hendley, was asked to come in, on Berrett's instructions, to the police-station.

Jefferies, aged twenty-one, lived with his mother, Mrs Emily Jefferies, in Cherry Court, 36 Castle Street, about ten minutes' walk from the scene of the crime, and worked as an errand-boy at Kingham's, a boot-and-shoe dealer's in Broad Street.

The lad told Berrett that his seventeen-year-old sister, Lilian, was critically ill in hospital, and that on the Saturday his employer had allowed him time off to go to visit her. He had returned to work around 3.45 P.M., and at about six o'clock took some parcels for his firm to the post-office in Friar Street. On his way back from the post-office he had passed through Cross Street. That would be at about eight minutes past six. It was then that he went into Oliver's to buy a packet of Player's cigarettes.

"I didn't know Mr Oliver to speak to, although I'd seen him several times standing at the door, and it was the first time in my life that I'd ever been into his shop. I went up to the counter. I had a half-crown in my left hand. No-one came to serve me, so I knocked on the counter with my knuckles. Then, suddenly, I thought I heard something move behind the counter. It was a sort of tapping. I thought it sounded as if someone's foot was tapping quietly on the floor. I leant over and saw the legs of a man. One of his feet was moving and making a tapping noise. I leant farther over the counter and could see as far as the waist of the man."

Berrett asked Jefferies to describe exactly how the man was lying.

"He was partly on his side and partly on his stomach, with his legs, which were slightly bent, close together. His right foot was resting on his left. Both feet were pointing towards the room at the rear of the shop, and he had his back to the counter. I didn't know who it was, and I didn't see his face."

Jefferies said that he became frightened and turned to leave the shop. It was only then that, looking over his shoulder, he thought he saw a little blood, just by the end of the counter. Thoroughly scared, he ran out. He was in the shop about two minutes in all.

The place was ordinarily lighted, he saw no signs of disorder, and at no time did he think that the noise he heard came from anyone in hiding.

"When I came out I still had the half-crown in my hand. I'd seen no one go into the shop or come out of it before I went in, and I saw no one in particular about when I came out. There were very few people in that part of the street. I did notice a woman walking down Cross Street, but I certainly didn't knock into her, or anyone else. I stood for a few seconds on the pavement undecided as to what I should do, then I went up Cross Street to Broad Street, left the parcel-book in at Kingham's, and went home."

The attitude of this slightly built youth of under average height and rather sullen mien puzzled Berrett. He was at a loss to understand how a young man of his age could leave a scene such as he had witnessed and do nothing about calling for assistance. There was a certain small discrepancy that worried him, too. He had been careful to keep Jefferies, Hart and Hendley apart at the station, and while Jefferies had told Berrett and Harris that he did not have his bicycle with him when he went to the post-office, Hendley said that Jefferies told him that he "ran out of the shop, jumped on his bike, went back to Kingham's and then home".

Berrett and Harris questioned Jefferies closely for more than four hours. Towards the end of the interrogation there was a dramatic interruption when a messenger arrived from Jefferies' home with the news that his sister was not expected to last out the night, and she did in fact die, of tuberculosis, in the Royal Berkshire Hospital, during the early hours of June 26th.

At half-past eleven Jefferies was allowed to leave the police-station. After he had gone, Berrett turned to Harris. "I think it's well on the cards we may have to see him again," he said.

Harris nodded. "It seems to me that there are a lot of people we're going to have to see again before we're done."

(8)

The funeral service for Alfred Oliver was held at All Saints', Downshire Square, at eleven o'clock on the morning of June 27th, a day of fitful sunshine.

Shortly after half-past ten the coffin was carried from the mortuary to the glass-sided motor-hearse. Then, slowly, the cortège crept through a network of side-streets until it reached the corner of Cross Street. Cross Street had been cleared of traffic, the blinds of its shops were respectfully drawn, and all business was temporarily suspended as the funeral car came to a standstill at the door of No. 15. For the space of two minutes every man in the street stood, bareheaded, at attention. Women, tears streaming down their faces, stood silent, with bowed heads. Even the children halted their games and chatter, perhaps not understanding, but awed by the weight of solemnity that filled that little street. All eyes, all thoughts, were fixed upon the flower-decked coffin in which lay the disfigured corpse of the man who had been described as "without an enemy in the world", and who had been battered to death in that shop.

There was a faint stir, a sympathetic rustle, as Mrs Oliver, the pallor of her face emphasized by the deep black which she wore, emerged. Staring bravely straight ahead, supported by her brother, her sister, and Mr Oliver's brother—who had come from London— she entered the second car. The funeral procession moved off, gliding through streets lined with silent crowds, and with white-gloved policemen posted all along the route to ensure that the cortège should pass smoothly on its way. Flags on the Town Hall and other public buildings were flying at half-mast. Blinds were lowered. Sitting, her face like carved alabaster, in the back of the big black limousine, Mrs Oliver saw that all Reading was in mourning for her husband.

At All Saints' the Reverend George Edwin Jenkins was waiting to receive the body and conduct a short and simple service. Efforts had been made to keep the time of the funeral secret, and only a small group of people had gathered at the church.

The coffin, with its over-spilling bank of wreaths, was borne in. Inside the church, the sun, at intervals, streamed through the windows on to the bier, flooding the beautiful wreaths with a pale golden light, throwing blood-red roses into vivid relief and touching the white of lilies with the rainbow-hued reflections, red and purple, blue and green, of the old stained-glass. From the church school next door came the sound of children singing merrily, but their voices were hushed when the first soft peals of the organ throbbed out the music of Mr Oliver's favourite hymn, "The Church's One Foundation".

Five minutes later, the coffin was reverently carried out of the church, to the slow and mournful tolling of the bell of All Saints', and once more the procession moved off, on the last stage of its journey to Reading Cemetery. And there Alfred Oliver was laid to rest in the grave that already held the remains of his first wife and their dead child.

Neither Mrs Oliver nor any of the women mourners was present at the committal. But Lance Martin, the coroner, was there, and, standing beside his old friend's open grave, he renewed the vow that he had made that he would never rest until he had played his part in bringing his murderer to justice.

(9)

Saturday, June 29th.

One week to the day since Alfred Oliver had been struck down. A good time to take stock.

For 170 hours the police had been keeping up a ceaseless barrage of questions. They had made house-to-house inquiries in various areas of Reading. Strangers in the town had been interviewed as to their movements: a difficult business because the population had been temporarily swollen by the people—many of them undesirable members of race-gangs—attracted to Reading by the Ascot and Windsor meetings. The town's taxicab-drivers had been quizzed as to whether any of them had picked up any stranger shortly after 6 P.M. on the fatal Saturday and driven him out of Reading. The police-forces of all the neighbouring counties had been asked to keep an eye open for any suspicious characters. The Birmingham police had been requested to do a bit of nosing around among their city's own race-gangs. Similarly, the Flying Squad had been asked to keep an ear to the ground concerning the activities of certain members of the horsy fraternity in Shoreditch and other districts of south-east London. And a whole succession of tramps and denizens of the seedy common lodging-houses of Reading and the small towns in its vicinity had been rakingly interrogated.

A great deal of activity, but, unfortunately, it had yielded little or nothing for the winnowing.

A close questioning of the various shopkeepers in Cross Street had been more productive. One, for instance, had come up with the information that for some time Mr Oliver had been worried over the possibility of a burglary, and about six weeks or a month before his death he had given instructions that the passage-door at the back of his premises should be kept locked at all times. He had, he said, been woken up one night by a noise as if someone was trying to enter his shop at the back, and he was so convinced at the time that a break-in was being attempted that he got out of bed, went downstairs, and made investigations.

Normally on a Saturday—market-day in Reading—Cross Street was thronged, although the stream of passers-by was apt to dwindle rapidly between five and six o'clock, tea-time. All the offices closed around midday, but, with the exception of Stock's, the newsagent's at No. 13, next door to Oliver's, all the shops remained open. Berrett had to accept that not a single shopkeeper had been aware that anything untoward was taking place at No. 15, but what he could not, would not, accept, was that *nobody* in the vicinity of Cross Street had noticed *anything* out of the ordinary—even if Cross Street had been unusually quiet on Saturday, June 22nd. And he was right. Gradually, bits and pieces of information began to drift in.

One of the first of these 'suspicious intelligences' was received from Mr J. Foster, licensee of the Bull in Cross Street. He told Berrett that at about three minutes to six that Saturday evening a rather shabbily dressed man of down-and-out appearance had knocked at his hotel door before the bar was opened and asked, in a broad Scots accent, to see the secretary of a local Scottish association which held its meetings at the Bull. When Mr Foster explained that the secretary did not live on the premises, and that the meetings of the association were in fact only held at infrequent intervals, the man showed him his worn-through boots, said that he had no money, and asked for assistance. This was refused. The man was described in the Press as: "Between 30 and 40 years of age. About 5 feet 9 inches tall. Broad, thickset and well built. Unshaven and full of face, with a ruddy complexion. Wearing a double-breasted blue suit and a cloth cap." Whether or not this was the same man as the one who, Berrett was told, had paid a visit to the mayor of Reading that Saturday, pleaded that he was destitute, and been given a ticket entitling him to a meal at a local restaurant, was never established. In any event, 'The Man in the Blue Suit' became the first of a series of mysterious strangers whom, according to the papers, the police were anxious to interview.

Berrett was giving nothing away to the Press at this stage, but it was perfectly true that a number of witnesses had come forward to make voluntary statements to him concerning a man in a blue suit who seemed to have been positively haunting Cross Street that day.

First of all there was Mrs Dorothy Gladys Irene Shepherd. She told Berrett that at about eight minutes past six she saw a man run out of Mr Oliver's shop and rush down towards Friar Street. She described him as being between 25 and 26 years of age, about 5 feet 7 inches tall, of stocky build, and wearing a blue suit.[1]

Mr A. J. Rivers of Tilehurst also saw a running man in Cross Street. He put the time at four minutes past six. He described the man as being six feet tall, slim, aged about thirty-three, and dressed in a dark suit. The man came across the road from the direction of Mr Oliver's shop.

And Mrs D. F. Lewington, of Pinewood, Wokingham, was actually knocked into by a hurrying man in Cross Street. It was, she said, between five and ten minutes past six when a rather tall man, middle-aged and fair-haired, crashed into her, knocking her bag to the ground. He appeared excited, or half-mad, and was talking to himself. "Clear out of the way," he said to her, and hurried on in the direction of Broad Street. He was not wearing a hat, and he looked to Mrs Lewington as if he had been fighting.

Mr Thomas Harold Windle, of Theale, saw a man acting strangely around 4.40 on the afternoon of June 22nd. He told Berrett, "I think the man had been drinking. He was peering into the shop windows and mumbling to himself. I saw him go into the Welcome Café." Mr Windle described the man as sturdy, thickset, broad-shouldered, and 5 feet 8 inches or so in height. He was wearing a raincoat, thrown over both shoulders cape fashion, a trilby hat, and a dark suit. He was big-jawed, full-faced, and had a swarthy, red complexion.

Mrs Kathleen Earl, of Reading, described a similar man to Berrett. She was in Cross Street at about 5.30 P.M., and saw a man with a very red face "behaving in a very peculiar way".

Mr William George Loxton, the manager who worked at Hieatt's shop—No. 19 Cross Street—made a statement to Berrett in which he said that at about 1.30 P.M. on June 22nd, a tallish, middle-aged, dark-haired man called at his shop, asked for some

[1] She subsequently revised her estimates of both the time and the man's age.

liver, and left without purchasing it. He saw the same man again at about 5.45 to 5.55 P.M., going towards Mr Oliver's shop.

But the witness whose statement immediately impressed Berrett as being of vital importance was Mrs Alice James. Mrs James had passed along Cross Street at about ten minutes past six, and she had seen a man—a man who was in all probability, Berrett had decided, Alfred Oliver's murderer—standing in the doorway of Mr Oliver's shop. Mrs James was unable to describe his clothing, but she said that she had had a pretty good look at the man himself. He was rather tall, of middle age, and had iron-grey hair. He was respectably dressed and wore no hat. There was blood on his face, as if he had had a nose-bleed or had been fighting, and he appeared to be talking to someone in the shop. Mrs James told Berrett that she thought that she would be able to identify him, and she, together with Mrs Lewington and Mr Loxton, was taken to Scotland Yard to look through the Criminal Records Office's picture gallery, but none of them was able to pick the man out.

On June 26th, Berrett had, at the suggestion of Chief Constable Burrows, taken the afternoon off and accompanied him to the sportsground where the Reading Borough Police Sports were being held. This was not quite the frivolous jaunt that it might seem, for, as Berrett had pointed out to Harris, it gave him the chance to make personal contact with many of the Chief Constables, Deputy Chief Constables and Superintendents whose districts surrounded the Reading locality, and the opportunity to enlist their co-operation without having to resort to lengthy correspondence.

While Berrett was watching the relay-races, the long-jump and the pole-vault, detectives of the Reading Force were concentrating inquiries in the neighbourhood of Reading Cattle Market and visiting the town's abattoirs. Men at the Cattle Market spoke of having seen a big, powerfully built man, who struck them as being a stranger to Reading, hanging about and acting rather suspiciously on the Thursday afternoon before the attack.

A cattle-drover named Daniels told the *Evening Standard*'s Special Correspondent that on June 22nd he had seen a giant of a man, six feet high, loitering near the junction of Friar and Cross Streets.

Now, 'The Big Man' joined 'The Man in the Blue Suit' on the newspapers' list of special suspects.

Mrs Jackson's story—that same Mrs Jackson who had been lectured by Berrett—also found its way into the newspapers.

The *Daily News* of June 28th reported how on the Saturday evening she "saw a man who roughly answered the description of the man who can be said almost to have haunted Cross Street on Saturday. He came rapidly out of Mr Oliver's shop doorway, collided heavily with her and, as he hurried off, almost shouted 'I'm sorry'." The paper's Special Correspondent adds: "This man referred to has been described to me by six different witnesses all of whom are employed in shops in Cross Street. Generally speaking his description is: Height about 5 ft. 8 in. to 9 in. Clean shaven, dressed in a dark blue suit with brown shoes, dark and of power-ful physique. He was first noticed at the Welcome Restaurant in Cross Street at 7.30 on the morning of Saturday, where he had breakfast and asked if he could have a wash. He looked, a mem-ber of the staff told me, as if he had been out all night, and as if he needed a shave. He was about 35 years of age and spoke with a Scottish accent. A butcher who was having breakfast in the restau-rant at the time told me that the man looked like 'a race-course tough'. This butcher said he saw the man at least a dozen times in Cross Street later in the day, the last time shortly before six o'clock. Two assistants in another butcher's shop in Cross Street also noticed the man who, one of the two said, appeared to be a queer customer. He went to the shop door and asked: 'Have you any calves' liver?' but before anyone could answer him he disappeared. 'Towards six o'clock,' said the other butcher's assistant, 'I saw him from half-way across the road and then he stopped and turned round and walked straight towards Mr Oliver's shop. That was the last I saw of him.'"

The *Daily Mail*'s version of Mrs Jackson's story christens the mysterious stranger 'The Man With the Staring Eyes'.

The affair of the 'bloodstained' clothing on Peppard Common had been another clue that never was. Peppard Common is a big expanse of open land six miles north-west of Reading, and the village of Peppard was a straggling one, built all round the edges of the Common. It was a visitor who first told Mr Harry Reed, landlord of the Red Lion Hotel, that he had just seen the clothing, which had been pushed far into the centre of a thick gorse-bush. Mr Reed, knowing that the police were anxious that anything of an unusual nature should be reported, telephoned to them at once. Detective Sergeant Knight collected the 'vital evidence'. Berrett took one look at the filthy, mildewed garments, and knew that they had nothing to do with the case. And so it proved. The stains turned out to be at least six months old—and they were not blood-stains, either.

At half-past four on this Saturday (June 29th), Berrett received a telephone message from a Detective Inspector Walter William Selby at Twickenham, telling him that he was holding a man who said that he knew who had murdered Alfred Oliver. This man, Frederick Charles Miles, had been talking in the Casual Ward at Isleworth the night before to Sidney Walter Coe, and Coe, of no fixed abode and freely admitting previous convictions for house-breaking, had told the police at Twickenham what Miles had said. Berrett promptly despatched Harris to Twickenham in a police-car, and he brought Coe and Miles back to Reading. Interrogated by Berrett, Miles made a long, rambling statement concerning three knife-grinders who were without money before the murder and suddenly had plenty of it on the Sunday morning. Two of the men were, he said, brothers, and had done time for violence. When he last saw them they were heading in the direction of Andover. Berrett subsequently discovered that the men Miles was referring to were named Nicholls, but they had no previous convictions for violence recorded against them, and Miles himself had been a patient in a mental hospital.

All in all, Berrett was not feeling that, at the end of seven days' hard slogging, he had much cause for self-congratulation.

Then, at 8.50 P.M., a message came through from the Winchester police. A tramp named Frederick Redvers Johns had made a state-ment that he had seen a man throw a bloodstained parcel over a railway bridge near Reading on the evening of June 22nd.

After a hurried consultation with Chief Constable Burrows, Berrett arranged to have Johns brought to Reading first thing in the morning.

Perhaps at last the tide of fortune was turning.

It was once again getting on for 4 A.M. when a weary Berrett left his little room at the police-station.

(10)

Mr Frederick Redvers Johns was duly delivered at Valpy Street on Sunday morning, June 30th.

By that time Berrett had a brief history of the man's movements before him. Johns had been arrested in London at 8.10 on the morning of June 23rd, for sleeping out in Hyde Park, and he had remained in custody until June 29th. On that day he had been discharged by the court on the condition that he left London.

Questioned by Berrett, Johns said that shortly after 7 P.M. on June 22nd he was standing on a railway bridge about a couple of miles out of Reading, waiting to get a lift to London, when a man whom he had previously seen at Ascot races came up and, after some conversation, threw a parcel over the bridge and on to a passing goods-train. As the parcel dropped it came partly open, and Johns had noticed that it appeared to be bloodstained. The man had then said good-bye and departed. He did not at any time offer any explanation as to why he had thrown the parcel away. Soon after the man had left him Johns had got a lift to London—and, next morning, was arrested in Hyde Park. He had not, he explained to Berrett, read of the murder of Mr Oliver until after his release on June 29th.

Johns was taken forthwith to Sonning Cutting Railway Bridge, and he pointed out to Berrett, Harris and Burrows the place where the man threw the parcel over. It was above the 'down' main line.

That afternoon Berrett decided to have the line searched, but no parcel or weapon came to light. He discovered that the train which Johns had seen was one composed of empty goods wagons, going from Old Oak Common to various destinations in South Wales. But, despite the subsequent assistance of the Great Western Railway Police, the parcel was never found.

The Press had been busy over the week-end, and Monday's papers came out with a tantalizing story concerning a man who had called at the People's Hostel in London Street, Reading, at 11.30 on the night before Mr Oliver was attacked.

Mr Simmonds, the night-porter, told a *Daily News* reporter: "He seemed to be under the influence of drink. I asked him for his name for entry in the book, but he refused to give it. He told me he came from Reading, but I knew that was not true. I could see he was a stranger and I was suspicious of him because he seemed threatening almost, and if there had been a policeman about I should have informed him of the man's refusal to give his name. I entered 'Reading' in the book and he watched me write it. He was looking very closely. I also saw that he was wearing a new blue suit and a new pair of brown shoes. He had a collar and a tie and was wearing a cap and I noticed that his eyes were staring and that he had two teeth missing from his lower jaw. He was dark and about 5 ft. 8 in. or 9 in., and I am sure I could identify him again. He paid a shilling for his bed and seemed to have more money. He went into the kitchen and then into the back, and when I said: 'What about going to bed?' he said: 'There's plenty of time, isn't there?' And when the man asked me to call him at 4.30 in the morning I was surprised, because it was late then. He gave me no reason for such an early call, and he did not say where he was going. He spoke with a sort of North Country accent, and I thought that he seemed eccentric in his manner. I showed him up to Bed No. 45, and I called him at 4.30. He went out, and I have never seen him since. He came in carrying no luggage."

The *Daily News* reporter added, "Mr Simmonds noticed that the man had a habit of passing his hand over his face. Three hours after the stranger left the lodging-house a man knocked at the door of the Welcome Restaurant. That was 7.30 A.M. He asked for breakfast and the waitress noticed that he looked 'rough' as if he had had little sleep. From that time until 6 P.M. the man was seen at least a dozen times in Cross Street, sometimes acting in an eccentric manner."

The newspapers of July 1st carried the following—so far as Berrett was concerned, totally unauthorized—description of the 'wanted' man:

Age about 35. Height 5 ft. 8 in. to 5 ft. 9 in. Broad build. Sharp features. Pale, thin face. Dark, staring eyes. Dark hair and high forehead. Two front teeth missing from lower jaw. On the day of the murder he was wearing a new blue serge suit, collar and tie, new brown boots and a cap.

Meanwhile, the police at Oxford had discovered the identity of Mr Simmonds' mysterious lodger. He was Stephen Smith, alias McLean, a hawker of no fixed abode. Interviewed on the morning of July 1st, Smith said that he was selling music in the streets of Reading on the day of the crime, stayed that night at a lodging-house, and the next day in the Casual Ward at Reading. His story proved satisfactory and he was released.

On July 3rd, Detective Sergeant Pope arrested Walter Canty, a travelling tinker and mat-mender, for attempting to slash William Henry Flitter, the manager of a Reading lodging-house, with a razor.

Canty appeared in court on July 4th, and was remanded until July 12th. He mentioned to Pope that he thought he could assist the police in their murder inquiries, and was taken to see Berrett on the morning of July 4th.

According to Canty, an Italian known as Mike had approached him with the suggestion that they should rob a shopkeeper in Reading. He [Canty] had refused, but later that Saturday (June 22nd) he met Mike, who told him, "I've just done it for a fellow, and I've got a poke." Canty went on to say that he had lost a hammer from his bag of tools, and boasted that he had once killed a man at Eastbourne with a soldering-iron.[1] "They call me the Spiteful Tinker," he said with evident satisfaction.

The Italian, whose parents kept a lodging-house in Reading, was brought in on July 5th. He was a great attender of race-meetings, and frequently did odd jobs for bookmakers. He vehemently denied all that Canty had said against him. He was, he told Berrett, at Ascot on the Saturday of the murder, taking down bookmakers' stands. He had also done a transporting job for a lady in Reading that day, and in the evening went into the Oxford Arms, in Silver Street, Reading, as soon as it opened, and remained there until twenty past seven. Fortunately, the licensee's sister-in-law happened to remember his being there, and Berrett was satisfied that he was completely in the clear.

The Inspector could not help wondering about Canty, though —the more so since he had in fact received anonymous letters alleging that both the Italian and Canty were responsible for the murder—and his misgivings increased when Mrs James and Mrs Earl both singled Canty out at identity parades as being very like the man that they had seen in Cross Street. However . . . a Mr Harold B. Phillips, who lived at the same lodging-house as Canty, came forward to swear that they were together in the Star public-house in Reading at eight minutes past six on June 22nd, and in the light of that statement—and the absence of any other evidence— Berrett had no alternative but to exonerate Canty. The latter's Parthian shot was to write from prison later, alleging that a man called Johnson, who played an accordion and had left for South-

---

[1] This proved to be untrue, although he had in fact struck a man named Edward Brewer over the head with a soldering-iron at Tunbridge Wells on June 3rd, 1924, and been sentenced to two months' hard labour for assault.

ampton, might have committed the murder. Predictably, Johnson turned out to be yet another red herring.

On July 5th, exactly thirteen days since their arrival, Berrett and Harris returned to London. The Reading end of the murder hunt was left in the hands of Chief Constable Burrows and Detective Inspector Walter Walters, head of the Reading C.I.D. There was still no sign of the murder weapon, although all the ironmongers in the town had been visited and questioned about their sales, and the public had been asked to look everywhere—particularly in their gardens—where the murderer might conceivably have jettisoned it. Neither had the search for the bloodstained bank-notes taken from the dead man's till been successful. A number of pound and ten-shilling notes bearing bloodstains on them had been handed to the police by various local banks, but they had not provided any clues.

A gentleman known variously as Maurice Powell and Bertram Childs was arrested at Brixton on July 8th for being drunk in charge of a child. Mr Powell was a character who generally managed to turn up somehow or other in any sensational murder case, and, sure enough, he lived up to his reputation once again by letting it drop to the officer who arrested him that he had been in Reading on the day of the murder and had picked up a few pounds. Naturally, this statement of his came to Berrett's ears. Berrett knew Maurice of old—hadn't Brixton been his patch for years? Anyway, on July 9th, Berrett and Harris made it their business to see Powell at Lambeth Police Court. It did not take Berrett long to discover that, as he had suspected, Powell knew nothing at all about the murder, and had probably only made his statement in the first place with a view to subsequently writing—and being paid for—something in the Press. When he saw his old friend Berrett, Powell knew that his little game was up—and swiftly made a second statement, withdrawing the first.

Sergeant Harris returned to Reading on July 11th, and Berrett joined him there the following day. But they both travelled back to London on the night of July 12th.

Then, shortly after midnight on Saturday, July 13th, Berrett received a message from Chief Constable Burrows that a man had been detained at Southampton that evening, and that the local police thought that he ought to be seen. So it was arranged that Harris should go to Reading next morning and accompany Burrows to Southampton.

There, they interviewed Bernard Campbell, a travelling street-violinist of no fixed abode. Campbell insisted that he had been in Portsmouth at the time of the attack on Mr Oliver—a statement which was later shown to be perfectly correct.

The last couple of suspects to emerge, briefly, from this shabby half-world, were John Macdonald and Ernest Collins. On July 15th information was received by a member of Scotland Yard's flying squad that Macdonald, a convict on licence, was the man who attacked Mr Oliver. The detective's informant said that Macdonald had gone to Reading with another ex-convict, Collins, for the express purpose of committing a crime. Collins proved easy enough to find—he was in custody, accused of being concerned with two other men in stealing a motor-car. Moreover, both Berrett and Harris already knew him. "An impossible man to approach without being in possession of some additional data," was Berrett's verdict. And since that additional data was never forthcoming, Collins was never implicated.

Macdonald was found to be missing from his registered address, and Berrett put out a general order for his arrest on the charge of breach of his licence. He was arrested on the evening of July 15th, and Berrett and Harris saw him at Carter Street Police Station, Lambeth. He appeared perfectly calm, denied all knowledge of the murder, and said that he had not been in Reading for the past five years. On balance, Berrett was inclined to believe him, and his belief was fortified by the failure of any of the Reading witnesses to pick out Macdonald's photograph from among those shown to them at the Criminal Records Office.

(11)

Wednesday, July 17th.
Berrett sat down to write his first report on the case.
Between June 23rd and July 17th the police had accomplished an enormous tally of work. They had gone over the scene of the crime with a fine-toothed comb. They had taken statements from more than a hundred people. The documents in the case totalled upwards of 2300 pages of foolscap. Intensive inquiries had spread over fifteen counties. Innumerable conferences had been held at Reading Police Station and at Scotland Yard. Berrett and Harris had travelled hundreds of miles, and worked indefatigably far into the night.

Berrett had seldom been in bed before 4 A.M., and he was always back in his little office at Reading Police Station by 9 A.M. at the latest.

And at the end of it all they had got precisely nowhere.

Mr Percy Taylor's cheque remained untraced. Even the forensic department at Scotland Yard had failed to produce anything tangible from an examination of the many things, including parts of the shop-fittings and a series of bloodstained bank-notes, sent to it.

Theories had been formulated—and rejected.

Suspects had been described, discovered—and dismissed.

Bulky sheaves of statements had been painstakingly transcribed, analysed, annotated—and added up to nothing.

At first, Berrett had thought that the crime was the work of a member of a race-gang badly in need of money because of losses at Ascot. Then he had wondered if it was the work of a motor-bandit in the town. For a long time he had not been able to make up his mind if the crime had been committed by one man or by two. The lad Jefferies had been a problem as well. The clothes he had been wearing when Berrett first saw him were, he had said, those that he wore when he went into Mr Oliver's. Berrett had made an excuse for looking at his jacket closely. It bore no signs of blood. Berrett had discovered afterwards that Jefferies' mother had sent a blue suit of his to be dyed black—for his sister's funeral, she explained. Inquiry was made at the dyer's. Nothing incriminating was found on the clothing.

Out of all this vast, many-tentacled mass of activity, a single shaky description of a man who might be able to help the police in their inquiries had emerged:

Middle-aged, rather tall, with iron-grey hair, of respectable appearance, dressed in dark clothes and in the habit of going about without a hat.

That was the sum and apogee of nearly four weeks' gruelling investigation.

Disconsolately grasping his handful of straws, Chief Inspector Berrett wrote:

At the moment we appear to be at deadlock. The evidence in our hands regarding the perpetrator of the crime is, even after exhaustive enquiries made, of a very meagre description. Beyond Mrs. James, no one has seen any person in or at the shop. No weapon has been found, and none is missing from the shop. The bloodstained impression has so far not been of value. It is, therefore, at present impossible to con-centrate upon any particular person or line of enquiry, but every pos-sible link will be followed up in the hope of bringing this dastardly crime to a successful end.

Ironically, Berrett was not in his office when, two days later, July 19th, the news for which he had been hoping, praying, and was by now despairing of ever receiving, came through.

At 6 P.M. the telephone rang.

Sergeant Harris took the call.

It was Chief Constable Burrows.

"I think we're going to be able to establish the identity of the man whom Mrs James saw in the doorway of Mr Oliver's shop," he said.

The tide had turned.

(12)

They sat in the Chief Constable's office at Reading Police Station, the three of them, Harris, Walters and Burrows, working out the exact wording of the message that was to be sent to the Chief Constable of Nottingham.

"Yes, I think that should do nicely," said Burrows at length.

The other two nodded.

Now all they had to do was sit back and wait.

Scene 3

STAR ENTRANCE

(1)

IT was fate, accident, pure chance, that first brought the name of Philip Yale Drew into what the newspapers were now calling the Reading Shop Murder Mystery.

It so happened that Chief Constable Burrows was a member of the Wellington Club, whose premises were in Friar Street, opposite the Royal County Theatre. Burrows was there one day in July when a fellow-member came over to him and said, "That chap you're looking for with the frizzy hair is Yale Drew, the actor fellow who was in *The Monster*."

Things had by now reached such a pass, or rather *impasse*, that Burrows was more than ready to seize upon any suggestion which embodied the smallest possibility of discovering the murderer, and he lost no time in tracing the whereabouts of the touring company that was presenting *The Monster*. They were, he found, currently appearing at St Helens, in Lancashire, and throughout the week commencing Monday, July 22nd, they would be in Nottingham, at the Palace Theatre, Trent Bridge.

That Monday Sergeant Harris had returned to Reading, and it was then that he, Chief Constable Burrows and Detective Inspector Walters had sent off the message to Nottingham, requesting that inquiries should be made as to whether or not Philip Yale Drew was still with the *Monster* company.

(2)

While awaiting a reply, Harris decided to look more closely into the position of the youth, George Charles Jefferies.

He began by seeing Mrs Jackson, of 35 Curzon Street, again. It so happened that she knew Jefferies, and consequently was able to say quite definitely that he was not the man who had bumped into

her in Cross Street. She had, however, some information of a decidedly startling nature to impart. It was that a Mrs Luckett, who
lived at 173 Great Knollys Street, in Reading, had told her that
Jefferies had on one occasion hit his sister over the head with a
jemmy.

Mrs Luckett was promptly interviewed, and it transpired that she
had simply been repeating gossip which she had heard, and when
Harris tackled Jefferies himself about it he said that there was not
a word of truth in the allegation. Harris had spread some sheets
of white paper over the surface of the table at which Jefferies was
seated during the interview in the hope that he would place his
hands on them. This he in fact did. The paper was subsequently
treated with black powder, and on it were developed some excellent
specimens of fingerprints and palmar impressions. These were in
due course submitted to Chief Inspector Battley at the Yard, and
he was able to say that the bloodstained print on the show-case at
Oliver's shop was definitely not that of Jefferies.

(3)

Next day—July 23rd—the news came through that Drew was in
Nottingham, and on July 24th, Berrett being away on holiday at
Margate, Sergeant Harris and Chief Constable Burrows drove there.

As soon as they arrived that evening they went to see the Chief
Constable, Lieutenant-Colonel F. Brook, D.S.O., M.C., and his
chief of C.I.D., Detective Superintendent J. Doubleday. Burrows explained the object of their visit, and the four police officers decided
that the best thing to do was to locate Drew's lodgings that night,
but to leave the interview until the following morning, so as not to
interfere with his stage performance.

Detective Sergeant Percy Ellington, of the Nottingham Force,
was detailed off to follow Drew home from the theatre after the
second house. This he did, and found that he was lodging at No. 37
Fox Road, West Bridgford.

(4)

Shortly after half-past nine on Thursday morning, Sergeant
Harris, accompanied by Superintendent Doubleday and Sergeant
Ellington, knocked at the door of 37 Fox Road.

Philip Yale Drew

Frederic Walter Drew,
Philip's father

Miss Abigail Tilden, Philip's
beloved Aunt Abbie

The Tilden homestead, where Philip grew up in
Marshfield Hills

Philip Yale Drew, partially dressed, was having his breakfast in a back room on the ground floor.

Harris introduced himself. "I am assisting the Chief Constable of Reading and other officers in inquiries respecting a murder which occurred at Reading on Saturday the 22nd of June, when I understand you were performing at the County Theatre there," he said, "and I would like you to come with me to the police-station to be interviewed."

Drew, understandably, was somewhat shaken. "Murder!" He seemed to be searching for words. "What do you want me for? I can't tell you anything. I don't know where I was that day. Are you accusing me?"

"I am accusing no-one. Will you come to the police-station?" asked Harris.

"Sure. I must tell my manageress, though." And Drew disappeared into the next room.

The officers heard him say, "Margaret,[1] there's three police officers here. They want me to go to the police-station about that murder at Reading."

Then Drew, followed by his manageress, Mrs Lindo, came back into the room.

Suddenly, hysterically, Mrs Lindo demanded, "Oh, Philip, what have you done now?" She staggered. Swayed. "Hold me—I'm going to fall."

The detectives, unaccustomed as they were to histrionics of this order, exchanged swift glances. Then, as one man, dedicated their best endeavours to the calming of this overpowering and very theatrical lady.

Eventually, she more or less recovered her composure. The swoon was averted and, with her best professional voice-projection, she summoned her husband, Frank Lindo, from upstairs.

He descended, listened in amazement, and then, with the authentic actor-manager's instinctive aplomb, delivered the appropriate line. "Oh, *this*", he boomed, "is ridiculous." The raised eyebrows, the spread hands. "If you want Mr Drew for murder I can prove where he was. Why not take the whole company? Why only him?" A sweeping gesture completed a neat performance.

But nothing was altered. They still wanted Mr Drew. And, after

[1] Mrs Marion Lindo, known on the stage as Marion Wakeford, and usually referred to as Margaret by Drew.

completing a hasty toilet, he accompanied them to the car outside
and was driven down to police headquarters at the Guildhall.

In a basement room there Chief Constable Burrows was waiting to
greet him. A caution was thrust into his hand. He was told to read it.

*I have been told that I answer the description of a man seen at the
scene of the murder and standing in a shop doorway, and have been
asked to account for my movements on the day in question. I have
been cautioned that what I say will be taken down in writing and may
be used in evidence.*

He read it.
And sign it.
He signed it.
Now the questioning began.

It lasted for nearly three hours. Then they told him that he
could go, adding that he would probably have to be seen again. It
was now one o'clock.

What Drew did not know was that he had left his finger and
palm impressions behind him, for, as in the case of Jefferies, a
'trap' of white paper had been laid for him upon the interview
table. And that very afternoon Harris sped with them to London to
submit them for examination by Chief Inspector Battley.

Meanwhile, Drew was talking his head off to various members
of the Press.

He told a *Nottingham Evening Post* reporter:

"I have never been through such an ordeal in my life. It was
worse than anything I have ever imagined. Of course I am completely innocent of the murder—I might almost say ignorant, as I
have not even read about it in the newspapers."

He went on to say that it was an unfortunate coincidence that he
happened to be wearing similar clothes to those of the wanted man
on the day of the murder—"But I always go about without a hat
and, of course, as an actor anxious to gain new experiences, I spent
most of my time in Reading that week walking about the streets
and visiting the shops. It might have been that in the course of
my wanderings I went into the shop of the unfortunate man who
was murdered for a packet of cigarettes.[1] If I did, I have no recollec-

[1] Berrett, who later read this piece in the *Nottingham Evening Post*,
was quick to note this alleged admission of Drew's, which was a complete contradiction of what he had said in his statement at the Guildhall
earlier that day.

tion of doing so, but it is the sort of thing that anyone might do when in a town. And how could I be expected to remember just when and where it was?"

Drew added that it was not until after he had left Reading that he had heard about the crime, his leading lady's telling him that there had been a murder in Reading while they were playing there.

"Fancy," he laughingly remarked, "suspecting *me* of a murder! Why, I just couldn't kill a fly. It certainly was a new experience, but it was not one that I wish to have again."

He was, however, emphatic about the gentlemanly way in which the police had treated him. "They had to question me about all manner of things, but they did it in a considerate way. They just did their job."

And then, recovering some of his old theatrical poise, Drew assured the reporter that the experience he had had today would, if anything, inspire him to an even more vivid interpretation of his part in the show.

That evening he chatted freely in his dressing-room at the theatre with a *Nottingham Journal* man.

"I shan't forget today for the rest of my life. The first inkling I had was whilst I was at breakfast this morning, my landlady telling me that three tall gentlemen wanted to see me. They had a look round my room, and then I went with them to the police-station. They suggested that I was outside this tobacconist's shop about 6.10 P.M. on the evening of the murder, but I couldn't have been, for we were playing the show twice nightly then, and I should most certainly be in the theatre at that time. They also said I was wearing a mackintosh. Well, now, I haven't got one, and didn't possess one then. I've had many queer experiences as a cowboy and an actor, but today's show has been the limit. Oh, gee, when my folk over home hear about it I wonder how they'll go."

Drew then answered his call—and went on-stage.

A big crowd attended the Palace Theatre, Trent Bridge, that Thursday night, and at the end of the second house Frank Lindo came out on to the stage and addressed the audience. An extraordinary thing, he said, had occurred to his company. One of their men had been taken to the Guildhall and been accused of being an accomplice in a murder. "We who know him realize that such a charge is absolutely futile and absurd."

Drew was then called to the front of the stage. He bowed and was about to address the audience when his emotions overwhelmed him. He broke down, and the curtain fell.

Backstage, later, Mr Lindo told reporters that Drew was dressing for the show at Reading when the murder was committed. "We, his colleagues in the company, have the greatest faith in Drew," he said.

At the Victoria Station Hotel, Chief Constable Burrows and Superintendent Doubleday were in conference with Sergeant Harris, who, shortly after 10 P.M., had arrived back from London with the news that Drew's finger and palmar impressions bore no resemblance to the loops and whorls of the blood-smear on the show-case in Mr Oliver's shop.

(5)

Philip Yale Drew was interviewed at the Guildhall by Burrows and Harris for the second time at 3.45 on the afternoon of Friday, July 26th.

By now Drew's nerves were strained to breaking-point, and when Burrows again read him the caution and asked him to sign it, it was the cue for an outburst of temperament.

As the police described it, "Drew then became very theatrical, said he was an American subject, said that we were interfering with his liberty, and that he would decline to say anything unless his solicitor was present. He walked about the room saying that in the country where he came from murders were not committed on innocent shopkeepers."

All that this meant to Burrows and Harris was that he was "acting a part with a view to avoiding further interrogation".

After about eight minutes, Drew sat down and began to cry. Then, pulling himself together, he quietly told them that if they would like him to sign any caution he would do so.

The barrage of questioning opened up again.

While the interrogation was going relentlessly on, Sergeant Ellington was paying a visit to a cleaner's shop—that of The Renovating Company, at 3 Wheeler Gate, where, on July 24th, Drew had put in an overcoat and a blue serge jacket and waistcoat for cleaning. These were handed over to the Sergeant by the manageress, Miss Doris Hamer.

That evening Burrows and Harris left Nottingham, taking Drew's blue jacket back to Reading with them.

(6)

By Saturday night—July 27th—Sergeant Harris was back in London, and first thing on Monday morning he delivered Drew's jacket to Dr Gerald Roche Lynch at St Mary's Hospital, Paddington, with the request that he should examine it for the presence of bloodstains.

That Monday, too, Alfred Oliver's will was proved at £2120 gross, net personalty £1978.

On August 2nd, back came Dr Roche Lynch's report—"I have detected no blood on this article". The partial decolourization of the fabric of the lining of the outer right-hand pocket might, he said, be due to the application of chemicals to remove a stain, and if that had been a bloodstain it would have been possible to remove it completely by chemical means. The coat appeared to have been recently chemically cleaned.

Berrett, reading this negative report, decided that it would be a good idea to obtain further particulars from the firm of cleaners, and a request was forwarded to the Nottingham City Police asking them to make inquiries regarding the state of Drew's jacket when it was first received at the Renovating Company's shop, and to find out as much as possible concerning the cleaning process employed.

In due course they reported back that a Miss Helen Budworth, who worked at the Wheeler Gate premises, remembered receiving the jacket from Miss Hamer. She had, she said, seen no sign of staining or bleaching.

Mr Errol Treece, principal partner of the Renovating Company, stated that only white spirit was used by his firm for cleaning purposes, and this would not cause bleaching of a garment.

By this time the *Monster* company had left Nottingham for Bolton, where they were playing the week of July 29th to August 3rd at the Theatre Royal, and Burrows asked the Chief Constable of Bolton to have discreet observation kept on Drew.

On the Sunday night when he arrived, he was heard by Detective Sergeant Robert Hall, of the Bolton Borough Force, crying in his lodgings, and on the Monday morning Mr Lindo called in a doctor, who suggested that a mental specialist should be consulted. All that happened in the end was that Mr Lindo made

Drew change his lodgings. The remainder of the week passed uneventfully.

(7)

On Sunday, August 4th, the Company arrived at St Albans. Again, the local police were asked to keep an eye on Drew, and Detective Sergeant Herbert William Thorpe reported that on the Monday evening he was seen to leave the County Theatre between the acts and drink a half-bottle of neat whisky on the bowling-green in St Peter's Street adjoining the theatre. He then returned to play his part, but during the final stages of the performance forgot his lines and nearly spoiled the play.

As a result of this there was a row with the Lindos. Frank Lindo dismissed Drew on the Tuesday morning, but they patched up their differences—Drew expressing contrition and being re-engaged before the evening.

Sergeant Harris travelled to St Albans on Wednesday, August 7th, and there, at the City Police Station in Victoria Street, he met Chief Constable Burrows, Inspector Walters, Acting Chief Constable George T. Wright of St Albans, and Sergeant Thorpe. After they had held a brief conference, Thorpe went round to the County Theatre, where he met Drew and told him that the officers who saw him at Nottingham would like to see him again, and at two o'clock that afternoon Drew accompanied him to the police-station.

For the third time Chief Constable Burrows read out the caution. For the third time Drew signed it. For the third time he submitted to a raking cross-examination. It lasted for the best part of three and a half hours.

"The police have been very nice to me," Drew told a *Daily Mail* reporter afterwards, "but their continued interrogation is becoming rather an ordeal. With the exception of three minutes, it has been established that I was in the theatre at the time the crime was supposed to have been committed. Although I know nothing about the details of this affair, it is rather preying on my mind. If I were asked what I was doing five weeks ago I should not be able to reply with any great precision—would you? It is not very nice for my friends in Massachusetts to read about my being interrogated, even though the police are trying to eliminate me and not incriminate me."

And he had this to say to a *Daily Herald* reporter: "It has been a horrible ordeal. To think that Philip Yale Drew should ever be interviewed in regard to a murder is just beyond comprehension. I don't know any more about it than this chop does [pointing to some meat on a plate]. As I was watching a man cutting and rolling a bowling-green outside the County Theatre a man came up to me and said, 'Are you Mr Drew?' I said, 'Yes, sir.' We went to the police-station, and there I went through it again. It is rather a difficult thing to be able to say eight or ten weeks afterwards whether you were standing at such and such a street corner at such and such a time, and on such and such a day. It is impossible! It cannot be done! I signed sheaves of papers and then was shown out of the station by the back door. But the stigma is there on a reputation of twenty-eight years in two hemispheres."

Later that day, Mr and Mrs Lindo were seen at their hotel—Drew was not staying with them, but in lodgings on his own—by Sergeant Harris. Harris did not reveal his hand, but it was obvious that the police were by now fairly sure in their own minds that Philip Yale Drew was the killer of Alfred Oliver—otherwise they would not have been contemplating, as they were, the re-opening of the adjourned inquest. Harris asked the Lindos to provide him with a list of the places that the *Monster* company was scheduled to visit during the forthcoming weeks, and warned them that the Reading coroner might require the presence of themselves and other witnesses at the inquest.

That night, Harris, Burrows and Walters returned to Reading, where Harris stayed overnight, leaving for London the following day.

It was while Drew was at St Albans that the mysterious affair of the vanishing trousers came to a head.

In order to understand this curious business it is necessary to go back to Saturday, June 22nd, the day of the murder. That night, at the end of the second house, Drew was packing his basket in his dressing-room at the Royal County Theatre, for the Company was moving next morning to Maidstone, where they were to play at the Palace Theatre. He was, as subsequent evidence was to show, somewhat the worse for drink, and found that he had—or so he thought—inadvertently packed the trousers of his blue serge suit in his basket. He looked around helplessly. Cursed. Well, they could stay there. He'd had a hell of a job closing the basket. Had to ask Stubbs, the stage-manager, to give him a hand. He wasn't going through all that again. He'd wear his grey trousers instead. And that was that.

However . . . when he came to open his basket at Maidstone the blue trousers were not in it. He promptly reported their loss to Mrs Lindo, adding, "And there were three pounds in the pocket". She wrote to the theatre manager at Reading,[1] who, after making a search, wrote back that the trousers had definitely not been left behind there.

"Then some son of a gun must have stolen them," was Drew's comment on hearing this.

Seven weeks went by.

At half-past twelve on the morning of August 9th, Mrs Lindo went into Drew's dressing-room at the St Albans County Theatre with an old shirt of her husband's for him to wear on the stage that evening, and, lo and behold, there, lying draped over the corner of his basket, was a pair of blue serge trousers which she immediately recognized as those reported lost. She left the theatre at once, with the intention of getting in touch with Sergeant Harris. Outside, she ran into Drew, and told him of her discovery. He expressed utter amazement, and then hurried round to the police-station to inform Sergeant Thorpe. Thorpe happened to be out at the time, but Drew saw P.C. Martin, and told him that he wanted Sergeant Thorpe to come and see them.

Thorpe arrived at the theatre shortly afterwards. Drew was not there, but, in the presence of Mrs Lindo, the Sergeant examined the trousers and retrieved from the pockets one pound-note, one ten-shilling note, five shillings in silver, one shilling and a halfpenny in copper, a book of stamps, a Yale key, one bone-backed collar-stud, three bone buttons, a telegram, and a printed circular advertising *The Monster*. At this juncture Drew appeared. He told Thorpe that the trousers had not been in his hamper the previous night, and that this was the first time that he had seen them since the night of their disappearance in Reading. With Drew's consent, Thorpe took possession of the trousers and their contents, and next morning travelled up to London and delivered them to Sergeant Harris at Scotland Yard.

They were submitted to Dr Roche Lynch for examination.

[1] Mr Charles Russell.

A week later he reported: "I have examined the pair of trousers and pair of braces. I have detected no blood on either."

A point—a small point—in Drew's favour. But not much to weigh against the balance of unfavourable points which Berrett had now gathered damningly together.

Here are the eight counts of Berrett's formidable indictment:

1. Drew denies all knowledge of Cross Street and the murder, but twelve people can speak of his presence, or at least of the presence of a man answering his description, in Cross Street on the day of the murder.

2. Mrs. James positively identifies Drew as the man she saw in the doorway of Mr. Oliver's shop with blood on his face.

3. Mr. Loxton positively identifies Drew as having been within a few yards of Mr. Oliver's shop at the approximate time of the murder.

4. Drew is unable to establish his whereabouts at the time of the attack.

5. There is evidence that Drew visited two other tobacconists' shops in Reading inquiring about pipes for which he could not pay.

6. On the evening of June 22nd, while he was in the Royal Berkshire Hospital, Mr. Oliver told P.C. William Parfitt, who was on duty at his bedside, "Just before tea I got some change for a man, I think he was from the Gas Office." Chief Constable Burrows states that there is an employee of the Gas Company who bears a striking resemblance to Drew. On the day in question this man was not in Reading. Drew was—and there is evidence to show that just before Mr. Oliver would have his tea Drew was in Cross Street.

7. According to the statement made by Mr. Alfred Fry, joint stage-manager of the *Monster* company, when Drew left the Royal County Theatre, Reading, in the early hours of Sunday, June 23rd, he was carrying something wrapped in newspaper under his arm. Drew says he does not remember doing so. But if he should be the culprit, it is possible that he carried away then, and later disposed of or destroyed, some evidence of his guilt.

8. At Maidstone Drew was heard to ask for some benzoline to clean some spots from his blue jacket. He states that he borrowed the benzoline from Mrs. Lindo in order to remove grease-paint from the collar of the jacket. This, he agrees, would take a matter of two or three minutes. But Miss Frances King, maidservant at Drew's lodgings in Maidstone, says that he spent half an hour in the garden cleaning his jacket.

Drew had, Berrett noted, a manner of being unable to remember anything of a vital nature concerning himself, and would always fall back on the statement, "I have no recollection", or "I cannot remember".

Pretty damning—but, as we shall presently see, the facts were not by any means so black and white, so cut and dried, as they might be made to appear. There was not a single one of those points of Berrett's which could not be demolished on analysis. Their cumulative effect *seemed* to point to the inescapable conclusion of guilt, but as each in turn is examined, amplified, the contradiction inherent in it is brought into focus.

Berrett had done his honest best.

Soon now it would be a matter for a jury.

(8)

Things are moving to a crisis. The forces of the law gathering momentum. By their different routes, Berrett and Drew are fast approaching their identical destination. Soon, very soon, they are to share star billing.

Berrett sits tight in London.

The miles unroll behind Drew—August: the Theatre Royal, North Shields; the Coliseum, Aberystwyth; Haverfordwest. September: the Palace Theatre, Neath; the Public Hall, Brynamman; Aberdare.

Wednesday, September 18th. While "Red" Mackenzie thrills Welsh audiences, mock-battling with the Monster at the De Valence Gardens Pavilion, Tenby, Berrett is in Reading. He, Harris and Chief Constable Burrows sit in the police-station conferring with the Reading coroner. They lay their facts before him. He puts a question here, scribbles an answer there. Yes, yes, yes. He nods. Right, then. Shall we say October 2nd? They agree. It's official now. The adjourned inquest on Alfred Oliver will be resumed on Wednesday, October 2nd, two weeks today.

Drew . . . travelling on . . . September 23rd, Merthyr Tydfil; September 30th to October 2nd, Brecon; October 3rd, Cirencester? Big question-mark!

Already the publicity, the advance billing, is starting.

The *Evening News*, September 30th:

MELODRAMA IN REAL LIFE

Secrets which Scotland Yard have kept closely guarded during months of keen investigation will be revealed this week, when the inquest is

resumed on Mr. Alfred Oliver . . . At least 50 witnesses will be called.
. . . Among those who give evidence will be:

> Home Office experts,
> Famous Yard detectives,
> A Finger-print expert,
> Actors,
> Actresses,
> Reading police officers,
> Doctors and surgeons.

Almost time for the star entrance.

(9)

The weeks between July 25th, when the police rang at the door
of his digs, near the junction of Fox and Hound roads (appropriate
names) in Nottingham, and October 2nd, 1929, when he was
bidden to present himself for examination before the coroner's
court at Reading, had not been happy ones for Philip Yale Drew.
On the surface, life had gone on much the same. *The Monster*,
twice nightly. Pubs, trains, more pubs, the odd day's rest. Rest?
Time to think. Time to worry. Time to drink—and try to forget
the worry. But you *couldn't* forget it. Alcohol had proved no
anodyne. Just a bigger headache. Back to work. *The Monster*, twice
nightly. But the nights were worst of all. After the curtain had
come down, the audience gone home, the world and his wife to
bed—then came the sweats and nightmares. Several times he had
woken himself—and everyone else—screaming. The whisky welling
up and forcing its way out as tears. Highly strung. Artistic.
Temperament, the artist's tax on talent. Or was it the D.T.s?
The anteroom to madness? It was his professional blessing—and
his personal curse—that he was a deeply imaginative man.

Now, for better or worse, the waiting was over.

Night again. The night of October 1st. Philip Yale Drew sat
on the bed in his room at the Great Western Hotel, Reading.
No seedy theatrical lodgings for him *this* time. He had decided to
do things in style. Rise to the occasion. Stay at a good hotel.
In a way, a very ironic and distorted way, it was like the old days
when, as Young Buffalo, he was top of the bill. How many
bottles ago? Now . . . top of the bill again. And he was right, for,
in a strange, pathetic sense, this *was* to be his greatest rôle.

He had never before, and was never after, to play to such packed houses in so bright a burst of limelight. His greatest rôle—and almost his last.

As Berrett and Harris came quietly into Reading and made their way to Mrs Forrest's modest hotel just round the corner, Drew began, slowly, to undress. His clothes fell where he dropped them, in an untidy heap on the floor. Naked, muscular, Young Buffalo stepped forth out of the crumpled remnants of drink-sodden Philip Yale Drew. His hand trembled a little as he took a long swig from the half-empty whisky bottle, then tumbled into bed.

The morning would come soon enough.

Intermission

In which we meet Philip Yale Drew,
discover what manner of man he is,
and trace the tortuous path which
leads him from a sleepy New England
village to a position of great peril
in the coroner's court of an English
country town.

INTERMISSION

(1)

I am the ninth descendant of Peregrine White, the first white man who was born in the United States.

It is Philip Yale Drew himself speaking to an interviewer.

My ancestors came from Dreux, in Scotland. I do not quite know where that is, but it is there all right.

The maps and gazetteers do not confirm his conviction. The precise location of 'Dreux' remains as enigmatic as that of Brigadoon.[1]

In my little parlour, home in Marshfield Hills, is my coat-of-arms. There is also one in Plymouth, Massachusetts, where my ancestors settled, and another hangs in the sacred halls of Westminster Abbey.

I was practically born in the stable. From the age of four years I was almost continually on horseback.

Certainly Drew was an outstandingly fine horseman. He was skilled, too, in the shooting and manipulation of guns, and was adept at rope and knife play. He explained that he had had instruction in these arts from "the Indians and Wild Westerners among whom I grew up".

My father had no connection with the stage, but the theatre is in my blood. Many famous actors and actresses are connected with my family. My grandfather was the famous Mr Drew, who owned the Arch Theatre in Philadelphia, and John Drew, the great Broadway actor, was also a relative.

Drew's paternal grandfather, Phineas Drew, who died about 1880, was actually the proprietor of the old Tremont House Hotel in Boston—a considerable achievement for a lad who had set out on foot from his New Hampshire home with less than a dollar in his pocket for his start in the big city. John Drew, of the famous Drew-Barrymore family, did indeed let it be known that he considered Philip Yale Drew one of his distant relatives.

[1] The mysterious village in the musical play of that title by Alan Jay Lerner and Frederick Loewe.

*I first went on the stage to play a small part in New York.
One of the actors in a 'Wild West' show was taken ill, and I took
his part.*

That simple statement was elaborated. In 1921, Drew told a
representative of the stage paper, *Era*, how, when he was riding
the range one day out in Canada, his horse stepped into a badger-
hole and threw him, breaking his leg. Stranded, helpless, miles from
anywhere, he kept firing his revolver as a distress signal until his
ammunition ran out. Fortunately, a Government interpreter heard
the shots and came to his rescue. This man took care of him, nursed
him until his leg mended, and, spotting signs of 'histrionic talent',
introduced his protégé to a theatrical manager who gave him his
first theatrical engagement.

The rather curious stage-name which Drew chose for himself,
Young Buffalo, was explained to the man from *Era* thus: he had
been born and raised in Indian territory, and while his parents
christened him Philip, it was his Indian friends who had christened
him Young Buffalo. It was, he said, the custom of the North
American Indians to name their children after the first thing that
they set eyes on after birth, and in his case, it was—a young buffalo.

This may all have been no more than an actor's truth, which
is often less exact than that of lesser mortals. For the currency of an
actor's life is make-believe, and in the end fantasy shades off so finely
into fact that the distinction becomes blurred. An actor's truth?
Perhaps. It does not really matter. It is a pretty story, and who
shall complain? The success which Drew had won after the long
apprenticeship in his chosen profession had surely given him the
right to write his own script. It is for us to try to sort the down-
to-earth wheat of fact from the high-flying chaff of legend. No easy
undertaking after the lapse of ninety years, but there are still
kinsfolk and friends of Philip Yale Drew's living in America, and
they have helped, contributed generously what they could towards
the reshaping of the jigsaw contours of his early days.

(2)

A dot on the map, 28 miles south-east of Boston, 14 miles north
due west of Plymouth, Massachusetts, Marshfield Hills is today a
pleasant northern suburb some four miles uphill from another dot,
Marshfield.

The embryo Thespian

The mature actor

A very young Buffalo

Marshfield Hills,
Summer 1913

Young Buffalo:
"Mighty Monarch of Melodrama"

Young Buffalo: Filmstar

Marshfield itself, a modest town in Plymouth County (pop. 1968, approx. 10,000), is situated on the Atlantic coast. Overlooking Massachusetts Bay, it is largely a summer tourist resort, although, recently, some visitors have begun to rent round-the-year houses there.

Both Marshfield and Marshfield Hills, once the homes of proud old Massachusetts families, have swollen with the advent of Boston commuters—lawyers, businessmen, investors, and so on. These newcomers are tolerated by the close-knit aristocracy of original inhabitants.

In Marshfield Hills, the houses, mainly white clapboard, are widely spaced apart, and the broad, tranquil streets are lined with maples and Japanese birch. Quiet, charming, it is a typical American 'small town', with little to mark it out.

Small today, it was smaller still in the 1880s, a sleepy New England village of no more than two or three hundred souls. It was here, into this self-contained, proud, and prescribed community, that, on Monday, March 15th, 1880, a child, christened Philip Yale Drew, was born, his roots deep in Pilgrim soil.

Monday's child is fair of face, and the infant Philip was certainly that—big blue eyes, a rich crop of curly fair hair. But he was also small and puny of body—so much so that his mother was almost ashamed to lift the bedclothes from him when people came to see the new baby.

Philip was the third child born to the young couple who lived in a small house on aptly named Pleasant Street. His eldest brother, Guy Frank, had been born four and a half years before, on October 28th, 1875. His other brother, Harry Tilden, on July 4th, 1878.

Their father, Frederic Walter Drew, who kept a hotel, was a distant cousin of the Honourable Samuel J. Tilden, Democratic nominee for President in the celebrated Tilden-Hayes campaign of 1876. Fred Drew had married Harriet (Hattie) Tilden, one of the six children[1] of Captain Charles Little Tilden.

This Captain Tilden—Philip's maternal grandfather—was a famous North River packet pilot. His business was ruined when the heavy baggage wagons began to operate between Marshfield and Boston. He took his last vessel from Union Bridge to Provincetown in 1870. Captain Tilden was also a musician, and, as a member of

[1] The others were Alice (1844–1909), Ellen (1848–1914), Abigail (1852–1937, Susan (1858–1943), and a brother, Edgar (1846–1924).

the East Marshfield Brass Band, gave concerts throughout Cape Cod. A friend of the statesman Daniel Webster (1782–1852), who owned a home in Marshfield, Green Harbor, the Captain also appeared at Webster's estate on historic occasions in his musical rôle.

Hattie, who is said to have been one of the sweetest and prettiest women in those parts, died, at the age of twenty-six, on August 4th, 1882, when Philip was not quite two and a half years old—"I was too young to remember even in the most fleeting way the tragedy of her death, but I know that another sweet woman stepped in to take me under her loving wing . . . this angel woman proved to be my guide, my anchor and my shield".

The 'angel woman' was Miss Abigail Tilden—Aunt Abbie, as Philip always called her—who lived with her father, the Captain, and her unmarried sister, Susan, in a lovely white clapboard house just across the street from Fred and Hattie Drew's, and when Hattie died, baby Philip and his brothers, Frank and Harry, went to live with Grandpa Tilden, Aunt Abbie and Aunt Susie.[2]

Grandpa Tilden, long-since retired from the sea and settled down on dry land, now had his own small farm, and also ran the Marshfield village store. The Tilden homestead, where Philip grew up, still stands. Unnumbered in those days, it is now 535 Pleasant Street, but apart from having acquired a number, it has altered hardly at all in the course of nearly ninety years. It was, and is, a two-storey, Colonial-style residence, one room thick, with a central front-door, built on a small hill above the street in the middle of the village.

Years later, looking back to those halcyon days, Philip wrote: "She was a wonderful woman that Aunt Abbie of mine, and I seem to think that I was always spoilt, always forgiven, and it was always love, love, love for me with her. Strangely enough, my earliest memory is of the pain I once caused Aunt Abbie through one of my infantile escapades. I suppose I was about five or six when it happened. One night there was a strawberry ice-cream festival in the Town Hall of our little village. How I wanted to go to that festival. How all the allure of the feast of ice-cream appealed to me!

[1] Fred Drew eventually married again, Luna Sanborn, a school-teacher from Weld, Maine, and had two daughters by his second wife, Philip's half-sisters, Ruth and Vera. Vera is dead. Ruth married Frank Silvernail, and is now living in the state of Vermont.

Fred Drew died on April 18th, 1923.

But I had no money. Aunt Abbie was out, and would not be back till it was too late. I knew that in a little cup upon a shelf she kept some money. Not much—just a little. I climbed upon a chair and reached down that cup. My little fingers closed over a 'quarter'— a quarter of a dollar, roughly a shilling. With the coin clutched in my hand I raced down to the Town Hall and paid the entrance fee. Never was a festival so devoid of pleasure to a boy as was that one to me. I knew that I had stolen. I knew that my beloved aunt would know that I had stolen. It was a sick-at-heart Philip who returned home that night to face that beautiful woman who had showered so much affection upon me. And when her big green eyes looked right down into my soul and she asked me quietly where I had gotten the money to pay for my evening at the festival I did not lie. 'I took it from the cup on the shelf,' I told her, and felt the first flush of shame that had ever come to my cheeks."

It was at the little white primary and grammar school in Marshfield Hills that Philip made his first nodding acquaintance with the three R.s, and the townsfolk knew him as a light-hearted boy who, though robust, high-spirited, and possessed of an adventurous disposition rare in a country boy of those days, embodied more than anything else a friendliness of character combined with an enormous lust for living. He was filled to overflowing with a bubbling stream of summer-morning wonder at the universe. The very act of being alive was in itself a prayer.

Next to his maiden aunts, Philip loved Grandpa Tilden better than anyone else in the world: "What a man! A direct descendant of the Pilgrim Fathers.[1] He owned a farm and a small ranch where I was taught to ride and plant and sow. I have wonderful visions of that time. Piling hay on the high carts, stowing it away in the lofts, pressing it down tightly beneath the eaves. Then, out into God's fresh air, with a stop in the kitchen for long draughts from huge mugs of chilled ginger water; then once again to the fields."

There were other rural delights, too.

"Hours by the bubbling streams where, by the exercise of due caution, and with the aid of rod and line, the wily speckled trout was to be had. Bears used to come and drink near by, and there

[1] Philip's descent from Peregrine White was through the Tilden family. Peregrine White was born in 1620 on the *Mayflower*, on the way to the New World, and was set down as "the first white child born in America".

was also a fine forest of white birch trees from which the Red Indians —with whom I became extremely friendly in after years—used to cut huge strips with which to build their canoes. My old grandad piloted many a new vessel down the river, which ran a short distance away, and it was on this river that I learned to handle the sailing craft of which I became possessed."

By the time he was fourteen, he could ride almost anything on four legs.

"At that age I was entrusted with an old horse called 'Frenchman' and a huge farm wagon. One of the greatest moments in my life was when a friend, who was connected with a travelling circus, loaned me one of his ponies. It was a lovely beast, and I used to hurry home from school, saddle up, and ride around the village. I taught it a number of tricks that it did not know, and I guess I got to know more about those four-footed fellers during that time than most men get to know in a lifetime."

Thus busily and happily the days of boyhood sped by. The school-room. The summer fields and woods and river. In winter, ice-skating, and the excitement of learning ball-room dancing. And, all the year round, solo singing in church on Sundays, with attendance also at several services during the week.

Innocent . . . idyllic.

(3)

Distance not only lends enchantment, it also brings a bonus of clarity to the view. The backward look imposes a discernible pattern on the hotchpotch of years whose days cluttered into shapeless-seeming weeks and months in the living. The whole wood comes into focus: the boles, high and low, coalesce.

Viewed from the standpoint of the biographer's hindsight, the landscape of the first forty-nine years of Philip Yale Drew's life resolves itself into three distinct terrains.

The first eighteen years were pleasant. A sunlit rural stretch of childhood, carefree youth, and theatrical apprenticeship. A time of hope and preparation.

The next twenty-four present a bright and varied panorama of promise fulfilled—eleven years of acting in America, mounting popularity, achievement piled upon achievement; seven of successful touring in Britain; four back in America again, a cavalcade of theatres and half a dozen or so films; two of stardom on the London West End stage. His heyday. His apogee. Highest point of the graph.

Then, down from the sun-flooded uplands. A seven-year span of shadowed and rocky country. Into the narrow-walled valleys. The sun in hiding. A tattered back-drop. The plaster and gilt of shoddy theatres; the drab wood of scores and scores of dingy little pubs and dreary out-at-elbows digs. The dip of the graph. The downward slide. The not-so-merry-go-round of third-rate provincial circuits. Drink, confusion, disillusion.

Finally, in his fiftieth year—catastrophe. The plunge. The nadir. The point of no return.

(4)

But back to the unsullied beginning . . . the clean slate, on which fate was, in time, to scrawl so crude and cruel a mass of hieroglyphs . . . the face of youth, as yet unlined by the scores that life was to groove into it. . . .

Philip Yale Drew, sixteen years old, working in Grandpa Tilden's village store, dreaming of the days when he will be treading, instead of sweeping, the boards.

Here, where you could buy anything from a tooth-pick to a side of beef, he took his first job. Strong and husky as a young jackass, and with an appetite so healthy that Grandpa said that he could digest nails, the work, though heavy at times, did not bother him. "I could put a barrel of flour on top of two, and haul up huge tubs of oil. A bag of corn—with the bag—weighed 113 lbs., and I could lift it from the floor to shoulder without the least difficulty."

What did bother him was the irksomeness of it. The boredom. He wanted to do something more romantic. He had, in fact, been bitten by the bug of the stage, and, fancying himself as an amateur actor, had joined the local dramatic society. Not only that, but in order to prepare himself for the stardom which he knew in his bones would one day be his, he was now journeying twice a week to Boston, where he had enrolled at Emerson's School of Oratory to study elocution.

"Each morning when I left the station at Boston to go to the School at 130 Beacon Street, I used to pass a theatre, and each time I registered a vow that one day I would play at that theatre." He was still, of course, working in the village store, but all the time he was begging and imploring Aunt Abbie and Grandpa Tilden to let him go on the stage.

And in the end he got his way. In the year 1898, at the age of eighteen, Philip left Marshfield Hills and went to live with Aunt Abbie's married sister, Alice, in Boston.[1]

Aunt Alice kept a boarding-house in Tremont Street, not far from the Castle Square Theatre, a repertory theatre at which the Castle Square Stock Company put on a different play each week. Many of the members of this company, along with others from other theatres, used to put up at Philip's aunt's, and, naturally, they showed an interest in this stage-struck youth who was so diligently preparing himself for a theatrical career.

One of them, a Frenchman named Louis Goullaud, did his best to get Philip a job with a well-known producer and theatrical manager of the time—Sam Harris. But nothing came of it.

Philip then got an introduction to Smith Russell, one of the finest character actors on the American stage. Mr Russell listened with a kindly smile as the lad poured out all his big hopes and ambitions in a vaulting torrent of enthusiasm.

"Look here, my boy," he said, "you join a good stock company. Work twelve months with them, good, solid, hard work, and when you've done that you can come to me again and tell me what you've done. I may then think about taking you on."

Philip went straight back to his friend Mr Goullaud, and told him what had happened.

"Good," was all he said. "We must see about that."

And see about it he did. "That good soul took me right around to that same theatre outside of which I used to pause and say to myself, 'One day I will play there,' and gave me an introduction to the manager. We set out together, passing along Park Square and Columbus Avenue. On the way we crossed a little bridge. I always shall remember that little bridge, for to me it was the bridge across which I passed to mount the first rung of the ladder of my career. It was in the middle of the bridge that we met an old actor, one of the real old-timers. He was on the way to this same theatre whither we were bound. Mr Goullaud stopped to speak to this man—I forget his name, although I remember him so clearly, his fine head with its

[1] She was married to George Wales Tilden, from another branch of Tildens.

wavy white hair. My friend explained how I was just going along to see the manager to ask for an engagement. I shall never forget the grace of gesture of that dear old seasoned Thespian as he gazed frankly and kindly into my face and said: 'Give up the idea, my boy; go back to your store and stick to it.' He placed his withered hand on my shoulders and with all the sweetness of a good soul, and in a voice as mellow as the tones of an aged violin, he repeated his advice. I know now that it was good, sound advice. I should say much the same today to my own son if I had one. He *knew*, did that old actor. He had experienced all the heart-aches, disappoint-ments, adversities, uncomfortable lodgings, long tiresome journeys, and all the rest of the game. He knew what it was to have too little to eat and too many lines to master. He knew all about the interminable rehearsals and the flurry, the commotion and the fault-findings. But I tugged impatiently at my friend's arm, and we turned to pass on. As we went on our way I gave one glance back and heard the mellow voice of the Thespian as he wagged his finger with an eloquent gesture and said, 'I've warned you—I've warned you'."

But Philip Yale Drew crossed that bridge and, heart pounding, entered the stage-door of the Castle Square Theatre. And there, white-haired, slightly bent with age, seated in a swivel chair before a roll-top desk in a dim and dusty office, was the grand old man of the theatre, Mr Pitman. His kindly eyes gazed at Philip over the rims of his glasses, all the time sizing him up as Mr Goullaud recited the litany of the youth's assets and aspirations.

Then Mr Pitman reached across the desk, picked up an enormous book, and handed it to Philip.

"There are 488 names in that book," he said, "and every one of them represents an ambitious young man or woman who is on the waiting-list. Waiting for a job—just like you, sonny."

Philip refused to be depressed. But Mr Pitman was not finished yet. The doleful tale unfolded. He told of how some embryo Thespians had been at the Castle Square Theatre a whole year—aye, and longer—without ever opening their mouths on the stage. Others, luckier, had actually walked on, carrying maybe a spear or a tray. And a few, a very few, the luckiest of all, had, dressed in gorgeous livery, known the all-but-impossible rapture of a *speaking* part—"The carriage awaits, My Lord".

Anger, plus Emerson School of Oratory training, lending an

impressive throb to his delivery, Philip threw discretion to the winds
and roundly declared that he was worthy of something better than
that.

Old Mr Pitman's eyes twinkled momentarily behind the defences
of his spectacles. "Oh, well, I'll give you a trial as a super," he said.

"I want a part. I can act, and I don't want to waste my time."

It was cheeky, ill-advised. It could have been the end of everything.
Actually, when he left Mr Pitman's office ten minutes later, Philip
had a ten-page part script tucked proudly under his arm, and
instructions to report for rehearsal the following Monday week.

The curtain had finally rung up on the career of Philip Yale Drew,
Actor.

(5)

Philip's first part was that of a Cockney cab-driver. The play was
an old English one, *The Guv'nor*,[1] and his rôle was listed on the
programme as 'No. 6666'. Came the first night. "The curtain went
up—so did my heart, into my mouth. Mr Pitman was in the prompt
box watching us all. I went on as in a dream. I spoke my lines and
did my 'business', and when the scene was over old Mr Pitman met
me in the wings. 'Well done, Drew,' he said quietly, and turned
away. Never was there such music in my ears as at that moment.
He turned round again and came towards me. 'So long as you can
do as well as you have done tonight, you can stay on with me.'
There was no higher compliment he could pay me. I was in the
seventh heaven of delight. I was eighteen years of age, and I was an
actor in a fine stock company."

Philip stayed on at the Castle Square Theatre for a year. It was a
wonderful school. During that time he played no fewer than forty
parts, ranging from Negro to leading man. And when, at the end
of that busy year, the opportunity came for him to go on tour, he did
not hesitate. He felt thoroughly equipped to take on anything. He
thought he knew it all.

"One week there came to the theatre two famous stars, Eugene
Canfield and George Richards, in a play written by that great author
Charles Hoyt. They stayed with us for two weeks, and then de-

[1] *The Guv'nor*—A farcical comedy in three acts, adapted from the
German by "S. G. Lankester" (Robert Reece). Vaudeville Theatre,
London, June 23rd, 1880. Revival, January 28th, 1893.

cided to start out on a tour of the last play which Hoyt had written. It was called *Temperance Town*. They required a young leading man for juvenile, and asked our manager, Mr Emery, whether he could recommend anybody. I was the lucky one, and so it was that I walked out of the Castle Square Theatre to play my first big part on tour. Immediately the tour ended I made my way back to Boston, back to the Castle Square Theatre, where I had been told I might always find a home. There, by the greatest good fortune, I came right in touch with Walter Perkins, one of the greatest comedians of his time. He was just going out with *The Man From Mexico*, and I told him that he must give me the juvenile lead. I was so persistent that he could not shake me off, and thus—without that terrible period known in the profession as 'resting'—I set out once more." At the conclusion of that tour Philip found himself in New York City, where he heard that the famous producer William A. Brady was sending out a company in *Way Down East*. He promptly bearded the formidable, cigar-chewing, actor-eating martinet in his den, and, surprising even his buoyant optimism, landed the plum part of David.

Three years, coast to coast, with *Way Down East*, from New York to the Pacific, way out west. A long trail of incident and adventure, its twists and turnings mainly lost for us in the mists.

Then, about 1904, Philip met up with Charles E. Blaney—and Young Buffalo was born.

Charles Blaney, brother of the actress Caroline May Blaney, was a producer and playwright. A young man of bright ideas and sharp visions, it was he who first saw the possibilities of a booted and buckskinned Wild Western folk-hero stirring beneath the patent-leather and fine stage linen of the matinée idol Drew. There was a visionary touch of genius in this sudden stab of perception, and Philip was quick on the draw in appreciating it. Charlie would write a play—plays—especially for him. They would be grand, impressive, spectacular, larger than life—sketched in bold, heroic strokes on a suitably massive canvas. They would be unashamed melodrama—towering mountains, rolling plains, rocky passes, the Wild West, the Land that God Forgot. Horses, real live Indians, all the many-feathered colour of the old frontier. "I hoped to write a big play, and I chose the fast disappearing frontier, where the mountains are big, the men big, the passions big . . . to catch the glory of the dying day and keep it for a moment from the encroaching darkness."

And it came to pass.

Philip's love of horses, his early experience with them in Marshfield Hills, were vital, invaluable ingredients. But these two young men were not the sort to do things by halves. Young Buffalo, Cowboy-Actor, had to be as near the real McCoy as the most dedicated resourcefulness could make him.

"It was Charles Blaney who suggested that in order to get the real colour I should go right into the heart of the West and spend several months on a ranch there getting to know my job. I could ride a horse as easy as some people ride a limousine. I was never happier than in the saddle, and I always reckoned I could ride anything with hair on. I was keen as mustard to carry out the idea, so away I went to a ranch down in Nebraska, and I shan't forget my first night there. I had ridden miles through the afternoon, and at length arrived saddle-sore and tired out. I asked for the foreman, and was directed to a bow-legged man with the complexion of autumn leaves, and as crinkly. 'Who the hell are you?' he greeted me, chewing an unlighted cigarette. 'Young Buffalo', I responded brightly. The old foreman gave a grin. 'My Gawd', he remarked, spitting with beautiful precision on to a tree stump. 'Young Buffalo —are you? You're the cove what's come along to show us how to break in the hosses, eh?' 'Not a bit of it, Bo,' I answered with a grin, 'I've jest come along to learn all that you can teach me.' 'Go and get a wash, then I'll be able to see you,' was his only comment to my little pleasantry. When I returned the foreman was sitting on the corral fence, still casually rolling a cigarette between his lips. There was a pony cavorting around the corral. 'Get across that,' he said laconically, and never shifted from his seat. One or two other of the boys had arrived to watch the fun. But I had been taught riding with the Indians. I had learned something of their tricks on bareback beasts, and could ride under a horse's belly or along its side as easily as I could eat a grapefruit. I could see that this pony was one which had been specially selected for me. He was a fine, spirited fellow with wicked flashing eyes, and ears that lay back so far you could scarcely see them. I sauntered across making a noise such as I had frequently made before. That pony was not having any. No matter how I approached him, I always found his heels lashing out a few inches from my nose. I was too old to be caught like that, and suddenly I made a feint which caused him to turn, and before he knew where he was I was astride him from the other side, and had got my feet in the stirrups. That pony was sure surprised. So were those cowboys. After a moment's pause, hell was let loose for me, and my mount went hurtling about the corral, rearing, kicking, plunging like a young tornado. From the fence came the raucous cry of the old foreman, 'Ride him, cowboy—ride him, blast you.' It rang in my ears as I put all I knew into sticking on that prancing beast beneath me. We always ride with our toes in the stirrups, legs outstretched, and clipping your mount with your thighs just above the knees. 'Ride him—ride him—you son of a gun.' This as I am doing all I know to remain in a perpendicular position. And then a crisp, 'Ah—serves you right, yer lubber. Threw yer—eh? Pity he didn't break yer so-and-so neck.' I picked myself up feeling rather pleased with myself. I knew enough of riding to know that I had not let myself down. I was bruised and breathless. I was also tired from my long journey, but I was determined that they should not get my tail down. I picked up my hat, brushed it carefully, and sauntered over to the corral fence. The foreman swung one bow leg across, and leaped lightly to the ground. 'Say,' I drawled quietly, 'I don't like 'em quiet like that. Give me something with a bit of devil in it.' He gave me one mighty thwack across the shoulder which resounded through the corral. 'All right, feller. Stick it. You're a good kid. We'll bring up Outlaw Harry in the morning, and I reckon as how he'll keep you'se quiet for a spell—hospital case if it ain't a burial service.' 'Right-o,' I replied, bucked to death with myself, 'bring up Outlaw Harry—or Outlaw Hell. I don't care one hurrah in Hades what happens to him or me. I'll stick to the son of a gun till I'm bleeding at the ears.'

"The next morning they brought out Outlaw Harry, notorious amongst them as the hardest beast to ride for miles around. I had had a good night's rest and was full of beans. I felt that I could master anything. I went down to the corral early. The other boys had said kind things to me over my performance of the night before, and given me a tip or two with regard to mastering this particular pony. He was a lovely beast. I can see him now as he stood there with a look in his eyes which seemed to say, 'God help us if this is the best they can do for me'. I could read the contempt in his eyes. The foreman came across. 'What did you call you'se-self?' he asked, and I told him again, 'Young Buffalo'. 'Well, if you can stick on that there 'oss, you can stick to the name.' I rode that pony for the best part of that day. I was thrown twenty-two times, but each time I

got up and mounted him and rode him some more. There was not a
trick that he did not know. He reared round corners. He bucked
like a catapult, and I was black and blue, and even bleeding by the
time he had finished with me. But I rode him, I earned my title, and
so stuck to the name which had been bestowed upon me years before
by old Chief King Philip of the Samosette tribe, that grand old
descendant of the original King Philip of the early Pilgrim days."

There was at least one occasion when this hard-sweat earning of
his cowboy spurs stood Young Buffalo in good stead. It happened in
Omaha.

"I was playing right in the heart of the Wild West country. Well,
this particular night Jake Isaacs, my manager, was standing in the
front of the hall waiting for the curtain to rise when suddenly there
was the clatter of hoofs outside, and he saw a bunch of cowboys
tearing down the street in the direction of the theatre. A tall, lank
fellow led the bunch, and he jarred up his horse like a trolley car
when he reached the door, and came loping across to Mr Isaacs with
an easy slouch and a sinister look in his eyes. The head boy had a
breath that smelled strongly of water that never freezes, and he bore
fruitful signs that planting time was near for precocious corpses.
'Manager?' he grunted. 'Yep', said Isaacs. 'Glad to meet you, pard.
Hear you've got a little friend what calls hisself Young Buffalo . . .
and I've been swallowing chunks of talk about him being a real
Westerner. Jest wanted to tell you that we've come along tonight to
give him the once-over. We're Colonel Coster's boys, and if that
Young Buffalo ain't the honestest, regular, roarin' cow-puncher,
then, by God, we're goin' to shoot up the whole damn shack. Got
me?' Jake was scared stiff. 'Give us all the boxes in the theatre, and
if he don't show up, then order all the hearses in the town, 'cos
there's goin' to be summat doin' with the undertakers round about
here.' Jake came right away backstage and told me what had happened. 'They look ugly, Buff', he said, 'and I'd look out that they
don't start a prairie fire'—meaning that they might start shooting
during the performance. When I made my first entrance I took a
quick glance in the direction of the boxes. These were the real stuff.
Their chaps were bloodstained with their work in the corral. There
was a weathered look about their big hats, and their feet with huge
boots and spurs were decorating the fronts of the boxes as they lay
back in their seats, hats cocked jauntily over one eye. I came in on my
horse at the gallop. I reined in, fetching him to his haunches, and

there he hovered like a circus horse, balancing on his hind legs for some seconds. It was a good entrance. It was good horsemanship. I knew that it would get those boys, and it sure did. They sat there and watched me work, and I put all I knew into the job. One mistake, one touch of crudeness, and I knew I should get the equivalent of the bird, with probably a dozen bullets through the crown of my hat. Came that last dashing entrance when I save the whole situation and claim my bride, firing off a six-shooter with both hands. Bang, bang, bang, went the guns on the stage, and from the boxes all around came an echoing bang, bang, bang, from the guns of the cow-punchers, who had been worked up into such a state of excitement that when I started off with a bit of a shoot-up they simply could not resist, and they drew their guns, firing into the air and liberally riddling the tops of the boxes and the roof of the theatre with real ball. And then there was a sudden dash. The audience got panicky, and there were cries from some of the women, who thought something had gone wrong. I was standing on the stage taking my calls through the pandemonium when there was a scuffling sound from the wings, and through the pass door came the long, lank figure of the head boy. I could see that his hand was hovering near his hip. He made straight for me and made a movement with his right hand. I grabbed his arm and held it tight. 'No, pard', I said, 'not jest now, there's ladies present.' 'You're all right, lad. Lemme go. You're the stuff. It's on me. Here—have a drink,' he said, and produced a hefty flask from his pocket. There was nothing they would not do for me, and afterwards we became great friends, and I went down with them on Colonel Coster's A Star A ranch in Nebraska, from whence they had come. And just here let me say that the A Star A ranch is 268 miles north-west of Omaha . . . and those toughs had ridden that distance to make sure whether I was the real thing or not."

The play which had so enthralled the A Star A Ranch boys was *The Sheriff of Angel Gulch*, high melodrama—"I have cut the high card, and you lose" . . . "Cheyenne Bill and Buck Wade, you are wanted for murder" . . . "You lie! The Golden Dollar Mine belongs to Young Buffalo"—in which, after a succession of hair-raising happenings, our hero, Young Buffalo, rides on to the stage on his beautiful and intelligent white horse, Major, just as his sweetheart's ranch is being sold to the villain, and, flinging 100,000 dollars in greenbacks in the air, outbids him. At once the boys draw their guns and start firing a triumphant salvo to celebrate this victory of virtue over villainy, and there is a wild scene of enthusiasm for the curtain.

After playing to capacity houses all over the States, this vivid piece was succeeded by another Blaney epic featuring Young Buffalo, the sheriff and pride of Angel Gulch. It was entitled *King of the Wild West*, and was an uproarious success. Young Buffalo rode triumphantly through the next five years. The cloud of dust from Major's flying hoofs hides much of that thundering time. But occasionally it clears.

Omaha, Nebraska. September 19th, 1907

Colonel J. Jordan, the founder of the Pine Ridge and Rose Bud Reservation, South Dakota, known as Big Bear, White Chief of the Sioux Indians, witnessed Young Buffalo's performance in *King of the Wild West* from a box at the Krug Theatre, and proclaimed it the best true to life Western play ever presented in a theatre. And he made this declaration from the box.

The hoofs drum on. Applause. Acclamation. "The Mighty Monarch of Melodrama." "America's Daredevil Rider." "The Great American Scout."

1909—Young Buffalo appears between the covers of a book— a 25-cent paperback, *Young Buffalo in New York*, by Charles E. Blaney, founded on the melodrama of the same title, complete with pictures, highly dramatic ones at that.[1]

Then, in 1910, something happened that was to change the whole course of Philip Yale Drew's life. It happened, oddly enough, at a place called Buffalo, in New York State.

" 'What a beautiful animal. I expect you trained him yourself?' A glorious voice spoke these words to me as I galloped on to the stage on Major. The speaker was a handsome lady with the kindest eyes I have ever seen. She was smiling at me as she spoke, and as I brought my steed to a standstill, and swung myself from the saddle, I swept off my sombrero, and replied, 'Yes, lady. I did.' And then, with a whistle which my horse knew so well, the beast went on his knees in front of the speaker. 'Major, hoss,' I said as he knelt there waiting for the signal to arise, 'allow me to introduce you to the lady with the wonderful voice. I am sorry I cannot give you her name.' There was a ripple of laughter, and then that voice, with

[1] J. S. Ogilvie Publishing Company, 57 Rose Street, New York.

its perfect diction and fine resonance, remarked, 'I am Ellen Terry.' That was all, but to me it meant more than I can tell. I had never seen Ellen Terry act, but I had read about her for years. Had read all there was to read about her wonderful partnership with Henry Irving. This great and gracious lady had come to Buffalo, where she was having a look round the various theatres. I was playing *King of the Wild West* at the Academy Theatre, and it just happened that I rode on to the stage at the very moment that Miss Terry and her daughter, Miss Edith Craig, were having a look round. You can imagine my delight when, later, at one of the matinée performances in Montreal, this great lady occupied a box. After the show, Miss Terry came round, and holding out a pair of gloves, which were tattered and in shreds, she remarked with a smile, 'Mr Buffalo, you owe me a new pair of gloves. I found the play so thrilling and exciting that I started to pluck my fingers in my agitation over the plight of yourself and the heroine, until I absolutely split them and tore them into shreds.' That is the greatest compliment that has been paid to me in the whole of my life. It was the genuine expression of a genuine woman, and she then went on to urge me to bring the play to England. 'It is a clean, healthy play, with an atmosphere of the wide open spaces, and honest drama. There has never been anything like it in our country, and I am quite sure it would do well.' That was the first idea I ever had of coming to England."

Excitedly, Philip broke the news of Ellen Terry's suggestion to Charlie Blaney, and after a good deal of discussion they decided to sound out the prospects.

When the summer break in touring came, Philip returned, as he had returned each summer for the past nine years, to Marshfield Hills, and while he worked his head off looking after the ponies and doing everything he could to beautify the old homestead for Aunt Abbie,[1] George Nathaniel Ballenger—who was the general manager of Blaney Productions, and who was, incidentally, married to Charles Blaney's actress sister, Caroline May—took an exploratory trip to England. He arrived there in July, and arranged with Frank Bertram to bring the *King of the Wild West* company over in the September.

The days of that summer of 1910 sped by for Philip. The weather

[1] Grandpa Tilden had died the previous summer—on June 27th, 1909.

was superb: Marshfield had never looked lovelier. He rode, gardened, did odd jobs about the house, and in the evenings spent long hours with Aunt Abbie telling her tales of his travels.

Then, suddenly, it was the fall.

The New England fall is a season quite unlike any other season anywhere else on earth. It is an Indian summer of blinding scarlet and gold, all the sadder because one knows that death is at the root of the glory. The sky, pierced by the white needles of the old Colonial churches, is unbelievably blue, but in its depths it holds the faintest shiver of the coming ice. From delicate maiden's-blush pink to blatant cock's-comb, every note of the chromatic scale of red is sounded, its singing intensity drowning all but the most strident evergreens. The sumacs flame, the maples blaze, the hawthorns glow vermilion. The lees of the blueberry-bushes turn into a wine-dark sea, lapping brown beaches of crumbling fern and bracken. Plump purple berries shine. Nut-brown ripened husks burst in a final swell of pride. Oaks riot in a Joseph's coat of variations on the theme of yellow, from palest lemon, through acid, to deepest-dyed old gold. And over everything climbs the perfume of wood-smoke, staining the clear air with its milky trail—the early plumes of summer's cremation.

As the last leaves were burning towards their brightest red-gold end, Philip set off aboard the *St Louis* for England, three thousand miles away, wrapped in the softer hues of her own brown autumn. There, from the windows of the train, he saw the stooks of alien corn standing in the fields, and hoped that he had come in time to gather some portion of the golden harvest.

(6)

The East End of the London of sixty years ago was a drab but livelier place than it is today. The poverty may have been greater, but so was the gaiety. The trio of districts, Stratford, Plaistow and Forest Gate, united in 1886 into the municipal borough of West Ham, contained a vast acreage of dreary streets of pinched and peeling houses. But the tenantry refused to be restricted. They found the spaciousness that their little grey homes in the east did not provide in the boisterous give and take of the public-house, the lively commerce of the street market, and in the scatter of theatres and music-halls that twinkled their bright invitation to an hour or two's popularly-priced escape. One of the most splendid of these was the Borough Theatre, on bustling Stratford High Street, and it was here, at 7.30 on the night of Monday, September 26th, 1910, that Young Buffalo made his English début.

Philip had left New York on September 3rd, but his old friend and fellow-actor Robert P. Oakman had preceded him across the 'herring pond'. Oakman came alone, bringing with him the four ponies—Major, Lady May, Karl and Buck. He landed at Tilbury, where he was met by George Ballenger. The ponies were shipped on to Fenchurch Street Station, where, later, Oakman picked them up and steered them through London to the stables in Globe Road, Mile End—a tricky job, having to pass at the left with animals that were accustomed always to go to the right, and not made any easier by the fact that by 8 p.m. it was growing dark.

When, in due course, Philip arrived in London, one of his first actions was to go along to the Globe Road stables and satisfy himself that the 'four-footed fellers' were happy and comfortable.

This, according to an old friend of Philip's,[1] was typical of the man. She writes: "I marvelled at his aptitude for training horses and dogs. How he trained! And how they loved and obeyed! 'All done by kindness and carrots,' he would drawl in that musical Western burr of his."

Stratford took Young Buffalo and the *King of the Wild West* to its heart. Every performance, including the Wednesday matinée, played to a packed house. These 'people of the abyss', as Jack London called them, revelled in the colour, the fascinating 'foreignness', and the larger-than-life drama of it all. And how they loved the daily parade of the cowboy band that swung, rum-tee-tum, through narrow Stratford, bringing a breath of the wide open prairies, a dash of Fenimore Cooper—Indians in full glory of wardress, Mexican horses, Young Buffalo prancing on Major at the head of the exotic procession, an urchin guard of excited almost beyond endurance youngsters hero-worshipping in its wake.

A six days' wonder. All set for an uproarious bonanza. Only the friendly eye of his old pard, Bob Oakman, glimpsed the shadow of the canker at the heart of the rosy prospect. "Phil was a very heavy drinker. I don't drink, never did, but I was told at the beginning that you folks over there in England felt insulted if anyone refused a

---

[1] Mrs Kitty Magnus, known on the stage as Kitty Clover.

drink when offered. I was always around with Phil, and when he was offered a drink I was offered one, too. Not wanting to offend, I accepted, and pushed my glass over to Phil on the sly, and he had to drink for both of us. That was bad enough, but in the play there was a bar-room scene and we had an advertisement on the wall for White Horse Whisky. For displaying that ad. Phil had four quarts sent free, gratis, to his hotel each week. And besides all he drank outside, he downed the four quarts, too. It got so that he, being a hard worker, would rehearse all day to straighten out something, drink nothing but coffee and liquor, and not have anything to eat till supper at midnight after the show. It sure had me worried."

But Buffalo was young and strong, and the drink—so far—did not seem to be doing him much real harm.

King of the Wild West moved on—the Prince's Theatre, Bradford; the Metropole, Birmingham; the Star, Liverpool; the Royal Court, Wigan; the Grand Theatre, Oldham; the Alexandra Theatre, Hull.

During the week at Bradford 17,000 people saw it. Buffalo was fêted. Became an honorary scoutmaster of the Bradford Group.

Gross receipts for the first four weeks of the British tour: a very healthy £1750.

After seeing the play at Stratford, Messrs Greening, the publishers, announced that it was their intention to publish a shilling novel entitled, *Young Buffalo, King of the Wild West*, and they planned to have it on the book-stalls some time in November.[1]

The band of Sioux Indians, "from Pine Ridge Reservation, South Dakota, and to procure and bring whom to Great Britain Mr. Ballenger had to deposit with the United States Government a bond for five thousand dollars," intrigued everyone, including the journalists, to whom Buff spun some good yarns.

King of the Wild West was to go on touring Britain for three years, and the interest which the public displayed in the show and its bunch of characters never waned. The majority of these were Americans, but in the summer of 1911 Philip engaged an English actress, Kitty Clover, to replace one of them who had decided to go back to the States. Kitty was under Buffalo's management for five years—"I can honestly say that it was the happiest and most com-

[1] The British Museum has no record of the publication of this book, and I have been unable to discover a copy of it.

fortable time that I had ever known"—and was to remain on the friendliest terms with him for nearly thirty years.

She writes: "Philip Drew struck me as the type of man to inspire —but never seek—confidence. And if you gave it, you would know that it never would be betrayed, no matter the price his silence might cost him. His kindly actions, unknown in many instances even to his intimates, endeared him to the hearts of all, and his utter lack of egotism and self-importance gained him the love and respect of the lowliest. Up and down the country he always made a point of entertaining Boy Scouts as his guests. He had a tremendous respect for the movement, and I remember how the Lewisham scouts called themselves 'Mr. Young Buffalo's Troop', and had his photograph on the wall of their headquarters. There was one young scout, who hankered after adventure and the cowboy glamour as depicted by Buffalo, who sought him out and told him of his great desire to go to this wonderful Wild West. He was not encouraged. Nor were many others who begged their stage hero to help them to go there. All the difficulties and hardships were pointed out to them. He drew deep comparisons between the stage picture, with its colourful trimmings, and the stern reality as he knew it. He said, 'It's all right mebbe for a man to call you aside and point out the setting sun as being the haven for abundant wealth, but the feller who manufactured that gabble was a bunko steerer of the first water. You little men here in Great Britain take my advice and stay here. I once heard a man say, "Go West, boy, go West," but if you take that cue I'm betting dollars to pennies that you never earn over sixty-dollars-a-month-and-found riding broncs.' But this particular young chap, this Lewisham scout, was not to be denied. With his parents' consent, he went, armed by Buffalo with letters of introduction to his late managers in New York City, and to Buff's uncle, further west in Boston. There, the lad broke his journey, and was entertained at Buff's uncle and aunt's home, before being seen safely on his way further to the West that beckoned him. And, carefully stowed away in his luggage, was a third letter, addressed to Colonel Coster of the A Star A Ranch, in Nebraska. Could any young adventurer ask for more—the passport, as it were, right up to, and through, the very doors of the great Wild West? But when this lad arrived, an event unforeseen by Buffalo had occurred. The old colonel had passed on. But the youngster got a job on the ranch just the same.

"Then I remember the occasion when we came across a badly stranded theatrical company in Wales. We were in Newport, and this troupe of players had come to grief during their tour of the Rhondda Valley. Their plight was pitiful; no money; manager absconded; lodgings unpaid; no means of transportation to London, or their various homes. Buffalo unhesitatingly dug down into his hard-earned savings—I say 'hard-earned' for he was ever a glutton for work, an eighteen-hour day was often his—to smooth the road for total strangers. The amount was a considerable item. His reply might well have been that he could not afford it *just now*, for he had spent the day in Corn's Studio, sitting with the members of his company for a vast number of photographs for the renewal of frames and for publicity purposes, at a cost of £70 or so. But he only said, 'It's terrible. I'm so sorry. Assure them at once that they need not worry!' Nor did they. Wales had no regrets. Not a farthing was left unpaid. They were safely transported to their homes —with enough to jingle in their pockets on their return as well. It was not he who went among them and doled out the pounds. He would not so embarrass the sensitiveness which he regarded as the artist's heritage. No, another did this, which he termed 'the donkey work.' But it affected a bank balance.

"I will not go into the details of innumerable charity performances, roofs saved over the heads of those less fortunate than himself, money-lenders bought off, people rescued from jail for debt, the setting up in business of some deserving youngsters. Buffalo himself has forgotten all these kindnesses—and I know that he would wish us to. But they happened . . . take my word for it."

One of the personal highlights for Philip of that first visit to Britain was when, in 1911, he was able to arrange for his beloved Aunt Abbie to make a trip to England. She left East Boston on the *Franconia* on May 30th, and arrived at Liverpool on June 7th.

That week Philip was appearing at the Shakespeare Theatre in Liverpool, and when Aunt Abbie docked she was met at the landing-stage by Philip, Caroline May Blaney, George Ballenger, and many of the *King of the Wild West* company, including Young Buffalo's Cowboy Band, which escorted her triumphantly through the town to the Victoria Hotel in St John's Lane. There, a gentleman was waiting to greet her. He extended his hand and said, "Welcome to England, Auntie Tilden!" This was Harry Lauder, a good friend of Philip's, who was appearing that week at the Argyle, Birken-

head, in *The Grocer's Boy*. He then recited the following poem
which he had composed especially for the occasion:

WELCOME TO AUNTIE TILDEN

I'm very pleased to meet you
   And shake you by the hand.
I'm very pleased to greet you
   And 'Welcome' you to our Land.
We folks o'er here are real sincere
   To you folks o'er the way,
May your stay be long and pleasant
   You're as welcome as the flowers in May.

Philip certainly did all he possibly could to ensure that Aunt
Abbie's stay was pleasant. It was Coronation year, and he wanted
her to see all the festivities. For three months he entertained her
royally. She toured England, Scotland and Wales, spent five days
in Paris, and then, on October 3rd, left on the *Franconia* for Boston.

Philip and his entourage travelled on—England, Ireland, Scotland
and Wales. The curtain rose. The curtain fell. The crowds cheered.
He made modest little speeches. "With all the adulation, however,"
George Ballenger commented, "he still wears the same size hat."
And he logged his progress and sightseeing adventures in a series
of letters and postcards, despatched with religious regularity to
Aunt Abbie every week of his life.

He is in Birmingham. Postcard view of Birmingham Art Gallery.
"I am in hopes to have time to go inside this before I leave. . . .
Some very fine pictures, I am told. Rather pretty don't you think?—
Philip."

A visit to Tintern Abbey. "I thought of you many times while
here and wished you could see it all. We met a wonderful old
man who told us many things. . . . Netley Abbey was beautiful,
but this is a wonder. Large parties go out here to view it all on
moonlight nights—Phil."

January 31st, 1913. Postcard of Chichester. "Had a fine gallop at
Southsea on 'Lady' this morning, and have motored out here alone
to see this beautiful cathedral. . . . Now going back to Portsmouth.
A very beautiful day. Lots of love to you all. Wish you were all
here. Love from your boy—Phil. x x x x"

Summers, he went home to Marshfield, with George Ballenger,

Caroline May, and his three favourite horses—Major, Lady, and the Indian pony, Buck.

His niece, Mrs Ruth Drew Damon, recalls: "Gay and popular, a handsome figure with his long curly hair and his sombrero, his advent at Marshfield each summer used to attract young people from miles around. As a young girl I experienced his patience and goodwill when I rode out with him on his Indian pony, Buck. I had had an accident, and was only allowed to ride if my mount was on a leading rein. I remember how on this occasion the three horses became entangled in the lead, and Philip's patience as he dismounted to straighten us out again. I suppose that would have been around 1913, when I was about twelve years old."

Mrs William Krusell, of Marshfield Hills, reports memories of a more boisterous Philip, "gleaned from some of the old-timers in town who knew him and remember his escapades". She writes: "There are many stories of his rather eccentric behaviour while here in Marshfield. He had a local following of hero-worshippers whenever he was in town. I am told that he wore chaps and a bandana, hair to the shoulders, and always brandished a gun in one hand. He would ride down the middle of our little village street shooting off his gun and hollering. In fact one night he got so excited at one of the local dances that he shot a hole through the floor of what was then our small library."

Although it was not until 1913 that the curtain descended upon the loud and cheerful climax of *King of the Wild West* for the last time, the show did not play continuously through 1912—as it had during the two previous years. Philip filled in time writing and producing plays in which he himself did not appear. Then for some months he toured the music-halls in a sketch, *The Cowboy and the Girl*, which he had written in odd moments on train journeys. But Buffalo did not care for appearing at music-halls. The legitimate theatre was his home, and he felt that he was, as he expressed it, "invading the variety artists' domain".

It was no easy task to construct a play capable of following so great a success as *King of the Wild West*, but Buffalo was nothing if not game. He put all he knew into the writing and producing of *The Frozen North*, and by June 1914 it was rehearsed and ready for George Ballenger's presentation.[1] It was a huge production,

[1] A sad little footnote. It was about this time that George Ballenger committed suicide. He had become partially paralysed, and the fear of

but it was ill-fated from the start, and the declaration of war a couple of months after its opening did not help. Nevertheless, it continued touring well into 1915.

In September 1915 he opened in yet another Western play, *The Texas Ranger*, produced by Frank Mundill. It was not a success. Philip was strongly advised to pack up and quit. Not he. He insisted on playing every contract signed, regardless. "I will keep faith," was his answer. He did—and went through three bank-accounts doing so. Finally, several thousand pounds the poorer, even he had to admit defeat and, early in 1916, he returned to America.

Five years of unremitting work had ended in failure, but at least he had some wonderful memories to look back upon. . . .

That Sunday night at Wigan when he and the company had been invited to see the moving pictures at the Pavilion Theatre, and the audience of one thousand five-hundred rose as one man and cheered him fit to raise the roof as he entered. . . . Visits to fine cathedrals. . . . Exploring old churches, ruins and antiquities. . . . Trips to historic castles, Rochester with Bob Oakman, Kenilworth with Caroline May. . . . Museums, art galleries, attending service at Westminster Abbey. . . . Happy stays at Hawes Hotel, South Queensferry, West Lothian, and Faulkners Hotel at Charing Cross. . . . Long blue days lolling on the beach he loved at Brighton.

But best of all, perhaps, that never-to-be-forgotten matinée when Ellen Terry came to see the show in London—"When I knew she was going to be in front I decided that I would let myself out a bit and show her what Major could really do. Major was ready for anything. Absolutely fearless when I was astride him, yet as temperamental as a Hollywood film star. Much more reliable though, and one of the best pals a man could ever have. There were several entrances where I had to ride him on to the stage at full gallop, and rein him up in his stride. I don't mind admitting that I liked this. So did the public. This particular afternoon I rode him on to the stage at one of my cues full pelt, but—instead of reining him up as I usually did I just put him straight at the footlights, and with the least touch of my tickle leathers, he rose

blindness preyed on his mind. He left a note: "Goodbye. I am going to Nottingham and shall sleep in the Trent." And he drowned himself. He was forty-eight. He was buried in Colwick Old Churchyard. Drew attended the funeral as a mourner.

like a bird and jumped the orchestra into the main aisle of the theatre. There was a gasp and some shrieks from one or two women in the audience, but I knew what Major could do. Without a pause I rode him full toss up the central gangway, reined him in at the top, turned him round as though he were on a threepenny bit, and put him straight at the orchestra again from the ground floor. Again those gasps of astonishment and fear; again that moment when I touched him lightly with my heels, and then—over the head of the conductor, over the footlights he landed, as beautiful a jump as was ever made by horse. Theatrical? Spectacular? Of course it was. It was intended to be. I *am* a theatrical. It is my life. And never shall I forget the tumult of applause which greeted this little stunt, holding up the performance whilst Major stood there quivering with delight, for he knew as well as I did that we had put it right across, and he was feeling as bucked as I was. And as for Ellen Terry she told me afterwards that she had never been so thrilled in all her life as during those brief seconds when she saw us tearing back towards the orchestra, and sensed what we were about to do."

Once more aboard a ship.

Sadly, Buff stares over the rails.

The shores of England recede.

But he will be back.

Just thirteen years from now he has an appointment in a Samarra named Reading.

(7)

Back in the U.S.A.—Marshfield, the Adirondacks, New York, and California.

Hollywood. Young Buffalo, star of silent films. The dashing Wild West hero of *Tex of the Timberlands, His Pal's Gal, The Law of the Border, The Hobo of Pizen City,* and *The Hold-Up Man.* He might have stayed on there to become another William S. Hart or Tom Mix of the talkies—he certainly had the voice for it —but he found the cranking camera a poor substitute for the warmth and enthusiasm of the flesh-and-blood audiences to which he was accustomed. He quit. Back to Marshfield.

In all this documenting of the stages—literally—of Philip's life we may seem to have lost sight of the man, to have been recording the choreography of a mere dissembling puppet, a creature that has theatrical height and breadth, but no human depth. What part, for instance, did sex play in his life? An important question in this psychiatrically orientated day and age. And the answer is— apparently little or none. If, as a young and virile man, he had affairs, no echo of them survives.

Mrs Krusell told me, "It is said that he courted Ruth Rose, who was the daughter of Edward Rose, partner of the producer, Henry Savage."

If he did, it came to nothing.

Later, his relatives told me, "No. Ruth was just a friend. No romantic interest."

I thought that I had unearthed the buried evidence of a long-ago and hushed-up marriage when Paul Myers, curator of the Theatre Collection of the New York Public Library, sent me a photostat of a clipping from the *Pittsburg Leader* of 1908. It read: "There will appear at the Academy this week a vaudeville shooting act in which Young Buffalo and his wife, known professionally as Mlle Marietta, do some really remarkable work. Young Buffalo and his wife were born in the West, and since childhood they have been associated together, each learning to shoot at an early age. Both, strangely enough, exhibited a prowess with rifle and revolver when scarcely old enough to hold a fire-arm. The young man joined the United States scouting service after reaching his majority and subsequently became one of its most intrepid members."

But when I took the matter up with Robert P. Oakman, he replied, posthaste: "Please forget that marriage stuff. Phil never married. He didn't seem to bother his head about women. In fact they were much more bothered over him. It was just a coincidence that Phil was playing around Pittsburg in 1908. At that time there was a fellow and his wife in vaudeville who were doing the sharp-shooting act, and he went by the same name as Phil. I remember that Charlie Blaney had a bit of litigation over it at the time."

And so the 'secret marriage' dissolved—even before it was contracted. The plain fact seems to be that Philip just was not interested in women in the romantic sense. It could well be that his drinking had something to do with this. Perhaps, as with the porter in *Macbeth*, it took away the performance, although, unlike that worthy, Philip apparently did not find that it provoked the desire.

And—no, he was *not* a homosexual.

January 1920. Four of those thirteen years gone by. The rope shortening. England is beckoning again. Buffalo has never quite managed to forget the splendours of the *King of the Wild West* tour. He had found something 'over there' that was lacking now, and sadly missed. He had liked England and the English, and they had liked him. He would not need much encouragement to return.

Right out of the blue the encouragement came; an invitation to appear in a Western play at the Lyric Theatre, on Shaftesbury Avenue, in the very heart of London's West End theatreland.

In Washington, on March 8th, 1920, American passport No. 181218 was issued to him. Just five weeks after that he was on the boat.

(8)

On April 23rd, 1920, Philip Yale Drew stepped once more on to English soil, and he was to remain here for the rest of his life.

On June 21st, he was issued with Aliens Registration Certificate No. 58486 at Bow Street.

He opened in a play by the American actor-playwright Edwin Milton Royle,[1] *A White Man*, at the Lyric in August. The show, presented by the distinguished London actor-manager, Andrew Melville, was a revival, and Philip took the part of Cash Hawkins. He spent the next three years under the management of Andrew Melville, whom he had first met back in October 1910, when *King of the Wild West* played at Melville's theatre, the Metropole, Snow Hill, Birmingham, and who was now to become one of his closest friends.

It was early in 1921 that Philip achieved a life's ambition—top of the bill, he trod those same boards that his heroine, Ellen Terry, and Sir Henry Irving had trod at the Lyceum. The play was *The Savage and the Woman*, a romance of the West, by Arthur Shirley and Ben Landeck. It was presented by Andrew Melville's brothers, Walter and Frederick.

Opening night was March 3rd, 1921. Kitty Magnus recalls: "Buffalo's performance as Indian Jim will take a lot of forgetting. And who of the countless thousands who saw it is ever likely to

[1] 1862–1942.

forget Hector, the 'Almost Human Horse', from which Buffalo removed a carriage harness, and which he so quickly trained. Hector, the wonderful animal upon which so much depended— would he do his stuff this opening night? Would he come down alone from the flies of that vast theatre, wending his way through the rocky pass that twisted and turned, reach the stage, come that deep distance to the footlights, roll his master over and over, find the bonds that secured him and gnaw on and on through them until they were severed? Would he? Dramatic suspense. Only once did he halt and seem to hesitate. The management were tense with apprehension. Would he fail, and ruin the scene . . . the act . . . the play? The crowded theatre held its breath. Horse and master alone. No one else could assist. Here indeed was the very acme of suspense. Was he acting, this beautiful animal that gazed from point to point, apparently listening? It would seem so, for he looked about as though he sought his master. Standing there without saddle or trappings, the lights playing on his satin-like skin, truly a wild picture in the mountain fastnesses. And then . . . quickly down to the helpless figure . . . and in his anxiety to get at the ropes he rolled Buffalo over and over until the very footlights were reached. From where I was sitting in the stalls this beautiful creature looked indeed gigantic in perspective. Slowly, surely, the ropes are loosened. Free, exhausted, torn, this master of his, with one last great effort hurls himself on to the eagerly waiting back. A flash of a turn, and away, up, up, up, and ever up, far above the scenery disappeared these two. Again and again the curtain rises as the faithful horse returns with his precious load, now seemingly unconscious, legs twisted about his mount's neck, head lolling against the rump, Mazeppa-like. Down, down to the very curtain came this beast, and bowed again and again. Did we cheer? Did we! The theatre rocked. Thus do I remember the first night of Buffalo's triumph in *The Savage and the Woman*. People who knew him best seldom mentioned that horse in his presence in after days. The animal was not his, nor could it be purchased. Its owner, Gardiner Hales, of Drake's Farm, Neasden, told how never afterwards would Hector perform for anyone else, and that he died of a broken heart. It was a long time before he plucked up the courage to tell Buffalo of the tragedy. Once, and only once, I mentioned it to Buffalo myself. A strange look came over his face and, gazing far into the distance, he began quietly to recite, as he had hundreds of times recited it after the performance with Hector's noble head closely snuggled to his shoulder, 'The Ol' Cow-Hawse'—

> *When it comes to saddle hawses—there's a difference in steeds,*
> *There is fancy gaited critters that will suit some fellers' needs.*
> *There is nags high-bred and tony, with a smooth and shiny skin,*
> *That will capture all the races that you want to run 'em in.*
> *But for one that never tires—one that's faithful, tried and true,*
> *One that allus is a stayer, when you want to slam him through,*
> *There is but one brand o' critters that I ever come across*
> *That will always stand the racket,*
>
> > *'Tis the Ol' Cow-Hawse.*
>
> *No he ain't so much for beauty, for he's scrubby and he's rough,*
> *And his temper's sort o' sassy, but you bet he's good enough,*
> *For he'll take the trail o' mountains, be it up or be it down,*
> *On the range a'huntin' cattle, or a'lopin' into town,*
> *An' he'll leave the miles behind him, and he'll never sweat a hair,*
> *'Cuz he's a willin' critter when he's goin' anywhere.*
> *Oh, your thoroughbred at runnin' in a race may be the boss,*
> *But for all-day ridin' lemme have*
>
> > *The Ol' Cow-Hawse.*
>
> *When my soul seeks peace and quiet in the home ranch of the blest,*
> *Where no storms or stampedes bother, and the trails are trails o' rest,*
> *When my brand has been inspected and pronounced to be O.K.,*
> *And the Boss has looked me over an' told me I can stay,*
> *Oh, I'm hopin' when I'm lopin' off across that blessed range,*
> *That I won't be in a saddle on a critter new and strange,*
> *But I'm prayin' every minute that up there I'll ride across,*
> *That big heaven range o' glory on an*
>
> > *Ol' Cow-Hawse.*

And without the usual 'So long, feller,' he turned away, nor did I see him again for weeks. But to go back to that opening night of *The Savage and the Woman*. How they rose to Young Buffalo. Eighteen curtain-calls he took after his big scene with Hector. Yes, truly, Young Buffalo had returned."

The play ran for seventeen weeks—149 performances—at the Lyceum. It grossed £22,845 9s 8d, and closed on June 25th. It was then taken out on the road under Andrew Melville's banner, playing such theatres as the Penge Empire and the Grand, Brighton. Brighton, by the way, was always a favourite spot of Philip's, and so popular was he with audiences there that at one time he was christened "The Uncrowned King of Brighton".

It was about this time, too, that Philip used to meet a certain C.I.D. detective in the lounge bar of the Brixton Theatre. His name was Jim Berrett. Eight years later, their paths were to cross again.

The following July (1922), he was back at the Lyric in another short revival of *A White Man*, and in August Andrew Melville presented Young Buffalo in a new Mexican play, *A Mystery Man*, which, under the name of Andrew Emm, he had written especially for him. It was the Wild West mixture as before. Nine swift scenes, the full American and English company, Young Buffalo as Don Delago, Cynthia Gordon as Rose Deering, a 'ray of sunshine' in distress, and Hector going through his paces once again. It toured—Grand Theatre, Brighton, the Wood Green Empire, the Number One towns and London suburban circuit—well on into 1923, and it has been said that of all Buffalo's great scenes his heart-rending vow of vengeance over the old man's body in *A Mystery Man* was his greatest.

In the latter part of 1923, Andrew Melville put on a production of George Bernard Shaw's *Sermon in Crude Melodrama, The Shewing-up of Blanco Posnet*, with Young Buffalo taking the title rôle. This was a short play—more of a sketch really. It opened the week of November 19th–24th at the Shepherd's Bush Empire, where it was played as the first act in a nine-item variety bill.

With Philip in *The Shewing-up*, were Miss Rose Ralph, Andrew Melville's wife, who played the part of 'The Woman', Marion Wakeford, playing Babsy, and her husband, Frank Lindo, who took the part of Elder Daniels. This was Buffalo's first meeting with the Lindos, whose lives were destined to intertwine closely with his own.

The first week in December, the production was at the Hippodrome, Bristol, and from December 10th–15th it was at the London Alhambra, where it was seen by the critics and Philip's acting was highly praised. Writing in the *Daily News*, E. A. Baughan said: "In many ways it was the best performace of this play I have yet seen. Philip Yale Drew, who calls himself 'Young Buffalo', as if he were another Tom Mix, is an actor quite unknown to me; but he certainly gave the best performance of Blanco Posnet I have yet seen."

The next year, 1924, brought the return of Don Delago in a

revival of *A Mystery Man*, now retitled *Under His Protection*. It opened on March 5th at the Lyceum, and was to be Philip's last appearance there. Cynthia Gordon as Rose Deering once more, still in distress, but no Hector. This time the Almost Human Horse was Dawn. Throughout the run of *The Savage and the Woman*, and the first run of *A Mystery Man*, Andrew Melville had been hiring Hector at a cost of ten pounds a week. This, he felt, was an expense which could be saved by the simple expedient of buying a horse of his own. So off he went to an auction at Aldridge's, at the top of St Martin's Lane, where he purchased a brown hunter, rode it bareback on a blanket through London, put it in a garage at Highgate, and presented it to Buff, who had to set to there and then to train it from scratch. This he did, with Melville's help, on Hampstead Heath. The new horse was named Rosy Dawn, after Melville's wife, Rose.

Under His Protection lasted only five weeks at the Lyceum. The run was killed by a bus strike lasting from March 21st–31st, and the play came off on April 5th, after taking a mere £3232.

Although this premature closure was no fault of Buffalo's, the Lyceum failure was symbolic of another and a deeper failure in Philip himself. Now, at the age of forty-four, the hard drinking which, fourteen years before, had put furrows in the brow of Bob Oakman, was seriously worrying Andrew Melville. For some time he had been aware that Buff's drinking was getting out of hand. At first, it had been a matter for regret, something to be discouraged as kindly and gently as possible. He had, for instance, volunteered to act as his banker, keeping back ten of the twenty-five pounds a week that Buffalo was earning, saving it for him, and thus diverting it from the pockets of the publicans. But by now this drinking had become a most acute problem. Not to put too fine a point on it, Melville had reached the stage where he was only keeping Buff on out of kindness. Kindness, and because of the very warm friendship which he felt for him. The sober Buff was indeed a most engaging person. He was loved by all. Great crowds waited for him at the stage-door. He was regularly mobbed by shop-girls and a sprinkling of rich widows. As he trotted down the street, always wearing brown corduroy breeches and coat, high boots with elevators, and a Stetson, people stopped to stare or shout a greeting, and children followed him like the Pied Piper. He was always signing autographs, always laughing and joking. Expansive, with a big, booming voice—"HULLO there"—he believed everyone was his friend, and was typically to be found with his arm round the shoulder of a chance pub acquaintance.

The drunken Buffalo was a horse of a different colour. He would lurch and bang through the doors into the theatre. He would scowl, use bad language, and look through people. No one trusted him. The horses always knew when he was drunk and would shy away from him, and his devoted Airedale slink warily off. Then, only Andrew Melville could handle him. "Now, Buff, get hold of yourself," and sometimes he would even slap his face. There would be emotional scenes, high drama, in which Buff swore to improve, and pleaded to be kept on. Down on his knees he would go. "I swear to God, Andy . . ." And it would end up with the pair of them in tears, Andy and Buff, two flamboyant characters, very, very fond of each other.

Andy was upset to see Buff beginning to neglect himself. His dressing-room had always looked like an arsenal hit by a hurricane, but now it smelt like a stable. An ugly film of grease-paint oozed, thick as fat, on his collar, and he would pretend that he had had a bath, when Andy knew perfectly well that he had not. It got to the point where Andy would take Buff along to the tub and give him a good scrubbing himself.

Oddly enough, no matter how drunk he was, Buffalo always remembered his lines. But he was a liability and a grievous source of anxiety to other members of the company. There was one little actress, Florrie Kelsey, who played the part of Floss Knight, a determined saloon-keeper, in *Under His Protection*, who wore one of those fringed cowgirl waistcoats on-stage. By the end of the run it was bald. She had plucked the entire fringe off as she waited in agonizing suspense, performance after performance, to see if Buff would fall down when he made his final curtain-speech. He *was* known to fall down . . . but the audiences did not seem to mind.

Things got worse. With increasing frequency Andy Melville would have to go on and play Buff's part, because he was 'at it' again. Obviously, it simply could not continue like that, and finally, worn out with constant expeditions to reclaim the drunken Buff, Andy Melville told him that he had broken his heart. This time tears, protestations, swearings on the Bible were no good. Andy threw on the fire the manuscript of a play about Nelson which he had been considering for Buffalo. It was the end.

After the break with Andrew Melville, Philip was at a loss to know what to do. There were months of wasted time, wasted talent. Meaningless parts, in meaningless plays, in meaningless, fourth-rate theatres. Hard work. Many lines to be learned. Study, study, study. But a lifeline.

Then he joined forces with the Lindos. For some time he had been writing, and pinning his hopes on, a religious play, *The Rock of Ages*. Through the dark hours he cherished the dream that it would eventually get to the Lyceum. It never did. Now, he completed it, in collaboration with Frank Lindo, and they, together with Marion Wakeford, appeared in it at the Royalty Theatre, Chester, in December 1924. Despite its optimistic self-advertisement as "The Greatest Religious Play since 'The Sign of the Cross'", *The Rock* crumbled into dismal failure.

Still with the Lindos, he embarked upon a long stint of touring repertory. Throughout 1925 they toured Somerset Maugham's *The Land of Promise*.

It was in May 1925, while he was doing *The Land of Promise* at some far-flung, flea-pit theatre, that a telegram reached Philip. Eddie Polo, it said, had had to leave the cast of *The Golden West*, a very successful revue, at the King's Theatre, Dundee, owing to his having been injured in a motor accident, would Buffalo take his place, "at your own figure"? Three times Tommy Mostel put the offer, until the figure reached £150 a week. Three times Philip refused it. Why? Because two hours before that telegram arrived he had agreed, verbally, to go to yet another small town to do repertory with the Lindos. His word was his bond. Eddie Polo's place was taken by Jack Willis.

September 1926. Resting. Address: 38 Edbrooke Road, Elgin Avenue, London, W.9. Hawking the manuscript of a play by the American author, Crane Wilbur, around managers' offices.[1] No takers.

More provincial repertory.

September 20th, 1927. A tiny part as Mexico Pete in *When Blue Hills Laughed* at the Criterion, Piccadilly. Now he is really slipping, and the whisky-and-ginger in ever-increasing doses does not steady him. Still hawking *The Monster*.

"For a year and a half, with that manuscript under his arm, he

[1] *The Monster*. First performed in New York in 1922 at the 39th Street Theatre.

Drew's decorative Aliens Registration Card

The Monster
Playbill

"A simple story to
be enacted for
simple folk"

had been, figuratively, he said, kicked off every theatrical manager's door-step," writes Kitty Magnus. "Nobody could see a penny in this thriller he was so sure of. He never claimed it a great play, but, 'There is a public for it,' he said. 'Once get the curtain up on it properly produced, and you will never need to touch the reserve capital.' One manager, and one only, was in agreement with him, Archie Pitt. 'Wait until September, Buff, and I'll do it,' he said. But Buffalo felt that to wait until September would be a mistake. He thought that the public were already showing signs of getting fed up with the numerous thrillers that had been offered to them, and that it should be launched as soon as possible. In this he was wrong. Thrillers had still a long life ahead of them."

George W. Alltree tells in his memoirs[1] how, in the autumn of 1927, Philip brought him a play which he said had been sent to him from America, and asked him to read it. Strangely enough, Alltree had recently been talking to Olga Lindo, Frank Lindo and Marion Wakeford's daughter, who had said to him, "If you ever come across a play suitable for my father and mother, do let me have it, as they are simply pining away when they're not acting." And he had promised, "I'll try to find something really good." And so . . . he offered her *The Monster*. And she took it.

Philip opened in it as "Red" Mackenzie—his 201st part in twenty-eight years on the stage in two hemispheres—at the New Theatre, Cardiff, on January 23rd, 1928, and made a distinct hit.

From there, the play went to the Theatre Royal, Nottingham, and the Royal Theatre, Torquay.

Kitty Magnus reports: "Yet when *The Monster* was eventually produced by Henry Oscar in London, it was without Buff in it. And without him it was not a success. I find a long explanatory letter received by him at Torquay, where he first learned that it would not be possible for him to play the part in the London West End production. It was produced, without him, at the Chelsea Palace, on March 5th, 1928, and moved to the Strand Theatre on March 19th. And there, Buff stood by as an understudy, while Edmund Gwenn played "Red" Mackenzie—an understudy at the Strand, while almost across the way stood the Lyceum, where, so short a time before, flashed huge posters proclaiming him as 'Star' and 'Attraction Extraordinary'."

[1] *Footlight Memories* (Sampson Low, 1932).

But there was a kind of rough, very rough, justice in the fact that long after the London production was in storage, long, long after, Philip was still continuing on and on, up and down the country—Douglas, Isle of Man, Sheffield, Wolverhampton, Malvern, Manchester—with the Lindos and *The Monster*.

It would be nice to be able to see this in terms of a vindicatory triumph, a well-earned reward for all that zealous nursing of the script, that shining faith in it as a sound commercial proposition, that good fight for it well fought.

But it was not really like that at all. It was, for the main part, a dreary trek of No. 3 dates, at No. 3 houses, in No. 3 towns.

"Surely the stars that watch over the Temple of Thespis must have wept in their paths as they traversed their journeys and foresaw the havoc that was to overcome, and well-nigh overwhelm, one of their favourites," lamented Kitty Magnus.

Drift, drift, drift . . .

January 1929: The Grand Theatre, Blackpool. March: The Prince of Wales, Grimsby. April: The Theatre Royal, Bognor, and the Hippodrome, Rochdale. May: The Pier Theatre, Eastbourne.

Drift, drift, drift . . .

June 10th–15th: The Winter Gardens, New Brighton.

The rocks are very near now.

June 17th–22nd: The Royal County Theatre, Reading.

The long-delayed appointment is upon him.

Act Two

The action takes place in the
coroner's court in Reading.
The time: Three months later,
October 1929

Scene 1

OVERTURE AND BEGINNERS

Wednesday, October 2nd, 1929

(1)

AUSTERE, precise, rectilinear and functional. A place of over-whelming wood—panelled wooden walls, hard and highly polished wooden pews, wooden boxes, wooden benches, wooden tables, wooden chairs, wooden desks—set out with the fixed and finicky exactitude of a tournament chess-board. A carefully planned war-game patterning of judicial furniture. Such was, and still is, the Reading Magistrates' Court in Valpy Street, where, since the Reading Coroner's Court in Duke Street was judged to be too small to accommodate the large number of witnesses to be called, the second act of the inquest on Alfred Oliver was staged. A fine and public place, entailed in far excess of four planks.

At 11.25 A.M. the coroner, Mr John Lancelot Martin, entered and took his seat in the high-backed leather chair on the long, raised dais. Next to him sat two local magistrates. Chief Inspector Berrett and Detective Sergeant Harris occupied seats immediately below the coroner, and on a bench facing him, and directly in front of the brass-railed dock sat Philip Yale Drew. He was flanked by Mr and Mrs Lindo. Farther along the same pew-like bench sat the youth Jefferies. Not far away were Chief Constable Burrows and Detective Inspector Walters, of the Reading Force.

The coroner, addressing the jury, recalled that he had adjourned the inquest on Alfred Oliver some three months before, in order to give Scotland Yard and the police authorities throughout the country a good chance of making inquiries with a view to finding the assassin of Mr Oliver. They had, he said, worked incessantly and, he hoped, with some measure of success.

Referring to "a tremendous amount of local rumours", Mr Martin asked the jury, as fair-minded men, to eliminate anything that they had already heard from their minds, and to apply themselves to listening with the greatest attention to the very great amount of evidence which would be placed before them.

"We cannot hurry or rush this case," he added, "and it may possibly last three days."

Actually, it was to last seven.

This overture concluded, the beginners were called—Mr Arthur William Crouch, brother-in-law of Mr Oliver, and Dr James Leonard Joyce. They listened as the evidence which they had given at the previous hearing of June 25th was read over to them, and to the jury.

Detective Inspector William McBride of Scotland Yard put in three photographs which he had taken at the scene of the crime, and the three which he had taken at the mortuary.

William Robert Wells, a tracing clerk in the Reading Borough Surveyor's Office, produced a detailed plan of the premises at 15 Cross Street.

Then, Mrs Annie Elizabeth Oliver, a slight woman of below medium height and dressed in deep mourning, entered the court and was led to the witness-box, where a chair had been provided for her.

Replying to the coroner's gentle questioning, Mrs Oliver said that she was now living at 40 Norris Road, Reading. She had not been serving in the shop on the day of the murder until the evening.

"I served first from 5.25 P.M. to 5.50 P.M., relieving my husband, and during that time served about six customers, all men, but I would not be able to identify any of them. They all made small purchases of a bona fide nature, and then left the shop at once. My husband had not complained of any suspicious man entering the shop or loafing about, either on that Saturday or on the previous day."

Mrs Oliver went on to tell of her discovery of her injured husband.

The coroner asked her to describe exactly what she saw, and, observing her distress, gently told her, "Try and bear up".

Berrett whispered to Mr Martin, who then asked, "While you were with your husband did you touch him, or anything in the shop?" Mrs Oliver replied that she did not.

The coroner said that he wanted to be quite sure about the time, and Mrs Oliver said that she was certain that she left with the dog at about five minutes past six, and was convinced that she returned at about 6.15 P.M. So that whatever happened had to take place within that short space of time. She added that she felt certain that when she left—between six o'clock and five minutes past—all was normal. She said how at first she had thought it might be that her husband had had a seizure, but that Mrs Taylor had suggested that it was a robbery, and that she should look at the till. She went on to recount how her husband was taken to the Royal Berkshire Hospital.

"I followed in Chief Constable Burrows's car. I was only at the hospital a few minutes and was told to return at 10 P.M. I went back to the shop, and one of the police cleared it up for me. When I examined the till, I think before I went to the hospital, I found all the notes were missing. I think that ten or twelve pounds would have been there. The silver and copper in the till was intact, so far as I know."

Mrs Oliver said that they had had customers that day of the racing type. Her husband had no connection with betting people, and was, in fact, against betting.

The coroner asked, "Do you see anyone in this court who may have been in the shop as one of the customers on that particular Saturday?"

Mrs Oliver looked carefully round the court, twice. "No," she said, "I see no-one."

She had given her evidence calmly, but as she left the witness-box she was unable to restrain her tears.

George Stannard Taylor, proprietor of the Welcome Café, 29 Cross Street, went briefly into the box to confirm the finding of Alfred Oliver.

He was followed by a succession of police witnesses.

P.C. Frank Chandler said: "I was in Hieatt's, the butcher's, at 6.25 P.M. in plain clothes, shopping. Mrs Taylor came into the shop and said to the manager, 'Will you 'phone for the police?' She then recognized me, and said, 'Will you come?' I said, 'What is wrong at your place?' She said, 'It's not my place, poor Mr Oliver has been knocked down and robbed.' I went at once to 15 Cross Street, and found the shop in some confusion. I looked round the shop for an instrument, but could find none. I stayed until Detective Sergeant Pope came and took over."

Police Sergeant Arthur Colbert said that at 6.25 P.M. on Saturday,

June 22nd, he received a telephone message from the manager of Hieatt's. He informed Detective Sergeant Pope, and also sent an ambulance.

Detective Sergeant Oliver Pope said that he went to 15 Cross Street, where he found Mr Oliver sitting in an armchair in the dining-room, and being attended by Dr Stansfield for severe injuries to the head. He examined every room at the premises, but could find no person there, nor any instrument with which the murder might have been committed. There were a number of tools underneath the counter, including a packing-case opener, for use by Mr Oliver, but these obviously had not been touched.

Chief Constable Thomas Alfred Burrows testified that at about 6.30 P.M. on June 22nd, he was in his office when he was informed that Mr Oliver had been badly knocked about, and his shop-till robbed. He went immediately to 15 Cross Street, and found that Mr Oliver had been taken to hospital. Sergeant Pope and other police officers were at the shop, so he followed the ambulance to the Royal Berkshire Hospital, where he saw Mr Oliver, who was conscious, but could not state how he came by his injuries. "During my conversation with him he said, 'There was a man came in. I thought he was from the Gas Office.' I left a constable—Parfitt—at the hospital in case Mr Oliver should say anything, and returned to the shop. Throughout the night, with the whole of my staff, we were making inquiries with a view to tracing the offender. The next morning I asked for assistance from New Scotland Yard."

P.C. William Charles Parfitt said that, at 6.25 P.M. on June 22nd, he went with P.C. Davis to 15 Cross Street with the police ambulance, and conveyed Alfred Oliver to the Royal Berkshire Hospital. "He was detained and I remained with him. At 8.30 P.M. he said, 'I was in the room behind the counter when Mrs Oliver went out to Wellsteeds,[1] leaving me to clear away the tea. I had an attaché-case on the table containing about £30 in notes and silver which I last saw just before tea, when I got some change for a man—I think he was from the Gas Office.' At 9.5 P.M. he said, 'Sitting in shop, six or five-past, reading book, *A Day From London to Penzance*. Remember no more.' He spoke after this to the doctor, but not to me again."

Chief Inspector Harry Battley, of the fingerprint bureau, said that

---

[1] Wellsteeds, Ltd. A departmental store at 125–133 Broad Street.

he had found a bloodstained imprint on a show-case in Mr Oliver's shop, and that it had now been definitely established that this impression was identical with part of the palmar surface of the hand of one of the witnesses.[1] It could not, therefore, have any further bearing on the crime.

The lad George Charles Jefferies was called next.

The coroner told the court that Jefferies had signed three different statements which he had made to the police, and these were read. In his third statement he said that it was between 6.8 P.M. and 6.10 P.M. when he went into Mr Oliver's.

The foreman of the jury asked: "Can you give any reason for your hesitation in coming forward to give information?"

"I didn't know what to do," said Jefferies. "I didn't think it was serious till I saw the papers."

"Your mother told you that you ought to come forward, but you still hesitated. Why?"

"I might have been scared of the police," he said.

The coroner asked: "What is your age?"

"I was twenty-one last May."

"That is old enough to be a man and not be scared, is it not?"

"Yes," said Jefferies.

"Why did you not ask for help outside?"

"I was dumbfounded when I saw the man on the floor."

"Did you notice anyone suspicious in the street?"

"No."

The witness's mother, Mrs Emily Jefferies, told the court, "My son came home about twenty-past six and sat down on the sofa with his head buried in his hands. I said, 'What's the matter, George?' He said, 'I've been scared to death.' I said, 'In what way? Have you run over anyone or met with an accident?' He said, 'No, Mother. Something worse than that. I went into Oliver's shop to get some cigarettes. I looked over the counter, and thought I saw the body of a man lying in a pool of blood.' I said, 'Have you reported it?' He said, 'No.' I said, 'Why?' He said, 'I was too spellbound over Lily.' That was his sister, who was dying in hospital. That is all that was said. Then he changed his clothes. He was wearing a wine-coloured coat and vest and blue trousers. There were no marks on them. He wears them to work, and they

[1] That of Mr George Stannard Taylor. Battley had taken palmar impressions of Mrs Oliver and Mr and Mrs Taylor.

have not been washed or cleaned. Then he went out—about a quarter to seven. I saw him at about half-past seven in West Street, talking to two friends, Hart and Hendley. He came home about 11 P.M. On Sunday morning my daughter saw in the paper about the murder and showed it to my son. He said, 'They've got it in the paper now, Mother.' And I advised him to report it to the police. But he said, 'If I go there I might get the sack. Mr Kingham might hear.' He was still upset on Monday and didn't eat his meals. I again suggested he went to the police. He said, 'I can't. I've got to look after my work and you.' He gets twenty-one shillings a week, and gives me twelve to fifteen shillings. He had no extra money about him that week-end. I read that half a crown had been left on the counter, and I asked my son if he'd left it. He said, 'I don't earn enough to leave half-crowns on counters.' His wages are sometimes paid at dinner-time, and sometimes as he is going to the post. He said after that he wished he'd reported it. I would have done so myself had not my daughter been dying. My boy keeps good company and is well conducted at home. He has been in his place four years. He has never threatened any of us. I think he would have gone to the police, only he was upset over his sister. I said that if he didn't, I would go."

And Jefferies' friends, Frank Hart and Walter James Hendley, both gave evidence.

"About twenty-past seven on June 22nd, I was standing outside the Billiard Hall,' said Hart, "when Jefferies told me that he left work about six o'clock, went to the post-office and on his way back called in Mr Oliver's. He said that when he came out of the shop he went up Cross Street, went to the workshop and then went home. I said that I would go with him to the police, but he refused. We passed along Broad Street later, and Jefferies said, 'Come along, let's get away from here.' I asked him if Mr Oliver was seriously hurt, and Jefferies said he thought he would die from loss of blood. On Saturday and Sunday nights I noticed he was very nervy and his hands were shaking. He told me he rode up Cross Street. I took it to mean on his bicycle."

Said Hendley: "The first time I heard of the murder was about seven o'clock on the Saturday evening. About half-past seven I met Jefferies outside the Billiard Hall. I asked him if he'd heard about the do in Cross Street. He said, 'Hush, I'll tell you more about it later on.' When Hart arrived later he told us. I asked what he did, and he said, 'I ran out, jumped on my bicycle and went back to my work, and went home and told my mother. I took some water because I felt queer.' I said if I was in his place I should have found some assistance. He said, 'I was too dumbfounded to do anything.' Both Hart and I advised him several times that night to go to the police."

The first real sensation of the day came with the calling of William George Loxton.

Mr Loxton was a butcher, employed in Hieatt's shop, next door but one to Mr Oliver's.

"About 1.30 P.M. on June 22nd," said Mr Loxton, "a man came to the shop-door. He didn't come in, but asked, 'Have you any calves' liver?' Then he turned, and before I could say yes or no he went away. I said to the other man in the shop, 'That gentleman's a bit of a lad. He's either a Scotchman or an Irishman. At any rate, he's not an Englishman.'"

Loxton explained that he had noticed the man's pronounced accent.

"He might have been an American?" asked the coroner.

"He might have been anything," replied Loxton amid laughter.

Witness went on to say that between half-past five and six o'clock, he was looking through the shop-window when he saw the same man. He was by Bradley's wireless shop, which was at No. 14, opposite Oliver's. "He was coming towards my shop. He came half-way across the road, stopped, turned, and went towards Mr Oliver's shop. He appeared to be very agitated and undecided. After that I lost sight of him."

Mr Martin then interposed that, according to another statement which Mr Loxton had made regarding the time at which he had telephoned a message from his shop to the police at Mrs Taylor's request, the second occasion when he saw the man would have been at about at about 6 P.M. or 6.5 P.M. Loxton agreed, and the coroner then asked, "Will you give me a careful description of this eccentric man?"

"His height was about 5 feet 8 inches. He had dark hair and a sallow face. He was clean shaven with a full face. He was wearing no hat, and his hair was long and in a rough state. He had on a navy-blue suit, brown shoes and he wore a collar and tie."

The Coroner: "Is there anyone in this court who resembles that man?"

The first arrow of suspicion was out of the quiver.

Loxton: "Yes, sir. . . ."

A buzz of excitement.

"That gentleman sitting there."

And he pointed straight at Philip Yale Drew.
Mr Martin asked Drew to stand up. He did so.

The Coroner: "Are you positive that that is the man?"
Loxton: "I am."
The Coroner: "Remember you are on oath. Do you swear it?"
Loxton: "Yes, I swear it on my oath."

There was another buzz of excitement as Drew resumed his seat.

Continuing his evidence, Loxton said that he subsequently made a statement to the police, and, on July 25th, he and a Mrs James were taken in a car to Nottingham by P.C. Woodward of the Reading Force. There, at about 6.20 P.M., he was standing at the corner of a street and was asked to keep a look-out for anyone he might recognize in connection with the crime. After about five minutes he saw the man to whom he had just pointed.

"I believe the man in question is Mr Drew," observed the coroner.

Philip Yale Drew stood up and said, "That is correct."

Mr Martin turned to Drew. "Do you wish to put any questions to this witness? You are entitled to do so if you wish."

"No, thank you," said Drew.

The inquest was then adjourned until eleven o'clock the following morning.

What did the day's evidence amount to? Not very much.

The police witnesses had made it clear that the murderer, whoever they might think he was, had not left a single clue to his identity at the scene of the crime, and that no possible weapon had been traced.

Mrs Oliver, although she had every opportunity to do so, had been unable to identify Drew as having been in the shop.

It was clearly established that Mr Oliver himself had been incapable of throwing any significant light upon the identity of his attacker.

Neither had George Charles Jefferies' account of his discovery of the injured tobacconist added anything.

The one seemingly positive contribution was Mr Loxton's conviction that Philip Yale Drew had been in and around Cross Street at the approximate time of the attack. That in itself did not prove that Drew had perpetrated the attack, but it was enough to alert him to the potential danger in which he was placed, enough to send him that evening, on the advice of a friend,[1] to the office of Mr Frederick James Ratcliffe, solicitor, of 4 Blagrave Street, with the request that he should represent his interests when, the next day, the inquest was resumed.

There was no telling what the police might not have up their sleeves.

[1] Bernard O'Donnell, crime reporter of the *Empire News*.

Scene 2

WHAT THE CARETAKER SAW

Thursday, October 3rd, 1929

(1)

MRS Alice James, a plump, homely body, seemed ill-cast for the rôle of Nemesis, but hers was to be a vital strand in the rope of circumstantial evidence which, as the days of the inquest wore on, was to come perilously near lassoing Young Buffalo, and putting a running noose about his neck.

Shortly before eleven o'clock that Thursday morning, Drew, a striking, burly figure in a grey suit and brown belted overcoat, was waiting in the corridor outside the glass swing-doors of the police court, where a case was just finishing before the magistrate. He stood in the middle of a small knot of people—Mr Ratcliffe, his newly retained solicitor, Mr and Mrs Lindo, and Alfred George Fry, stage-manager of the *Monster* company—chewing continually on the stub of an unlit cigar, stuck Yankee-style in the corner of his mouth.

Then came the usher's cry, "Witnesses this way, please." And Drew, his light brown hat still set firmly upon the mass of curly hair above his rather Cromwellian features, led the file of fifty-odd witnesses into the court. There, he took his place at the solicitors' table, removed his hat, and placed it carefully on the bench in front of him. Mrs Lindo settled herself down on his left—a slim, nervous figure, wearing a close-fitting blue hat, a black satin coat with a fur collar, and incessantly fingering a bottle of smelling-salts.

Mrs Alice James made her way to the box. People in the sardine-packed court leant forward attentively.

Mrs James was a caretaker. She lived with her husband, William James, a labourer, at 17 Blagrave Street, Reading. Just after six o'clock on the evening of June 22nd, she had left her home to go shopping. She had walked along Friar Street, crossed over by the post-office, turned into Cross Street, and headed towards Broad Street. She remembered the time clearly because she had looked at the Town Hall clock as she passed, as she had wanted to get back home extra early, and had noticed that it was ten minutes past six. About midway up Cross Street she had passed a tobacconist's shop on the left, but did not register its name. She said that as she went by the shop she saw a man standing just inside the doorway. He was wiping some blood off his face and nose—whether with a handkerchief or not she could not say. She thought he had been fighting.

Asked to describe him, she said, "He was fairly tall, of stoutish build, with a full face, and was dressed in dark clothes. He was between forty and fifty. He had no hat and a lot of hair, roughish, which appeared to be iron-grey. He wasn't wearing glasses."

The man was very respectable-looking. He seemed to be muttering to himself, and to be dazed.

Mrs James then told the court that on July 25th she and Mr Loxton went with the police to Nottingham. She said that at about 6.20 that evening she was standing in a street in Nottingham— "There were a tidy few people about, and I saw a man come round the corner and recognized him. He was the man I saw in Cross Street, standing in the shop-door with blood on his face."

The Coroner: "Can you recognize anyone in this court as the man you saw standing in the doorway of Mr Oliver's shop?"

There was a tense silence as Mrs James glanced round, and then, without hesitation, she pointed to the well of the court. "That is the man," she said firmly.

The Coroner: "Will you stand up?"

A half-smile flitting across his face, Philip Yale Drew stood up.

The Coroner: "You are positive that is the man?"
Mrs James: "Yes."

Mr Ratcliffe then questioned Mrs James on Drew's behalf.

"Can you swear that whoever it was was wiping blood off his face?"

"Well, there was blood on his face and he'd got his hand up to it."

The coroner suggested, "He might have been trying to hide the blood?"

"Yes, I should think so," agreed Mrs James.

Mr Ratcliffe pounced—"But you said he was wiping it off?"

"He appeared to be doing so. I can't swear to it."

"Which would you swear to: that he was wiping it off, or that he was trying to hide it?"

"I can't say."

"Can you describe his clothes more particularly?"

"He was in navy-blue or black, or in something very dark."

"Did you notice the colour of his boots?"

"No," said Mrs James, "I didn't."

Three theatrical witnesses followed in rapid succession.

The first was Charles Russell, a Reading man, and stage-manager at the Royal County Theatre. He testified that it was Mr Drew's custom during the week that he was at Reading to arrive at the theatre between 6 and 6.15 each evening. Witness did not actually see him arrive on the evening of June 22nd, but he saw him play his part, without incident, in both performances. He had been drinking "fairly heavily" that week, and on the Saturday night the *Monster* company's stage-manager[1] packed his basket, which is not usual.

Russell said that at half-past one on June 22nd, he had gone to the Marquis of Lorne, in Friar Street, for a lunch-time drink with Drew and a Mr Grubb and a Mr Ingram. Drew had stood them a couple of rounds, and at approximately 1.45 P.M. left the party, saying that he had not time to have another drink as he had to go to Cross Street to get a special paper. "There's a paper-shop next door to Oliver's," Russell added.

In answer to questions put by Mr Ratcliffe, Russell said that it was a pretty strict rule that actors should be present half an hour before the performance began—which in this case was at 6.50 P.M.—and that before his appearance on the stage Mr Drew would have to go through a fair amount of preparation, as he had rather a big make-up for his part.

The next witness was Harry George Ingram, head flyman at the Royal County Theatre.

Mr Ratcliffe asked him if he had heard the previous evidence. He said that he had.

"Do you wish any of the witnesses to retire from the court?" asked the coroner.

[1] Mr William Norman Stubbs.

Philip Yale Drew in
The Monster
Rôle or reality?

Alfred Oliver:
Murder Victim

The very last person you would
expect to tangle with violence

THE SCENE OF THE CRIME

Alfred Oliver's 'superior' tobacconist's shop (*Above*)

The open till: the broken scales (*Right*)

The 'Trade Gap'—across which, one June evening, death reached out (*Below*)

"It's a bit late for that now," said Mr Ratcliffe.

"We have a particular reason for having them all in court," replied Mr Martin. "I will tell you about that privately."

Mr Ingram's evidence was simply that at 1.30 P.M. on June 22nd, he went to the Marquis of Lorne with Mr Drew, Mr Russell and Mr Grubb, and had some drinks. Ingram left the party at about 1.35 P.M., but not before Drew had told him that he was going to Cross Street to get a paper. Ingram said that during the week at Reading Drew wore brown boots and a blue serge suit. He never saw him wear a hat.

James Henry Grubb, an electrician at the Royal County Theatre, also stated that he went with Drew and the others to the Marquis of Lorne on June 22nd, but he put the time at about 1.15 P.M. He, too, had heard Drew say that he was going to get a special paper in Cross Street. "The last time I saw Drew," he continued, "was between 12.30 and 12.45 A.M. on June 23rd, when he said goodbye to me in the theatre yard. He was then wearing the beard which he wore during the play. That was unusual, as he had had plenty of time to change. He had a coat on, so I couldn't see his clothes. He went off towards Chatham Street."

The coroner asked if he was wearing a hat. Mr Grubb said that he was not.

Witness was sure that Drew did not go back into the theatre after he had wished him goodbye. He went out into the open street.

The Coroner: "Was there in his make-up any sign of an iron-grey colour?"

Grubb: "It was rather a ginger make-up."

The Coroner: "His appearance, in fact, was disguised when he went out into the street?"

Grubb: "Yes."

Mr Ratcliffe: "Do you suggest that it is unusual for an actor to leave in his make-up?"

Grubb: "Yes, at that time in the morning."

The last witness before the lunch-break was Thomas Harold Windle, a sanitary inspector, of Theale, near Reading. He stated that on Saturday afternoon, June 22nd, he had motored with his wife and child to Reading. He parked his car opposite the newspaper shop in Cross Street at 4.20 P.M. Some twenty minutes later he noticed a man in the street acting peculiarly. He had evidently been drinking. He was moving about in a short area, and gazing at the buildings—Mr Windle illustrated this by gazing round at different parts of the courtroom. The man was looking in the shops, mumbling to himself and staring at the bystanders. His manner was arrogant and bullying. Mr Windle had the impression that two girls were giggling at his antics. He went on to describe this eccentric man as sturdy, thickset, and broad-shouldered. His height would have been about 5 feet 8 inches or so. He felt pretty sure that he had a trilby hat on, and thought that he was wearing a suit that was on the dark side. He only saw his face three-quarters on, but noticed that he was rather a big-jawed man, full-faced, and of a somewhat swarthy, red complexion.

Mr Windle then demonstrated how the man was wearing a raincoat thrown over both shoulders, cape-fashion. He went into the Welcome Café, and closed the door.

The coroner asked, "Can you recognize anyone in court like the man you saw in Cross Street?"

Mr Windle glanced ostentatiously round.

"I recognize him here," he said, pointing.

"Stand up," ordered the coroner.

And, once again, Philip Yale Drew rose to his feet.

(2)

During the midday adjournment a *Daily Express* reporter chatted "over the luncheon table" with Drew at the Great Western Hotel.

"Mr Drew," he reported, "made a scrappy meal. He was obviously sensitive to the whispered conversation which was taking place all over the luncheon room. His hand trembled as he used his knife and fork, and he admitted frankly that he had been unnerved by his sudden entanglement in a sensational murder case. In court Mr Drew's face has not betrayed his emotions, but his hands were never still for a moment. 'I am the victim of a case of mistaken identity,' he told me. 'I have discussed everything with my solicitor. I am an innocent man; I have nothing to hide. There are some things I cannot remember. I have a bad memory, as you will discover yourself when I go into the witness-box, but I am perfectly clear on the main facts at issue. Fortunately I have an alibi. My life at present would be unbearable if this were not true."

Drew also told the reporter that he was no stranger to Reading. "I played here twice before my visit in *The Monster*. I starred in a play called *The Texas Ranger*, and I was also here in *The Land of Promise*."

At this point, Mrs Lindo—she and her husband were also at the table—broke into the conversation. She said that the performance of *The Monster* had had to be suspended because of the Reading inquest. "It has been impossible to carry on," chimed in Mr Lindo. "The police notified us only on Saturday that we should have to attend the inquest. We had to close down the show at Brecon on Tuesday instead of Wednesday, as arranged. We were to appear at Cirencester during the latter part of the week. We all have the greatest faith in Mr Drew, and we are confident that this case will end satisfactorily for him."

(3)

When the court resumed in the afternoon, Mrs Nellie Taylor, of the Welcome Café, went into the box. Having confirmed the evidence of the finding of Alfred Oliver given by her husband and Mrs Oliver the previous day, she told how, on Tuesday (June 18th) or Wednesday (June 19th), a man, who she now knew had taken part in *The Monster*, had come into her café at about 1 P.M. and ordered a meal of four fried eggs, two rashers, rolls and butter, and two cups of black coffee. He had struck her as "something out of the ordinary". He had been drinking, but did not act abnormally.

The same man came in again between 4.15 and 4.30 P.M. on Saturday, June 22nd, and ordered four fried eggs, two rashers, a cup of tea, and bread and butter. This time he was in an advanced state of drunkenness, but not "rolling drunk". When she asked for his money he was searching his pockets three or four minutes before he found it. Eventually, he produced some silver wrapped in a ten-shilling note. While he was waiting for his meal the man addressed remarks to other customers.

"He got up, walked to the door, and asked, 'Does this street lead to the County Theatre?' Nobody answered, and he repeated the question. When I said, 'Yes, straight up the street and turn to the left,' he replied, 'Thank God somebody has answered me.'"

He spoke good English at times, then lapsed occasionally into a very strong American accent. He left the café at three minutes to five.

Mrs Taylor described him as about 5 feet 9 inches tall, between

40 and 50, but nearer fifty, heavy, broad build, swarthy dark complexion, hair iron-grey, plenty of it and very rough, baggy under the eyes, and clean-shaven. He was well dressed, but very untidy. He was wearing a dark suit—it might have been blue—and had a collar and tie on. His appearance was quite respectable. He wore a coat over both shoulders like a cape. She could not remember whether or not he had a hat.

> The Coroner: "Is there anyone you can identify in this court as the man you saw?"
> Mrs Taylor: "That is the man." [She pointed].
> The Coroner: "Stand up."

Philip Yale Drew stood up.

Next came a quartet of witnesses, each of whom described variant aspects of the weird behaviour of the unconventional man in the street.

Sydney Eric Turnbull—"I am an estate agent in business at 20 Cross Street. Between 2 P.M. and 2.40 P.M. on Saturday, June 22nd last, I saw a man behaving peculiarly in Cross Street and thought he was under the influence of drink. He was nearly opposite the Welcome Café, and was looking for somewhere or somebody. He appeared to have some mission in the street, from my observation. He had on a navy-blue suit, brown shoes, a fawn-coloured mackintosh, half on and half off, or as a cape, and a grey—I think grey—trilby hat. His age was between forty and fifty-five, his height between 5 feet 8 inches and 5 feet 9 inches. He was very thickset and his face was rather flushed, which made me think him partly under the influence of drink. He was staggering about between the Welcome Café and the International Tea Company's Stores at No. 25 He went in somewhere—I did not see where. From ten to six to ten past six that evening I was in the Liberal Club yard repairing my car. The yard doors were open to the street, but I had my mind on the car and saw nothing unusual in the street."

> The Coroner: "Can you see the man in court?"
> Turnbull [pointing to Drew]: "If that man will stand up perhaps I shall be able to say."
> The Coroner: "Stand up."

Philip Yale Drew did so.

Mr Turnbull looked intently at him. "That man resembles him," he said.

George Thomas Nicholson—"I live at New Mill Road, Eversley, and I am a gardener. I remember being in Cross Street about 5.20 P.M. on June 22nd. My wife was in the International Tea Company's Stores, and I went into Mr Oliver's and made a purchase. He came from the inner room, and spoke to someone as he came to me. There was no-one else in the shop. He was all right then, and passed a remark about the dry weather. I then went to the International, and as my wife was still inside I stood outside. A man came from Broad Street and passed me. He had his mac on his arm, dragging along the pavement. He seemed to me to be drunk. He was staggering, and reeled off the pavement on to a stationary car. He got to the lamp-post near Oliver's, and appeared to be counting with his fingers all down the lamp to the bottom."

"He was measuring the lamp-post?" asked the coroner.

"I don't know whether he was measuring it," said Nicholson. "He was pointing with his finger."

Continuing his narrative, Mr Nicholson said that the man then threw his mackintosh over his shoulder and walked into Friar Street. That would be at about 5.30 P.M. He was a very big-built man, dark-complexioned, aged forty to fifty, wearing a navy-blue striped suit, not a decent-looking one but rather shabby, and a brown (he thought, but could not swear to the colour) trilby hat.

Invited by the coroner to see if the man was in court, Mr Nicholson looked all round, and said that he could not see him.

"Have a good look," insisted Mr Martin.

"No, I don't see him," said Mr Nicholson emphatically.

Herbert Booth, an Alfred Doolittle-like character straight out of the pages of Shaw, provided a little much-needed comic relief.

"I am a stableman," he said. "Between half-past ten and eleven o'clock on the morning of Friday, June 21st, the day before the Windsor Race Day, I was standing opposite the post-office in Friar Street, and I saw a stranger ask a postman where he could get some food. He sent him to the Welcome Café. The stranger came up to me, and I said I'd show him the Welcome. So I went down Cross Street with him and said, 'Here's the Welcome.' He said, 'Can we get a drink?' I said, 'Yes. In the Bull.' And he said, 'Let's go in and have one.' So we went in and had one together. (Laughter.) He said he could do with a feed of eggs and bacon, and I said, 'You'll get it in the Welcome.' So he said, 'Have another drink.' (Laughter.) While we were talking he was excited, and he said, 'I don't know, actors don't seem to be appreciated'."

Mr Booth then pointed out Drew as the stranger whom he had met.

"Stand up," ordered the coroner.

And when Drew did so, Booth touched his forelock and said, "Quite right, sir, ain't it?"—a remark which made the court laugh again, and brought a smile from Drew.

Mrs Kathleen Earl—"I remember being in Cross Street on June 22nd, as near as possible at 5.30 P.M. I went to the butcher's. I saw a man walking in the middle of the road, behaving in a very peculiar way. He was muttering to himself and looking at the windows above the shops both sides. He turned round twice, quickly. His face was very red. I was in the butcher's two minutes, and then saw he was at the end of Cross Street, near Broad Street."

Mr Martin put the inevitable question.

Mrs Earl pointed to Drew.

"Stand up," said the coroner curtly.

The next witness was a hairdresser, Mr Reginald Percy Collins, recently employed at 10ª Blagrave Street.

"I remember that at about 1.45 P.M. on June 21st, someone came in our saloon. There was one customer in, and the other hung round the front shop looking about. He was looking through the cases. I was rather suspicious. Then I shaved him, and he said, referring to my razor, 'What a fine piece of steel you have.' After shaving him I went in the front shop and he followed. He told me he had just seen two lovely pipes at 15s. 6d. and 26s. I showed him one at 7s. 6d., and he said, 'Good God, man, don't tempt me. I've got no money.' He told me that he sent pipes to America to a friend who ran a ranch there. He said he'd be in next day, but he didn't return. While I was shaving him he said he acted in *The Monster* at the theatre. He had a little grease-paint on his face, and I brushed his hair very flat as he had to wear a wig."

The Coroner: "Do you see that man here?"
Collins: "Yes . . . there . . ."
The Coroner: "Stand up, Mr Drew."

Mrs Marion Lindo stepped into the box.

Although this was not—was not supposed to be—in any sense a trial, you could say that she was the first witness for the defence.

Mrs Lindo began her evidence with an account of the events of

June 22nd. She said that when the *Monster* company, of which she was the proprietress, was in Reading she and her husband lodged at 77 Vastern Road. Drew stayed in King's Meadow Road opposite, but had his meals, other than breakfast, with them. She said that Drew was an embarrassment to her—that she had to look after him to a great extent because of his one weakness—taking too much whisky. Occasionally he had spoilt his acting by this, but not much, he was such a good actor.

"On June 22nd Mr Drew had lunch with us between 2 P.M. and 2.30 P.M. I couldn't say he was drunk. He was flushed, but he'd come in late and said he'd been hurrying. It was a hot day. My husband advised him to have a nap, and he did sleep for a little while on the sofa. I sat and wrote letters, and then went upstairs. I wasn't up there long. I was collecting things to pack. I came back to the sitting-room about four o'clock, and when I came in it woke him up. I noticed in his side trouser-pocket the outline of what I took to be a whisky bottle. I asked him to give it to me. He denied that it was whisky, and refused to give it up. I asked several times, and I got very angry. He was making for the door, and I said, 'You must give me that.' And he said, 'No, you must not touch that,' and went out. I went over to his lodgings about ten minutes later. He was not there, so I went to the kitchen and asked if I might go upstairs. I did so, and found him lying down in his bedroom. I again asked for the bottle, and he said, 'You can search where you like, but you won't find it.' I searched but could not find it. Then the landlady told me that Mr Drew had gone out. This would be a little after five o'clock. I went home. Just after five, near my lodgings, I saw Mr Drew, who said, 'You're going early.' I said I had some shopping to do. We spoke as it were in passing. He was going home for tea. Later, I went to the theatre, where my dressing-room was next to Mr Drew's. The half-hour call that night would be at 6.20 P.M. I heard Mr Drew enter a few minutes before the call. At least I took it to be him, I didn't see him or hear his voice until half-past six, when he spoke to someone. Before that I'd heard things being moved in his room. The curtain went up at 6.50 P.M. Twenty minutes before that Mr Drew came in my room and asked if his make-up was right. He appeared to be normal, only one eye was made up heavier than the other. Then his landlady came and said did I know a murder had been committed, and is Mr Drew all right? I said, 'Of course he's all right.' She then left. I don't think I mentioned this to Mr Drew. He played his part all right. We left at 11.20 P.M., and Mr Drew said he would come to supper. We waited till midnight, but he did not come. He came to breakfast on Sunday morning, and later we all went to Maidstone. He said his blue trousers had disappeared with three pound-notes in the pocket. I wrote to Reading about them, but they were not traced. I was paying Mr Drew four pounds a week, and everything paid. I gave him some money at Victoria, as he said he had none at all. He stood to share one-third of the profits. It was not a good week at Reading."

Mrs Lindo then told the court of the strange reappearance of Drew's missing trousers.

A pair of blue serge trousers were handed to the coroner.

The Coroner: "Did you notice that new pockets had been inserted?"
Mrs Lindo: "I shouldn't say they were new. I should say they have been cleaned."

The trousers were passed round the jury, and Mr Martin remarked that he had noticed several holes. Inspector Berrett thereupon rose and whispered to the coroner. He was explaining that the holes had been made by the police.

The coroner asked if it was customary for actors and actresses to leave the theatre in their make-up, and Mrs Lindo said that she would not expect any good-class actor or actress to do so—certainly not a man of Drew's calibre.

"Did you notice on Sunday morning what clothes he was wearing?" asked Mr Martin.

"A pair of grey tweed trousers and a navy-blue coat and waistcoat," was the reply.

The foreman of the jury asked Mrs Lindo if she knew why Mr Drew's landlady visited the theatre and made the inquiries that she did.

Mrs Lindo replied that that had always puzzled her and her husband, but that she had had no opportunity to find out, as she left Reading early on the Sunday morning.

Mrs Lindo said that she had known Drew for over five years, that he was exceedingly kind, and that she had never seen him threaten anyone. "His character is splendid."

Mr Ratcliffe asked if Drew was financially embarrassed?

Mrs Lindo said that he couldn't have been because he'd been in constant work for so long. And anyway, he was entitled to one-third share in the profits of the company.

She added that she could not understand the evidence of a previous witness, who had said that Mr Drew left the theatre wearing his beard. It seemed an extraordinary proceeding to put it on again. And, replying to Mr Ratcliffe, she confirmed that on the night of June 22nd Drew went through his performance in a perfectly normal way, and had arrived in good time for the show.

She then left the box.

William Norman Stubbs, stage-manager to the *Monster* company during the week it was playing at Reading, said that the first time that he could swear to seeing Drew on the evening of June 22nd was during the performance.

"Drew was drinking heavily that week, which is his normal habit. After the performance Fry and I saw the stage props cleared and, well after midnight, I saw Drew come out of his dressing-room. I found his trunk had been packed, but he couldn't close it. I helped him to close it. He was the worse for drink then. So far as I know, he was sober after the second house, so he must have had liquor in his dressing-room. If any tools had been missing the stage carpenter would have reported it to me. Drew borrowed three shillings from me at Maidstone. He was unwell there on the Monday (June 24th). He shook like a leaf, and his understudy, Mr Fry, took his part that night."

Replying to Mr Ratcliffe, Mr Stubbs said, "I know Drew had a breakdown at Woolwich about three weeks before coming to Reading. When he came out of the theatre in the early hours of June 23rd, he had some of the crêpe hair left on his face. It would make him look unkempt, but it wouldn't be left on to disguise him."

Just as the day's sitting was drawing to a close, a surprise was sprung by the police when they called Miss Frances King, a domestic servant employed at 31 Brewer Street, Maidstone, the theatrical lodging-house at which Drew and Mr and Mrs Lindo stayed during the week after the murder.

Miss King said that when Mr Drew arrived, at about half-past three on Sunday afternoon, June 23rd, he had on a blue jacket and a pair of old grey trousers. He was wearing a felt hat, and carrying an old overcoat over his arm. His shirt-front was disarranged over the top of his trousers. He had been drinking, and was very excitable, shaky, and nervy.

The Coroner: "Did he appear to be in his right mind?"
Miss King: "I should call him almost mad the way he behaved."

She went on: "He went out during the Sunday evening. I saw him come in and he was carrying a stone ginger-beer bottle in his hand. I don't know whether it was full or empty. I found it in his bedroom when he left the following Sunday. I threw it away. I didn't see his clothing during the week, as he stayed in bed each day till it was time to go to the theatre. We've had theatricals before. They're not famous for early rising. He usually got up about half-past four, and came home each night with Mr and Mrs Lindo. On the Saturday (June 29th) he asked Mrs Lindo if she would get him some benzoline to get some spots off his coat. She brought him benzoline and rags. I saw him go into the garden where he took off his jacket, laid it on the ground, sprinkled liquid out of the bottle on it and rubbed it with the rags. I should think he spent half an hour over it. The old grey trousers looked very dirty, but he didn't clean them."

Miss King also said that on the Monday evening after Drew arrived a doctor was called. When Drew heard that the doctor was coming he ran out of the house. The doctor came next morning when he was in bed. Miss King took his breakfast up, and Mrs Lindo took up his lunch. Witness did not think that anyone stayed with him. Nor did she know why he stayed in bed. He always appeared to her to be very shaky, but otherwise normal.

Replying to Mr Ratcliffe, she said that Drew used the benzoline on his coat in the garden in the full view of everyone. He made no secret of what he was doing.

So ended the second day of the inquest.

(4)

"Of course I shall go into the witness-box! Why not? I am innocent. What have I to fear?"

Philip Yale Drew was talking to a *Daily Mail* reporter that Thursday evening on his return to the hotel after a long consultation with Mr Ratcliffe.

"He looks," wrote the reporter, "the typical actor of a thousand black and white drawings. His grey, wavy hair falls back in leonine fashion, and he draws his overcoat to him as if it were a flowing black cape. He speaks with a deep resonant voice, with the faintest trace of an American accent. 'I have grown to feel myself an Englishman,' he said. 'I have got enough confidence in English justice to be without a worry in the world. I am of best British stock. My people were Scottish and went over to America in the *Mayflower*. I am very proud of the part I have taken in English theatrical life. When I was tackled by Scotland Yard detectives at Nottingham I did not worry considerably. I know what the duties of citizenship are, and I told them all I knew. Since then, however, things have advanced so much that I wou¹d not care to say that I am without a worry. It seems to me that when I am clear of this suspicion I shall still suffer. Publicity is good for an actor, but I doubt whether notoriety is. I have sufficient belief in the infallibility of British justice to know that the fact that a man cannot remember every point of what happened months ago will not make people think that he is guilty of something of which he is innocent. Meanwhile I suffer, although I am only a person trying to give answers to the police to help the course of justice.' "

The position as established by the proceedings of the second day's hearing was that the drunken and eccentrically behaving presence of Philip Yale Drew—or someone incredibly like him—in Cross Street, at various times between 2 P.M. and 5.32 P.M. on Saturday, June 22nd, was definitely attested by four witnesses. Mr Turnbull spoke of the Staggering Man; Mr Windle of the Gazing Man; Mrs Taylor of the Theatrical Man; and Mrs Earl of the Jay-walking Man. All identified Drew. Mr Nicholson spoke of the Measuring Man, seen in Cross Street between 5.20 and 5.30 P.M. He alone did not identify Drew.

Some of their evidence was, however, flatly contradicted by that of Mrs Lindo, who claimed to be able to account for Drew's whereabouts between 2 P.M. and 5 P.M.

Less definitely, a solitary witness, Mrs James, swore that she had seen Drew standing in the doorway of Oliver's shop at about eleven or twelve minutes past six. Not that *she* was indefinite in her identification of him, but her observation was not confirmed by that of any other witness.

But neither, so far, had any witness been brought forward to say where Drew *was* at 6.11 P.M.

There was still nothing that you could call cast-iron evidence to show that Drew was guilty of murder. What there was, was a cumulative weight of insinuation that added up to palpable unease.

The statements of Russell, Ingram and Grubb, suggested that he knew Cross Street by name— a fact which he was to deny—and was familiar with the paper-shop (Stock's) next door to Oliver's.

Grubb's testimony that between 12.30 and 12.45 A.M. on June 23rd, Drew walked off in disguise towards Chatham Street—the opposite direction from that in which his lodgings lay—invited a sinister interpretation.

The affair of the missing trousers, and the prolonged cleaning of his jacket at Maidstone, seemed to hint that they might have borne incriminating stains or marks, although again there was not yet a jot of evidence to substantiate this.

But, in the charged atmosphere of that courtroom, with the coroner's oft-repeated order, "Stand up," and the witnesses' invariable, "That is the man", the overall effect was—unfortunate.

It required no gift of prophecy to foresee that the next few days were going to be crucial for Philip Yale Drew.

Scene 3

THE THEATRICAL LANDLADY'S TALE

Friday, October 4th, 1929

(1)

MRS Mary Eleanor Goodall was a pert, robin-like little woman with grey hair, bright brown eyes, and a ready tongue. She and her husband, George, lived at 9 King's Meadow Road, Reading. The house was small, but not so small as to prevent their taking in the occasional lodger. And if there was one class of lodger that the vivacious Mrs Goodall enjoyed doing for, it was theatricals. So, when Philip Yale Drew came to Reading during the third week in June 1929 he found himself a welcome guest at Mrs Goodall's.

Now, in consequence, this first week in October, Mrs Goodall found herself a prominent witness at the ordeal of her erstwhile lodger.

(2)

If you were to seek particular themes with which the individual hearings of the inquest had been, as it were, orchestrated, you could say that days one and two had been set against a background music of identification, with the recurrent refrain of "Stand up ... That is the Man". But this third day was to be swamped by the insistent rhythm of time.

This dominant note made itself heard within minutes of the commencement of the examination of the first witness of the day, Alfred George Fry, joint stage-manager of the *Monster* company.

"Just before two o'clock on June 22nd last," said Mr Fry, "I went into the Marquis of Lorne. I saw Drew inside, and we had drinks together. He was drinking ginger-ale and was quite sober. We came out together and parted at the call of 'Time'. I didn't see him again until the evening at the theatre, where I arrived at roughly 5.45 P.M."

It was, according to Fry, at approximately six o'clock that he heard Drew singing as he came in through the stage-door, and it was at 6.15 or 6.17 P.M. that he first saw him at his dressing-room door. He had by that time changed into his stage clothes and was making up. "I have done this make-up," said Fry, "and I find I want forty minutes to do it comfortably. I don't think Drew would do it as quickly as I. I next saw Drew at twenty-eight minutes to seven. He was coming out of his room, going towards Mrs Lindo's. He was then practically made up—only wanting finishing touches."

The last time witness saw Drew that night was at about 12.30 A.M., leaving the theatre. He was then certainly intoxicated. He had removed his make-up very, very carelessly. Spirit-gum, crêpe hair, and grease-paint adhered in little bits here and there, as though he had wiped his face with his towel with no great care. He had a vague recollection that when Drew left the theatre in the early hours of that Sunday morning he had some laundry under his arm, wrapped in a newspaper. He also thought that he was carrying a walking-stick. He was not wearing a hat.

Examined by Mr Ratcliffe, Fry said that he did not hear Drew mention his intention of going to Cross Street for a paper while he was in the Marquis of Lorne, but explained that he (Fry) was not in the company of the others. He was lower down the bar.

He also said that Drew was not a man who was violent in liquor—"Just the opposite. Mr Drew is a big baby at any time, and a bigger baby when he has had a few drinks than at any other time."

A Miss Nellie Drew—no relative of Philip Yale Drew—then made a fleeting appearance to tell how, between five o'clock and half-past five on the afternoon of Thursday, June 20th, she saw a man looking in the window of the tobacconist's shop, Newbery's, at 155 Friar Street, where she worked as an assistant. She was behind the counter, and the man came no farther than the step of the shop, but called in to her and asked the price of two pipes in the window. She told him 30s. and 25s. respectively. He said it was a big price to pay for a pipe, but that he wanted one to send to a friend abroad. He said he would call next day, as he had not the money with him. He did not return on the Friday. The man, she said, had on a dark suit. He was not wearing a hat, and his hair was rough and darkish in colour. He appeared to be rather intoxicated. It was, she now recognized, Mr Drew.

> The Coroner: "Do you think it was his honest intention to buy a pipe, or simply an excuse to look into the shop?"
> Miss Drew: "I think it was his honest intention to buy a pipe."

The foreman of the jury asked: "It did not strike you as suspicious?"
"No," said the young girl, "it didn't."

(3)

And now the time had come for the theatrical landlady to tell her tale. With quick, bird-like movements, Mrs Goodall trotted briskly towards the box.

Mr Drew, she said, rarely got up before one or half-past, but on Saturday, June 22nd, he was up early—for him. He left the house at eleven o'clock, and it was between 3 P.M. and 3.30 P.M. when he returned.

"He rushed in and up the stairs, and Mrs Lindo rushed in behind him and stood at the foot of the stairs. She told me she wanted to take some whisky from him, and asked my permission to go up to his room, which I gave her. There were high words. I heard it all from downstairs. She said, 'Give me the whisky, or don't dare come to the theatre tonight.' I heard her bang the bedroom door. Then she came down and went into my sitting-room, and I followed her in. 'What shall I do?' she asked. 'If he has that whisky he won't be able to do his work tonight.' Whilst we were talking Mr Drew came down and went out. I saw him from the window. He was wearing his usual navy-blue suit which he had worn all week, and no hat. He came back at a quarter-past five. I was having tea and he came and sat in my sitting-room, and I gave him a cup of tea. His hands were shaky and he spilt the greater part, some on his trousers and some on the floor. I gave him a piece of rag to wipe it off. He was always more or less the worse for what he had had, and he had had plenty."

Mrs Goodall's piquant phrasing frequently provoked ripples of laughter that relieved the strain of the inquiry, but she was always compelling in her vivid narrative.

The Coroner: "Can you estimate what time he went out again?"

Mrs Goodall: "Not before ten past six, and it might have been a minute or two later."

The Coroner (incredulously): "Ten past six?"

Mrs Goodall (emphatically): "Ten past six. I drew Mr Drew's attention to the time—that it was after six o'clock—and told him he'd be late. But he said he would have time enough."

The Coroner: "In your statement you say: 'I should say he was in my house half an hour or more'. Five-fifteen and half an hour . . . that would be a quarter to six. Why did you say half an hour? You say you cannot remember the time in your statement."

Mrs Goodall: "I said I couldn't verify the time by the clock."

The Coroner: "Have you got any good clocks in your house?"

Mrs Goodall: "I've got a clock in every room, but we've not got the correct time."

The Coroner: "They are all against one another. (Laughter.) Well, then, that is not much good."

After consulting a typewritten statement, Mr Martin said, "You have got a clock in the sitting-room, and you told the police that it is always twenty-five minutes fast."

"Sometimes more, sometimes less," said Mrs Goodall thoughtfully.

The coroner raised his eyebrows. "You will never miss a train with that clock," he remarked. (Laughter.)

Amid further laughter, Mrs Goodall added, "When the 7.15 train went out this morning it wanted one minute to eight by the clock."

The coroner resisted the temptation to make further comment.

Continuing her evidence, Mrs Goodall said that Drew told her that he could be from her sitting-room and on the stage in seven minutes. She could not be sure of the time Drew left for the theatre, but it was certainly well after six o'clock.

"Mr Drew ran out of the house at a good sprint and threw his overcoat round his shoulders like a cape. I went out at about a quarter to seven, and was in Broad Street at 6.55 P.M. by Samuel's clock. I went, as I usually do on a Saturday, to Reading Cemetery, and got back to Broad Street by tram at eight o'clock. I saw a crowd in Cross Street, asked what was the matter, and was told there had been a terrible murder."

The Coroner: "Did anything enter your mind with regard to that? Tell me quite candidly."

Mrs Goodall: "That is what I am here to do. Mrs Lindo said she didn't know why I went to the theatre to see her. The reason was that she had dared Mr Drew to go to the theatre, and I went to see if he was there. I didn't feel disposed to sit up half the night if he was running wild."

The Coroner: "After you heard of this murder you had something in your mind?"

Mrs Goodall: "Yes, I worried over it. I wondered if Mr Drew had not gone to the theatre, and whether he was concerned in it. I didn't say so . . ."

The Coroner (interrupting): "But that *was* in your mind?"

Mrs Goodall: "Yes."

Replying to Mr Martin, Mrs Goodall said that she sat up that night waiting for Drew to come home.

"He returned at 1.15 A.M. I was waiting at the door for him, and I watched him coming. He ran all the way down from Reading Bridge corner right to the gate. Anyone would imagine he was being chased. He had his old stage clothes on that he performed in, his overcoat on, and his collar and tie in his hand. He didn't have a hat. There was a small portion of false beard adhering to one side of his face, he hadn't taken any of his grease-paint off and he was in a great state of perspiration. His hair was rough, but it always was, and it always appeared more grey than it does now. I can't say whether he was drunk, but he was very excited. I told him I'd been waiting for him. He didn't apologize. He seemed to be wanting to talk, but I asked him not to disturb anyone, and he went to bed quietly. I called him about ten o'clock, and saw him leave the house in a taxicab with Mr and Mrs Lindo. He was dressed almost the same then as when he came in. He looked a bulk of clothes. Judging by his appearance, I think he had a blue suit under the grey suit and overcoat."

In answer to a question by Mr Ratcliffe, Mrs Goodall said that Drew was absolutely no trouble "except that he broke our rest at night with his rambling and raving".

The Coroner: "So he rambled and raved, did he?"

Mrs Goodall: "Oh, something terrible."

The Coroner: "Every night?"

Mrs Goodall: "Yes. On the first night it was beyond description. That night I was scared."

The Coroner: "It was not very pleasant."

Mrs Goodall: "No. I thought he had his business on his mind. To me
it seemed as if he were rehearsing all night."

Mr Ratcliffe: "You think his raving was a private rehearsal in his
bedroom?"

Mrs Goodall: "Yes, and when I saw him perform in *The Monster* I
understood what his weird noises were."

When Mr Ratcliffe asked her about the occasion when Mrs
Lindo tried to take the whisky bottle from Drew, Mrs Goodall said,
"She seemed to be trying to mother the man."

This remark caused Mrs Lindo to sob and burst into tears, and
Drew, who was sitting next to her, leant over to comfort her and
patted her gently on the shoulder. She buried her face in her hands,
but revived when the coroner's officer gave her a drink of water.

"Had you any reason to think that Mr Drew would murder
anyone, or be murdered?" asked Mr Ratcliffe.

"No, there was nothing, in my opinion, in the man which was
murderous or brutal."

"Was he a well-behaved man?"

"I cannot say anything different."

The coroner asked Mrs Goodall if she had seen a performance of
The Monster.

She said that she had, on the Friday night.

"From what I remember of it, it went into darkness a lot, and
there were collapsing beds, collapsing floors, doors flying open, and
groans . . . and I don't wonder Mr Drew's nerves were racked."
(Laughter.)

"You would not like to perform in it yourself," remarked the
coroner.

"No," said Mrs Goodall with great emphasis, "I would not."

Mrs Goodall concluded her evidence by saying that the road by
which Drew returned home in the early hours of that Sunday
morning was not a way that she would have chosen from the
theatre; that she had not missed any tools or implements from her
house; that Drew never brought a walking-stick home; that she had
seen no ginger-beer bottles in his possession, only flat, pocket-size
whisky bottles, and that she could not tell what colour boots he
wore to save her life.

The most important point in Mrs Goodall's evidence had been
her statement that Drew did not leave her house until *after* 6 P.M.
on the evening of June 22nd.

The next two witnesses confirmed this.

Mrs Elizabeth Crouch, of 16 King's Meadow Road, said that on the evening of June 22nd she and her husband walked home from town. They passed the Town Hall clock between five and ten past six, and at ten or twelve minutes past six they saw a man rush out of No. 9 King's Meadow Road—Mrs Goodall's—and run very fast up the road, "as if he had a minute to live". She identified him as Philip Yale Drew.

Mrs Winifred Greenwood, of 7 King's Meadow Road, said that she had seen a man, whom she knew to be Drew, rush out of the gate of Mrs Goodall's house on Saturday evening, June 22nd, and run very fast towards the town. She could not say whether it was just before, or just after six o'clock.

"It is obvious that he was not in Cross Street at the time," said Mr Ratcliffe.

"It is also obvious that he was not at the theatre at the time," commented the coroner.

Mrs Greenwood added that she had seen Drew earlier that afternoon in Friar Street. He was going towards the Town Hall, between 3.30 P.M. and 4 P.M.—nearer four o'clock—and was then very drunk. He was staggering a bit, walking with his hands in his pockets, and his coat under his arm—dragging on the ground.

Mrs Dorothy Gladys Irene Shepherd was with her children in Cross Street on June 22nd, looking into Hieatt's, the butcher's shop. The time by Hieatt's clock was between 6.11 and 6.12 P.M. It was then that she saw the Running Man.—"I saw a man come running out of Oliver's shop, and he ran, slanting, across the street up towards Friar Street, and then turned to his left towards the station way. I didn't see the man's face, but he was of middle height and rather broad, and had on a navy-blue serge suit. I can't say if he wore a hat or not. I can't remember if he had a coat, and I didn't notice his shoes."

At six o'clock that same evening, Mr Bertie Hathaway, a one-legged man who walked with a crutch, was standing outside Attwell's music shop in Friar Street, talking to a Mrs Williams. He told the court: "I left her at five or seven minutes past six, and went along Friar Street towards the theatre, where I had arranged to meet my brother-in-law. Between Cross Street and Queen Victoria Street I noticed a man, a broad man with dark curly hair, blue trousers, a coat thrown over his shoulders, no hat, hair very curly and rough. He was a powerful man and full-faced. He appeared to be intoxicated, and was also very excited, which is what drew my attention. He was muttering to himself. He came up alongside me on my left near Hickie's.[1] He seemed in a desperate hurry. Everybody was in his way. I followed him and kept up with him. At Queen Victoria Street we were side by side, and a bus crossing Friar Street held us up while it passed. He was very much annoyed by it, and I heard him mention the rush of traffic in a muffled voice. He seemed to be cursing. I thought a bit of fun was coming, he was acting so peculiarly. I saw him turn into the theatre yard. I spoke to the pit attendant at the theatre and asked, "Who's that client gone up there?' But he said he didn't know as he hadn't seen him. As near as I can work it out, I should say it was 6.15 when the man entered the theatre. You might perhaps give him a minute and make it 6.14."

"We had a lot about jazz clocks this morning," said the coroner. "Your watch is a good watch?"

"Yes, and I keep it true."

Mr Hathaway said that he saw the man's face sideways all the way, "and I say he was Mr Drew".

George William Henry Hawkins, bus-driver, and Wallis Ernest Wells, bus-driver, both testified that at 6.12 to 6.13 P.M. on June 22nd, they were passing down Queen Victoria Street, driving their respective buses. Neither of them had noticed the Angry Man, who so diverted Mr Hathaway.

Miss Doris Hilda Hamer, manageress, and Miss Helen Pretoria Budworth, assistant, of the Renovating Company's shop, at 3 Wheeler Gate, Nottingham, were then called.

Miss Hamer told how at 2.30 P.M. on Tuesday, July 23rd, Drew came to her shop saying he was from the theatre, and asking how long it would take to clean some of his clothing.

"I said if I had it before one o'clock Thursday, he could have it Friday evening. He returned next day—Wednesday—and handed in a light tweed overcoat to be cleaned. I turned to enter it in my book, turning my back on him. I then found that he had taken off his hat, navy jacket, and navy vest. He said he wanted them all cleaned. I was surprised at his doing this. I just said, 'I am feeling rather nervous'. And he said, 'You needn't worry, I'm not taking

[1] Hickie & Hickie, Ltd. A musical-instrument dealer's shop at 149 Friar Street.

these off,' touching his trousers. He left the shop, saying he would walk to Trent Bridge in his shirt-sleeves."

Miss Budworth said that she had unpicked the corner of the lining over the right-hand pocket of the blue serge jacket left by Drew, and cleaned it out. The insides of the pockets were very dirty and very sticky. In fact the whole coat was dirty—but she had noticed no stains.

Mr Ratcliffe suggested that the stickiness might have been due to sweets in hot weather, and Miss Budworth said that she had thought it might be due to Mr Drew's make-up.

Finally that session, Detective Constable Charles Woodward of the Reading C.I.D. took the oath.

He was described by 'R. E. Corder' in the *Daily Mail* as "the youngest looking detective constable I have seen".

Said Woodward: "I made some tests as to the time in walking, normal pace, from 9 King's Meadow Road to 15 Cross Street, by various routes. Going via Vastern Road, Valpy Street, Blagrave Street, and Friar Street, it took 4 minutes 45 seconds. I then retraced my steps along Cross Street and Friar Street to the theatre stage-door. This took 2 minutes 20 seconds. Total time for the journey, 7 minutes 5 seconds."

> Mr Ratcliffe: "I congratulate you on your walking. Do you suggest that an ordinary man could do it?"
> Woodward: "Yes."
> The Coroner: "I could do it myself, easily."

In another test Woodward was accompanied by Mrs Crouch. She set the pace, and it took six minutes to walk from the clock-tower entrance of the Town Hall, via Blagrave Street, Valpy Street, and Vastern Road, to 9 King's Meadow Road. Mrs Crouch said that she walked at the same pace and by the same route on Saturday, June 22nd.

Woodward continued: "At 2.5 P.M. on Thursday, July 25th last, I left Reading in a private car with the witnesses Loxton and James. We arrived at Nottingham at 5.50 P.M., and were met by the Chief Constable of Reading and a Nottingham detective officer. This officer took the witnesses and myself to one of Nottingham's main streets near Trent Bridge. The witnesses were asked to stand in the street and to communicate with me if they saw anybody whom they recognized in connection with Mr Oliver's death at Reading.

I then took up a position about thirty yards away from them, the witnesses being some yards apart. At 6.20 P.M. the witness Loxton came to me and pointed out a man who had just passed me. A minute later, the witness James came and pointed out the same man. He was a stranger to me. I know him now as Mr Drew."

Adjourning the inquest until 11 A.M. on Monday, October 7th, Mr Martin said that on that day the court would be fully occupied with police evidence. He would not, therefore, require the attendance of the other witnesses who had given evidence, but they would have to be in readiness to be recalled, perhaps on Tuesday.

(4)

Looking back on the events of the day, things seemed to have taken a decidedly more favourable turn for Philip Yale Drew. What had been suggested as damningly clear-cut was now fuzzy with doubt, the benefit of which would surely have to be given to him. As witness had succeeded witness, the timetable of Drew's movements on that all-important 22nd of June had become more and more complex, more and more conflicting.

Alfred George Fry had sworn that Drew was in the theatre at 6 P.M. (heard singing), and definitely seen at 6.15 or 6.17 P.M.

Mrs Goodall had sworn with equal conviction that he was just leaving her house at 6.10 P.M.

And there were two completely uncommitted and disinterested women witnesses—Mrs Crouch and Mrs Greenwood—to testify to his emergence into King's Meadow Road at, one said, 6.10 P.M., and the other said around six o'clock.

If Mrs Goodall, Mrs Crouch, and Mrs Greenwood were correct, even allowing for the disparities, then Mr Fry must be wrong. It was not physically possible for Drew to have been in King's Meadow Road at six o'clock *and* in the theatre at six o'clock.

But equally, if he was in King's Meadow Road at 6.10 P.M., it seemed impossible for him to be in Mr Oliver's doorway, the crime committed, wiping blood from his face at 6.12 P.M., as Mrs James had sworn. Even Detective Woodward's athletics required 4 minutes 45 seconds to accomplish that journey.

And what of the Running Man, seen in Cross Street at 6.12 P.M. by Mrs Shepherd? She did not, could not, identify him as Drew.

That Drew was the Angry Man, seen in Friar Street at about

6.11 P.M. by Mr Hathaway, and followed by him to the theatre, where he arrived at about 6.14 P.M. or 6.15 P.M., seems most probable. That, at least, would tie in with the Goodall-Crouch-Greenwood narrative.

But no amount of juggling with the figures can make all three of these variant sequences of testimony coincide. Either Fry was right (improbable), or the Goodall-Crouch-Greenwood-Hathaway faction was right (probable), or Mrs James was right (problematic).

On the other hand, if we postulate that ALL the witnesses were fractionally wrong in their various estimates of the material times, then the sum of their differences could add up to a significant margin of error which would allow for the possibility that Drew had had the opportunity to commit the crime.

Suppose that it was 6.4 P.M. and not 6.10 P.M. when he left Mrs Goodall's. Add 4 minutes 45 seconds. That would bring him to Oliver's shop at, say, 6.9 P.M. Allow 3 minutes for the commission of the crime, and at 6.12 P.M. Mrs James could have seen him standing in the shop doorway. Then, between 6.12 and 6.13 P.M., Mrs Shepherd could have seen him running down Cross Street towards Friar Street. And it could have been between 6.13 and 6.14 P.M. when Mr Hathaway encountered him there. From Queen Victoria Street to the theatre—say 2 minutes. That would bring the time of his arrival there to 6.15 or 6.16 P.M., and suppose it was 6.18 or 6.19 P.M. when Mr Fry first actually saw him. A tight, split-minute schedule, stretching it a bit—but, on these moderate assumptions, not totally impossible.

When Drew reached the hotel after the day's proceedings at the coroner's court an old friend was waiting there to see him. He was a London taxicab-driver named Noone. He came from Brixton, where he had first seen Drew over the footlights of the Brixton Theatre, and he had driven his cab from London to Reading to bring him his good wishes in person. Drew's face twitched with emotion as he gripped Mr Noone's outstretched hand. "You can take it from me that it's all going to come right in the end," he said, "and I can't tell you what I feel in my heart about your coming here today." When Mr Noone left he kissed Drew's hand. "You know where to find me," he said. "One word and I shall be here. I would drive you round the world if you wished it."

Later that evening the *Daily Express* Special Correspondent

chatted with Drew and the Lindos. "The *Monster* touring company
is to be disbanded. Mr and Mrs Lindo have decided that they
cannot carry on in consequence of the Reading murder inquest.
Mrs Lindo, who is the business organizer of the company, told
me why tonight. Mr Drew was with her during the interview,
and he was almost in tears when she told me of her misfortune.
'It is all my fault,' Mr Drew said in a broken voice. 'I have brought
all this on you.' 'No, no, Philip,' protested Mrs Lindo, laying her
hand on his arm, 'you must not say that. You cannot help it—
it is the hand of fate.' Turning towards me, Mr Drew said:
'Mr and Mrs Lindo have been mother and father to me. They have
stood by me in my darkest days. When everything was black they
helped me out. I do not know what I should have done without
them. Now I have caused them all this trouble, and I cannot bear
it.' Mrs Lindo said: 'Who could have imagined when we set off
on tour in this thriller that we should suddenly find ourselves
tangled in a real murder drama? Do you believe in dreams? Well,
I am rather psychic, and some time ago—it was before Mr Oliver
was killed—I had an extraordinary dream. I saw a shrouded figure
in deep black and I heard the words "Reading murder".'

(5)

Three days of the inquest gone. The halfway mark—surely?
At any rate, the coroner had indicated that he was thinking in
terms of concluding his inquisition on Wednesday at the latest.
For that relief, much thanks. But the worry was lying heavily on
Philip. And now it was the weekend. Two days of suspense and
nerve-stretching inactivity to be lived through.

A *Star* reporter who saw him on the Saturday described him as
"a pathetic figure wandering about the hotel, trying to busy himself
about little things and trying to relieve Mrs Lindo of some of the
inquiries that are reaching her every hour".

The 'little things' about which he was busying himself included
the writing of his life-story for a newspaper, and working upon a
stage thriller.

Of the latter, he said: "Remarkably enough, it opens with a
scene in court. The chief character in the play is a man who,
through force of circumstance, is under a cloud of suspicion. It is
a strange coincidence that I thought out the plot and started to

write the play before the Reading murder was committed. My idea was to write a thriller to appear in myself with a part that would give me scope to portray a number of different characters. So I decided to make the principal character a man wrongly suspected of a crime who has to keep assuming different disguises to escape arrest until he is in a position to prove his innocence. I have to take the part of seven different characters."

Asked if he had decided on a happy ending, Philip replied, with a magnificent gesture, "My dear sir, it will have a terrific ending. The hero is driven mad by his ordeal."

During that week-end Philip was visited by a woman clairvoyant, who said that she had come because she considered it her duty. She did not belong to Reading, but declared that she had had a vision, and that she was convinced that a visit to the workhouse at Basingstoke would enable the police to throw light on the affair. "I don't even know if there is a workhouse at Basingstoke, except for my vision," she added.

Daily News reporter who saw Philip on the Sunday quoted him as saying, "I am feeling fine, and, thank goodness, am sleeping like a top and eating like a horse".

Perhaps he was just showing a brave face, for the previous day Mrs Lindo had had this to say: "My husband and I were attracted to Philip during the first time we met him at rehearsals. He appealed to us as a thoroughly lovable fellow, and he has always so proved. No one has ever seen him do an unkind action. Although he is a big man, there is a great deal of the little boy about him. The suspicions that have been hanging over us since we were questioned about this matter many weeks ago have been terrible. Even when we were sent for to attend the inquest on Wednesday last we did not think anything like this was before us. We imagined an inquiry lasting an hour or so, a few questions, and then permission to leave. Instead, this terrible calamity descended upon us. No one could imagine my feelings as one person after another got up in court and said, 'That is the man.' I have never been in a court of any kind in my life before; I thought I should scream. I knew the impossibility of it, and was powerless to make others feel it too. Since the first implied accusation life has been a nightmare. But what must it have been for Philip? I find it easy to forget my own troubles in his. He has a nervous temperament, and, since the horrible business began, he has become a nervous wreck. Sleep became impossible for him, and I had to give him a sleeping-draught. Then I found it necessary to administer the same thing to myself in order to get my rest."

That week-end Mr Ratcliffe advised Philip that he had managed to retain the services of Mr William Arthur Fearnley-Whittingstall, the exceptionally gifted young barrister who had so successfully watched the interests of Thomas Sidney and Mrs Grace Duff in the Croydon poisoning case inquests the previous August. And although Mr Ratcliffe was far too tactful to say it in so many words, Philip was far too intelligent not to divine the undertow of anxiety signified by this move.

Scene 4

THE TALE OF THE MEN OF LAW

Monday, October 7th, 1929

(1)

AND suddenly it was pandemonium. . . .

Nobody could call the Reading of forty years ago anything other than a quiet and conspicuously law-abiding town. You would have had to look back to 1895 to find murder being perpetrated within its decorous boundaries—and then the violator was an immigrant from Bristol, a black bombazine Victorian bogy-woman, Mrs Dyer, the infamous Reading baby-farmer.

In the three decades since her despatch into the arms of the hangman, only one killing had taken place actually in the town. That was some twenty-eight years before the Cross Street affair, when a poor crazed creature named Fox cut her baby's throat in Soho Street. She was not hanged, but sent to Broadmoor. The odd murder in the town's far-flung environs—yes; such as the notorious Gallows Tree Common murder of 1921, and, at a remove, so to speak, the case, in June 1929, of a man who was once a Reading grocer, found guilty, but insane, of murdering his wife at Maidenhead. And that, until the killing of Alfred Oliver sullied the bloodless record, was the full tally of Reading's fringe brushes with the crime of homicide.

Despite the lack of opportunities afforded them for practice, the Reading police had, however, twice in recent years shown themselves to be dab hands at the capturing of itinerant murderers who trespassed upon their manor. In October 1920 Detective Purdy of the Reading C.I.D. had played a significant part in the laying by the heels of George Arthur Bailey, the Marlow wife-killer, and in 1922, Sergeant Phillips arrested Thomas Henry Allaway, the Bournemouth slayer, in Reading.

In these circumstances, you might expect the novelty of a murder case of its own to produce instant excitement in Reading—but no, strangely enough the Oliver inquest got off to a relatively quiet start.

. . . And suddenly it was pandemonium.

(2)

At half-past eight that Monday morning of October 7th, 1929, a good two and a half hours before the fourth session of the hearing was due to start, a long line of people had formed up outside the police court.

By half-past ten Valpy Street was virtually impassable, and a worried-looking inspector of police, plus a handful of equally worried-looking constables, was doing his best to control an excited crowd of well over a thousand.

All the way from the Great Western Hotel in Station Road to the police court the pavements were lined with people, and as soon as Philip Yale Drew appeared they started to clap. This was taken up all along the street—and then they began to cheer, too, the cheers swelling to crescendo at each point as he reached it, marking his progress with a running fuse of explosive sound.

There were lusty shouts of "Good luck!", "Cheer up!", and "Don't be downhearted!" Men waved their hats and yelled, "Keep smiling, old chap!" One man, stretching over the shoulders of the others, thrust his fingers into Drew's hair and ruffled the curls. Women and girls pressed around him as he walked, and seized him by the hand. A woman stuck a bunch of white heather in his buttonhole. Another stepped forward from the crowd and handed him a little embroidered purse in which was a small piece of coal wrapped up in paper. "Keep that for luck," she said.

Drew was obviously deeply touched by this spontaneous demonstration. His eyes were wet, and he bowed and raised his hat repeatedly as he struggled to get through to the court. Several times he said, "Thank you, people. Thank you."

Never in its entire history had Reading witnessed anything remotely resembling the scene.

It is difficult to account for this sudden surge of popularity, this great warm wave of sympathy and friendship, which all-unexpectedly engulfed him. Perhaps it was the Establishment's treatment of him as much as anything that veered public opinion so

strongly in his favour. An Englishman—unlike so many foreigners
—cannot stand the spectacle of what he considers to be a helpless
victim's being pilloried. He cannot stomach bullying, tolerate auth-
ority rampant. The sight of poor bewildered Drew being consistently
told—"Stand up." "Sit down." "Turn round." Never a please or
thank you, as he smilingly, meekly, did as he was bid—outraged
their sense of fair play, enlisted their sympathy as nothing else
could, and they expressed their contempt by heroizing Drew.

So, this man at bay was swept on the wave-crest of a remarkable
display of public affection and concern to the very doors of his
personal Star Chamber. And only when his figure finally disappeared from view inside did the football-roars of the crowd
gradually subside. The pattern had been set, and it was to continue
in this way from now to the end of the inquest.

But in the wider world the enthusiasm for Drew was signally
less heated. H. F. Maltby recalls in his memoirs[1] how about this
time he and his friend, George Tully, were talking one morning
in the old Sailing Club at Brighton to which they both belonged,
about the Drew case, and Tully picked up a membership-proposal
form, filled it in, and handed it to Maltby, saying, "You'll second
him, of course." Maltby saw that he had proposed Drew for
membership. He duly signed the form, and they stuck it up on
the notice-board and sat back to await events. Presently, one of the
old members came in. He glanced casually at the board . . . started
. . . put on his spectacles . . . and looked again. Huffing and puffing,
he beckoned another old member over. "Here, look at this!" The
other turned a wrathful red. "By gad! Philip Yale Drew! Isn't he
the feller they suspect of doing the Reading murder?" At this,
Tully leapt to his feet. "Pardon me, Mr Drew happens to be a
personal friend of mine. In this country every man is innocent until
he is proved guilty. No charge has been brought against him, and
I propose him as a member of this club." "And I have great
pleasure in seconding him," said Maltby. And then the hurricane-
force row blew up—Maltby and Tully, neither of whom had ever
so much as seen Drew, stoutly defending their 'friend' in the teeth
of a storm of furious protestations, threatened resignations, and a
gale of demands for extraordinary general meetings, until, finally,
Tully gave in. "Ah, well," he sighed, "I suppose we'd better wash
it out," pulled down the form, and tore it up.

[1] *Ring Up the Curtain* (Hutchinson, 1950).

(3)

When the court opened there was a great pressure from people trying to bulldoze their way in, but there was not room for more than a tenth of those who had waited lined up in order on either side of the road by the shepherding police.

Inside, the scene was much the same as it had been on each of the preceding days. Drew sat on the solicitors' bench, opening and reading letters while he waited for the proceedings to begin. On his left was Mrs Lindo, her bottle of smelling-salts on the ledge in front of her. Facing them, at a desk immediately below Mr Martin, were Berrett, Harris, the Chief Constable of Reading, and other police officials. On the desk a litter of carefully docketed exhibits, including a pair of navy-blue serge trousers, with check braces attached.

The coroner entered.

Mr Ratcliffe rose and announced that he had instructed counsel, Mr Fearnley-Whittingstall, to watch the case on behalf of his client. He explained that counsel, having been instructed somewhat late, was engaged in another court during the morning and would not be able to attend until the afternoon, or possibly tomorrow. "In these circumstances," he said, "and in view of the gravity of the case, I feel sure that if counsel thinks necessary you will allow witnesses to be recalled."

"I will consider it," said Mr Martin. "I will proceed with the evidence. We cannot wait."

The first police witness, Percy Richard Ellington, stepped smartly forward. Took the oath.

"I am a detective sergeant in the Nottingham City Police. At 9.35 A.M. on Thursday, July 25th, I accompanied Detective Sergeant Harris of the Metropolitan Police to a boarding-house, No. 37 Fox Road, West Bridgford, and we saw Mr Drew, who accompanied us to the C.I.D. of Nottingham Police. At 9.45 A.M. the following day, acting on instructions, I kept observation on 37 Fox Road. At 10.5 A.M. Mr Lindo left the house in the Chief Constable of Reading's car. Five minutes later Mr Drew left, and made a purchase at a shop on Loughborough Road, and returned to the house. Within a few minutes he again left and had with him a dog. He went to a tobacconist and barber's shop on Radcliffe

Road. He was in there ten minutes and came out without the dog. He proceeded along Radcliffe Road and stopped two men and asked to be directed to a butcher's shop. He then walked along Loughborough Road, where he entered a butcher's shop and purchased some bits of meat and asked if they had any liver. He returned via Radcliffe Road, called for the dog, and went home. On entering the house he met Mrs Lindo, who was coming out, and he stood and conversed with her and fed the dog with what appeared to be some of the meat. I kept the house under observation until he left ten minutes later, when he called at a public-house, the Trent Bridge Inn, after which he proceeded to the Palace Theatre."

At 4.5 P.M. that same day, "in consequence of what came to my knowledge", Ellington went to the Renovating Company's shop at 3 Wheeler Gate, where he collected Drew's navy-blue jacket and waistcoat from Miss Hamer—"I examined it and found in the right-hand jacket pocket much discolouring of the lining."

"It had by then been cleaned, I believe?" interjected the coroner.

"Yes," said Ellington, adding that he had later handed the coat and waistcoat to Detective Sergeant Harris.

P.C. John Thomas Martin, of St Albans City Police, gave brief and formal evidence that at 12.55 P.M. on August 9th Drew walked into the St Albans police-station, where he was in charge of the office. Drew asked for Detective Sergeant Thorpe, said that he wanted to report that his missing blue trousers had turned up, and that he wanted Sergeant Thorpe to come and see them.

And Detective Sergeant Herbert William Thorpe testified that in consequence he went at 1.35 P.M. to the County Theatre, where he did indeed see the newly materialized trousers.

"Let us have a look at the pockets," said the coroner.

Thorpe turned the pockets inside out.

The Foreman: "In your opinion, do you think they are new pockets?"
Thorpe: "I do."
The Coroner: "They are clearly new pockets?"
Thorpe: "Yes, there are no stains here."
The Coroner: "All the pockets seem to be renovated."
The Foreman: "Did it appear to you that they had been treated by cleaning, or not?"
Thorpe: "I couldn't say."
The Foreman: "There was no smell?"
Thorpe: "There was nothing to show they had been cleaned."

The Foreman: "When you examined those trousers were these moth holes in them?"

Thorpe: "No, sir."

The Coroner: "I ought to make it clear that those holes which you call moth holes are not moth holes, but the marks where certain parts of the material have been taken out by the police. You will hear more about that."

Call Detective Sergeant John Harris—and the most important police witness of the day heaved his impressive bulk up into the witness-box.

Sergeant Harris gave his evidence in a confident, matter-of-fact way. No ifs and buts, just plain statements of fact as he saw it. No mincing of words, no hedgings, no hesitations. Sergeant Harris knew what he knew.

Having described his visit to Drew's Fox Road lodgings with Detective Superintendent Doubleday and Sergeant Ellington, he added, "And I may say, Mr Coroner, his hair that morning was not the same colour as when this inquest started. It was greyer then than it is now. And his hair today is much greyer than when the inquest was resumed on October 2nd. It was much browner then."

"How do you know?" asked the coroner. "You have made observation of this at the time?"

"Yes, while I have been sitting in court."[1]

Harris then gave evidence regarding the first statement which he said that Drew had made at Nottingham Police Station on July 25th. The statement had been taken in the form of question and answer.

Harris: "Do you know Cross Street, Reading?"

Drew: "No, I do not know the name of the street."

Harris: "Would it be correct to say that you were drinking heavily during your week at Reading?"

Drew: "I cannot say. I do drink, and sometimes may have more than others."

Harris: "Did you visit any tobacco shops in Reading during your stay there and speak about sending pipes to a friend abroad?"

Drew: "No, sir, I didn't. In York I bought one, but have not sent it off yet. I sent a friend many from Grimsby."

---

[1] According to several newspaper reports, Harris then added, "The dye is going off now." He was later to deny having made this remark. "There is no suggestion in my evidence respecting dye," he said. And the coroner agreed, saying, "I do not remember your saying it. I think you said it was brown and the colour had changed."

Harris: "If shopkeepers come forward and say that you did do so, what do you say the position would be?"

Drew: "Either they or I would be mistaken, but I know I did not ask anyone about pipes in Reading."

Harris: "Were you drinking with members of the theatre staff on the Saturday?"

Drew: "Yes, I may have been. I cannot keep account of all that. I cannot even tell you the name of the street where I lived in Reading. I do not book my lodgings myself. Mrs Lindo always does all that. Mrs Lindo and her husband were staying at the same address that I did."[1]

Harris: "Would it be correct to say that a female member of your company demanded a whisky bottle from you at your lodgings on Saturday?"

Drew: "No, I don't think so."

Harris: "And that you were under the influence of drink at Cross Street in the afternoon?"

Drew: "I have no remembrance of that either."

Harris: "Did you tell anyone in Reading on Saturday that you had to go to Cross Street to get a special paper?"

Drew: "No, I did not."

Harris: "Would it be correct for anyone to say that when you arrived at your lodgings at 1.15 on Sunday morning, June 23rd, you had your old stage clothes on and a part of your make-up?"

Drew: "It would not be true."

Harris: "At what time did you leave your lodgings for the theatre on the Saturday evening, and did you have a mackintosh or coat round your shoulders, and were you wearing a blue serge suit?"

Drew: "I cannot say the time. I was wearing a blue suit, and probably I had my coat with me. I did not go home in my blue trousers. I thought I had packed them, but found afterwards I had lost them, with three pounds in the pockets. I have reported this to my manager at the County Theatre, Reading. It is quite possible I was without my hat. I cannot say definitely. Sometimes I go out without a hat."

Harris: "Can you tell me if you went to get a paper in Reading on the Saturday you were there?"

Drew: "No, sir, I cannot say. I don't think I did."

Harris: "Did you at about six o'clock on June 22nd go into any tobacco shop in Reading?"

Drew: "I cannot remember doing so."

Harris: "Would it be possible for anyone to say you were in the door-way of the shop where the crime was committed about 6.10 on

---

[1] In this particular Drew's recollection was quite wrong.

Saturday evening, June 22nd, wearing no hat and with what appeared to be blood on your face?"

Drew: "I might not have been wearing a hat, but I would not have had blood on my face, and I have not the slightest idea where the murder was committed. I know nothing about the murder at Reading, and would not have known one had been committed if Mrs Lindo had not told me. I do not know the name (of the victim), although you mentioned it just now."

Harris: "Would it be at all possible that you had any blood on your hands, face or clothing on the Saturday evening in question?"

Drew: "No, sir, it is impossible. I cannot say if I went into any tobacco or other shops that night to buy anything. It is so long ago."

Harris: "When were you last in the Mitre public-house—Mr Plumb's—in Reading?"

Drew: "I cannot tell you."

Harris: "Did you go there after the show on Saturday night?"

Drew: "No, I didn't."

Harris: "You could not, could you?"

Drew: "I didn't leave the theatre until very late. I made no call after leaving the theatre at Reading. I sometimes go for a walk after the show. I remember I went home alone that Saturday."

Harris: "Do you know the post-office in Reading?"

Drew: "Yes. It is in the same street as the theatre."

Harris: "Do you know the street almost opposite the post-office?"

Drew: "I am afraid I don't."

Harris: "Do you ever buy anything to take from the theatre or shops to your home, such as calves' liver?"

Drew: "Yes, I am very fond of calves' liver."

Harris: "Did you ask a butcher in Reading for any on the Saturday?"

Drew: "Very likely I did. I asked three or four for it during the week."

This concluded the statement.

Sergeant Harris told the court, "He was quite calm, I would like to say, and he left the police-station at 1 P.M. We told him then we should probably have to see him again, and he offered no objection. I next saw Drew the following day in the same room at the police-station, at about 3.45 P.M. Mr Burrows was again present. Drew then became very excited. He walked about the room waving his arms and wiping his hands across his face like that ..." (Harris illustrated the action by drawing his hand smearingly across his face.)

The coroner asked Harris to repeat the gesture.

Harris complied.

"That happened on several occasions?"

"Yes," said Harris. "I took particular notice of it. That is a regular habit when he gets excited."

Mr Martin looked across to the jury. "You had better make a note of that in your minds," he told them.

Resuming his narrative, Harris went on: "Drew took his coat off and put it on again once or twice before he made the second statement. This continued, I should think, for about eight minutes."

Mr Martin interrupted again. "How many times did he take his coat off?"

"He came in with it on, took it off, put it on again, and finally made his statement with it off. When he sat down he banged the table with his fist. He then said, 'Now what have you got to say?' I said, 'Read that,' and pushed the caution towards him. Neither the Chief Constable nor myself had spoken during this little outburst. He then commenced to cry."

"He broke down?" queried the coroner.

"He was under the stress of great emotion undoubtedly. He then intimated that he would sign the caution if it would do us any good. I said, 'I don't care whether you sign it or not. In any case I shall question you.' He then became much quieter, read the caution and signed it."

Harris then produced Drew's second statement.

"I have now been told that two witnesses have identified me. They came from Reading and saw me in the streets of Nottingham last evening and picked me out—one as being the man who asked for calves' liver in a butcher's in Cross Street, Reading, and the other who states I am the man seen standing in the doorway of the late Mr Oliver's shop . . . I again say I did not go into any shop in Reading and commit a murder. I would like to sign this about four times and underline it."

The statement continued, again in question and answer form:

Harris: "Do you know that so far no one we have interviewed has been able to satisfy us that you were in the County Theatre, Reading, when the crime was committed, and can you tell us anyone who can inform us? We have already seen Mr and Mrs Lindo and Mr Norman Stubbs, your stage-manager."

Drew: "If the three people you have mentioned cannot say, I am afraid I cannot tell you the name of any person who can definitely satisfy you on that point."

Harris: "Did you at Maidstone ask for some cleaning material, benzine, of Mrs Lindo, whom you address as Margaret?"

Drew: "Yes, probably I did, in order to clean grease-paint off my coat collar, which would get on there when turning up my collar to go home. And later I sent it on to the dry-cleaner's to be done properly."

Harris: "Is that why you sent your coat and vest to the dry-cleaner's in Nottingham?"

Drew: "Certainly, and the only reason."

Harris: "Are you in the habit of having stone ginger-beer?"

Drew: "I often have a dry ginger, and often I have those white stone ginger-beer bottles in my room at the theatre. I drink quite a lot of this, and possibly had ten bottles at Reading, but I do not know definitely. I again wish now to tell you that I know nothing about the murder at Reading, and have never committed any crime. I could not and would not kill a man. Although I realize that what is said may seem wrong, owing to my not being able to tell you where I went on the afternoon in question, I certainly committed no murder, and cannot understand the witness picking me out as being in the shop doorway, as you say she did. There could be no blood on my face or clothing."

While this was being read out, Mrs Lindo, dressed in black, with furs and a tight-fitting blue hat, made frequent notes.

Harris: "Can you tell me what was wrong with you so that you could not play your part on the Monday evening at Maidstone?"

Drew: "I had fever and ague, and Mr Lindo said, 'I don't think you had better go on'. This was the first time in all my career of twenty-eight years on the stage my understudy has had to take my place. I have nothing more to add."

End of statement . . . and end of the morning's proceedings.

(4)

When Drew left the court for the luncheon adjournment he was clapped and cheered as he walked down the centre of the street. There were cries of, "Good luck, Philip Drew!", and, taking his hat off and waving it, he shouted back, "I am quite happy, boys!"

At the Great Western Hotel Mr Fearnley-Whittingstall was waiting to hold a brief conference with him.

A hurried lunch, and then it was time to return to court, and once again he had to slow-march his way through streets loud with enthusiasm for his cause, and pavements buttered with supporters.

Buoyant upon this risen tide of goodwill, Philip Yale Drew was swept out of the sunlight, back into the panelled gloom of the court.

(5)

First to take the stage when the court resumed at 2.30 P.M. was Mr John Lawrence, a dark, somewhat nervous man, who had acted as stage-manager to the *Monster* company.

Lawrence had written from Manchester to the coroner asking if he was to be called. The police had been informed that he was unfriendly with Drew, and in view of the fact that his statement was at variance with those of all other witnesses as to times, it had not been their intention to call him. But, on receipt of his letter, he was warned to be present on October 7th.

Lawrence now told the court that on the evening of June 22nd he arrived at the Royal County Theatre at 5.30 P.M., or shortly after. On his way in, as he went to the letter-rack, he saw someone coming down the corridor from the direction of Drew's dressing-room. He thought that it was Drew, and said "Good evening". He did not actually see the man's face, but he did notice that he was carrying an overcoat or a mackintosh, and was not wearing a hat. The man either went to the lavatory or into the street. He could not swear that it was Drew, but he usually arrived at the theatre about fifty minutes before the curtain went up, and he had never known him to arrive less than half an hour before the play started, on account of his difficult make-up.

After he had put further questions, and received lengthy, rather over-elaborate answers, Mr Martin said to Lawrence: "Frankly, you talk too much. With all due respect, we get a blunt witness who is just a working woman and she tells us what we want to know, but you go on talking."

Mr Lawrence had got off on the wrong foot with Mr Martin. He was about to establish that foothold.

"I think the next time you saw Drew that evening was just before the curtain went up at 6.50 P.M.," began the coroner.

"No," says Lawrence emphatically, "that is not correct."

"Well, that is the statement you made to the police," snapped Mr Martin.

"I next saw Mr Drew about five minutes past six, when I went into his dressing-room to get a revolver," said Lawrence imperturbably.

"Why make one statement to the police when the matter was more fresh in your memory, and another statement to me today? Your statement to the police says: 'The next time I saw him was just before the curtain went up'."

"That statement is incorrect."

"Well, take your statement to the police and read it through, and tell me where it is wrong."

In his statement, which was then read out by the coroner's clerk, Mr Lawrence had said that five minutes after he reached the theatre he distinctly remembered seeing Mr Drew and saying 'Good evening' to him.

"You say there that you distinctly saw Mr Drew," said Mr Martin.

"I was under that impression at the time."

"You are on oath. We want the truth, not vague impressions."

The statement continued: "The next I saw of him was at one minute before the curtain went up, when he moved to take his position on the stage."

The Coroner broke in again, "Is *that* true?"

"It was true to the best of my recollection at that time."

"Do you mean," asked the coroner tartly, "that your memory improves with the passage of time?"

"May I explain? After making that statement I remembered an additional incident. There was a stage revolver used in the play. Mr Drew used this revolver in the last act, and then took it to his dressing-room and kept it there. As juvenile lead, I used this revolver in the second act, and it was my routine to fetch it from Mr Drew's room every evening before I made up. On the evening of June 22nd I got to the theatre and started my packing. I had replaced most articles in my basket. Then I walked across the road and set my watch at six o'clock by the Town Hall clock which had just finished striking. I went back and put my watch on my dressing-table, where I keep it whilst making up. I put two shirts in my basket, glanced to see if the properties I used in my part were on my table, saw my notebook and pencil were there, but not my revolver. I went along to Mr Drew's room, and knocked at the door."

"What time would that be?" asked Mr Martin.

"Not more than five-past six. Mr Drew called out, 'Come', and I went in and said, 'I've just called for the revolver, Mr Drew.' I don't think he spoke, but just grunted, and I went across and took it from the shelf of his dressing-table. I went back to my dressing-room, changed into my stage clothes, and as I commenced to make up Fry came in and said, 'It's the half-hour'. I overlooked the revolver incident when I made the police statement. I recalled it the day after I made the statement, but I did not take much notice of the fact that Mr Drew had been questioned by the police, but when I subsequently realized the importance of time in the case I wrote to the coroner, giving my address and asking to be called."

> The Coroner: "Do you now withdraw the statement which you made to the police: 'I distinctly remember seeing Mr Drew'?"
>
> Lawrence: "I can only put it like this: I went into the theatre and there was apparently nobody in the theatre. I saw someone coming from Mr Drew's dressing-room, and it did not occur to me that it was anyone else than Mr Drew."
>
> The Coroner: "I think it is incomprehensible. I should never commit myself to that extent when I was not sure I saw the person by saying, 'I distinctly saw him'."
>
> Lawrence: "I can only say that, seeing someone coming from that room, I thought it was Mr Drew, and I didn't realize that there was any significance in it."

That really was too much for the coroner. "I should think that when Scotland Yard men came to you you would have thought it very serious. They don't come down here for fun, you know; only in very serious cases. In other words, you were not telling the truth."

"I was doing my best."

Mr Martin was not to be placated. "Your memory cannot be so good now as it was then—unless you have been talking it over with someone," he added acidly.

"I have not had a chance of talking it over with anyone."

> The Coroner: "The next time you make a statement to the police I should be very careful to tell them what you know to be the truth. One does not know what to believe."

Lawrence: "May I say this, sir—"

The Coroner (interrupting): "You have said too much already, I think. You are the one witness who has failed to keep to his statement out of something like fifty of them. It is not a credit to anybody to do that."

Lawrence: "May I say this—"

The Coroner: "Yes, but do not say too much."

Lawrence: "The officer did not stress that—"

The Coroner: "They do not stress. That is the whole point. They ask you for a statement and leave you to tell the truth."

Lawrence: "I am doing my best."

The Coroner: "It is a very bad best to tell the police one thing, and tell me another. It is not creditable to an Englishman."

Mr Fearnley-Whittingstall, who had by now arrived in court, rose and questioned Mr Lawrence about a man whom he had mentioned in his statement to the police. This man, who was aged about thirty-five, dressed in a dark or blue suit, wearing a cap, with very thick hair bulging from under it, and of Jewish appearance, had stopped him outside a paper-shop in Reading on Sunday, June 23rd, and had spoken to him about the murder.

Asked by the coroner if he would ever be able to identify that man, Lawrence answered that he thought he would.

The foreman of the jury asked: "Did you definitely give that description to the police and request them to find him?"

Lawrence replied that directly the police came to him he had given them that description.

"How long after June 22nd?" asked the foreman.

It was the coroner who replied. "Two months exactly," he said.

"It did not occur to you, I suppose, to give the police a description of the man," observed the foreman.

"Well," said Lawrence apologetically, "it seemed almost ludicrous to me to think there was anything in it. Events had not assumed the seriousness they have now."

The choice of the word 'ludicrous' was unfortunate. It seemed to sting the coroner like an outsize hornet. "When you say ludicrous, what do you mean? Especially when we lost one of our citizens. No murder is ludicrous. It may seem nothing to you, of course."

Embarrassed, Mr Lawrence muttered something about its having seemed ludicrous that there should have been anything important in the meeting with the man outside the paper-shop, and, red-faced and perspiring, was obviously relieved to escape from the box.

After those fireworks the evidence of the remaining three witnesses heard that afternoon seemed flat and uninteresting.

George Stanley Pike said that he was formerly business manager to the *Monster* company, but had left because of a difference of opinion with Mr Lindo. He spoke of a "lot of unpleasantness" in consequence of his having had to reprimand Drew, who was "muzzy" with drink, for forgetting his lines at the end of the play. He also said that he thought that the Lindos were frightened of Drew to a certain extent.

Quick as a flash, the coroner was asking, "Have you ever seen Drew violent?"

"Never," admitted Pike.

"Did he ever tie a man up in a bag?"

Pike looked surprised. "Yes—but only in the play."

"Do you know if this unfortunate individual left the company in consequence?"

"He left because he didn't like the general run of things in the company."

"Did he say anything about Drew?" persisted Mr Martin.

"Only that he was a trying man and that he found it difficult to work with him."

Mr Pike added that he remembered that Mr Lindo was upset one night because Drew was not dressed properly. He was partly exposed.

Mr Fearnley-Whittingstall then asked Pike, "What makes you say that Mr and Mrs Lindo were frightened of Mr Drew?"

"It would have been a serious thing if he had left the company. I don't know how they could stand the treatment for such a time —this continual drinking."

"You mean they were frightened he would go?"

"Yes."

"Not physically frightened?"

"No."

Miss Phyllis Moore, an office clerk at the Royal County Theatre, Reading, testified that she was on duty at the theatre at 6.15 P.M. on the evening of June 22nd. "I caught an Erleigh Road tram from Whitley Pump at 6 P.M. I got out at Sands,[1] between Cross Street

[1] Sands, milliners, 26 Broad Street.

and Queen Victoria Street, and went through Cross Street somewhere about ten-past six. I ran through the street so as not to be late, and saw nothing wrong. I went along Friar Street, then to the theatre." She also said that when she got to the theatre yard she noticed a one-legged man, Mr Hathaway, whom she knew. "I went through the stage-door and saw Mr Drew in a navy-blue suit near the letter-rack. He had no hat and wore no grease-paint. He had not started to make up at all. I saw Mr Drew go into his dressing-room, dressed as he would be in the street. I should put this at 6.15 P.M. roughly, but probably later. It couldn't have been earlier as I couldn't get to the theatre before." Miss Moore said that she could not speak as to Drew's condition, whether he was drunk or sober, and added that she did not see him with an overcoat.

Replying to Mr Fearnley-Whittingstall, she said that she had first been asked to give evidence that morning, and that that was when she had in fact first made a statement.

The last witness was John Caleb Povey, a coal merchant of Sonning Eye, near Reading. His evidence was to the effect that he was in Cross Street from 5.5 P.M. to 5.25 P.M. on June 22nd. "I had my car with me and was looking in the antique shop[1] near Oliver's. The car was standing halfway between the antique shop and Oliver's, with its bonnet facing Broad Street. I saw a man fall on the back of the car and start stroking and patting it and mumbling to it."

The Coroner: "Making a fuss of it like a dog or a cat." (Laughter.)
Povey: "Three or four people watched him."
The Coroner: "Were any remarks made?"
Povey: "I made a remark. I said, 'He's had more than I have.'" (Laughter.)

Mr Povey was invited to look around the court and see if he could identify the man.

He pointed at Drew. "That's the man," he said.

"Stand up," ordered Mr Martin.

The Coroner: "How was he dressed?"
Povey: "In a dark suit, I think. I don't remember if he had a hat or a coat. I only remember his antics."

Mr Fearnley-Whittingstall was asking Povey whether he had seen accounts and photographs in the newspapers, when the coroner

[1] Jesse P. Ballard's, 21 and 23 Cross Street.

cut in with: "I think Mr Drew has supplied his own photographs pretty freely, hasn't he? He has advertised himself pretty well."

And on that sour note the inquest was then adjourned until 2 P.M. the following day.

At his hotel that evening Drew told a *Daily Mail* reporter: "I feel almost light-hearted. It has been a brighter day for me. You do not have to be an actor to appreciate the demonstration I have experienced in the streets today. Every man who has been in a somewhat similar position to myself has wondered what the world is thinking. You can understand my wondering whether there would be prejudice against me because I am what some people would call a foreigner—a foreigner of British stock, of course—or because I am what some people would call a strolling player. These demonstrations tell me there are no such prejudices in this country. Tomorrow I expect to give evidence. Whenever the call comes, I am ready to say just what I know about my week in Reading and events since."

Scene 5

THE ACTOR'S TALE

Tuesday, October 8th, 1929

(1)

THERE were never queues like this at the Royal County Theatre. Not since the days of *King of the Wild West* had Philip Yale Drew drawn such crowds.

Although the day's proceedings were not due to start until two o'clock in the afternoon, people began clustering around the police court before 8 A.M. Women and girls outnumbered men in the queue, and many of them had brought camp-stools and picnic lunches with them. Several times during the morning the police had to clear the street, as the growing throng was impeding the traffic, and a passage had to be made to enable the magistrates to enter the building for the morning courts. But as soon as the officers' backs were turned the crowds swarmed resolutely back and settled down patiently for their long wait.

At about one o'clock, further crowds started to gather outside Drew's hotel, where he had spent a busy morning in consultation with Mr Fearnley-Whittingstall and Mr Ratcliffe, and there was another friendly demonstration as Drew, accompanied by Mr and Mrs Lindo, emerged, cheers following the trio all the way as they walked—between the eager spectators lining the streets—to the court. At every step Drew turned round to thank his sympathizers, raising and waving his hat and seizing the hands that were proffered to shake his. He was wearing his usual light-brown overcoat, a sprig of white heather which had been presented to him for luck in the buttonhole. Just before he entered the court a woman shouted, "Three cheers for Mr Drew," walked up to him and thrust a pound-note for his defence costs into his hand, crying,

"Good luck, sir!" Drew was taken by surprise and said, "You shouldn't have done that. This will go to Mr Lindo."[1]

Then, amidst the clapping, the cheering, and the shouts of "Good old Philip!" he disappeared from view, to the accompaniment of one great, final ear-splitting cheer.

In the crowded court Drew again sat next to Mrs Lindo, immediately behind Mr Fearnley-Whittingstall and Mr Ratcliffe. On Mrs Lindo's left sat her husband, a typical actor of the old school, grey hair, keen brown eyes, and a mobile mouth.

When Mr Martin entered every available seat in court was occupied.

Silence.

The coroner cleared his throat.

The fifth hearing was in session.

(2)

The first couple of witnesses to be called were Reading Corporation Tramways' employees, Albert William Walker, a motorman (that is, a tram-driver), and Donald Arthur Goodall, a tram-conductor.

They gave evidence regarding the time that their tram—the one which the witness Miss Phyllis Moore had stated that she caught to work—had arrived at Queen Victoria Street on the evening of June 22nd. Both testified that their vehicle did indeed reach Queen Victoria Street at about 6.10 P.M.

Mrs Florence Wheeler, a widow, who lived at 4 King's Meadow Road, Reading, told the court that on Saturday evening, June 22nd, she was shopping at the Co-operative Stores in Cheapside. "When I finished my purchases I looked at the clock in the stores, and it was just six o'clock. I went out and turned into Friar Street, pushing a push-car with a little boy, and stopped to make another purchase at a shop in Friar Street. That took one or two minutes. When I came to Queen Victoria Street I turned down Station Road, and turned to my right into Blagrave Street. I then crossed the road and turned into Vastern Road. As I turned the corner into Vastern Road I practically collided with a man walking towards the town at a very fast pace."

[1] Mr Lindo had announced that he was initiating a fund to cover the costs of Drew's defence.

She could not remember if he was wearing a hat, but he had a coat draped over his shoulders and was wearing a dark suit. He walked quickly, and his coat was flying open. She had seen the man on the Friday—the previous day—from her bedroom window as he came along King's Meadow Road. He was wearing his coat over his shoulders in the same way then.

"Can you see that man in court?" asked the coroner.

Mrs Wheeler looked slowly round at the faces upturned towards her. Her gaze travelled over the detectives, sitting immediately below, to the jury, then to Mr Fearnley-Whittingstall and those who sat behind him, until at length her eyes rested on Philip Yale Drew. She pointed. "I think that is the man . . . sitting there," she said.

Mr Fearnley-Whittingstall then asked: "When did you first tell this to the police?"

"On Sunday last."

"How long would it take you, pushing the cart, to get from the Co-operative Stores to the point of this encounter?"

"I can't tell you exactly. Somewhere about a quarter of an hour."

"This would happen, then, about a quarter past six?"

"It may have been a little more or a little less."

"Certainly not before ten past six?"

"It couldn't have been."

The foreman of the jury said, "You say that the Co-operative Stores clock said six o'clock. Can you certify as to the accuracy of the clock?"

And when Mrs Wheeler replied that she could not, the foreman commented, "My experience of these clocks is that they are not very correct."

Detective Sergeant John Harris was now recalled.

He said that on the afternoon of July 26th he received from Sergeant Ellington, of the Nottingham City Police, a blue coat, which he retained in his possession. "I examined the lining of the right-hand pocket. It was stained brown. At 7.15 that evening, with Detective Superintendent Doubleday, I visited the Palace Theatre, Trent Bridge, Nottingham, and saw Mr Drew in his dressing-room. Mr Fry was also there. They were both preparing themselves for their parts. I said to Drew, 'I understand this is your coat. I am going to retain it for the present.' Mr Drew examined the coat and said, 'Yes, that is my coat. I left it at the cleaner's. I don't mind your having it.' On August 7th, at about 2.10 P.M.,

I again saw Drew at the City Police Station, St Albans, in company with Chief Constable Burrows and Detective Inspector Walters of the Reading Force. A further caution was read to Mr Drew, which he signed, and then I took down a third statement from him."

It was, like the two previous ones, in the form of question and answer:

Harris: "Who was the friend you sent the pipe to from Grimsby?"

Drew: "Justin P. Lapham,[1] of Marshfield Hills, Massachusetts, U.S.A. But that was years ago. I should think in 1911. I also sent him one from Canada, Montreal, and another from Birmingham or Sheffield. It is a long time since I sent him one, and I cannot definitely say the year, but it was before the war, and the same week I was made a member of the Royal Ancient Order of Buffaloes at Grimsby."

Harris: "What was in the parcel which you took from the County Theatre, Reading, on the Saturday night you finished there?"

Drew: "I did not know, until Mrs Lindo told me that a certain member of the company had said that I left the theatre with a parcel and a stick, that I had done so. I do not remember leaving with a parcel, and I cannot understand anyone's saying that I had a stick there, because I lost a stick which Mr Lindo gave me before I went to Reading. I may have left it in a public-house or a train, but I certainly had not a stick at Reading."

Harris: "Would you care to tell me any particulars of your present financial position?"

Drew: "I have a banking account at Lloyds, Chatham Bank. It is only a small amount. My credit is about £35 now, I should say. I also have a credit in a savings bank at Bradford of about £4."

Harris: "Did you leave Reading wearing two suits?"

Drew: "I did not."

Harris: "Can you remember what you left in?"

Drew: "The grey suit I have on now."

Harris: "Did you change on the way to Maidstone?"

Drew: "No."

Harris: "If anyone said that when you reached Maidstone you were

---

[1] Justin P. Lapham was a kind of 'uncle-in-law' of Philip's. He was the brother of Eliza Lapham, who had married Philip's mother's brother, Edgar Tilden. He worked as a sort of general handyman at Aunt Abbie's, caring for the grounds, horses, cows, and so on. Back in 1913 he had been brought over to England by Philip to play the part of Black Horse Bill of the Wild Flower Mine in *King of the Wild West*. Philip kept up a sporadic correspondence with him over the years, signing his letters and cards 'Nusie', short for 'Nuisance'.

wearing a blue jacket and grey trousers would you think they were wrong?"

Drew: "Yes, they must be, because I have a trunk which I leave in the theatre and do not carry clothes with me, and what I left Reading Theatre in I should be wearing on arrival at Maidstone. I did not, and could not, change on the journey to Maidstone."

Harris: "Have you ever looked at the lining of the right-hand pocket of your blue suit?"

Drew: "I do not ever remember doing so. I do not think I can tell you the colour of it."

Harris: "Have you ever used any hydrogen peroxide or other chemical upon your pocket or jacket?"

Drew: "I have occasionally used Mrs Lindo's for abrasions, and also for my teeth, but never have I had a bottle of my own for years, and never have I used any on my clothes."

Harris: "What did you clean your jacket with at Maidstone?"

Drew: "I might have used some benzine to clean my collar, which benzine I should buy from Boots, the chemists. I might have had some benzine from Mrs Lindo also, but I cannot remember whether I had any at Maidstone, or cleaned my jacket collar there."

Harris: "Can you explain to me how the pockets of your jacket—the blue one—had been stained or bleached?"

Drew: "I cannot understand why there should be any stains in any part of my clothing."

Harris: "Have you ever attempted to remove any stains from the lining of your pocket?"

Drew: "I certainly have not."

Harris: "What would there be in your pocket that would be sticky and dirty?"

Drew: "I cannot imagine. I sometimes buy sweets, peppermints, but I do not remember anything being in my pocket. They are usually sold in a packet."

Harris: "Have you ever attempted to remove any stains from your pocket, or could you have had blood in your pocket?"

Drew: "There could not be any blood in my pocket, or anything of an improper nature."

Harris: "You now say you cannot remember whether you cleaned your coat collar at Maidstone?"

Drew: "No, I cannot definitely say. I may have done so."

Harris: "How long would it take you to clean the greasepaint off your collar?"

Drew: "About a couple of minutes I should say. A piece of rag and some benzine; it does not take long."

Harris: "Do you remember being told that a lady had identified you as the man she saw in Mr Oliver's shop-door who looked as if he had been fighting and had blood on his face? Is it possible she is correct?"

Drew: "I told you before, there could have been no blood on my face. I certainly do not remember being in the shop in question."

That concluded Drew's third statement.

Harris then told the coroner: "There is one point I should like to mention. I read an article in the paper called the *Empire News*, dated September 10th. It was headed 'What I Told the Police After the Shop Crime', and purports to be written by Mr Philip Yale Drew. In the last paragraph of the first page, Mr Drew is supposed to have been asked after some questions about calves' liver, 'Did you carry it home in your pocket?' And on the next page in thick type there appears an explanation as to how blood from the liver may have got into the pocket. That question was never asked Mr Drew."

"Who makes this explanation in the article?" asked the coroner.

"Mr Drew, apparently, as the author of the article," said Harris.

"A scientific explanation. Possibly well thought out and considered," observed Mr Martin.

Continuing, Sergeant Harris said, "On August 10th I received from Detective Sergeant Thorpe the pair of blue trousers previously referred to, which I retained. There was, and still is, a cleaner's green cleaning tab at the top left-hand inside."

"Have you traced that cleaner?" asked the coroner.

"No."

Harris was about to read out the number on the tab when the coroner said, "Will the Press please take careful note of this number."

The number, said Harris, was A 8819, with possibly another figure following, then a dash and a 3. It was on a piece of light green tape 3¼ inches long by half an inch wide.

Said the coroner, "Will the Press, on our behalf, appeal throughout the country to any cleaners who will help us in this matter of identification, and find where these trousers were cleaned. Probably new pockets were inserted. The pockets appear to have been renovated entirely with ordinary buff pocket material—two side-pockets, one hip-pocket and the fob. This is very urgent, and any communication should be sent to the Chief Constable of Reading."

Mr Fearnley-Whittingstall stood up. "My client instructs me to

say that these trousers were twice cleaned, and he will help the
police by telling them where. They were cleaned at Rochdale and
Swansea. It may also help the police to know that the suit was made
by Burton's at Stratford Broadway."

"What we want to know is the last date of cleaning, and the
last place of cleaning," said the coroner.

Fearnley-Whittingstall now began his cross-examination of
Sergeant Harris. The two stood facing one another. The one, young
—and looking even younger than his years—tall, slender, boyish,
with a keen, clever face and an incisive manner. The other, middle-
aged, wary, and worldly-wise, with vast experience. Both of them,
strong personalities.

The opening was gentle. "How did you take the statements from
Mr Drew?" inquired counsel mildly.

"I wrote the question down before I asked it, and wrote his
answer down afterwards. They were written in longhand. The
Chief Constable of Reading and I were the only two who asked
questions, with the possible exception of Sergeant Thorpe, who
may have asked a minor question."

"You said yesterday that Mr Drew's hair had changed?"

"Yes."

"Are you suggesting that Mr Drew is dyeing his hair?"

"I am."

"You stated that Mr Drew's hair looked as if the dye had been
wearing off. Are you suggesting that Mr Drew had dyed his
hair?"

"I am giving evidence of what I see."

"*Have* you any evidence—any suggestion, any data—on which
to base that statement?"

The gloves were coming off.

"My own eyes."

The gloves were off.

"When you say your own eyes," snapped Fearnley-Whittingstall,
"do you mean your own guesswork?"

"Certainly not." There was an edge to Harris' voice now, too.
"Why, it's apparent to everybody in court. It is my job to notice
things like that. I have noticed something about yourself, for
instance. I have noticed since you have been in court that the
handkerchief in your pocket has a red laundry mark."

Laughter. Definite score to Sergeant Harris.

He added: "I only mention that because it is my job to notice those things."

"In spite of the eminence of your art," rejoined counsel with heavy sarcasm, "Mr Drew will let any chemist in the country examine his hair to prove that he has had no dye on his hair at all. When you say hair-dye, and you tell us of your detective powers and your own eyes, are you aware that Mr Drew is prepared for any chemist whom the police like to choose to come and examine it?"

Harris remained unperturbed—unperturbable. "I give evidence of what I see. I don't know anything about that. It may have been peroxide."

"But you said *hair-dye*."

"I merely said that it was not the same colour now as when the inquest started."

Counsel was not to be put off. "As you have suggested on oath that it is dyed, can you suggest when he dyed it?"

"I have made a statement on the difference in the gentleman's hair."

"Are you suggesting he dyed it?" persisted Fearnley-Whittingstall.

"Since I saw him on August 7th his hair has changed in colour. Then it was brown; now it is not brown."

"Are you suggesting that he has dyed it recently?"

As though answering a tiresome child, Harris said, "Surely between the seventh of August and now *must* be recent?"

"Surely," counsel flashed back, "you can say yes or no whether he has dyed it recently?"

"The question," responded Harris tartly, "does not call for yes or no."

"*Will you answer m*e—and say, can you, out of fairness to Mr Drew, on behalf of the police take the step to prove whether you are right or wrong?"

As Harris was replying, "It does not lie with me" the coroner turned to Fearnley-Whittingstall and observed, "You can take that step yourself."

End of skirmish.

Fearnley-Whittingstall changed tack. "Is it not true to say that Mr Drew has given you all the help he could, and answered all your questions?"

"Certainly," said Harris.

"He answered questions he need not have done?"

"Yes."

"He has helped you all he could?"

Harris would not commit himself. "So far as I know he has helped us all he can," he said.

"Of your general knowledge and experience as a detective and a man, have you ever gone into the street and seen a man whom you could have sworn was a friend of yours, and on closer investigation found he was a perfect stranger?"

Harris considered. "I have seen people, certainly, I thought might have been friends of mine from a distance, but on getting closer to them I have found that they were not."

A clever bit of side-stepping. The fangs of implication drawn.

"Have you ever been smacked on the back by a person who thought you were a friend of his?"

Harris had to capitulate. "Yes, I have."

Fearnley-Whittingstall went a step further. "It happens every day?"

"It is quite a common thing."

Now counsel drove his point home. "And if it is easy to make a mistake with a friend or acquaintance, it is still easier to make a mistake with a stranger?"

Harris saw the danger. Parried. "There are degrees, and it is a matter of opinion."

"In your opinion, do you agree with me?"

Harris took evasive action. "Oh, I am not going to go so far as that. I am not here to give opinions."

Fearnley-Whittingstall lunged. "But you *have* given an opinion —about his hair. Is *that* not an opinion?"

"No. It was my observation. I have only spoken of what I have seen."

Adroit.

Fearnley-Whittingstall had one more try. "Did you say yesterday that the dye was wearing off?"

"No," said Harris.

Fearnley-Whittingstall raised his eyebrows in surprise. He had not been expecting that denial. "It is in every paper, almost."

"Very likely," said Harris evenly.

"We are not responsible for the papers," interjected the coroner.

Addressing Harris, the foreman of the jury asked: "Have you

ever heard of a water cosmetic used by theatrical people to colour their hair which washes off and which is really a sort of water paint?"

"I am not a hairdresser," said Harris. "I take it that if anything changes the colour of hair it must be a dye. That is my experience. I suppose peroxide changes the colour of hair. I have known ladies change the colour of their hair."

"Yes, I have noticed in this case that Mr Drew's hair is certainly greyer than it was. The jury is satisfied that Mr Drew's hair has changed colour while he has been in the court the last few days. We have noticed that," said the foreman.

"On behalf of Mr Drew," said Fearnley-Whittingstall, "I am not stating that Mr Drew's hair has not changed. I do not wonder if it has. I say it is not dyed."

The coroner broke in, "You are not giving evidence on his behalf, I suppose?"

"Those are my instructions," said counsel.

Just before Sergeant Harris left the box Mr Fearnley-Whittingstall was given permission to ask a further question.

"Mr Drew will say that you did ask him if the calves' liver might have stained one of the pockets?"

"I did not," replied Harris. "If I had, it would have been taken down in the statement. I say I did not ask him. I am definite on that."

Chief Constable Burrows was recalled.

"Can you remember if Mr Drew was asked about how liver was taken home?" Fearnley-Whittingstall asked him. "Did he say: 'I cannot tell after five weeks how I carried it home'?"

"No," said Burrows, "I cannot remember such a question. I am confident Mr Drew never made such an answer."

A buzz of interest in court. Chief Inspector James Berrett entered the box.

Quietly and graphically, he described his examination of Mr Oliver's shop. Reconstructing the crime, he said that in his opinion Mr Oliver was attacked while standing between the two show-cases. The positions of the blood-splashes on the premises gave him the impression that the murderer struck from the front of the counter, never passed behind it, stole the contents of the till by leaning over the right-hand show-case, and knocked the scales on to the floor in making the attack. He also, and finally, stated that the coat and trousers belonging to Drew had been submitted for microscopical examination by experts, with negative results.

A buzz of incredulity in court as the spectators realized that this meagre contribution was his all—and Chief Inspector James Berrett left the box.

Now the day's preliminaries were over. The bit players had done their parts. Time for the star actor to tell his tale. The moment for which everyone had been eagerly awaiting had arrived.

(3)

After a short adjournment, the coroner turned to Mr Fearnley-Whittingstall. "I understand," he said, "that your client, Mr Drew, wishes to give evidence."

And counsel's assenting reply was almost drowned as Philip Yale Drew jumped smartly to his feet and in ringing tones boomed, "Certainly."

He walked briskly to the witness-box. There he stood, a pictur-esque figure in his grey suit and brown overcoat, his mass of curly hair brushed straight back, looking every inch what he was—a melodramatic actor. Clean-cut features and, as one court reporter described them, "the eyes of a marksman—keen, steadfast eyes that are in curious contrast with his artistic temperament".

Mr Martin was the first to speak. "I shall consider it my duty formally to caution you that whatever you say will be taken down in writing. You need not give evidence unless you wish to do so."

Ominous.

"I understand that," Drew replied, drawing himself up and speaking in a firm, confident voice. "I am going to tell the truth."

He took the oath in a dramatic way... "and nothing but the truth," he intoned slowly and impressively. He kissed the book, and glanced around the court.

Deep silence. Not an eye in that crowded place that was not turned upon him. Not an ear that did not listen keenly.

The first question put to him by his counsel was, "During the course of the last year what has been your financial position?"

Drew said that he had earned a splendid salary—between £18 and £20 a week. In Reading he was getting £4 a week, all expenses paid, plus one-third of the profits.

"There has been," said Fearnley-Whittingstall, "some suggestion about your drinking. What had been your inclination towards drink during that week in Reading?"

"I should say probably about the same as usual. Surely not less; possibly more. I am not denying the fact that I do drink. I am not denying that I had, perhaps, what one of the witnesses said ... one too many. Most of the people I have met in my life have been in the same boat."

"Are you by any manner of means regularly drunk?"

"I am certainly not." Then, blandly, "Perhaps I do not quite know what 'drunk' is. I have heard so many definitions. I presume some people are drunk after having only one drink. If you mean by drunk falling down and not being able to get up, I am certainly not regularly or habitually drunk."

It was not meant as a quibble, but as a whimsical observation.

"Whatever you have taken to drink in your opinion has not interfered with your performance?" said the coroner.

"I fail to remember when it has to any noticeable extent," replied Drew.

"When," asked Fearnley-Whittingstall, "did you cast your mind back by force of circumstances to your movements on June 22nd? When was the first time you had to recollect what happened then?"

"When I was interrogated by Sergeant Harris in Nottingham."

"July 25th," said counsel.

Drew nodded.

"You remember Saturday, June 22nd?"

Drew nodded again. "I shall have to say this. I never check the time of my movements. They may be a bit erratic. I am afraid I cannot tell you in the morning what time I leave my lodgings. I cannot tell you exactly the time I may arrive at the theatre, the time I leave it in the morning, whether I went for a walk, which place I went to buy fruit or anything else I might be shopping for. I feel I am at liberty to do as I like during the day. It is my business and nobody else's. I always know I can account for my movements when I am supposed to be in the theatre, and when my work makes it necessary for me to be there. I am responsible to the owner of the production and my stage-manager. It is my living."

"Don't be punctilious over time if you don't remember, but what did you do in the afternoon, say after luncheon?"

"And swear on my oath to the time where I was? I can't do it."

Counsel tried again. "What is the first memory you have of

June 22nd—the first thing you remember doing, now, looking back?"

Drew pondered. "Being in the theatre on time."

"And what time was that?"

"I have made it a rule of my life to be in the theatre one hour before the performance begins."

"What time did this performance begin?"

"Six-fifty P.M."

"How long did it take you to put on your make-up?"

"I do not rush into my room and tear my things off. I have to strip first of all to the skin. I wear nothing on the stage that I have on in the street. It takes a man about three minutes to strip. If there are any artists in the world who can put on the clothes I have to wear—ragged and torn clothes tied up with pieces of elastic, and shoes tied on with string—if there are any who can do that in less than fifteen minutes I should like to engage them if I had a production."

"How long does it take you to do this?" the coroner inquired.

"I cannot do it under fifteen minutes after I have stripped."

"Does this include your make-up?" asked counsel.

"Certainly not. I cannot do that in under fifteen minutes. In hot weather it would be a bit longer. It is difficult to get stuff to stick whiskers on your face if you are perspiring, and my middle name is 'Perspiration'."

"That is a minimum of thirty-three minutes?" commented Fearnley-Whittingstall.

"I would like to add that I have yet to remember the time when the half-hour has been called and I have not been in my stage clothes."

"When is the half-hour called?"

"At Reading it would be at 6.20 P.M., or perhaps a few minutes earlier on a Saturday night."

"Can you tell me what time you had your last meal that day before going to the theatre?"

"No. I am very irregular with regard to food."

"Which way did you walk to the theatre?"

"I could better take you there than explain it. I came from the house, down the street, to the left and under a bridge, and I don't know exactly what the turnings are. I always passed the post-office on the way."

The coroner raised his head. "Then you would come by the Town Hall clock-tower."

"I travel by locality," Drew told him. Then, pointing to his forehead, "I have bumps of it up here. I don't know anything about the landmarks of the streets."

"You never look at the landmarks?" asked Mr Martin.

"I wouldn't say never. I probably do, unconsciously or sub-consciously."

Fearnley-Whittingstall took up the questioning again. "Can you remember what you were wearing?"

"Certainly. The suit I see here." Drew pointed to the blue serge suit lying in front of him.

"What else were you wearing in addition to that suit? What colour boots?"

"Black. I have never owned a pair of brown boots in my life."

"That you are positive of?"

"*Positive* of it. Neither have I had a mackintosh for more than five years."

"What about your hat?"

"Sometimes I wear one, and sometimes not. If I am by the river or at a seaside town like Weymouth or Tenby or any of those places, I very often go without one."

"Do you think the chances are that you had one on or not?"

"Very likely not."

"What about the coat?"

Again Drew's answer was completely noncommittal. "Very often with, and very often without."

"Can you recollect whether you were with or without?"

"I would not swear on oath."

"Did you go into any shop between your lodgings and the theatre?"

"Not to my remembrance."

"Did you go to Cross Street?"

"I had no occasion to deviate from my usual route."

Once again the coroner raised his head. "Now answer a plain question, Mr Drew."

"I'm sorry," apologized Drew. "No I did not. I must have passed the end of it."

"It is alleged," continued counsel, "by one witness, if not by two other witnesses, that you said you were going to Cross Street to buy a paper."

"If three thousand say it, it is not true."

"Is there any expression you might have used?"

"Yes, we often use it at home. I might have said, 'I am going across the street for a paper'."

"That is an Americanism?"

"Yes, meaning somewhere near at hand."

Fearnley-Whittingstall then asked Drew if he could remember the first person that he spoke to at the County Theatre on the night of June 22nd, and he replied that he could not.

Asked what time the show was over on the night in question, Drew said that he did not know. "I'm afraid you'll have to inquire of the stage-manager," he added.

Fearnley-Whittingstall: "What did you do when the play was over?"

Drew: "Well, I probably said good-bye to the boys. I might have stood on the stage a minute or two with them, then picked up my props, took off my make-up, and packed."

Fearnley-Whittingstall: "How long would that take you?"

Drew: "If I hurried it wouldn't take very long."

Fearnley-Whittingstall: "What time *did* it take you?"

Drew: "I can't tell you."

Fearnley-Whittingstall: "Did you leave in your make-up?"

Drew: "I certainly did not—though many actors do."

The coroner suggested that perhaps he had been careless in removing his make-up, and Drew replied that considering that he had had only cold water and two heavy make-ups that night, possibly the removal would not take it all off.

He explained that he removed his beard before the last act. "I go to my dressing-room and am only away a few minutes, and I entirely remove my beard to the best of my ability. I also remove the moustache at the same time, but before I return to the stage I put on another moustache, for the reason that the one I have had on has become so stiff, and as it is necessary in the play for me to rip off my moustache, it is necessary for me to put on a new one so that it does not take the lip off as well." (Laughter.)

"Wig, moustache, whiskers and beard, or whatever you call it, all come off?" asked the coroner.

"Yes," said Drew, "in the last act I appear without any wig or hair on my face."

"So," commented Mr Martin, "the electrician and your land-lady are mistaken when they say you had part of your make-up on?"

"I should say so."

Fearnley-Whittingstall remarked, "Mr Fry said in his evidence, 'He had removed his make-up carelessly. A little was left as though he had taken a towel.'"

And Drew chimed in with, "It might have been carelessly removed. Not having any hot water, I daresay there would be a suggestion of make-up. More than you have on your face at the moment." And everyone laughed.

"There is none on mine," said Fearnley-Whittingstall rapidly. And everyone laughed again.

"Well, I certainly didn't make up on the way home," said Drew. And there was more laughter.

"What clothes did you wear on leaving the theatre?" asked counsel.

"Grey trousers and blue coat and waistcoat," said Drew.

And then he embarked upon the story of how his blue trousers had mysteriously disappeared, and Fearnley-Whittingstall made the point that it was Drew himself who had drawn attention to the fact that his trousers were missing.

After that the question of the cleaning of his blue serge suit arose.

Fearnley-Whittingstall asked, "How often have you had this suit cleaned?"

"I can't tell you how many times I've had it cleaned since I bought it," replied Drew.

"Where was the last place you had it cleaned prior to Reading?"

"Rochdale."

"Trousers, or the whole suit?" asked the coroner.

"Prior to Nottingham I have sent the whole suit twice. The whole suit went in Rochdale, and before that at Swansea."

Fearnley-Whittingstall took up the questioning again. "When was the Rochdale cleaning done?"

"I should have to ask the manager of the cleaning company."

"Tell me roughly."

Drew did not reply.

The coroner interposed, wearily, "His memory is so bad it is not much use asking him."

But Fearnley-Whittingstall persisted. "Was it before or after you went to Reading?"

"Oh, long before."

Some questions were then put about the cleaning of grease-paint off his coat-collar with benzine at Maidstone.

The Coroner: "You heard the servant-girl[1] say you were half an hour on the lawn cleaning the coat?"

Drew: "I did."

The Coroner: "And you say that was incorrect?"

Drew: "I do."

Fearnley-Whittingstall: "Did Detective Sergeant Harris ask you whether you were fond of liver, and whether you had ever carried it home in your pocket?"

Drew: "I wouldn't like to say the question was put to me deliberately, 'Do you ever carry it home in your pocket?' To the best of my memory the question was, 'Would it be possible you might have carried it home in your pocket?' And I replied that, since it was five weeks back, I defied anyone to say what I carried home in any particular pocket, but I could not think I should do such a thing as carry liver home in my pocket. To the best of my recollection, it was put to me that, if it was wrapped up in paper, the blood might have oozed through. I certainly did not dream that."

Fearnley-Whittingstall: "Have you ever dyed your hair?"

Drew: "Never in my life have I had any dye on my hair."

Fearnley-Whittingstall: "Not even with water dye?"

Drew: "Not any sort of dye. The same man has had charge of dressing and cutting my hair ever since I first came to this country."

Fearnley-Whittingstall: "The suggestion has been made that your hair is less brown now than it was when the inquest opened."

Drew: "Well, a few more days here and it will be dead white. (Laughter.)

Fearnley-Whittingstall: "Have you ever in your life had the finger of suspicion pointed at you before?"

Drew: "Never."

And that concluded Drew's evidence.

(4)

When he stepped down Philip Yale Drew had been in the box for an hour and twenty minutes, and as a witness he had acquitted

[1] Miss Frances King.

himself well. Never once did he hesitate or bungle. His replies to his counsel, often divertingly ingenuous, had been excellently phrased. His manner to the it must be admitted somewhat hostile coroner had been politely correct.

It is true that he had inclined at times to be verbose, and was unable to resist the ingrained habit of striking an attitude, as if he were on the stage, but his evidence, given in a clear, well-pitched voice—American more in phrasing than in intonation—carried conviction.

When trying to remember something he would gaze out of the window towards the ivy-covered wall beyond it in deep concentration. And at such moments he was an impressive figure. At other times he would grasp the ledge in front of him and crane his head forward, the better to hear his counsel's questions. Then, shoulders and head thrown back, hands—big, powerful, broad-fingered hands —gripping the sides of the box, he would deliver his vividly couched replies.

His general demeanour suggested earnestness and candour, the straightforwardness of an honest man—admitting his faults, regretting them, but never seeking spuriously to excuse them. If it was acting, then it was acting of a high order.

It was considered wise that Tuesday evening to smuggle him out of court by a back door. By then the October dusk was deepening, but the waiting crowd discovered him before he reached his hotel.

Again the cheers rang out, and the cries of "You are all right!" and "Don't lose heart, Philip". And a woman gave him a fancy comb in a case—"To comb your lucky curls".

In a blaze of flashlights he passed through the besieged doors of the Great Western Hotel, and went enthusiastically to thank Mr Fearnley-Whittingstall for what he called "a good afternoon's work".

Scene 6

THE BUTCHER'S TALE

Wednesday, October 9th, 1929

(1)

A long, lofty hall. Elaborate, decorated ceiling, and walls painted, seemly, in two merging shades of grey. Tall windows slot one side, framing a scene of waving treetops. The other walls are hung with massive, gilt-framed oil-paintings. At one end, a raised platform. Behind it, two elegantly arched niches, each, cameo-like, tenanted by a marble statue—classical deities or nymphs in flowing robes. Usually, this place is the scene of concerts, amateur dramatics, dinners, and dances—the gayer things of life. But today, for the first time in its 54-year history, it is the setting for an inquest. It is what is generally referred to in Reading as the Small Town Hall, a sort of lateral adjunct, a decorative sidepiece, to the main municipal building, and because the police court is required for other purposes, the sixth hearing of the resumed inquest on Alfred Oliver has been transferred to this unusual venue.

A table has been set upon the platform for the coroner. Behind it are ranged rows of benches for the Press. Immediately below the platform is a long table covered with red baize. Here, the Chief Constable of Reading, Inspector Berrett, Sergeant Harris and other police officials are to sit. On the coroner's left, at ground-level four feet below him, are the jury's chairs, placed closely together before a narrow table. And on the opposite side a tiny platform with a smaller table standing upon it has been provided for the use of the witnesses. A veritable witness-stand. Beyond a sort of railing, the rest of the hall is filled with neatly serried phalanxes of chairs for the public. There is accommodation for something over a hundred of them. At twelve o'clock, the time the proceedings are scheduled to begin, every one of those chairs will be occupied.

Now it is just after 11 A.M., but the square outside the Town Hall is already black with people, and the raised plinth of Queen Victoria's statue in the centre of this open space is doing duty as a sort of makeshift grandstand. An immense queue, its head beneath the glass-canopied entrance to the Town Hall, snakes the length of Blagrave Street, and curves, serpentine, into the hopeless distance.

While the crowds have been gathering Philip Yale Drew has been paying a visit to the house in King's Meadow Road where he lodged during that week in June, and chatting with Mrs Goodall, his former landlady.

The Town Hall clock chimes the half-hour.

There is a rumble of excitement among the crowd who have collected outside the Great Western Hotel. Drew emerges. He is still wearing the sprig of white heather given to him on Monday in his buttonhole. Smilingly he acknowledges the cheers that greet him. Slowly he makes his way on foot to his solicitor's office in Valpy Street, which is on the way to the Town Hall. There, he has a brief interview with Mr Ratcliffe and Mr Fearnley-Whittingstall. The news that he is inside the building flashes through the crowd. They move towards Valpy Street to meet him. Wait patiently. Presently he reappears. The crowd presses forward. More cheers. A wild scramble to accompany him along the street. An elderly lady hands him a bouquet of red roses. She is Miss Lily Burn. She tells him that she has come specially from London. She says that she is "gifted with spiritual influence", which has forced her to come to Reading. He thanks her. Pats her shoulder. "Good old Drew!" yell the crowd. "I owe much to your kind sympathy," he calls back to them. He bows. Waves his hat. Then exits with solemn dignity into the Town Hall.

(2)

The Town Hall clock chimes twelve.

Mr Martin, accompanied by Mr Tom Rowland Kent, the deputy coroner, Alderman John R. Rabson, the Mayor of Reading, and other local magistrates, enters and takes his seat on the platform.

There is a hush. In the silence Drew's voice is heard. In answer to a polite inquiry from Fearnley-Whittingstall as to how he is feeling today, he replies, "Very fine, thank you"—in tones which resound all over the hall.

Five minutes past twelve. Time for curtain-rise.

This is to be a day of surprises.

The coroner turns to Mr Fearnley-Whittingstall. "I allowed you yesterday to examine your client in your own way. I should like to know now whether you have any further questions to put?"

"I have finished my examination, sir," replies counsel.

"Very good. Then I shall proceed to put some questions myself."

Drew immediately walks to the small witness-platform, mounts it, and sits down behind its little table.

The Coroner: "Now, Mr Drew, in your evidence yesterday, taken from you through the means of your learned counsel, you said that you did not know Cross Street, Reading."

Drew: "No. I said I did not know the name of that street until I was interrogated in Nottingham. I didn't say I didn't know the street."

The Coroner: "There was a certain witness, a stableman—I expect you heard him?"

Drew: "I think I have heard all the witnesses, sir."

The Coroner: "He told us that you took him into the Bull Hotel, which is at the end of that street . . . and that you had a couple of drinks together."

Drew: "It wasn't an unusual thing for me to do. I can remember it, but I can't swear on oath."

The Coroner: "Is it possible?"

Drew: "It is possible. Everything is possible."

The Coroner: "You cannot remember?"

Drew: "Not on this book, sir." (Picking up the testament.)

The Coroner: "We must try to keep your memory up as well as we can. I don't want to press you. Can you remember going to the Welcome Café in that street? A woman says you visited there on two occasions, and she describes your meals—fried eggs and bacon. Might that be correct?"

Drew smiled before replying, "It would be a most unusual thing. I can't remember eating eggs that way. I break them into a glass with a little butter and pepper and salt, which is an American idea. I eat them that way, and I can't remember eating them otherwise for years. But it might be correct."

The Coroner: "There is a paper-shop in that street with the name Stocks, I think. Have you ever been in that shop?"

Drew: "Yes, I might have been."

The Coroner: "There again, you cannot say?"

Drew: "Very likely I was. I can't say."

The Coroner: "I think you told the police in one statement that you are fond of calves' liver?"

Drew: "I did, and it is true. I am fond of calves' liver."

—Here Drew paused, looked out of the window and up to the sky, before adding brightly—

"Had some this morning."

The Coroner: "Do you think it is possible that you visited a butcher's shop, or went into the doorway of a butcher's shop in Cross Street on Saturday morning, June 22nd, and inquired whether they had any calves' liver?"

Drew: "I think it is possible . . . but I am equally sure that I am not such a 'simp' as to ask and not wait for an answer."

The Coroner: "You have heard what the witness said?"

Drew: "Perhaps he didn't say no, but a negative nod of the head or something assured me that he didn't have any to sell, but I surely waited for some answer. Had he said yes, I should have bought some."

Mr Martin next questioned Drew as to the times of his movements on the Saturday evening.

"Now you told us yesterday also that it takes you approximately thirty-three minutes to strip, dress and make up for your performance. You worked it out."

"Yes, to the best of my ability. I don't see how I could do it much quicker than that."

"So that had you arrived at the theatre at about 6.15 P.M. you would have had time to dress completely and properly for your performance before 6.50 P.M.?"

"Not to have been complete—to accomplish my entire make-up and to call on Mrs Lindo to pass the make-up as correct and put the finishing touches."

"With a bit of a spurt you might have done it?"

The coroner had gone too far. With great deliberation and emphasis Drew took him to task. "I have too much love for my profession to *spurt* when dressing," he answered.

Turning then to the matter of the mysterious missing trousers, the coroner asked, "Have you any theory or explanation as to what happened to those blue trousers between June 22nd and August 9th?"

"It occurred to me that they must have been taken from my dressing-room during some part of the Saturday night's performance in Reading. That thought came to me when I could not find them in Maidstone when I turned out my basket."

"Did you suspect theft of those trousers?"

"What else?" said Drew.

"Well now, when those trousers mysteriously appeared again on August 9th, it is common knowledge that in the pockets was money. Approximately thirty-five shillings. . . . Does it strike you as peculiar if a thief had taken those trousers he would have left money in the pockets?"

"Most peculiar," said Drew emphatically. "*Most* peculiar."

"You would think he would value the money more than the trousers, as a man of the world?"

"I should imagine that he might take the money, and perhaps destroy the trousers."

"But"—and the coroner was hammering the point home—"it was most peculiar?"

"I think so," agreed Drew. "Why bring them back at all?"

"Can you remember the time when you left the theatre in the early morning of Sunday, June 23rd?"

Drew gazed reflectively up at the ceiling. "I can't," he said at length. "It may have been rather late. My time is my own when the curtain descends."

"Is it possible you left there at 12.45, according to the evidence of the electrician[1] who locked up and said good-night to you?"

"It is quite possible. I don't think I looked at my watch."

"Was there any reason why you should have stayed on so late?"

"I know no particular reason. I often do."

"Your hamper was packed ready?"

"My innovation trunk had not been closed."

Drew was gazing soulfully through the window at the sky, as he added:

"Somebody said I am a bit of a baby.[2] Well, all the years I have been in the profession, I still love to see them getting the scenery in and out."

"You stayed and watched them?"

"Yes. Often I have sat in the empty, darkened theatre during the day, for I love the atmosphere. . . ."

[1] James Henry Grubb.
[2] He was referring to the evidence given by Mr Alfred George Fry.

And he went on to explain that he was writing an atmospheric poem called 'The Theatre Speaks'.

Mr Martin brought matters firmly back to earth. "When you left the yard entrance to the theatre ultimately, and apparently said good-night to the electrician, you heard him say that probably the direction you took was towards Chatham Street?"

"That was not my way home."

"No—but do you agree with that?"

"Only to this extent: that I often take walks after the performance. Why I should turn to the left, I don't know."

"You can give no reason?"

"I have no reason."

"You may have turned to the left?"

"I may have."

"But if you had turned to the left, it would be taking you *away* from your lodgings?"

"Yes, it certainly would. I only know one road to the lodgings; that is to the right."

"Would there be any reason for you take a longer route to the lodgings?"

"None whatsoever."

"I think your landlady, Mrs Goodall, said you returned home about 1.15 on Sunday morning?"

"I heard her say something about clocks."

Mr Martin ignored this. "It was half an hour later, after the time you were alleged to have left the theatre."

Drew did not reply.

"Did you also hear her say you came running up from the direction of Reading Bridge?"

"I did. I don't know Reading Bridge. I only know one route, which is by way of the railway bridge."

"It is very close to where you were lodging, you know."

"Probably."

"You can't say whether it is correct, or otherwise?"

"I am willing to say that I have only returned from the theatre by one route. That took me by the railway bridge. I know it now because I was there this morning."

"Reading Bridge is the bridge across the Thames."

Mr Martin continued: "Now supposing Mr Grubb, the electrician at the theatre, is telling the truth, and supposing Mrs Goodall is telling the truth, it took you half an hour to get from the theatre to King's Meadow Road?"

"It would appear so," Drew agreed. "I would like to know how the electrician knows he is correct."

The coroner did not reply. "The route you generally took would not take you half an hour," was all he said.

"Certainly not. I would estimate it as ten minutes."

For once they were in agreement. The coroner nodded. "I should think you are about right. And would it be probable, as some of your colleagues at the theatre have stated, that you were very drunk after the last house on Saturday, June 22nd?"

That was handing it to him on a plate. A drunken man might stagger about and lose twenty minutes without any sinister significance attaching to the loss. But Drew did not grasp the ready-made excuse. He was not having it. "I should say they were mistaken. I may have had one or two drinks after the curtain came down, but had none to interfere with my work. It has happened more than once—but not drunk." Thus he refused to stagger, as it were, through the perfect loophole, rejected the semi-demi alibi out of hand.

"While you were playing at St Albans . . . were you discharged by Mr and Mrs Lindo from the company?"

"I have never been discharged from the company."

"I understand that Mr or Mrs Lindo, or both, gave that information to the police: that you were discharged for messing up—those are the words given to me—the third act of *The Monster*, and then they re-engaged you the next day. Is that correct?"

Drew replied that at one time he was handed "what is known in our profession as my notice", by the manager of the company. A notice, he explained, consists of two weeks' notice either way. "I have got it still," he added, "and will have it framed one day."

Mr Martin next asked, "Were you ever turned away from your hotel and told to get fresh rooms?"

"From my hotel? Not within my recollection. You said hotel?"

"Yes," said the coroner. "You cannot remember?"

"It never happened."

"Have you ever been turned out of apartments?"

"I've been asked to leave before now because of dogs; for no other reason so far as I can remember."

"As regards Saturday afternoon, June 22nd, and the early evening, you say you have no memory of where you were?"

"I cannot swear on oath where I was at the time, and it is not fair for me to say now where I was since I have heard other witnesses. It would sound as if I had listened or talked it over."

"And yet you remember leaving your lodgings in King's Meadow Road to go to the theatre?"

"When I am round about during the day I pay no attention to time or where I am wandering, but I am quite sure I am going to leave my diggings in order to be there one hour before the rise of the curtain."

The coroner asked Drew if he remembered playing at North Shields. He said that he did. He was, he said, there about the middle of August last, and had to spend three days in the Tynemouth Union Hospital,[1] as he was suffering from acute alcoholism. He also agreed that during the week he was at Reading he had probably been taking more than the usual amount of alcohol.

The coroner asked: "On that Saturday afternoon, June 22nd, have you any recollection of Mrs Lindo going to your bedroom at your lodgings and asking you for a bottle of whisky?"

"Since hearing her evidence it would hardly be right for me to answer that question, because I'm afraid that prior to her making that statement I would have said that I had no recollection of it," said Drew.

"You have no recollection of it still?"

"Sometimes one's afterthoughts are the best."

"Very often."

"But not to swear on always."

"You do not recollect?"

"It is a long time ago."

The coroner having concluded his examination of Drew, the foreman of the jury then rose and put a series of questions.

"Do you agree with the evidence that on your arrival at your lodgings at Maidstone you were in an exceptionally disordered state of nerves? It has been given in evidence that the witness thought you were mad."

"I heard that witness," replied Drew. "I can't possibly understand how anybody could have thought I was mad—in a very nervous condition generally, yes."

"Do you still agree with the statement to the police that you were

[1] Drew said he thought that the hospital was not in North Shields, but in South Shields.

unable to take part in the play on the Monday night at Maidstone for the first time in twenty-six years?"

"For the *entire performance*, that was the first in my experience . . ."

"Is it not a rather strange coincidence—the first time in twenty-six years?"

"It was not the first time in twenty-six years, because in Woolwich I only played the first act, owing to a seizure."

Reverting to the week in Maidstone, the foreman then asked: "Do you deny that you remained in bed all day that week, and only visited the theatre in the evening to take your part, returning with Mr and Mrs Lindo at night?"

"I do not deny it."

"Do you agree that in that week, when about to be visited by a doctor, you rushed out of the house?"

"I don't remember rushing out of the house, but I do remember while I was in bed I was told a doctor had been called, but I didn't consider that I required a doctor. I was upset previously to that. Many times when Mr Lindo has said, 'Don't you think you ought to have a doctor?' I have said, 'No, please'."

"But the evidence is that you rushed out of the house."

"I heard it. I should rush out now if a doctor asked me anything, probably."

"Do you think it would be acting with discretion?"

"I don't say it would be acting with *discretion* . . . but it would be *me*."

"But you will agree with me that it was a strange performance for a patient to rush out of the house when the doctor came?"

"Yes," said Drew, "it might be strange, but I *am* a strange man." This last spoken slowly and thoughtfully as if he were deeply engaged in probing his own psychology, and with his eyes lifted to the sky.

"Do you consider your acting in Nottingham, in the way you divested yourself of an overcoat, jacket and vest, and left them to be cleaned, and walked through the streets to a theatre for some considerable distance, to be the ordinary rational procedure of a person having his garments renovated and cleaned?"

"When I walked back from the renovating place I had a belt on and was in my shirt-sleeves. I fail to see the difference whether I went there with this coat, jacket, and vest over my arm, or wearing them. It might not be a thing that the average man would do. Very likely not."

The foreman was repeating the question when the coroner interposed, "That is your answer—of a sort. He has given you your reply, in a great many words."

"I am sorry, sir," said Drew humbly.

The foreman went on: "As you cannot give any explanation of your movements on Saturday, June 22nd, before arriving at the theatre, do you suggest that the sworn testimony of the witnesses as to your movements in regard to Cross Street and to the theatre is perjury?"

Fearnley-Whittingstall jumped to his feet. "I suggest that that is not a fair question."

The coroner—to the foreman—"No. Say, 'Are they correct?' "

And Drew replied, "If I say I cannot remember my movements during the entire afternoon, and there are so many witnesses against me, with so many different accounts of time, I'm afraid I would not like to say they had committed perjury."

The coroner broke in again. "I should not labour that question," he told the foreman. "The witnesses are on their oath."

The foreman had no more to say.

And that concluded Drew's evidence.

It was 1.12 P.M. when he left the witness-platform, and the coroner announced that the court would adjourn for lunch.

(3)

When the proceedings were resumed that afternoon, Philip Yale Drew again took his place on the witness-stand while his evidence was read over to him. Several times he interrupted when he felt that the deposition did not accord with what he had actually said, and amendments were made by the coroner's clerk. Drew then signed the deposition and returned to his seat next to Mrs Lindo.

He had given evidence for—including Tuesday—a total of two and three-quarter hours, and had done well. He had said some things that sounded almost quaint, but was always emphatic and deliberate when his art was mentioned. Although obviously suffering from strain, he had made an excellent witness, and today he had been even more composed than on Tuesday, and had dropped the somewhat theatrical mannerisms which had characterized his first appearance in the box. But, always, he remained the Actor, speaking in sacrosanct tones of his love for the Profession, and exhibiting little fugitive flashes of the Artistic Temperament. Nevertheless, he had most ably withstood the ordeal of Mr Martin's sharp examination, and was never once manifestly perturbed. His replies came readily, and while they were being written down he stood with his hands behind his back, gazing thoughtfully at the trees that swayed outside the windows of the hall.

Mr Fearnley-Whittingstall called as his next witness Mr Frank Lindo. Of medium height, handsome, benevolent-looking, and with long white hair, he stepped up on to the small platform which Drew had just vacated.

Speaking in a raised, resonant voice, he began his evidence by saying, "I know of no man in our profession who is more honoured, loved and respected than Mr Drew. That is speaking with a vast knowledge."

Mr Lindo added that he had known Drew by name and reputation for more than fifteen years, and intimately for about six. For the last five years Drew had lived with him and his wife, and in that time they had learned to know him and to love him, too. He said that during that week at Reading Drew and the entire company were paid their salaries on Friday night, June 21st.

"Can you," asked Fearnley-Whittingstall, "shortly describe what Mr Drew is like when he is drunk?"

"Well, I hardly like the word drunk," protested Mr Lindo. "There are degrees of inebriation, and degrees with effect of alcohol, and drunk is a word that has a bad sound."

"Never mind. I am going to use it," insisted Fearnley-Whittingstall. "Drunk is drunk."

"Well, when Mr Drew had more whisky than was good for him —or when he was drunk, as you call it—he became very like he was in this court, only more theatrically dignified, and rather more proud, if I may say so, of his importance in the profession. A little more dignified."

"Is he likely to stroke a motor-car?"

"Quite impossible."

"He is not a stroking man?"

"No, sir."

"Is he more likely to fight anybody?"

"Absolutely no."

"Have you ever known him rough?"

"Never."

The coroner then interrupted with some questions of his own. "What time were you at the theatre on the night of June 22nd?" he asked.

"About half-past five, I think."

"Did you tell the police you left the picture palace—the Central —about six o'clock?"

"About six."

Mr Martin pounced. "So you could not have been at the theatre that night at about half-past five?" And he read from Mr Lindo's statement to the police: " 'I went to the pictures in the afternoon. I think it would be somewhere about 6 P.M. that I heard Mr Drew's voice in the theatre.' "

"That is quite possible," said Mr Lindo.

"Can you remember anything that would help you to tell us when you imagined Mr Drew entered the theatre on that evening?"

Mr Lindo shook his head.

After some further questions, Mr Martin asked, "Did you ever have any trouble with Drew owing to his habits?"

"No trouble," replied Mr Lindo, "but I used to reprimand him as a father."

"As a *father*?" asked the coroner in surprised tones. "Not as a theatrical proprietor?"

"Well, partly. But I looked upon him in a fatherly way. I am an older man than he."

"He is old enough, I suppose, to look after himself," observed Mr Martin icily.

"Some men, sir, never grow up," said Mr Lindo in a gentle voice. And one of the court reporters, looking at Drew, noticed that his eyes were full of tears.

"Did you ever hand a notice to him to retire from your company?"

"If I answer yes or no, it might be misconstrued. I certainly did instruct my manager to hand him his notice. That was merely in a way to threaten him. It was never intended to be carried out."

"Bluff?"

"Purely."

It was, he explained, intended to frighten Drew. The notice was handed to him in the February or March of that year, when the company was at St Helens, in Lancashire. And it had the desired effect, Drew pleading and promising that he "would be a good boy in the future".

"What was the special reason for your serving that notice on him?" asked Mr Martin. "There must have been something serious, I think?"

"To my mind anything that is wrong on our stage is serious."

"Now, what was the incident?"

"Well, I thought on a particular occasion he had had too many whiskies and was not giving the full value to his performance. I knew that there would be nobody more sorry than Mr Drew if that happened. But I thought it was serious, and I am rather a martinet in that respect."

"From your point of view, his performance was suffering in consequence of his habits?"

"From my point of view, yes."

Continuing his evidence, Mr Lindo said that on Monday night, August 5th, when the company was at St Albans, he had told Drew that he was not to appear again. Drew had, Mr Lindo explained, played his part very well the whole evening, but he had had some friends in to see him in his dressing-room—"And there is a convenient, or perhaps I should say an inconvenient, club next door to the theatre and very easy of access."

"A great temptation for some people," observed the coroner.

"Absolutely. I think Mr Drew had succumbed to that club and his friends."

"You noticed the effect during the play?"

"No, there was no effect during the play. It was at the end . . . in the last scene."

"Then you had words with him?"

"May I say why? Mr Drew had to come on at the finish of our play, and there is some very important business indeed for him to perform, part of that business being to tie a gag round my mouth. I don't think it has been mentioned that I am the Monster, but I am . . ."

The coroner smiled. "Oh, you are the Monster. You certainly don't look it."

"A monster of iniquity, sir. To prevent my calling out, it is Mr Drew's business to tie a gag round my mouth. On this particular night he failed to do so."

"He fumbled it, or forgot it?"

"He forgot it. As I have said, as regards anything connected with the stage I am old-fashioned and a martinet. I wish that to be understood, because it accounts for what I said."

"One of the old-timers?"

"Absolutely. Forty-odd years."

The foreman of the jury asked Mr Lindo, "What time did you actually see Mr Drew on the evening of June 22nd?"

"I can't answer that question, but I know for a positive fact that he was in the theatre before a quarter past six."

Asked by the foreman if Drew was the worse for drink at lunch on the Saturday, Mr Lindo replied: "I should not have taken much notice, as Mr Drew might have taken a little too much and have recovered before the evening performance. I should not have noticed it."

> The Coroner: "You did not notice it. There are so many words that you theatrical people use!"
>
> Lindo: "Necessary words."
>
> The Coroner: "I do not agree with you."
>
> Lindo: "I think so, at any rate. And *I* am telling the jury."

The coroner received this rebuke in silence.

The foreman then asked, "Is it your opinion that Drew was not always responsible for his stage work owing to his drinking habits?"

"Well," replied Mr Lindo slowly, "he was not always as good as he should have been if he had been perfectly sober. His drinking habits affected his performance to the extent of not satisfying me as a martinet, but nobody else. No one has ever complained to me about his performance from the front of the house."

"I asked your opinion," said the foreman.

Once again Mr Lindo showed his claws. "And I have given it," he answered curtly.

"There is no disguising the fact that he does have drinks," said the foreman.

"I have not attempted to disguise the fact," replied Mr Lindo.

Mr Lindo had duly signed his deposition and stepped down, when Fearnley-Whittingstall dropped his bombshell.

In his pleasant, even voice, he said, "I call Alfred John Wells."

(4)

The calling of Alfred John Wells, butcher, for the defence, eleventh-hour witness, was a surprise, a shock, and—for the defence —a triumph.

With all the suddenness and startling effect of an arresting line shouted in the final act of a stage drama, a new witness, the very last in a long procession, came dramatically forward.

The last-minute emergence of this vital witness was entirely due to the ingenuity, the persistence, of a newspaper reporter, Bernard O'Donnell, crime man of the *Empire News*, aided and abetted by another newspaperman, Henry de Winton Wigley of the *Daily News*.

Back in June, when the story of the murder first broke, O'Donnell was one of the many national newspapermen who descended upon Reading. Ferreting about in search of an angle, he had interviewed a number of tradesmen in the Cross Street area who said that they had seen a strange man in Cross Street at various times of the day, as well as at the time of the murder. They all described him to O'Donnell as an unkempt sort of individual, rather heavily built, wearing a blue or dark suit, hatless, and with a shock of dishevelled hair, who had attracted attention to himself by his peculiar behaviour.

Among these tradesmen was a young butcher's assistant named Wells, who worked at Geary's, No. 22 Cross Street, and Wells had told O'Donnell and de Winton Wigley that he had not only seen the stranger with the unkempt hair on two or three occasions on the day of the murder, but had actually spoken to him.

O'Donnell, sitting through each session of the inquest, and watching witness after witness identify Drew as the man in Cross Street, remembered something—something that disturbed him greatly. It was his conversation of three months before with Mr Wells. And he recalled that Wells had said two very important things—that the strange man of Cross Street was wearing *brown* shoes, well worn down at the heels, and that he spoke with a pronounced *North Country* accent.

What was more, Wells had told O'Donnell that within three hours of the murder he had gone to the police and made a voluntary statement, giving a full description of the man whom he had seen.

But, by the end of the fifth day of the hearing, O'Donnell realized that Wells was not going to be called as a witness, and it was this realization which was worrying him.

That evening—Tuesday, October 8th—O'Donnell talked the matter over with his fellow-reporter, de Winton Wigley, who declared himself as puzzled as O'Donnell by the fact that Wells was apparently not being called, and, encouraged by de Winton Wigley, O'Donnell decided to seek out Wells again.

So, before breakfast on Wednesday morning, O'Donnell went along to Geary's shop, found Wells and reminded him of their previous meeting.

"You've seen the pictures of Philip Yale Drew, I suppose," said O'Donnell.

Wells nodded.

"Are they pictures of the man you saw in Cross Street on the day Mr Oliver was murdered?"

Wells was, quite properly, cautious. "I couldn't say for certain off-hand," he replied, "but I don't think so. It's so difficult to tell from a photograph, but I'd be absolutely sure if I heard him speak."

"Will you come along to the hotel and see Mr Drew?" asked O'Donnell.

"All right," said Wells.

When they arrived at the Great Western Drew was in the lounge talking to the Lindos. O'Donnell pointed him out. Wells shook his head. "No. That isn't the man I saw. He had a mop of hair, and it was very untidy. *That* hair could never get dishevelled. It's too crisp and wavy."

O'Donnell led Wells over to Drew. "Meet a friend of mine," he said.

Drew turned and smiled. "Any friend of Bernard's is a friend of mine," he said.

Wells looked across to O'Donnell. "Good Lord, no—that's not the man I spoke to," he said. "There's no North Country accent about that voice."

"Would you be prepared to swear that on oath?"

"Certainly I would," answered Wells.

And O'Donnell, joined by de Winton Wigley, rushed the young butcher round to Mr Ratcliffe's office, where he swore an affidavit. Then Ratcliffe, Fearnley-Whittingstall, and Drew held a rapid conference, and it was decided to put Alfred John Wells in the box.

(5)

"I call Alfred John Wells."

There was an excited stir as Mr Wells entered the court, and every eye was turned on him as he took the oath.

Fearnley-Whittingstall: "Can you remember June 22nd?"

Wells: "I can."

Fearnley-Whittingstall: "Were you in the Welcome Café about 7.30 in the morning?"

Wells: "I was, having breakfast."

Fearnley-Whittingstall: "Did anyone come in while you were there?"

Wells: "They did. A man."

Fearnley-Whittingstall: "Can you describe him?"

Wells: "About 5 feet 9 inches to 5 feet 10 inches, as near as possible."

Fearnley-Whittingstall: "Did he speak to you?"

Wells: "Yes."

Fearnley-Whittingstall: "Did you notice anything else about him?"

Wells: "Yes. He had long dark hair, pushed right back in front, blue coat, blue waistcoat, grey trousers and brown shoes, trod over at the heels. He asked me where the lavatory was, and I directed him. After about ten minutes he came back."

Fearnley-Whittingstall: "Did you notice any gesture that he made?"

Wells: "He came back, and when he sat down he started brushing his hair back with his arm, and wiped his hand and part of his sleeve across his face. I may say he looked as if he could have done with a nice haircut to start with."

Fearnley-Whittingstall: "About how old was he?"

Wells: "Thirty-five to forty, as far as I can say."

Fearnley-Whittingstall: "Middle-aged?"

The coroner glanced up. "Would you like to be called middle-aged at thirty-five to forty?" he asked counsel. "You have not reached that age yet."

Fearnley-Whittingstall: "When he spoke did you notice anything about his speech?"

Wells: "He had a North Country accent."

Fearnley-Whittingstall: "Did you see him again that day?"

Wells: "Yes. I was wiping off just inside the shop window. . . . I saw him two or three times. He passed to my knowledge about twenty minutes to six. I was going round Friar Street corner into Cross Street, and I saw the same man carrying his mac over his shoulder.

He was walking out from Cross Street into Friar Street. He passed me at an angle, not front face."

The Coroner: "Can you say that was the same man?"

Wells: "To the best of my knowledge."

Fearnley-Whittingstall asked, "Would you recognize him again?" And then, without waiting for an answer, "Stand up, Mr Drew."

Drew stood up smartly and looked towards Wells.

Like a gunshot, Wells said, "Sit down, Mr Drew. That is not the man."

"Thank you," said Drew, with emphasis on the second word.

After the tension of those last few moments there was a great rustle of movement through the court. People half rose in their seats to survey the scene.

Fearnley-Whittingstall turned back to Wells. "You were so impressed by seeing this man that you at once went to the police?"

"I did," said Wells. "Voluntarily."

"And they didn't think much of your statement, obviously, or they would have called you," commented Mr Martin, somewhat pointedly.

"They didn't seem to be very sharp," rejoined Wells.

Counsel resumed his examination. "When did you hear of the murder?"

"As near as I can tell, it was about three minutes before Mr Oliver was carried out."

"And did you mention about this man at once?"

"I mentioned it to a policeman outside the Liberal Club, and he said, 'Go to the police-station.' But I can't leave my business, as you know."

"You went to the police-station later. What time would that be?"

"About twenty minutes to nine—or nine o'clock."

"Whom did you see?"

"I don't know his name, but I could tell you if I saw him. He was a sergeant."

"Can the sergeant be found?" asked the coroner.

"He's outside the court now," said Wells.

It was yet another of the extraordinary coincidences with which the whole case had been riddled.

"Bring him in," ordered Mr Martin ... and Sergeant Arthur Colbert, who was assisting in controlling the large crowd outside the Town Hall, was brought in.

"This man says he came to see you about 9 o'clock on June 22nd," the coroner told him.

"I don't remember it," said Colbert. "So many people came in that night."

Wells broke in—"Do you remember that while you were taking the statement a very small man came running in and said he'd just heard a woman say she knew a man she'd seen, and Mr Burrows rushed two men out to find him?"

"No," said Colbert stolidly.

The coroner resumed his questioning. "Did you take a statement from this man?"

"I cannot recollect it."

"It would have been put in if you had?"

"Yes. I took three or four other statements that night, and I may have taken one from him, but I don't remember."

"Perhaps Mr Burrows can help me?" said the coroner.

Burrows rose to his feet. "Possibly. We took sixty or seventy statements that night."

"Obviously you did not attach much importance to it, or I should have seen it," said Mr Martin.

Then, turning to Wells, he asked, "Having made the statement, were you not surprised that no-one questioned you further?"

"I was."

"You knew the gravity of this case, why did you not go to the police again?"

"I tried to help them all I could."

Mr Fearnley-Whittingstall stood up. "The day you saw the man you went and told the police?"

"I did."

"Having made that statement, did you wonder why Scotland Yard officers did not see you?"

"Yes, but I thought there was no reason why I should make the statement twice."

"Well," said the coroner, "what has brought you here today? We might have finished last night, you know."

"A gentleman came running to me this morning and asked if I could tell him about it."

"And that is why you are here? Do you know who the gentleman was? He was not a police officer?"

"No."

Heading a phalanx of supporters, Drew makes his way down Valpy Street to court
With him: Alfred Fry (far left), Mrs Lindo, and Frank Lindo. Right, with glasses:
Bernard O'Donnell

The Men of Law
(Front row) Sergeant Harris, Chief Constable Burrows, and Inspector Berrett
(Back row) Sergeant Ellington and Inspector Walters

Alfred John Wells:
Butcher for the
Defence

The eleventh-hour witness

Mrs Mary Eleanor
Goodall, the
Theatrical Landlady,
wishes Drew well
outside his Reading
lodgings—9 King's
Meadow Road.
Inquest Day Six

The coroner returned to his previous point. "As you heard no more about it, and knew the gravity of this case, why did you not come forward again?"

"Well, I have to work hard for my living," said Wells. "I can't afford to lose time. I tried to help them all I could, didn't I? I would help them still. I hope to bring someone to justice, as he should be. I would do anything. I always respected Mr Oliver."

"You seem to have dropped for a considerable period your efforts to help," observed Mr Martin.

That brought Fearnley-Whittingstall to his feet again. "You told all you could and all you knew, and any step which lay after that did not lie with you?"

"No," said Wells, "I couldn't make a statement three or four times."

"It is very strange that the police have no record of this statement," commented the coroner pointedly.

Counsel then said to Mr Wells, "Very well, then—do you swear that you made that statement?"

Wells seized the Testament, kissed it, and held it aloft. "I do, by Almighty God."

"Do you swear you made it to Sergeant Colbert?" asked Mr Martin.

"I do."

"Very well, we will have Sergeant Colbert in the box," said the coroner.

Having taken the oath, Sergeant Arthur Colbert said that on the evening of June 22nd he was on duty in the charge-room at Reading Police Station. He had first heard of the murder at 6.25 P.M., when he took a message on the telephone asking for help. During that night he had had more people coming in to make statements than he could remember, and he certainly did not remember Wells.

Fearnley-Whittingstall stood up. "May I ask a question?"

Amidst dead silence, the coroner issued the following solemn warning: "I will tell you one thing before you ask a question. Inquiries will be made tonight, and Detective Pope and the Chief Constable will be called tomorrow respecting what was done on that evening with regard to these papers. . . ."

At this point a sheet of foolscap was handed up to the coroner from the table at which the Chief Constable and the detectives were sitting.

Mr Martin read it through in silence. Then—"This clears it up. I think this is the statement you took." He passed it across to the Sergeant.

As everyone leant forward to catch his words, Colbert said, "That's right. It's marked 27. It's the one I took from Alfred John Wells." And the Sergeant then read the statement out. Its contents tallied almost word for word with the evidence which Wells had just given.

"Now the statement has been found I have no questions to ask," said Fearnley-Whittingstall.

Immediately, a busy hum broke out. The coroner irately demanded order, then asked Mr Fearnley-Whittingstall if he wished to call anybody else. Counsel replied that he did not.

Mr Martin turned to the jury. "So far as I am aware, we have now concluded the examination of the witnesses in this case. We have spent a great amount of time about it, and a great deal of concentration. We have not lost much time, and we have not hurried it. I think we have given every witness a fair chance to give his testimony without being hurried or pressed, and I am now going to review that evidence quietly and shall therefore adjourn this court until tomorrow at eleven o'clock in this hall, when I propose to sum-up.'

(6)

Some inkling of that last dramatic scene staged in the court had filtered out to the crowds waiting in the streets, and the police inside the hall offered to let Drew out of a side-door.

"No, thank you," he said. "You're wonderfully kind to me, but I am not afraid of these people. They are my friends, and I will go the usual way."

So out he went, and was at once swallowed up by the jostling, cheering mob—which was bigger than at any time since the inquest began, for Wednesday was a half-holiday in Reading, and the town had turned out in force.

Women and girls surged round Drew, struggling to embrace him, nearly tearing the clothes from his back.

He stood there helpless, without space to make his usual graceful bows, unable to move, until six constables came to his rescue and carried him through the crush to his hotel.

It was a gratified but exhausted Drew who finally sank into a chair in the lounge of the Great Western and breathlessly begged for a cup of tea.

Later that night, Drew, accompanied by Mr and Mrs Lindo, went to see a revue called *Coo-ee* at the Reading Palace of Varieties, in Cheapside. He sat in the corner of a box unnoticed by the rest of the audience. But afterwards, when he came out, he was recognized and was immediately surrounded by a crowd.

Inspector Berrett, Chief Constable Burrows and other police officers prominently engaged in the case, also paid a visit to the theatre that evening. They went to the Royal County Theatre.

The show that they chose—*Dracula*!

Scene 7

BALCONY SCENE

Thursday, October 10th, 1929

(1)

NO matinée idol had ever at any time aroused such excitement in Reading as the popular hero of the hour—Philip Yale Drew.

And at no hour was that popularity greater than at the time when he was to come up for final judgment.

This seventh and ultimate day of the inquest, the queues were forming and the crowds massing a full three hours before the Town Hall chimes struck the call of the reckoning.

The morning was cold, and, nipped by the first pincers of autumn, those who waited huddled beneath heavy overcoats. At the head of the line was a housewife clutching a bouquet of bronze chrysanthemums and a single vivid carnation. "The bouquet is for Mrs Lindo, bless her heart," she said. "And the carnation is for Philip's buttonhole."

By now, Drew was 'Philip' to the crowd, who, day after day, had waited to see and cheer him on his way. They seemed to have established a very special relationship with him.

A contingent of police kept the centre of the roadway to the Town Hall clear, but as soon as Drew appeared, walking as usual from his hotel, a Pied Piper followed by his flocks, the road behind him filled, and the police were powerless to control the overspilling throng.

Reaching the Town Hall steps, he turned and faced the crowd, and in ringing tones that echoed to the outermost fringes, he said, "Thank you for your sympathy—and God bless you all," and threw kisses to them.

Before the coroner arrived, a woman entered the court, and the spectators in the public seats, mistaking her for Mrs Lindo, began to clap. Mr Fearnley-Whittingstall appeared, and the clapping intensified—until a police sergeant ordered them to stop, and warned that if there was any repetition of the demonstration those responsible would be ejected.

Then Drew came in, and people all over the hall stood up to get a good view of him. He paused before going to his seat, turned so that he looked down the hall, and smiled at them.

Almost at the same moment the coroner entered.

A police officer shouted, "Open the court".

Mr Fearnley-Whittingstall instantly rose.

Mr Martin looked across to him. "Do you wish to say anything?"

"May I address the jury for a few moments?"

"I think," said the coroner, "you know as well as I do that that is not permissible in this court."

A sharp passage between them ensued.

Fearnley-Whittingstall: "When you say 'not permissible' I join issue with you. It is sometimes the practice."

The Coroner: "You will not be permitted today."

Fearnley-Whittingstall: "It is not a case of not being permissible. It is sometimes done. It is often done."

The Coroner: "It is against all our rules, and every learned counsel knows that quite well."

Fearnley-Whittingstall: "It may be a local rule; it is certainly not the general rule."

The Coroner: "It is not done here, at any rate."

Fearnley-Whittingstall: "It may not be done here, but it is done in a great many coroners' courts."

The Coroner: "I have nothing further to say."

Fearnley-Whittingstall: "And I have nothing further to say, but I merely point out that it is not a case of not being permissible."

And having registered his protest, counsel resumed his seat.

Then, without further ado, the coroner began his summing-up.

He first told the jury: "I want again to ask you to start your consideration of the evidence taken during this inquiry and still to keep your minds open and to eliminate anything you may have further read in the Press or heard outside. Now as regards Mr Whittingstall's application, I gave him somewhat unusual licence in this case to lead his client through the evidence he gave, and I think I have given him every chance to call witnesses and cross-examine in every shape and form, as I did to Mr Ratcliffe, who represented Mr Drew before Mr Whittingstall appeared on the scene."

Having recapitulated the events of June 22nd, Mr Martin said that there was no doubt that Mr Oliver was murdered between 5.50 P.M. and 6.15 P.M. on that day, and that the first person to see him after the attack appeared to be the young man George Charles Jefferies, who put the time at 6.10 P.M.

"I think his evidence and actions were somewhat unsatisfactory, and I think you carefully noted that in your minds. If his story is true, the task of the police would, in all probability, have been very much simplified if he had raised the alarm at once. But you have heard what he said. He was afraid. By his age he should be a man." A reasonable enough comment, but to be fair to Jefferies, people do not always act rationally when suffering from shock.

Mr Martin then pointed out that the chief evidence naturally concerned Philip Yale Drew.

"The times and identification play most important parts, and where witnesses cannot be certain as to times you must be guided by any corroboration of their story which is put forward. Most important of the witnesses is Mrs James, I think, who swears she saw Drew inside the doorway of Mr Oliver's shop with blood on his face at 6.11 P.M. Just previous to that, Mr Loxton swears he saw Drew in Cross Street coming towards his butcher's shop, and he then turned back towards Mr Oliver's shop. Now are you satisfied as to the identification of Mr Drew by these two witnesses?"

While the coroner was speaking, Drew's face worked from time to time, and he crushed a handkerchief in his hands. He looked up at the ceiling, his mouth set firmly, his forehead wrinkled. Then his face began to work again. No amount of fine acting could mask the tension that he was obviously feeling.

Mrs Lindo, sitting beside him, was all eyes, and, as a reporter who was in court wrote, "There was a depth of agony in those eyes that was almost painful to watch".

The coroner continued: "Mr Loxton has told you that he had a man asking for liver at about 1.30 P.M. His shop is in Cross Street, three doors from the paper-shop. You have heard three witnesses—Ingram, Russell and Grubb—say that Drew told them he was going to Cross Street for a special paper. Drew said he was fond of calves' liver, and probably asked for some in Reading. Mr Loxton recognized Drew in Nottingham in a busy and crowded thoroughfare. Mrs James's identification took place there also. This method of identification has been described by Mr Ratcliffe as 'primitive and crude'. Nothing, in my opinion, could have been fairer or more perfect in the way of identification than that at Nottingham. It is for you to be satisfied as to whether the witnesses are correct. Neither Mrs James nor Loxton were shaken by cross-examination. If they are correct, the theatrical witnesses who stated that Drew was in the theatre at 6 P.M. or earlier must be wrong.

"Then there was the witness Mrs Taylor, at the Welcome Café in Cross Street, who identified Drew as a man to whom she served two meals of fried eggs and bacon in her café. Drew said he did not eat eggs fried. Which is right, Mrs Taylor or Drew? That is for you to judge.

"You also need to give your attention to the statement of Miss King from Maidstone, who told you that she saw Drew take half an hour to clean some spots from his coat on the lawn. Drew told you that he would use benzine to clean the collar of his coat, and that the operation would take him a few minutes.

"Now we come to the mysterious blue trousers, their disappearance and reappearance. Drew could not give you any explanation respecting these, and it is peculiar that, although Drew says that three pounds were in the pockets when he last saw them at Reading on June 22nd, there was only about thirty-five shillings when they reappeared at St Albans. He suggests that they were stolen, and replaced by the thief at St Albans. But do you think that thieves generally return money?"

Mr Martin spoke next of the evidence of Mrs Shepherd, who was with her children in the butcher's shop in Cross Street, a few doors from Oliver's. He said that she swore that she saw a man run out of Oliver's at eleven or twelve minutes past six. She saw him run quickly down Cross Street, and turn left into Friar Street. "That," said the coroner, "would be in the direction of the theatre."

"Now take Mrs Goodall for a moment. Why did she visit the theatre after she heard of the murder to see if Mr Drew was all right? It has been stated that it was a unique occurrence for a landlady to go to the theatre to inquire after her lodger. She told you what she had in her mind, although she did not say anything about it to Mrs Lindo, except to tell her that a murder had been committed.

"Is it possible in your minds that, to the three witnesses who have sworn it, Drew, in the Tudor Restaurant—or the Marquis of Lorne, is it called?—on the morning of June 22nd, expressed his intention of going to Cross Street to get a special paper? Drew explained that he told them he was going *across* the street. Now you must judge between those statements. Drew has told Sergeant Harris that he did not know Cross Street. Again, it is for the jury to say which is right.

"The possibility of Drew's having been in Oliver's tobacco shop is possibly strengthened by the evidence of two other tobacconists, who said that he called and asked questions about some pipes he wanted to send to a friend abroad. Drew denied that he had visited shops in Reading for this purpose, but admits that he has sent pipes to a friend abroad some years ago. Now, are these witnesses mistaken, or is it a coincidence?

"You must bear in your minds the evidence of Drew. He seemed to be quite indefinite as to time. He has told you the first thing he remembers is being at the theatre in the evening. And the time of his arrival there is very important. Now, when did he arrive? Mr Lawrence and Mr Fry say before 6 P.M. Mrs Goodall, Mrs Crouch and Mrs Greenway say he was in King's Meadow Road then, and after, up to between 6.10 and 6.15 P.M., when some people say he left his lodgings running very fast. Then Mrs Wheeler, with a pushcart, I think it was, said that she saw him in Vastern Road somewhere about 6.15 P.M.

"Now we come to Mrs James again. Mrs James says without any hesitation that she saw Drew at 6.11 or 6.12 P.M. in the shop doorway, and she had looked at the clock previously at the Town Hall when she passed, I think at 6.10 P.M., and she came straight down.

"Then we have Mr Hathaway, who has sworn that he saw Drew held up in Queen Victoria Street at 6.13 P.M.

"Miss Moore, who was engaged at the theatre, has sworn that she saw Drew in the theatre, not made up or dressed for his part, after the theatre had opened at 6.15 P.M.

"Hathaway has told you that he estimated that when Drew entered the theatre yard it was about 6.15 P.M.

"Mrs Lindo has told you that she heard Drew 'asked' a few minutes before the half-hour call, which would be somewhere about 6.20 P.M. This would be in keeping with the times given by Mrs James, Hathaway and Miss Moore. If you are satisfied as to this evidence, then Mr Fry and Mr Lawrence are incorrect.

"As to the question of the time to make up, Drew told you

thirty-three minutes approximately. That would still leave it possible for Mrs James to be correct as to time.

"I would also bring to your notice the fact that neither Drew nor his learned counsel or solicitor referred to the evidence of Mr Loxton or Mrs James, although Drew said he did not go to Cross Street that night.

"I think we can safely say that Drew did not go home in the early hours of Sunday morning, June 23rd, in his stage clothes, as suggested; but probably, from the evidence we have heard, some of his make-up was still on his face, as stated by Mr Grubb, the electrician, who said goodnight to him and locked up, and his landlady, Mrs Goodall, who received him at his lodgings about 1.15 A.M. on the 23rd. Another point; did Drew go straight home from the theatre to his lodgings, or by a roundabout way, as stated by Mr Grubb and by Mrs Goodall? Drew says that he does not know. Now Grubb definitely states that Drew turned to his left down Chatham Street, which was right away from the route he would follow—as he told you, the only route he knew. This is borne out to some extent by the evidence of Mrs Goodall, who was waiting up, apparently anxious about Drew, and says that he came running up from the direction of Reading Bridge. If these witnesses are correct, he had therefore taken half an hour to get home from the theatre to his lodgings.

"Drew has been unable to help us as to where he actually was when this murder was committed. The witnesses have picked him out in various places during this day, and I think you must give great consideration to the evidence of Mrs James, which is most important. You remember she picked Drew out without any hesitation at Nottingham. Can it be possible that all these witnesses could be mistaken, and the man they saw was not Drew, but the man mentioned by Mr Wells yesterday? Mr Wells in his original statement speaks of a man with a growth of beard. I think it must be admitted that Mr Drew has not a beard, but was clean-shaven on the day of the murder.

"I think I have reviewed the evidence. You have heard examined something like sixty witnesses, but I think I have put the times before you, and it must be for you to judge whether the witnesses are correct or incorrect, or mistaken as to those times and places. There is no doubt as to the cause of death, which was given to you by Dr Joyce, the surgeon who made the post-mortem examination. Therefore, it is for you carefully to consider whether you find a verdict of murder against some person or persons unknown, which means an open verdict, or whether, after considering all the evidence which has been placed before you, you find any particular person was guilty of that murder, having due respect to the strong circumstances put before you. I am expressing no further opinion myself. I put these points before you, and I am asking you to retire and very carefully consider all you have heard during this long and, I hope, careful inquiry."

When the coroner ended his summing-up he had been speaking for twenty-seven minutes.

Before the jury went to their room the police sergeant in charge stepped up on to the witness-stand and read to them the customary oath to keep "without meat, drink, or fire" until they came to their verdict.

It was exactly 11.35 A.M. when the eleven jurors filed out, a police officer following them with a suitcase containing most of the exhibits which had been produced during the long hearing.

A minute later, the coroner and his clerk, the Chief Constable, and other officials left the court.

Surrounded by hundreds of people, foremost in the minds of thousands more, never in the whole of his life had Philip Yale Drew felt more isolated, alone, unreachable in his private Gethsemane. Like an automaton, he rose to his feet and, for once looking neither to right nor left but fixedly, unseeingly, in front of him, walked out of the hall, followed by Mr and Mrs Lindo.

(2)

The actor's traditional mask adjusted foursquare once more upon his face, Philip Yale Drew stood in the long and gloomy arched corridor outside the improvised court-room. All unknowingly, he took up a position just outside the locked door of the committee-room in which, in charge of a sergeant, the jury were deliberating, and was glued there for more than an hour. Every now and then he would glance at the frosted-glass door-panels at his right elbow, through which the shadowy forms of the jurors could be seen bending their heads in consultation. Nervously, he puffed away at an endless succession of cigarettes and cigars.

Bernard O'Donnell, who was standing beside him, said, "Now

look here, old son, leave everything to us. There's no need for you to worry about anything. Fearnley-Whittingstall's quite happy about things, and you'll know that there's a host of friends working for you outside."

The clock ticked on. . . .

12.35 P.M.

The strain of waiting was beginning to tell on all the chief personalities in the case. Mr Martin paced up and down the corridor smoking a cigarette. Mr Fearnley-Whittingstall started to walk back and forth with long strides. Berrett stood there tugging reflectively at his neat beard. Harris was standing beside him. The affable Chief Constable of Reading, Tom Burrows, was cheerfully busying himself sorting out documents for the jury. A harassed-looking constable flitted to and fro automatically requesting people not to smoke in the corridor . . . and they, automatically, went on smoking.

Meanwhile, outside the Town Hall, a temporary car-park had been established to cope with the increasingly long line of motor-cars which were bringing spectators from long distances. Motorists were climbing on to the roofs of their cars to see over the heads of the people thronging the roadway. Unattended bicycles stretched for two or three hundred yards down a side-street. The crowds had swarmed over the iron chains guarding the Queen Victoria statue, and were sprawled across the stone plinth at the base of the memorial. Until two o'clock, when they had to return to school, children stood in hundreds on the inner fringe of the watchers, but as the clock struck they dwindled away, until once more only adults stood in the freshening wind, many of them bareheaded and coatless, but unworried by the chilly blasts.

Back in the corridor, everyone was discussing an article by 'An Eminent Criminal Lawyer' which had appeared in that morning's *Daily Mail*. It had condemned the growing practice of trying unarrested persons in a coroner's court. Most people heartily agreed with the writer's views. Drew was delighted with the article. "Perhaps it will prevent some other poor fellow from being put in the same position I have endured," he said. "I hope the murderer of Mr Oliver will be caught, if only to convince the few doubting Thomases that may still exist."

His old perkiness was now reasserting itself. He laughed and jested with the Lindos, making a brave effort to conceal the mental anguish which he must obviously have been suffering. His hands shook slightly as he lit yet another cigarette, but he spoke cheerily, and from now on always had a grip on himself.

Fearnley-Whittingstall came along and asked Drew whether he had had any lunch. He replied that he did not feel hungry, as it was not so long ago that he had had his breakfast. "Calves' liver, of course," he added with a mischievous twinkle.

Drew lit another cigarette and became interested in a bust of a heavily bewhiskered old gentleman—a former mayor of Reading— standing on a pedestal. He asked who it was. "Old Buffalo!" said O'Donnell promptly. "But his hair has gone much whiter since he has been here, and he forgot to remove his make-up." They all laughed.

Seemingly at ease, Drew chatted with various newspapermen. He told Henry de Winton Wigley that whatever verdict the jury returned, he was confident that his future was safe.

Reporting that conversation in the *Daily News*, de Winton Wigley wrote: "Next to him, pale and wan, was Mrs Lindo, whose pluck and fidelity to the man she looked upon as her big boy have caused the women of Reading to bring her bouquets of flowers and to call out blessings on her name in the streets. Philip Drew searched his pockets to show us the little mascots that had been given to him. We related stories to each other as we waited. Philip Drew told me of the man who asked at an hotel for his bill for his bed. 'You had no bed,' said the manager, 'you slept on the billiard table.' 'What!' said the customer, 'at sixty cents for half an hour.' We all laughed—but not very heartily. We hushed almost at once because of a tap at the jurymen's door. The jury only wanted a certain statement made by Sergeant Harris. Someone pressed Philip Drew's hand and told him to cheer up. He smiled and said, as he had so often said this last week, 'I'm fine; I am absolutely physically fit, you know.' He smoked a cigarette, still waiting, the corridor filled with police, every sense on the alert at the sound of an opening door or a movement. 'Do you know,' Philip Drew remarked to me suddenly, 'I can't believe this is Philip Drew. I have a strange impersonal sense.' We stood silent for a moment, and someone remarked that the jury had been out for two hours."

The clock ticked on . . .

1.35 P.M.

"'Well, my patience is good,' said Philip Drew, 'although there is such a long interval between the first and second acts.'

"We talked," de Winton Wigley continued, "of last night's revue, which Mr Drew attended, of juggling and burlesque, and in some way got on to the subject of alligators in America, and from that topic to camels and elephants. The face of the actor in front of me was drawn, and his eyes were haunted; but he joined in all this talk. He told us he took a great interest in things psychic, and was psychical himself. The next minute he was humming. I know quite well that he did this to reassure poor Mrs Lindo, whose eyes were always anxiously searching his face. I leaned against the wall at his side and he turned to me spontaneously, and, staring thoughtfully at the mosaic-tiled floor, said, 'Whatever happens, my faith in British justice will remain unshaken by this ordeal. As far as I am concerned it is mistaken identity and I maintain my innocence.' He was silent a moment, and then went on, 'I have confidence in British justice—absolute confidence. British justice is famous the world over. It will remove this shadow that has fallen on me.' He might almost have been communing with himself. I heard another voice say quietly, 'Fate plays tricks with coincidence that fiction would never dare. Do you remember that, Philip?' It was Mr Lindo, and he had recited a line from *The Monster*. Drew sighed, and said, 'Yes, I remember'."

A tall, burly man in wig and gown passed along the corridor. "Who is that?" asked Drew. "Sir Henry Curtis-Bennett," whispered O'Donnell. He was on his way to attend a case at the Quarter Sessions.

Among Drew's post there had been a letter containing a little silver horseshoe for luck. He had tucked it into the buttonhole of his overcoat—upside down. Now someone noticed it, and turned it up the right way.

Just before 2 p.m.

The corridor crackled with excitement. All eyes were turned towards the jury-room. The foreman was seen to be approaching the glass-panelled door, and everyone became suddenly silent in anticipation of a verdict. But all he wanted was to intimate that, owing to the noise of conversation in the corridor outside their room, the jury were unable to concentrate on their consideration of the evidence.

The clock ticked on. . . .

2.5 p.m.

Chairs were brought, but Drew refused to sit down. He stood

with a handkerchief clutched in his hand, his eyes often staring away into the gloom.

He began to feel 'a trifle peckish'. Fearnley-Whittingstall came up and suggested that they should go out and get a sandwich. But events overtook them.

Just coming up to 2.20 P.M.

A sudden noise. Peremptory orders by the police. Word was passed along the corridor that the jury were returning. There was a hurrying and scurrying of feet. A rush towards the court.

Mrs Lindo, on the verge of tears, took Drew's arm. "Come along with Mammy," she said.

And so, followed by Mr Lindo, arm-in-arm they entered the court.

(3)

The feet of the jury clattered noisily on the bare boards as they filed back to the seats which they had left two hours and forty-eight minutes before.

As the foreman passed by him, Drew glanced down and registered the meaningless fact that he was wearing brown boots with a rather wide welt.

Absolute silence fell on the two hundred or so people packed into the court, wedged against the walls. In that great silence every sound the jury made in reaching their places echoed loud and harsh.

The coroner sat on his platform motionless as the statues in the niches behind him. Drew, sitting between Mr and Mrs Lindo, leant forward in his chair, perfectly still, his eyes shiny. The Chief Constable of Reading, Berrett and Harris were in their places at the table below the coroner.

Eyes searched the faces of the jury for a ghost of a sign. Found none.

The roll of the jurymen was called. Eleven names read out by the coroner's officer. Eleven replies of "Present". A formality taking only seconds, seeming to occupy hours.

Mr Martin leant forward. Then, in his quiet voice, "Mr Foreman, have you a verdict to give me?"

Ears cocked. Breath held. Knuckles shining white.

The foreman—burly, grey-haired, impassive—stood up. He had a sheet of paper in his hand. "Yes, sir."

"If it is in writing will you hand it to me, or will you read it out?"

"It is in writing, and I will read it out, Mr Coroner."

"Read it slowly, then."

Mrs Lindo's face began to twitch and her lips to tremble. Drew's stillness and pallor were eburnean.

And in that strangely hushed court the foreman slowly read out:

"Mr Coroner, the jury have, after very careful deliberation on all the evidence submitted to them, unanimously agreed that the evidence is too conflicting for them to definitely establish the guilt of any particular person, consequently they return a verdict of wilful murder against some person or persons unknown."

There was the most dramatic pause when the foreman's voice ceased. Then . . . like a crash of surf. . . . came a great shout of joy from the body of the hall . . . a tremendous outburst of clapping from the back of the court.

Drew looked up, flushed and happy, and glanced around the crowded hall with a quiet smile.

Mrs Lindo, who was in a state of collapse, was shaking so violently that he slipped his arm under hers and patted her gloved hand comfortingly. She just breathed the words, "Thank God".

There were cheers, loud hurrahs. The silent court became a bedlam. Women sprang to their feet. Men stood and waved their hats—some throwing them high into the air—and shouted, "Three cheers for Mr Drew." There was hand-clapping, the shrieking of women, the fluttering of handkerchiefs, the waving of papers, and the stamping of feet. Those spontaneous cheers—not a single cheer, but a succession of swelling cheers—that rang through the court carried the news of the jury's decision to the huge crowd waiting outside, and presently fainter cheering from the street was heard by those inside the building.

A police inspector, a woman superintendent of police, and other officers immediately rushed from the front of the court and went among the people. The inspector thundered out a warning against the demonstrators, called vigorously for order.

When, at last, quiet had been restored, the coroner said, "Mr Foreman, that amounts to an open verdict."

"Yes, sir," agreed the foreman. "That is so."

"Thank you, Mr Foreman," said Mr Martin.

The coroner's officer formally pronounced the court closed.
The inquest on Alfred Oliver was over.

(4)

Reading had long ago made up its mind that Philip Yale Drew
was innocent. Now, Reading, proved right, its instinctive belief
ratified by a jury's decision, went completely mad.

The hysterical scene enacted in court was merely a mild prelude
to the frenzy which was very soon to engulf the town. It was the
most fantastic explosion of relief at the end of this extraordinary
inquest, which had been bouquets and kisses for the chief witness
nearly all the way.

Mrs Lindo was the first to be greeted by Drew. He shook her
hand warmly and affectionately embraced her. Then he shook hands
with Mr Lindo.

Friends clustered around and struggled with each other for the
privilege of shaking Drew's hand. He gave them both hands at
once.

Just as Drew and his friends were about to leave the court, Mrs
Lindo finally collapsed. She did not faint, but sank back in her
chair, crying softly, and incapable of movement.

O'Donnell and another of Drew's friends—one on either side—
took Drew by the arms and hustled him out of court.

The instant he appeared at the top of the Town Hall steps a
mighty roar went up, and the crowd, completely out of control,
flooded all over the street. "I want my hat," said Drew, who had
left it behind in the court. But there was no opportunity to get it,
for the people behind him were as solid a pack as those he had to
face outside.

Surrounded by police, he and those with him charged—there is no
other word—down the steps. An attempt was at once made to rush
him, but for a moment or so the police were able to stem the tide. It
was only for a moment, though, for as soon as Drew reached the
foot of the steps—where the police had managed to keep an open
space—and crossed the pavement to the roadway there was a great
surge, and Drew and his companions disappeared as if they had been
swallowed up by a huge wave. A dozen hefty constables fought their
way to where Drew was struggling to get along, and forced the
people back. The crowd did all they could to break through the

BALCONY SCENE
October 11th, 1929

(Above) Drew takes a curtain-call on the portico of the Great Western
Hotel, Reading

(Left) It was the most
wonderful audience of his
life. He addressed the
wildly cheering crowd like
a king from a balcony

Philip Yale Drew with Frank and Marion Lindo
The ordeal by inquest was over. A little hour of triumph

police guard and reach Drew, who seemed to be in physical danger from their enthusiasm. There were shrieks and cries from the women, many of whom held up above their heads bouquets of flowers which they were hoping to present to their hero. But they were unable to get anywhere near him, and, from the Town Hall steps one could see the waving flowers floating back towards the side of the street.

The police, turning their shoulders towards the people, adopted the tactics of rugby forwards, and, elbowing and shouldering, cleared a way for him through the mob of cheering, shouting, clutching humanity.

This was hysteria. Women were weeping for sheer emotional relief, fighting to embrace him, jostling to hang on to his coat. Some fell to the pavement as Drew's procession heaved by. Then, as he passed, the excited crowd, breaking into many sections in his wake, ran through the side-streets in order to get ahead of him and be there to greet him when he reached his hotel. Athletic girls sprinted past women who were running with babies in their arms. A bicycle, left on the kerb, was trampled into wreckage.

Waving and smiling broadly, Drew was borne along by four stalwart and sweating constables, their helmets bobbing like corks in the sea of spectators. Yard by struggling yard, foot by foot, inch by inch almost, down Blagrave Street, round the corner into Station Road . . . a flash of police helmets . . . a heave of broad blue shoulders . . . a sudden scattering of close-packed bodies to right and left . . . and the four policemen, with Drew in their midst, hurled themselves across the pavement and through the doors of the Great Western Hotel with such impulsion that two of the constables lost their footing and fell flat on their faces in the hall. The doors were instantly locked, and a dozen policemen stationed inside them to make sure that the crowd did not force its way in.

(5)

The cheers of the crowd roared through the windows. They wanted Drew—and they meant to have him.

How could he deny his public? He hurried upstairs and stepped out on to one of the hotel balconies.

A roar of applause greeted him.

For a minute or two he just stood there, looking down on the vast sea of upturned faces, his hair rough and tousled from his battle through the mob. It was the most wonderful audience of his life, and he faced them like the bred-in-the-bone actor that he was. Held up his hand in a magnificently dramatic gesture.

The cheering subsided.

His voice throbbed with emotion. "Just one moment, please, before you all go to your several homes. . . ."

Weeping women shouted, "Don't cry". Members of the hotel staff were sobbing at the windows. A waiter wiped his tear-filled eyes with a napkin. Emotion was palpable on the air. It was a welter of tears and cheers.

Drew raised his hand again. Commanding presence. Leonine head. Caesar, Lear, Henry V, rolled into one.

"I want to thank you and to let you know just how much I appreciate this wonderful demonstration. The prayers that have been sent up for me, and the glorious sympathy extended to me, have meant much. The One Above, like myself, knows that I had nothing to do with it in any way. I shall never forget this demonstration, and from the bottom of my heart, and on behalf of Mr and Mrs Lindo, who have been so kind to me, I thank you. I shall never forget the wonderful courtesy and wonderful things that that glorious Press has unanimously accorded me. Good afternoon—and God bless you all."

A little bow. He stepped back through the window, and was gone.

The crowd cheered . . . and cheered . . . and cheered.

It had been the balcony scene to end all balcony scenes.

How could he deny his public an encore?

A moment later he was on the balcony again. This time with Mr and Mrs Lindo on either side of him.

Mrs Lindo was once more teetering on the brink of collapse, but, stout trouper that she was, managed to pull herself sufficiently far back to gasp, "Thank you, thank you," to her yelling, beside-itself audience. And there she bravely stood, her Titian hair blowing in the wind, her arms about the shoulders of her husband and Philip, who supported her. Then, disengaging herself, she went to the front of the balcony, smiled a weary little smile, and threw three kisses to the crowd. As she did so, Drew stepped forward, seized her hand and raised it to his lips. Then he put his arms round her and kissed her on the face.

The cheering became deafening, and Mr and Mrs Lindo and Drew remained on the balcony for several more minutes acknowledging their reception.

Somebody in the crowd shouted, "Are you coming back?"

"Yes," boomed Drew, "I shall be coming back."

A final wave . . . a last-blown kiss . . . and the three of them vanished into the wings.

Weeping, cheering, waving tear-sodden handkerchiefs, the multitude lingered hopefully on outside the hotel for more than an hour. The excitement and the sentiment were infectious. One woman crying would set half a dozen others sobbing. Everybody seemed to be attacked by a sort of weeping fever.

In fact, Philip Yale Drew had at this moment no need of weeping. This was his little hour of triumph. His sympathizers should have taken John Pudney's poetic advice, and kept their tears, for him in after years. But this was indeed his moment, and the Press was waiting to set it all down in glowing and perishable prose.

The Press did not have to wait long. Having done his duty by his public, Drew's first consideration was to meet all 'The Boys'—as he called the newspapermen who had been staying in his hotel. And so, with the cheers of his well-wishers still echoing in his ears, he, together with the Lindos and one or two members of the *Monster* company, went along to Mr Lindo's room and let it be known that an immediate Press reception was to be held there.

Drew walked to the window, selected a red rose from a vase, and put it in his buttonhole. While they were waiting for the late-comers to be rounded up he asked one of the reporters to read over his shorthand note of the balcony speech for the benefit of Mrs Lindo, who had missed it. Then, standing there with his hands buried deep in his overcoat pockets, Drew asked, "Are we all set?" And the audience of reporters, brought up to full strength, said that they were. Drew thought for a moment or two before speaking. In the silence they could all hear the shouts of newspaper-sellers announcing the result of the inquest, and the low rumble of the crowd, still waiting outside in the hope of seeing Drew again.

Then . . . "Really," he began, "I hardly know what to say. I can't think of anything fresh. It is possible now the shadow has been lifted from over me that I am perhaps more calm than at any time since I was first interrogated by the police at Nottingham. I do not hesitate for one moment to say—and I am not ashamed to admit it

—that after I received at Merthyr Tydfil a subpoena to attend the inquest, I was not only most concerned, but had many a sleepless night. Had I been alone I would not have minded it so much, but I realized that I was innocently involving, or was the part-cause of others being involved, particularly Mr and Mrs Lindo, not forgetting Mr Fry and other members of the *Monster* company. I frankly admit that when I took my seat in the well of the coroner's court on the first day of the inquest I experienced a sensation that I have never known before, not even on the first nights of new productions. Something seemed to jump up and down inside me. Outwardly, I might have appeared calm, but inwardly I was all turmoil. As the days went on I gradually became more calm, possibly more collected, and possibly not so fidgety. Prior to going to the court in the morning I trusted in God that the right words would be put into my mouth, and I am confident they were. I had no real doubt as to what the ultimate outcome would be. I hope never to leave the stage, but that is in the hands of Mr and Mrs Lindo. I don't feel I require a holiday, in fact I feel fit enough now to go on the stage and play my part in *The Monster* tonight, and I would like to—only unfortunately that can't be done. I have no complaint to make against the way in which the police have treated me over this very serious matter. I feel deeply that the system of the coroner's court, as I have seen it, is wrong. I can't say it is exactly a sort of third degree or a crucifixion, but anyone who has been through what I have will realize what a terrible ordeal it is. Now we have a reunited family, and there is every possibility that *The Monster* will be revived again. And I shall act in it as I have never acted before."

In his account of this Press conference, the *Daily Express* Special Correspondent wrote somewhat more fully: "Philip Yale Drew revealed himself at last today. Almost to the end of the inquest he was fully reconciled to the prospect of a verdict of murder against him, and he expected that he would have to stand his trial before a judge and jury at assizes in order to establish his innocence. It has not been possible before to tell the story of what has been going on behind the scenes—of the evenings when Mr Drew has returned from the coroner's court feeling that the hand of fate was against him. There were many anxious conferences in his hotel when—to use Mr Drew's own words—everything looked black for him. Every preparation was made in anticipation of an adverse verdict at the inquest. Mr Frank Lindo was arranging an appeal for public subscriptions to raise money for the defence. Mr Drew faced the possibility of an assize court trial with quiet resignation. Only on Tuesday night (October 8th) when he returned from the court he said to me, 'I am afraid that it will go against me here, but it will be all right higher up.' It was not until last night (October 9th) after evidence had been called on his behalf, that he felt at all hopeful about the inquest result. He talked to me quite frankly over the breakfast table this morning about the prospects of the verdict. He said to me: 'On Wednesday night I did not expect the case to end with the inquest'. He was silent for some time, as if contemplating the ordeal of a trial for murder. When he spoke again it was with studied emphasis and pause between each word. 'Last night. . . . well . . . I thought maybe it would end here.' Then, with that sudden change of mood which is so typical of the man, he laughed inconsequently, and said, 'You see, I'm having calves' liver'. A few mornings before he had made a jest that he dared not order liver because it had been made to appear significant at the inquest that this was his favourite dish. Someone came up to say 'Goodbye' before he was engulfed in the crowd outside that was waiting to cheer him on his way to the court. 'Not goodbye,' said Mr Drew with a whimsical smile. 'I shall see you again later—today.' "

Every scrap, every utterance, was fair copy for the poised pencils and hungry pads of the reporters. Naturally, the Lindos came in for their share of interviewing.

Said Mr Lindo: "From the start I knew that Philip was absolutely innocent, and I have never faltered from that opinion for one moment. I have never had a moment's worry or uneasiness about the final result. I realize, of course, that at this inquest things might have gone temporarily against us, but I knew that in the long run we should have the truth."

Mr Lindo added that he contemplated giving a public concert or entertainment of some kind at Reading before he left. "Probably it will be held in the Town Hall," he said. "Mr Drew will positively appear at that concert, because, apart from anything or whatever he does in the programme, he certainly feels that he would like to thank publicly the people of Reading for the way they have rallied round him in the hour of his trial."

Asked about the future of the *Monster* company, he said that his plans were a little indefinite. "I have this morning received an offer from a well-known London manager who says that he will be able to book important dates all over the country, and he suggests that the play should be given a run of some weeks in London. I have not yet replied to this offer, but I am seriously considering accepting it."

Said Mrs Lindo: "I am crying out of sheer relief and thankfulness. Not that I had any real doubts, but it has been a terrible time for all of us."

Asked by a reporter from the *Daily Mail* how she accounted for the tremendous scenes of public weeping and enthusiasm, she replied: "Women understand that most men are helpless creatures, and in no calling more than ours. If there is anything a woman can do for them they will let her do it. I have been the woman to help Philip Drew. I have nursed him through three illnesses."

The Press conference broke up.

Drew, accompanied by Mr and Mrs Lindo, drove in a taxi to the Town Hall, where the inquest witnesses were signing their evidence and receiving their fees and expenses.

When, at the Town Hall, it was pointed out to Drew that he had forgotten to collect his witness' fee he said, "Oh, it doesn't matter." But Chief Constable Burrows, overhearing the remark, insisted that it did matter. In fact, Drew and Mr and Mrs Lindo all donated their fees and travelling expenses—amounting to about £21—for the benefit of the Police Orphanage.

In the Town Hall corridor Drew met the foreman of the jury. They shook hands. "Good luck—and goodbye," said the foreman. "Thank you very much. Goodbye," replied Drew.

Seconds later, Chief Constable Burrows came up to Drew. Out went his hand. "Goodbye, Mr Drew." And the two men held each other's hands in a warm grasp.

That evening there was a continuous stream of calls from private friends who were anxious to offer their congratulations. Drew remained in the hotel, chatting with his visitors and reading through an immense postbag, which included more than 130 telegrams. And among the letters was one very special one. It bore a Nebraska postmark. It came from the Lewisham boy scout—a boy no longer—who, all those years ago, Young Buffalo had sent West to Colonel Coster's A Star A Ranch. He was living now in the thriving city of Omaha. The West had been good to him, and he had prospered. He wrote an anxious letter to his onetime hero and benefactor. He wanted him to know that he was remembering him, and praying for him in his time of trouble.

Another vast crowd gathered outside the Great Western, and when, as the evening wore on, Drew went out to them, a woman rushed forward and pressed his hand to her lips. It was the day's final act of homage.

Gradually the crowd thinned . . . drifted away.

Alone at last in that same room where, ten nights before, he had wondered so anxiously to what scene the call-boy of fate was about to summon him, Philip Yale Drew, exhausted, prepared to go to bed. He undressed, slowly. Then crossed to the window. Opened it. Looked out. Under the single undoused lime of the October moon, the street was empty. The audience had gone home. He thanked God that he had not been called upon to play out a tragedy.

He could not have been more wrong.

Intermission

In which we mark how five
words spelled not the end
but the beginning of the
ordeal of Philip Yale Drew.

INTERMISSION

(1)

Some person or persons unknown . . .

The suspect dismissed. Free to step out of the black limelight, back into the safety of the shadows from which he has so briefly, and alarmingly, emerged.

A man arraigned for murder before judge and jury is found guilty or innocent, and once the legal process of trial is complete the rest is silence.

Trial by coroner is different.

(2)

The duty of a coroner is clearly defined and decisively laid down by statute. It is to discover the cause of death: to hold an inquiry upon the dead body of a person lying within his jurisdiction as to how, when, where and by what means the deceased came by his death when there is reasonable cause to suspect that that person has died either a violent or an unnatural death, or has died a sudden death of which the cause is unknown, or that that person has died in prison, or in such place or in such circumstances as to require an inquest.

The Coroners (Amendment) Act 1926 introduced several important changes to the Coroners Act 1887. It provided that a coroner is permitted, with certain exceptions, to hold an inquest without a jury. The exceptions are those cases in which murder, manslaughter, or infanticide is suspected. And it further provided that if a person has been brought before a magistrate on a charge of murder, manslaughter, or infanticide, the coroner is obliged to adjourn his inquest pending the finding of the criminal proceedings.

No comparable safeguard was enacted, however, in respect of persons *suspected* of committing such crimes. This was undoubtedly a very serious defect, for while magistrates and judges are strictly bound by well-defined rules of evidence and stringent methods of procedure in their courts, the coroner is virtually a law unto himself. He may or may not, for example, permit cross-examination of witnesses. He may or may not allow counsel or solicitor to appear before him. He may constitute himself both judge and prosecuting counsel, for he is in a position to ask questions and make suggestions which no judge would permit. He may proceed to a fishing inquiry of any length, in which the suspected person may be positively encouraged to make those damning admissions against which the police are bound to warn a man before they charge him. Hearsay evidence can be admitted. His court may, in short, be turned into an inquisition—literally.

It is not surprising that, having regard to the coroner's wide powers, a careful eye was customarily kept upon his activities by the Press and public. On the whole, there has been remarkably little room for complaint or cause for misgiving, but just occasionally a coroner's actions have given rise to widespread concern.

A case in point was that of Mrs Beatrice Annie Pace, who, in 1928, was committed to Gloucester Assizes, charged on the coroner's inquisition with the murder of her husband. At the conclusion of the inquest, which had extended over four months, the coroner's jury returned an open verdict. It left the police at liberty to continue their inquiries, and meant that in the event of their obtaining further evidence they could have brought a charge against Mrs Pace.

However, the coroner, Mr Maurice Carter, sent the jurors back to their room with the instruction that they must name somebody. After an absence of twenty-five minutes the jury returned, and the foreman announced, "We have revised our verdict as follows: We find that the deceased, Harry Pace, met his death at Fetter Hill on January 10th, 1928, by arsenical poisoning administered by Beatrice Annie Pace." Mrs Pace was then arrested on the coroner's warrant and charged.

The matter was immediately taken up by the Press. Mr Albert Arthur Purcell, Labour M.P. for the Forest of Dean, whose constituent Mrs Pace was, set about raising a public subscription to provide her with adequate defence at her trial, and Norman Birkett was briefed on her behalf. In fact, the defence was never called upon. Mr Birkett submitted to Mr Justice Horridge that there was no case to go to the jury on the indictment. The learned judge accepted that there was not sufficient evidence and directed the jury to return a verdict of 'Not guilty'.

Less than a year later, similar disquiet followed the long series of inquest hearings held between March and August 1929 in the Sidney-Duff Croydon poisoning case, in which, when the inquests opened, the nature of the questions framed by the coroner, Dr Henry Beecher Jackson, led the public to believe that the court's suspicions were centred upon one person, and as the inquests proceeded an atmosphere unfavourable to that person was created.

And now, two months after that, came the Alfred Oliver inquest, with its seeming pillorying of Philip Yale Drew.

On Friday, October 11th, 1929, the *Star* had this to say: "Mr Philip Yale Drew has never been charged with the murder, and yet he has been subjected to an ordeal which in effect amounts to a third degree examination conducted on a public stage."

Commented the *Daily News* of the same day: "Mr Drew was not treated as an innocent man. He was subjected to a public ordeal which no person should be required to undergo at a coroner's inquest because he happens at the moment to be under a certain suspicion."

Stung no doubt by the widespread criticisms, Mr Martin was constrained to offer a public reply and refutation: "To speak first of the Reading inquest. I should like to repeat that I gave Mr Drew's counsel more licence than is usually given at an inquest. I consider that the inquest was conducted in a most fair way throughout. The detectives and also the police were most anxious that this should be the case, and, from my own knowledge of the statements given to the police by all those whom they interviewed, I think Mr Drew was treated most fairly. Mr Drew showed that he recognized that when he thanked Mr Burrows, the Chief Constable of Reading. There has been no variation to my knowledge as regards the conduct of inquests. I have been coroner for eighteen years and I have never yet received a complaint as to the way in which I have conducted any inquest. I have received a large number of threatening and abusive letters from various parts of the country. On the other hand, I have received some congratulations as to the conduct of this inquiry. If there is to be any change, I am rather in agreement that a coroner's duty should be limited to determining the cause of death. I think that the police authorities should then become responsible for any further action. I am also against the practice of naming individuals. In this case I resumed my inquiry at the express wish of Scotland Yard. I think it is up to the Government to take such action in this matter as they think desirable. I feel sure that all the coroners in England and Wales would be grateful if their powers were more definitely defined than at present. There has been so much criticism of the present system that I think it is up to the Government to legislate."

The *Star* of October 11th announced that a Bill to limit the powers of coroners was to come before the House of Commons at its next session. Mr Edward Clement Davies, K.C., Liberal M.P. for Montgomery, had told the *Star*'s representative that he was already at work drawing up an amendment to the Coroners Act.

Commenting on the Reading inquest, Mr Davies said that Drew was subjected to a criminal inquiry which was disgraceful.

It was also announced that, "in view of the recent proceedings in coroners' courts at the Reading inquest, the Duff inquiry and the Pace inquiry", Mr Harry Day, M.P., intended, immediately the House of Commons resumed, to ask the Home Secretary (Mr John Robert Clynes) if his attention had been called to the procedure adopted and the examination of witnesses during recent inquiries in coroners' courts, and if he would consider—in conjunction with the Lord Chancellor—the appointment of a committee for the purpose of introducing legislation which would have as its object the amending of the Coroners (Amendment) Act and the further clarifying of the powers of coroners during such inquiries.

Despite all this uproar, this to-ing and fro-ing of official and un-official opinion, no revolutionary changes in legislation were immediately forthcoming.

It was in 1953 that the Coroners Rules were enacted. They provided a codification of a great deal of what was established practice and embraced several of the recommendations of the Wright Committee on Coroners of 1936. They also laid down firm rules of procedure and unequivocally defined the scope of the inquest itself.

(3)

Some person or persons unknown . . .
For Philip Yale Drew those five words were not an end but a beginning of an ordeal. The worst ordeal of all. A slow, inexorable disintegration.

If this were simply a book about a man who committed murder, was accused, tried, and convicted—or acquitted—it would now be at an end.

But Drew was never accused of murder. Neither, by the same token, was he ever exonerated.

And so this book cannot end with the curtain-fall at Reading.

There has to be one more Act.

Act Three

The action takes place mainly
in London, and moves against a
backcloth of mean streets and
seedy lodgings.

The time: Late 1929 to mid-1940.

Scene 1

THE KISSES OF DOLORES

(1)

STORMS left behind. Barometer set fair. Trial and tribulations past. The future a blank cheque.

As one, marginally warped, member of the theatrical profession put it, "If Drew can't make a success of it after all *that* publicity, he must be a real dud."

Certainly one would have thought so. Indeed, many people *did* think that his fortune was assured, and were quick to hitch their wagons to his star.

Contemptuously, the *Daily Express* of October 10th reported the first of these endeavours to cash-in:

A remarkable attempt to 'commercialise' the ordeal of Mr Philip Yale Drew, the actor-witness in the Reading murder case, will culminate tomorrow in a 'trade show' in London of films in which he appears. Box-office managers of cinemas are now being invited to attend the show, and the invitation and publicity matter leave nothing to the imagination of the possible film renters. The invitation reads:

"—— Ltd. requests the pleasure of your company at the trade and Press show of a selection of their recent pictures, featuring

PHILIP YALE DREW

the prominent witness in the Reading murder case.

MILLIONS OF PEOPLE ARE READING ABOUT HIM. MILLIONS WILL WANT TO SEE HIM."

The date, place and time of the trade show then follow. The firm state:

"Every newspaper in the country is carrying a story. A million pounds worth of advertising for nothing. Wise showmen—get busy! Or get left."

The show took place before a packed audience, the majority of them women, at the Avenue Pavilion, on London's Shaftesbury Avenue,[1] on Friday, October 11th.

The three films screened were good, old-fashioned Westerns—plenty of ranch scenery, galloping horses, barking guns, saloons and sheriffs. In the first, Drew, the hero, was seen holding up and robbing a coach. He is masked, but a woman in the coach says, "He turned his back and I saw his long, wavy hair. You could never mistake him." In another, Drew was suspected of a murder he did not commit, and one of his accusers says, "I know him by his hair". There is talk of 'suspicion' and 'the long arm of the law'. He is, however, eventually cleared.

"The films," wrote a critic in the *Daily Chronicle*, "are worth seeing in themselves, being about as good as most of the more sophisticated films now shown. Mr Drew not only shows himself a competent actor, so competent that he makes everyone else in the films look amateurish, riding a horse, paddling a canoe, carrying a crippled woman with unusual muscular strength and dexterity, but he shows real artistic magnetism. In appearance and professional skill he is the typical hero of the Wild West film. Perhaps it was because he was able to take this appearance and skill and magnetism into the coroner's court that he became the centre of such extravagant sympathy."

That Friday, while his celluloid shadow was diverting the London film-goers, Drew himself was relaxing in Reading. He spent most of the time indoors at his hotel, and groups of people who watched outside throughout the day saw nothing of him.

A *Star* correspondent did, however, see him, and reported: "Mr Drew was smiling and he looked particularly fit. 'The sleepless nights are over,' said Mr Drew. 'Last night I slept soundly and well, and today I feel more refreshed than I have felt for many days.' Rising early today, Mr Drew walked through the almost deserted streets. A few persons who waited outside the hotel gave him warm greetings as he strolled past them. He returned for breakfast with Mrs Lindo. Afterwards, surrounded by newspapers, he sat in the lounge reading the accounts of yesterday's remarkable scenes of which he was the central figure. The little black dog,[2] that is his constant companion, lay at his feet."

---

[1] It stood in the block where the Columbia Theatre—No. 93—now is.
[2] Actually Mrs Lindo's dog, Pip.

Having completed his reading of the papers, Drew set to work answering his enormous mail, that morning's post having brought him a further 140 letters of congratulation.

He was interrupted when, later in the day, Inspector Walters and Detective Sergeant Knight called at the Great Western to return to him and to Mr and Mrs Lindo the witness fees which they had donated to the Police Orphanage. It was explained that Chief Constable Burrows felt that, in view of the expense to which they had been put, they should accept the money due to them.

It was also announced that *The Monster* had been leased to the London theatrical manager, J. Bannister Howard, and that Drew and the Lindos would be appearing in it. "It will open on Monday, November 4th," Mr Howard told a *Daily Express* representative, who saw him at his office at 45 Chandos Street, "and after a spell in the provinces it will not be long before *The Monster* will make an appearance in suburban London."

Berrett and Harris returned to London that Friday, leaving the hunt for the shop-crime murderer in the hands of the Reading Force.

Said Chief Constable Burrows: "Our position at the moment is just this—we are resuming our search for the murderer of Mr Oliver."

Said Inspector Walters: "The police in Reading will not relax their efforts to bring the offender to justice. You may rest assured that we shall leave no stone unturned."

In fact, they had already been questioning a local amateur boxer whom they suspected of being implicated in the murder—and had exonerated the youth.

Some further evidence was put into their hands on the morning of Saturday, October 12th. This was in the form of a letter addressed to Mrs Lindo at the Great Western Hotel. It had arrived on the Friday morning and was delivered, with a pile of other letters, to Mr Lindo while he was in bed. He did not have time to read them properly then, as he had to go to London on urgent business that day, and took the correspondence with him to go through on the train.

The letter, which was anonymous, unpunctuated, and written in rather small handwriting, bore a Leeds postmark, but no address. It read:

DEAR MRS LINDO,

I am writing to tell you something which may be of interest. When I was employed as a general in London last winter I met a man and got very fond of him. After he courted me for two months he suggested robbing my employers, and after doing so made my life such a misery that I went off with him and got situations and did the thieving. We do all the races, and were at Ascot, and actually in Reading at the time of the murder together until four o'clock, when he suggested he did a job and got back to London. I was to wait about by the Post Office till he returned, and I waited, and was just beginning to go and see if I could get a bun, as I was hungry, when he turned up looking scared. He said he had done a job, and the cops were about, so we parted, and that was exactly 6.12, and he said we should meet in London, on the corner of Burdett Road,[1] on the Monday, about five. We met and went to Epping Forest for a picnic, but when we got there he undid his case and said he was getting rid of the suit and coat and shirt, also his cap. He poured petrol over his suit, and also over his fawn gaberdine coat, and burned the case, as it was stained. He told me it was red paint. While it was burning he said, 'My name ain't Brown, old girl—he was caught with the goods on him.' After that he went into the undergrowth and hid something, and when he came back I asked him if he got rid of it, and he said, 'Yes. I can easily get another spanner if I want it.' All went well until he got to York last month for the races. He said I pinched a quid off him, and the last time I saw him was when he was lifting a pair of field-glasses from a gent's pocket, and he disappeared and left me stranded, and I haven't a bean, only what I get by begging. But I am writing this out of spite, to spite the man that brought me in the gutter and left me. He did the murder all right, and that's why he burnt his clothes, and I hope he will get caught, and then I will give evidence and know he will not plug me. I am afraid of writing to the police; they bring up all sorts against you, sometimes what ain't true. I have been to Doncaster, and he isn't there, but I will spend my last penny to get even with him.

After reading it, Mr Lindo decided that he ought to pass it on to the police on his return from London. He took it to Reading Police Station in the early hours of Saturday, October 12th, but, finding neither the Chief Constable nor Inspector Walters there, said that he would come back later, which he did at 11.15 A.M.

[1] In the East End of London.

Inspector Walters asked for the envelope in which the letter had arrived, and Mr Lindo went to the hotel to fetch it, but could not find it. It must, he said, have been burnt as rubbish, along with a heap of other envelopes that he had left in his bedroom. He was, however, convinced that the letter was genuine. "It rings true," he said. "If the police do not act on it, we shall. Mr Drew is lying in bed late today after his long ordeal of the past few weeks. When he read the letter he said to me, 'Slowly but surely I am walking out of the shadows'. And the tears were in his eyes as he said it."

Inspector Walters seemed less impressed. He said that the letter did not contain any information likely to assist the police in any direction. He then delivered himself of the following somewhat enigmatic statement: "This anonymous letter is very similar in character to many other such letters we have received in connection with the Oliver murder. We are going as far as possible to try and trace the author of this letter, and, for the moment, I would not express my own opinion of it. There are certain characteristics which, although they have no bearing on the investigations, might have some bearing upon the author."

One suspects that the slightly American tang of the word 'cops', and the phrase 'plug me', stuck in Inspector Walters' craw.

Regarding the Inspector's misgiving, Mr Lindo was subsequently to say, "It was my duty to hand the letter over to the police, and I cannot believe there is any insinuation that the letter was not genuinely received. There could be no object in us handing over such a letter unless it was genuine now that the inquest is over."

Saturday's papers contained two interesting items.

The first was that the cleaner's tab attached to Drew's blue trousers[1] had been identified. Mr E. Midgley, general manager of Messrs Martin, cleaners, of Waterloo Mills, Bramley, Leeds, told a *Daily Mail* reporter that he had had no difficulty in recognizing the mark—A 8819–3—as that of his firm. The figure 3 indicated a complete suit. It was received from their Sheffield office on May 10, 1929, and returned from the mills on May 12th.

The second item was that Mrs Oliver had sold the premises at Number 15 Cross Street. She told a *Daily News* representative: "I could not possibly carry on business in Cross Street, the associations would be too distressing."

[1] See page 177.

Mrs Oliver had, the report stated, bought "a pretty little cottage in the hope of being able to secure rest and seclusion after her great tragedy".

She had also written to the *Daily News* asking, "*Need* the crowds add to my torture by cheering *anyone*? Are they *glad* that an upright, loyal fellow-citizen, a Christian gentleman, was gashed and beaten to death? Crowd psychology is truly a curious thing."

But the cheering at Reading was over. There were no cheering crowds to see Drew off when that Saturday, October 12th, he left the town. He simply shook hands with the hotel staff, waved to a few people in the street, the drivers on the taxicab rank outside the station, and a handful of railway officials and passengers on the platform. Then, quietly, he and Mr and Mrs Lindo boarded the London train.

Only Mr Lindo showed any sign of distress. He said, "If ever I return to Reading it will be as a paid actor. I am going back to *The Monster* as a paid actor after years as an actor-manager. I am getting old, and this ordeal has left its mark on me. I feel I shall never undertake management again. We shall probably have a few days' rest in the country. We all need quiet and a relief from the trying atmosphere of the last few weeks."

Very few of those waiting to meet friends at Paddington recognized Drew—until a small boy dashed up, autograph book in hand, and asked him for his signature. As Drew signed the book a number of people realized who he was. They pressed round to shake him by the hand, and his friends had some difficulty in getting him away from the crowd that surrounded him.

Mrs Lindo left immediately to visit her daughter, Olga. Mr Lindo accompanied Drew to a hotel where they were to stay the night.

The following day's *Empire News* carried on its front page an exclusive—"My Trial: By Philip Yale Drew". It is a skilful, highly coloured and melodramatic piece of writing, and one detects in it the practised and 'ghostly' hand of Bernard O'Donnell.

"For six days I have been pilloried as a drunken ruffian who was capable of going into the shop of Mr Oliver, and battering a poor, inoffensive old man to death.

"For nearly three months I have been under suspicion of a murder as foul as any that has ever been commited: murder for a few paltry pounds, if the evidence is correct; and whatever may be the real legal technicalities of the facts, I HAVE BEEN TRIED FOR MY LIFE.

"I have looked at death many times during a somewhat adventurous career, and I am not afraid. But this time I have looked at a different sort of death. During the past two months, since that fateful day the police descended upon me at Nottingham, I have been looking at death through a noose.

"That was the grim reality which stood out before me the whole time, death at the hands of the hangman, a shameful death upon the gallows for the brutal murder of an old man.

"We are a temperamental people, we actors and actresses. Therein lies much of our art. If we were not, if we had not that sense of drama, then we should not be able to entertain you on the stage.

"All my life from the age of eighteen I have been playing in drama, the drama of make-believe made to look real, but this time I have been playing in a drama of life and death on a stage set in the grim surroundings of a coroner's court, where I have been pointed at by the fingers of honest witnesses—most of whom who identified me not having seen me for four months—recollected and described as reeling drunk, of a 'bullying and arrogant' manner, and, in fact, as one capable of this fearful crime.

"It is an ordeal that few men, thank God, are called upon to face. To me it has been something more than a grim reality, it has been a lesson, a lesson I shall never forget.

"I am glad this terrible ordeal is over. I am grateful for the wonderful loyalty and support of all my friends. I have made many new ones, and I tell them here and now that I will never let them down."

(2)

For Philip Yale Drew the Reading ordeal was over, but for the Reading police the murder file was still very much open, and for many weeks, months, to come, reports of their continuing investigations were to appear in the newspapers.

First of all came the announcement—on October 14th—that a new witness, a man who worked as an assistant in a shop in Cross Street almost opposite Mr Oliver's, was claiming that he had seen a mysterious drunken man in Cross Street on the night of the murder. This man was definitely not Drew. He was aged about forty, about 5 feet 9 inches in height, wore a blue suit, and carried a fawn raincoat, which he trailed on the ground. Said the witness: "It was a few minutes after five o'clock when I saw him, and he was standing in a peculiar attitude at the lamp-post which is on the same side of the street as Mr Oliver's shop. He was clutching the lamp-post. His behaviour was so queer that I remarked, 'That fellow is drunk'. That man may have been the same man, judging by the description, that Mr Wells saw. He went away in the direction of Friar Street."[1]

There were newspaper reports that on October 20th and 25th the police carried out dragging operations in the Thames in an unsuccessful search for the murder weapon, and that on October 27th they had the river-bed in the Caversham area searched by a diver.

Yet other 'new avenues of inquiry' were referred to in the *Daily Express* of October 17th.

One was the possibility that Drew had a double, who was in Reading on the day of the murder. It was stated that the police had in fact received a number of letters from informants describing a man bearing a close resemblance to Drew.

Another was an alleged statement claimed to corroborate the details given in the anonymous Leeds letter to Mrs Lindo. This statement, which came into the possession of the *Daily Express* on the night of October 16th, declared that on the evening of June 22nd, about two hours after the Reading murder, a motor-car stopped at a public-house in the Camden Park Road district of London. Four men and a girl alighted and entered the bar, and drinks were ordered. The man who seemed to be most intimate with the girl answered exactly the description which the anonymous correspondent gave in her letter of the man in whose company she was at Reading earlier that evening. This man used bad language to the girl, and made for her as if intending to hit her, but two of the others held him back. When remonstrated with about his language, the man said, "What does she want to mention names for?" Soon afterwards the party, who all seemed worried, left in the direction of central London.[2]

---

[1] The man may well have been the same one that Mr Nicholson saw (see p. 133), and stated was definitely not Drew.

[2] Since the letter—the text of which is given on p. 246—does not contain any description of the man in question, the value of this evidence seems dubious.

The issue of *John Bull* published on Saturday, October 26th, contained an article strongly critical of the police and their non-production of the witness Alfred John Wells.

> With the police constantly in conference with the coroner, and a mass of vague evidence which would not have been admissible in another court being called, the inquest might have had another and unjustified result but for the last-moment appearance of a vital witness. This witness was Mr Alfred J. Wells. The essential information he gave to the court—in the end it cleared suspicion from Mr Drew—was in the possession of the police on the night of the murder—nearly twelve weeks before the inquest opened. Yet the police did not intend to put Mr Wells in the witness-box. In fact, they had not even told the coroner about the statement they received from him. It was, we have found, the earliest and by far the most exact description given to the police of a man who had been hovering suspiciously near Mr Oliver's shop for eleven hours before the crime. Mr Wells had sat a foot from the stranger, studied him closely, and spoken with him. But the description and accent given to the police were not those of Mr Drew. It would probably never have been known that Mr Wells had laid this quick and definite information before the police, and he certainly would not have been produced as a witness but for the intervention of two London journalists. It is the imperative duty of the Home Secretary to ascertain and inform the public why Mr Wells and his statement were forgotten.

It was an apt and timely broadside from a magazine whose masthead motto was: "For the People—The Right to Justice and Truth".

One by one, all these 'new avenues of inquiry' petered out into culs-de-sac. The author of the Leeds letter was never traced. No murder weapon of any sort was ever found, in the river or anywhere else. Nothing more was heard of Drew's double, or of the members of the mysterious party in the Camden Park Road public-house.

Then, at 2.20 P.M. on Sunday, October 27th, a man walked into Glasgow Central Police Station. He gave his name as Joseph Barrett, his age as forty-five, said that he was of no fixed address, and told Lieutenant James Mulherrin, the officer in charge, that he wanted to confess that he had murdered Alfred Oliver.

Mulherrin was, naturally, very surprised, and at first assumed that the man was mentally unbalanced. He soon realized, though, that, whatever his mental condition, Barrett was in earnest, and that mental trouble does not stop people from committing murder. So he

summoned members of the Glasgow C.I.D., who took Barrett off
to the C.I.D. office. There, he was examined by the police surgeon,
Dr Walter Weir Galbraith, who could find no evidence of mental
abnormality. Barrett then proceeded, in a calm and collected manner, to dictate a long statement which filled several foolscap pages.
He was, he said, a tic-tac man, and his occupation took him to
racecourses in all parts of the country during the summer. On June
21st, 1929, he had been at Kingston-on-Thames in company with
two men, Ernie Carter and James McGuire. Carter he described
as a hairdresser living at Reading. McGuire, he said, was a tic-tac
man. After drinking together they parted, but not before they had
arranged to meet next day at Reading. Barrett said that he spent
that night at Ewell, leaving there at about 5 A.M. on June 22nd,
and reaching Reading between 6.30 and 7 A.M. At Reading he
spoke to a policeman with a view to finding Carter's address. He
also picked up a spike or iron bolt on a railway siding, and carried
it with him. He duly met Carter and McGuire, and the latter told
him that Mr Oliver kept about £50 or £60 in a drawer below the
counter of his shop. Barrett went on to describe how he had entered
the tobacconist's, hit Mr Oliver over the head with the iron bolt,
taken a few pounds and some silver from the till, and then run off,
wiping the blood from his hands with a handkerchief, which he
afterwards threw away, along with the iron bolt, on some allotments. He then caught a bus to London, to King's Cross, where
he had arranged to meet McGuire. He gave McGuire some of the
money, stayed the night with Darby Sabini,[1] later went to Liverpool, and from there to Glasgow, staying in lodging-houses.

Having signed this statement, Barrett was formally charged with
murder. The Glasgow police then telephoned to Chief Constable
Burrows, who telephoned Inspector Berrett, and also ordered that
at daybreak a search should be made on the allotments adjoining
the Sutton Trial Seed Grounds, which were situated beside the
main Reading–London road, along which the bus route to King's
Cross passed.

On the Monday morning Barrett made a brief appearance before
Mr George Smith, the stipendiary magistrate, at the Glasgow
Central Police Court, and was remanded until the Wednesday.

[1] The notorious race-gang boss who, with his brothers, Harry and
Joseph, led the Sabini Mob. He died, aged 62, at Hove, in the odour of
respectability, in October 1950.

Back in Reading the search on the allotments had resulted in the finding of an iron bolt bearing the initials G.W.R., and, in a tank of water close by, was a piece of white rag, such as might have been used as a handkerchief. It was stained with what looked like blood.[1]

In addition to this, it was established that the man Carter, known in Reading as the "Mad Barber", had indeed been in the near vicinity of the scene of the crime at about 5.30 P.M. on the evening of the murder.

Having found all this apparent corroboration of Barrett's story, Chief Constable Burrows lost no time in going along to Scotland Yard, where, after consulting with Inspector Berrett, it was decided that Burrows, accompanied by Sergeant Harris, should catch the 1.30 P.M. train to Glasgow.

On their arrival there, soon after 10 P.M., they went at once to the Central Police Station, where they were informed that Barrett had now been identified as Philip Joseph Dickens, who lived with his wife and son at 18 Bankhall Street, Govan, Glasgow.

Mrs Dickens was seen that night, and made a statement. She said that she and Dickens had been married for twenty-four years. He had joined the Army a week after war broke out, and had served until he was discharged in 1919, in consequence of injuries sustained when he was buried by a shell-burst on the Somme in 1916. When he came home he was a bundle of nerves. Although he had spent several prolonged periods in hospitals and institutions, he had not, since March 1929, been away from home any night, except for a week's holiday in September.

This statement was supported by the couple's twenty-year-old son, Joseph Dickens, and both he and his mother said that Dickens was all right until he drank whisky, adding that he had been drinking since the Wednesday—October 23rd. He had left home on Sunday morning, October 27th, and had not been back since.

Burrows and Harris held a conference with Chief Constable Smith of Glasgow and Detective Superintendent Forbes, head of the Glasgow C.I.D., on the morning of Tuesday, October 29th, at which it was agreed that Dickens should go back with them to Reading.

Early next morning Inspector Berrett travelled to Reading and

[1] All this turned out to be mere coincidence. In fact, two more iron bolts were later discovered on the same allotments. The Great Western Railway line was only about a quarter of a mile away.

interviewed Dickens, who repudiated all that he had previously said. He told the Inspector that he was an engineer, but had had no regular work since 1924. He said that he suffered from 'confusional psychosis', and had a military pension of thirty shillings a week. On October 23rd he had heard voices accusing him of the Reading murder. Ernie Carter and James McGuire had both been fellow-patients in Ewell Hospital with him. He had seen neither of them since 1926.

Berrett decided that Dickens was obviously in a very bad state, and was convinced that he had had no connection whatsoever with the killing of Alfred Oliver. A number of inquiries were put in train, and the results amply confirmed Berrett's belief in Dickens' entire innocence.

So, in the end, this most promising 'new avenue' also crumbled into a farrago of tragic delusions and extraordinary coincidences.

There was one more coincidence, too. On that same Sunday, October 27th, another ex-inmate of Ewell Hospital, one Joseph Cassidy, walked into another police-station—at Blackheath Road, London—and accused himself of the murder of Alfred Oliver. And he, too, proved on investigation to be the completely innocent victim of morbid self-deception.

(3)

While the police were diligently picking their way through an abortive maze of new avenues, Philip Yale Drew was valiantly picking up the threads of his old life.

On Monday, October 21st, he made his first post-inquest appearance on the stage. In fact, he made five; two at the early and late houses at the Empress Theatre, Brixton,[1] and three at the Croydon Hippodrome,[2] alternating between the two theatres from the matinée onward.

Mr and Mrs Lindo accompanied him on to the stage, Mrs Lindo nursing her little black dog, Pip, in her arms. Frank Lindo made a short introductory speech, in which he emphasized that the appearance was not a stunt performance, but a means of thanking the public for their sympathy, which had been accorded to Mr

[1] Where Sam Mayo's revue, *The Calcutta Sweep*, was being presented.
[2] The programme there consisted of two films, *The Last Warning* and *Kid Gloves*.

Drew, Mrs Lindo and himself in their trying time. They were, he said, appearing in their ordinary capacity as actors and actresses.

Drew, still wearing the horseshoe mascot that he had had in his buttonhole at the inquest, then stepped forward. He was nervous. His hands clenched and unclenched. He wiped them with a handkerchief which he pulled out from the sleeve of his dinner-jacket. He thanked the audience for their applause, and referred to Mr and Mrs Lindo as "the staunchest friends that any man could ever have. They have stuck to me through thick and thin in my darkest hours." He then enumerated the many plays he had been in, and went on to recite "*The Ol' Cow-Hawse*," after which he delivered a dramatic monologue describing his feelings and experiences from the time when he was first seen by the police in Nottingham to his 'acquittal' at Reading. He told of his interrogation by Scotland Yard detectives, his ordeal at the inquest, and how after the jury's verdict he went back to his hotel, and, behind the locked doors of his room, went down on his knees and thanked God that he was a free man. "Although I am an American subject, I never for one moment doubted or felt uneasy over the ultimate result. I knew I was safe, and could rely on good old British justice. Can you conceive," he asked, "the sensation of knowing you are free?" He concluded by saying, "Good night—and God bless you all."

Writing in the *Daily Express* of the following morning, the paper's 'Special Representative' commented: "I have been sorry for Mr Drew. His experiences at Reading were obviously torture to him—as they would have been to anyone similarly placed. I am no longer sorry for him as I was for the Mr Drew of that Reading time. He was a different person on the stage last night. He was, to speak as frankly as he did himself, an actor commercializing—and he had a perfect right to do so—a tragedy which affected his private life. He recited a poem, and recited it well. He delivered a monologue. It was a good, dramatic monologue, excellently declaimed. The audience applauded, but Brixton was not hysterical like Reading."

After this trial run, Drew opened at the Bristol Empire, playing his old part in *The Monster*. He arrived in the town on Sunday, November 3rd, at 12.35 P.M., and although his train was twenty minutes late he found a crowd of nearly two thousand waiting to greet him. No sooner did he appear on the platform than he was practically swept off his feet by the surge of people anxious to shake him by the hand or clap him on the back, and hundreds of shop and factory girls swooped on him, thrusting autograph albums under his nose. Overwhelmed, he promised that he would be available daily in the foyer of the Empire to give signatures, at a charge of from threepence upwards for the benefit of the local hospital funds, and made his escape.

That Sunday's *Empire News* contained a hard-hitting article by Bernard O'Donnell, demanding further information as to whether any fresh inquiries were being made to trace the author of the Leeds letter. "I happen to know," he wrote, "that the police suspected me of writing this letter by way of a journalistic stunt, and on this account it may be that they attached even less importance to it. I can only declare on my oath that I had nothing whatever to do with the writing of that letter, and that Mrs Lindo did in fact receive that letter in an envelope bearing a Leeds postmark on the morning of the 11th October. The obvious course for the Yard to have taken was the same course which was taken in reference to the tracing of the green tab on the mystery blue serge trousers. Ask that the Press throughout the land should publish a facsimile of the letter inviting the writer to go to the nearest police station where she would be afforded adequate protection against any possible reprisals, and no other offences in which she might have been concerned mentioned. If this course had been taken, and this wholesale publicity had been given to the letter, it might well have been that information of tremendous importance would by this time be in the possession of the police. It is dangerous to ignore any piece of possible evidence in an inquiry of this sort. I am also in a position to state that most important evidence has been laid before chief Inspector Berrett by a London man who has placed in the hands of the Yard the written statement of a man who said that he knew who had done the murder. This man's name is known to the Yard, and it is possible that investigations will produce the most startling developments in the near future."

By the week of November 11th–16th Drew was back in London, doing *The Monster* at the Bedford, Camden Town. The *Daily Express* reported: "The production shows that it would have been a failure if brought back to the West End. Mr Drew is signing autographs for 3*d*. each from noon till one every day, in aid of the local Christmas treat for children. In the foyer there are photographs showing the crowds at Reading, and others of the ovation Drew received at Bristol last week."

The last two weeks of that month saw *The Monster* being played at the Hammersmith Palace (November 18th–23rd) and the Islington Empire (November 25th–30th).

(4)

December.
Tuesday the 17th.
Christmas eight days away.
Drew and *The Monster* are in Scarborough.
A poignant letter has reached the *Daily Mail*. The editor, to whom it is addressed, prints it.

> *98 Hamilton Road,*
> *Reading.*

Sir,

Will you of your courtesy grant me space in your paper to make an appeal to anyone who is able to give information that may lead to the arrest of the murderer of my husband, Alfred Oliver, to do so?

Surely someone knows who did it, and will not that one now show me the pity up to now shown to the murderer by shielding him?

Think. The bells will soon be ringing in Christmas. The choirs will be singing their carols, and last year my husband and I listened together, thanking God for the gift of His dear son and for each other.

This year I am alone, with a battered face for memory.

I think if the murderer or his confederates do not confess their Christmas will be as hopeless as mine, and perhaps the bells will torture them as they will torture me.

ANNIE E. OLIVER

A *Daily Mail* Special Correspondent went along that day to see Mrs Oliver's sister-in-law. She told him: "Mrs Oliver is feeling her grief today as much as she did when she found her husband battered and dying in the shop that was their home. She has not cried from that first moment when she found him. Her grief rises above tears. I have looked at her and wondered why her mind does not fail—but her determination to live to see justice done is such that she keeps her mind clear and unfaltering. She has never given up hope that justice will prevail. Sometimes she goes alone to the chief police-station here. They meet her with kindness, but they have to tell her that they have no message for her. They are still seeking the murderer, they say. But there is little progress to report. She does not come back entirely crushed by what seems at times to be the hopelessness of it. She just works on without tears or breakdown."

And, finally, on December 17th, Inspector Berrett, at Scotland Yard, wearily reports: "There are no fresh developments to the case".

December 20th. Friday. Drew's week at the Opera House, Scarborough, is drawing to its close. That night a bombshell explodes backstage. Mr and Mrs Lindo tell him that they are leaving the cast of *The Monster*. He is staggered. Hurt. Puzzled. But violently loyal. All that he would say to a probing reporter was, "We have parted just the same as we have parted many times before. There is no difference of opinion as far as I am aware. I believe they have another play in hand, and have left me to carry on with *The Monster*". Then he packed his hamper and caught the meandering Sunday train to Dunfermline.

There, December 23rd–28th, at the Opera House, Reform Street, he played *The Monster*, the Lindos' parts being taken by their understudies.

The second week in January found him at the Empire, Preston, still working with understudies. The show must go on.

On January 10th, 1930, Mrs Lindo sailed for South Africa in the *Windsor Castle* with her daughter, Olga, whose company was to tour a repertoire of *Her Past*, *The Stranger Within*, *The Patsy*, and Pinero's *The Private Room*, there.

Mr Lindo told a *Star* reporter that he would not be accompanying his wife and daughter. "After forty years of touring the country I feel I want a rest," he said, adding that he intended to take up dramatic recital.

Drew, at the Empire, Preston, reading the news of Mrs Lindo's departure, realized that she had finally severed her connection with him, and that he was now desperately in need of a new leading lady.

He was soon to find her.

Her name—*nom d'art*—borrowed with unconscious aptness from Swinburne's poetic *belle dame*, was Dolores.

> *What shall rest of thee then, what remain,*
> *O mystic and sombre Dolores,*
> *Our Lady of Pain?*

Poor Dolores, she was indeed a "lady of pain".

Born, on March 11th, 1894, Norine Fournier Schofield, in fairly humble circumstances at 23 Doughty Street, London, her only assets were a beautiful face and a classically lovely, lithe, and slim body. Her father, George Edwin Schofield, was a Lancashire man—from Ashton-under-Lyne—who had had a very varied career. He had been a professional dancer, had sung in grand opera, and was said to have financed several theatrical productions. Her mother, half French and half Spanish, was the Vicomtesse Marie Honorine Melfredine de Fournier, and Dolores' baptismal name, Norine, was a diminutive of Honorine.

As a child, Dolores attended Tiller's Dancing School, where a fellow-pupil was Gaby Deslys. Dolores did well, and appeared as an eleven-year-old juvenile in various shows for John Tiller. After leaving the Tiller Troupe she went to Paris, to *L'Opéra Comique*, under Mme Mariquita, the celebrated ballet-mistress, and met Sarah Bernhardt—"Sarah Bernhardt gave me a bunch of violets, which I clasped in my hand that night when I went to bed. They were dead in the morning, and I cried my heart out." Later, she appeared in the *Folies Bergères* for André Charlot, and with Adolph Bolm at the Théâtre Royal de la Monnaie, in Brussels. It was there, at a command performance, that she danced before the German Kaiser. He afterwards received her in the royal box, thanked her for her beautiful performance, and presented her with a gold powder-box. She danced with Pavlova, and with Bolm again at the Alhambra. She also appeared—as a Russian—on the opening night of the Victoria Palace.[1] She sang in opera on the Continent, and is said to have given a notable performance in *Ivan the Terrible*. She toured the whole of the Stoll and McNaughton circuits in a sketch entitled *Harlequin's Lover*.

After years of drudgery—albeit much of it well paid—her moment

[1] November 6th, 1911.

of fame came when, in 1920, Jacob Epstein, artistically attracted by her physical enticements, chose her as his model. He saw her sitting one spring day in the Café Royal, walked straight over to her, and asked, "Will you be my model?" Without hesitation, she replied, "Yes".

Epstein captured all of her brooding, coiled-spring vitality and tragic beauty—which even then was on the wing—stayed its flight, and preserved it for all time in bronze.

But flesh and blood are less durable material, and Dolores, caught up in the punishing Bohemian fringe of the old Café Royal society, was playing the game of life too hard. Soon the inevitable forfeits began to show themselves—those hard little lines around the mouth; the weariness behind the sparkle in eyes that have looked too much and stayed awake too long too often; that drying and shrinking of the plump and supple skin of cheeks and neck. Those melancholy grey eyes, that beautiful pale face, deep and still, framed by raven-black hair and set upon a neck firm as a pillar of marble—they were being altered only too swiftly by the dissolving alchemy of time.

> *Fruits fail and love dies and time ranges;*
> *Thou art fed with perpetual breath,*
> *And alive after infinite changes,*
> *And fresh from the kisses of death.*

Craving affection, she sought it—in all the wrong places. A dedicated daughter of joy already clearly bespoke by sorrow, she was determinedly gay with a gaiety that always skimmed the hysterical edge of despair. She was up or down in a trice, for ever on the verge of the most wonderful experience in the whole of the universe, or, bleakly, waving a tear-stained farewell to all the joy of life.

At twenty-one she had married an Army officer, Second-Lieutenant William Frank Amsden, at St Pancras Roman Catholic Church. Naturally, it proved a mistake.

Characteristically, she tried again at twenty-four. This time she chose Richard Harry Farwell Peckover Sadler. They were married at Kensington in 1918, and divorced in 1924. Another mistake.

And yet again, at thirty-one, she married. Her third husband was a coloured gentleman, George William Lattimore, an American film and theatrical producer. By this marriage she lost her British nationality . . . and gained no lasting happiness. The couple were never divorced, but they had not been married two months when Mr Lattimore decamped. She never saw him again.

Three times unlucky—marriage, it seemed, was not for her. Henceforth she settled for the unsatisfactory romantic substitute of frenetic, short-lived affairs. And, as it was her custom to surround all her activities with a blaze of secrecy, she rapidly achieved wide notoriety as a scarlet woman. It was a reputation not strictly merited. She was not really a *femme fatale*, just, behind all the surface sophistication, the Chelsea *chic*, a naïve, generous, and love-hungry woman-child, who never grew up emotionally.

This immaturity of hers was tragic not only for herself, but for others, too. Most tragic of all for a young man named Frederick Atkinson.

Atkinson, the artistically talented and inward-turning son of a Rotherham miner, always wanted to paint, to be an artist. He left school at fourteen, and, for a time, worked down the pit in his native Yorkshire, saving every penny he could scratch together. Then, in March 1926, with fifty shillings in his pocket, a small parcel containing his painting materials under his arm, and a cloth cap on his head, this young man came to London. He brought with him, too, considerable artistic ability and high hopes. He found . . . disappointment, disillusion, Dolores, and death.

It was in October 1928, in the studio of a fellow-artist—where she was posing for a picture in the nude—that he first met Dolores, and promptly fell in love with her. They began to spend a great deal of time together. He painted portraits of her and wrote sheaves of love poems to her. He took her out and bought her expensive dinners, lavished jewellery, clothes, and other gifts that he could ill afford upon her, all paid for with reckless disregard for his slender and fast-diminishing capital of savings. In the end, he ran into debt, owed his rent, was unable to go on sending home the money that he used to give his parents from the sale of his pictures, and became agonizingly worried. Then, suddenly, there came the realization that Dolores, fond of him and kind to him though she was, could never return his love.

And so, some time in the dark hours of the night of January 2nd–3rd, 1929, the twenty-year-old youth, despairing, embittered, lonely, locked himself in his studio in Blomfield Road, Maida Vale, lay down upon the floor, wrapped his head carefully in an eiderdown quilt, placed a rubber tube in his mouth, and turned on the gas.

He went back—a corpse—to Rotherham in the old green motor-van that used to take his pictures to the galleries; back to the little house in Lindley Street from which he had set out three years before so full of hope, and was buried in Haugh Lane Cemetery, after a service in the Parkgate Spiritualist Temple.

The inquest was held by Mr Henry Robert Oswald, at Paddington on January 7th, and in the course of it some harsh things were said of Dolores, who was not present.

When she was seen by reporters in the small, barely furnished, attic room of the drab house in Pelham Street, South Kensington, where she was living, she spoke of her association with the dead artist. Dressed entirely in black, a black veil over her head, Dolores wept nearly the whole time she was speaking. She was wearing in a little leather purse around her neck what she described as the most cherished treasure in her possession. It was Atkinson's love poem to her beginning, "O Dolores, fatal one".

"I thought," she said, "he was only a young and simple fellow who was smitten with calf-love. I think now that he really did love me. If only I could communicate with him tonight, just to tell him how much I value his love. I am a spiritualist. My father is a confirmed spiritualist. Atkinson, too, was a spiritualist, and in this way we had much in common. Soon I am going to get him to come back and make people realize that the genius which was his still lives—lives more than ever it did before. Atkinson is more to me now than he was before his death. I feel he is all around me wherever I go, and that thought comforts me."

> *Did he lie? did he laugh? does he know it,*
> *Now he lies out of reach, out of breath,*
> *Thy prophet, thy preacher, thy poet,*
> *Sin's child by incestuous Death? . . .*

> *Wilt thou smile as a woman disdaining*
> *The light fire in the veins of a boy?*
> *But he comes to thee sad, without feigning,*
> *Who has wearied of sorrow and joy . . .*

A few days later Dolores collapsed in the dance-room of a West End night-club. She was in straitened circumstances. Her clothes were old and bedraggled, she had gone hungry, and, having had to leave Pelham Street, lacked the means to find a bed. She had all her worldly wealth—eight shillings—in her purse.

On January 23rd, a *Daily Mail* reporter interviewed her. She was lying in an old-fashioned, iron-railed bed in a sparsely furnished, gas-lit room in the Fulham Road. Her emerald-green silk dressing-jacket and the blue net boudoir cap round her black hair were pathetic in contrast to her surroundings. She was suffering from bronchial pneumonia and pleurisy, coughing painfully and moving restlessly on her pillow. And yet even in these unlikely circumstances she had dignity: somehow every unconscious pose of Dolores' was a thing of marvellous grace.

Dolores had always rather fancied herself as an actress,[1] and it was in this rôle that she was to play a brief part in the life drama of Philip Yale Drew. Their paths ran stormily together for a few months, then forked, before converging to an oddly similar end.

It was four years after she and Philip had separated that Dolores died, of cancer. Her last days were made bitter by the pinchings of severe poverty.

In November 1931, Dolores was living in Meard Street, London, W.1. In July 1932, she was reported to be lying dangerously ill in a nursing-home in Dorset Square, N.W.1. In January 1933, she was occupying a dank little basement room in a narrow court behind Oxford Street. And there is a quality of sheer Dickensian horror in the fact that while the growth that was so soon to kill her was eating into her ravaged body, she was exhibiting herself, fasting in a barrel—Roll up! Roll up! See Epstein's Famous Model, Dolores, in the Flesh!—in a booth set up by a showman in a fun-fair amid the desolate northern marches of the Tottenham Court Road.

In October 1933, the *Daily Mail* reported an interview with her

---

[1] After her careers as a dancer and an artist's model, Dolores turned to the stage. In 1922–23 she appeared in *The Nine O'Clock Review*, at the the Little Theatre, John Adam Street, Adelphi, and in 1923–24 in its successor, *The Little Review*, in which she was in a sketch called "The Empty Easel". Her part was a non-speaking one, entailing no more than the striking of a number of poses in *tableaux vivants* representing famous pictures. In 1926 she was in the short-lived *Riki-Tiki* at the Gaiety, and she later appeared at the Prince of Wales. This was followed by a spell as a dancer once more, doing the halls in a double turn with a partner. In February 1929 she was at the Pavilion Theatre, a twice-nightly house in a working-class district of Leicester, acting in a somewhat full-blooded murder melodrama, *By Whose Hand?*, by Herbert Darnley. She was still touring with this production in the July and August of that year, when she was at Mexborough, and at the Theatre Royal, Sheffield.

in "A Town in Yorkshire", in the course of which she said: "A few days ago the doctors who have been attending me in a nursing home came here and told me that I could not expect to live beyond April".

They were wrong—by three months.

Shortly before she died, Dolores told a friend: "A few days ago I was sentenced to death. The doctors tried to hide it from me, but I insisted on knowing the truth. 'Are you brave?' they asked, and I said, 'Yes, I am.' But, of course, I realized the truth then. They need say no more, but I let the doctor who was speaking go on. I have wondered how a doctor approached the passing of life. Perhaps he was wondering how I would take the news he had to break to me. 'Well, you certainly have plenty of pluck, Dolores,' he said, 'and you are shortly leaving this world. Be prepared. Don't be frightened; get all you can out of these last few'—and he hesitated. 'Weeks, or months, or years?' I asked. 'Let me have the whole truth.' And he told me it would be a question of a few more days. I had hoped for a little longer respite than that. I asked him if it would be painful, would this growth hurt me very much. 'It can't hurt you, Dolores; your body never hurts you; you only hurt yourself by thinking about it. Control your thoughts, and let them dwell only on pleasant things. There has been much in your life that has been pleasant and happy, so reflect on that.' My first reflections were that I had got a good deal out of life. Now my life has no future I wondered how I could help others. So I told my doctors that they could make any experiment on me that they liked. . . . To be frank, I do not now view this passing from life with any misgivings, nor have I many regrets. Now in my passing I am sure I am going to find that great beauty and idealism which all great artists strive so earnestly to create in this life. I am leaving a drab world, occasionally brightened by great artists, for a sphere of idealism and beauty. I feel that, and that is why I am preparing for the passing. I will not hasten the passing—nor will I lengthen it. I am ready."

She died, brave and gay to the last, a single pound in her purse, in St Mary Abbott's Hospital, Marloes Road, Kensington, on August 7th, 1934. Aged forty-two. Burnt out.

They buried her in a public grave (No. 90 c. G.) in a corner of St Mary's Roman Catholic Cemetery, at Kensal Green. There were only four mourners. Philip Yale Drew was not one of them.

> *Dost thou dream of what was and no more is,*
> *The old kingdoms of earth and the kings?*
> *Dost thou hunger for these things, Dolores,*
> *For these, in a world of new things?*

This, then, was the woman, who, early in 1930, entered Philip Yale Drew's life. His new leading lady.

(6)

Dolores joined the cast of *The Monster* at the Theatre Royal, Hanley, on Monday, February 3rd, 1930. She had been offered Mrs Lindo's old part—Julie Carter—by J. Bannister Howard, who had taken *The Monster* over, and she had also signed a contract to appear under Howard's banner with Philip Yale Drew in a new drama by Adelaine Foster and Bernard O'Donnell, *The Thirteenth Hour*. The plot, which was said to bear in parts a certain similarity to incidents in the Reading inquest, concerned a suspected murderess (Dolores), who is subjected to a terrible third-degree ordeal by a detective (Drew).

Before her arrival at Hanley, Dolores had told newspaper reporters: "Mr Drew and I feel that we shall be able to pull well. We both think we have been badly treated. I think it will be a wonderful opportunity. We are temperamentally suited to each other."

And on February 6th, Philip sent a postcard to Aunt Abbie: "I have a new leading woman, a great French actress, Epstein's greatest model—Dolores. We hope to do big things together, she is simply *glorious*."

But *The Thirteenth Hour* ran into troubles. In fact, it never struck. It was to have been produced at the Opera House at Dudley, in Worcestershire, on February 10th, but the opening was postponed to February 17th, when it was scheduled to take place at West Bromwich. It did not. A rift had occurred between the backers of the play, one of whom had promised financial support, and unexpectedly withdrawn his promise. On February 23rd a writ was issued, and a claim was said to be pending in respect of £250 spent on preparations for the play, which had been extensively rehearsed, and for which a considerable amount of scenery had been constructed. "Its production", said the *Star* of February 24th, "has been dropped for the time being."

The following day's *Daily News*, however, was more optimistic. "The play will be produced," it announced, "at Reading during the week beginning March 31st."

This fairly put the cat among the pigeons.

The very next morning Mrs Oliver called at Scotland Yard and told Inspector Berrett that she was very upset to read that Drew was likely to appear again in Reading. She said that friends had told her that she ought to get her brother to thrash him. Berrett advised her to tell her brother that he must do nothing of the sort, and said that it would be in the interests of all concerned if she were simply to ignore Drew's presence in the town.

The Reading Watch Committee were also aghast at the prospect of Drew's reappearance, and the Town Clerk promptly wrote off to the Lord Chamberlain—who had already licensed *The Thirteenth Hour*—asking whether he had any power under the Act of 1843 to prohibit the acting of the play on the ground that it might lead to a breach of the peace. He was advised that the Lord Chamberlain had no such power.

Mr Milton Bode, the proprietor of the Royal County Theatre, said that, according to present booking arrangements, Drew and Dolores would definitely be visiting Reading, if not in *The Thirteenth Hour*, then in another play.

As it turned out, they need not have worried. *The Thirteenth Hour* never saw curtain-rise, and well before March 31st Philip Yale Drew had given his last performance but one on any stage.

While all this kerfuffle was going on, Dolores and Drew were still playing *The Monster*. The tour ended at the King's Hall Theatre, Dover, on March 1st.

Five days later a small paragraph appeared in the *Daily Mail*:

DOLORES ENGAGED TO MR DREW

Dolores told a *Daily Mail* reporter last night that the wedding will take place in London probably within the next few days. With a smile at Mr. Drew, she continued: 'I adore him. He is the most wonderful man I have ever met. I fell in love with him almost to desperation when I first saw him playing the part of the tramp in *The Monster*. I adored his long whiskers, his dirty clothes, and his ragged boots, and when we finished the play at Dover last week and he threw some of his dirty rags in a corner, I went outside on to the stage and wept all to myself. I am certain we are going to be wonderfully happy.' 'I think Dolores is the most wonderful woman I have ever met,' Mr. Drew said. 'She has a great big heart. She is as temperamental as a leaf in a wind.'

This announcement brought something other than congratulations to the happy couple. Saturday's *Daily Mail* contained this unwelcome corollary:

The *Daily Mail* yesterday (March 7th) received the following letter concerning Mr Philip Drew and Dolores:

To the Editor of the *Daily Mail*

SIR,

Reading my *Daily Mail* this morning I came across an article 'Dolores and Mr. Drew.' I am greatly concerned in Mr. Drew's whereabouts, he and Dolores having stayed at my house last week.

My wife keeps a professional boarding-house situate as below, and Mr. Drew engaged five rooms for the week commencing February 23rd for their two selves and his man and Dolores's maid.

Upon arrival they informed us that as they had just recently got married to each other and they were making this their honeymoon they would only require one bedroom for their two selves. They ran up a bill of £8 7s. and went away suddenly on Sunday morning.

A few minutes previously they called up my wife and stated they had been robbed at the theatre during their week's performance at the King's Hall Theatre, Dover, and had not sufficient money—only enough to take them to London. Mr. Drew promised that he would wire the money (£8 7s.) on the next day, Monday, as soon as his bank was opened, but up to the present moment we have not heard of or from them or received any money.

We, my wife and self, unfortunately are poor people and depend on our boarding-house for our living. I am out of employment through old age and illness.

Can you assist us in any way as to their address and as to procedure to recover this money?

GEO. MATON

Marine House,
35 Liverpool Street,
Dover.
March 6

A reporter had been immediately sent to interview Dolores and

Drew. He found them living as Mr and Mrs Drew at 35 Devonshire Street, Islington.[1]

His report, headed "I HAD NO IDEA—Dolores's Statement", was printed below Mr Maton's letter:

A young woman—who was afterwards described by Dolores as her maid—said that Mr. Drew was out, but Mrs. Drew was in. Dolores was surprised when she read a copy of Mr. Maton's letter, but she did not deny any part of it. 'There is no need for you to see Mr. Drew,' she said. 'He is in such a highly strung state that this shock would put him in bed for a week or two. I am doing all the business and I will settle this myself. I had no idea the bill was not settled. I will send a cheque off immediately.' Dolores read the letter carefully again, and then said mysteriously, 'This must be the valet. He has been sacked. It is quite true,' added Dolores, 'that we were robbed of our money at Dover. Several members of the *Monster* company were also robbed, but we said nothing, as we did not want to appear to blame anyone who was with the show.' Dolores would say no more, declaring that the letter was a private one. 'Mr. Maton could have found our address,' she concluded, 'for we are aliens and have to register at the Aliens Department.'

The end of the affair was duly recorded in the *Daily Mail* of March 12th:

Mrs. George Maton, a letter from whose husband was published in the *Daily Mail* on Saturday, received the following letter yesterday from Dolores, once famous as an artist's model, addressed from a house in Devonshire Street, Islington:

'Dear Madam,
Herewith I send you money order for £8 7s in payment of hire of rooms etc.

Yours, etc.,
DOLORES.'

[1] The house still stands, a three-storey, somewhat dilapidated Victorian property now known as 35 Devonia Road. In March 1930 it was owned by Frederick David Mann, and was divided into three flats. Joseph and Ada Coleman occupied the top storey. William and Florence L. Davidson the first floor. And Frederick David Mann, Beatrice Mann, and Frederick David Mann (junior) were the tenants of the ground-floor and basement. In 1968 I found Mrs Davidson still living there. She remembered Dolores and Drew, and told me that Mrs Mann used to let rooms from time to time to theatricals from Collins' Music Hall, and it was she who let the ground-floor front to Dolores and Drew.

No sooner was that little *contretemps* behind them than another small squall blew up. On March 27th, Dolores appeared before Mr Theodore Wilfred Fry at Bow Street Police Court, on a summons under the Aliens Act, charged with having failed as an alien to notify a change in her address. She arrived in a taxicab with Drew, and they sat together in the well of the court until her case was called. The magistrate accepted her apology and fined her one guinea.

(7)

During the next three months the couple's financial—and emotional—situation steadily deteriorated. The honeymoon period was over, and with poverty at the door love made a decided move towards the window. It had been a strange mating from the first. An odd alliance. There were fifteen years between them. He was an ageing drunk of fifty. She was a fading beauty of thirty-five. Dolores, it seems, made the running. Drew was really more interested in drink than in women. Their destinies crossed. Their lives intertwined for a little time. It was ill-starred from the start. They were both in love with the idea of being in love, rather than with each other. Fate had brought them together, and, theatrically, they conceived the romantic notion of carrying their union over beyond the footlights. But when the floats went out, this new-found romance was also soon extinguished, this *folie à deux* foundered. It ran its ten months' course through what seedy rooming-houses, threadbare boudoirs, and ups and downs of drunken rows and maudlin peace-makings, until neither could sustain the pretence any longer, and, without bitterness, without regret—or joy—they simply parted. No bang. No whimper.

On the afternoon of April 19th, 1930, Drew sat in Islington Post Office and scribbled an article. He called it, "A Leaf From Life After Midnight".

> It was cold—d—— cold. A bitter cruel winter's night. Behind me I had left the bright lights of Leicester Square. Fingering a few odd coppers in my pocket one—a small one—surely a sixpence, I thought. Then, under the brilliant lights of the Coliseum, I discovered it to be —a farthing. I laughed aloud.
>
> I wonder why I remember such things. I wandered into St Martins in the Fields. Here is shelter, I thought. Here is rest for the soul. Here

In Post Office Islington
London N.1
april 19th 1930

<u>A</u> LEAF FROM LIFE By Philip Gale Drew
"AFTER MIDNIGHT"

It was cold - I — cold.
a bitter cruel winters
night - Behind me I
had left the bright ~~lights~~
lights of Leicester Square—
fingering a few odd
coppers in my pocket—
one - a small one—
surely a sixpence I
thought — then under
the brilliant lights of the
Collisium & discovered
it to be a farthing — I
laughed aloud —
 & wonder why I re—
— member such things
 I wandered into "Saint
martins in the Feild"—
here is shelter I thought—
here is rest for the soul.

Facsimile of Part of Drew's 'Life after midnight' Article

may one escape from chill winds, sleet and blinding rain; broken boots may be dried. How long I knelt and prayed I do not know.

I am on the street again. The storm has ceased. The moon is riding high. By her bright beams I stumble down the steps. The lions in Trafalgar Square seem to greet me, and as Big Ben booms out the hour of two, I am conscious of a few stragglers passing by. And as they reach up with well-gloved hands and snuggle 'neath their huge fur-lined collars, so do I instinctively, with red and cracked chapped hands, reach for my ragged collar, and gazing up, as clouds apart do drift, the moon peeps forth, and silhouetted against its face Nelson's head and shoulders are, aye with hand upon his sword.

Again the coppers jingle. I know a coffee-stall nearby. Not long ago I halted there with pockets lined with treasury notes. But not so this morn.

Wearily I wander toward the Embankment. The lights flicker from across the Thames. A late tramcar crawls over Westminster Bridge. Another, far away, over Waterloo. Big Ben tells me 'tis four o'clock. Here and there recumbent figures stir in the shadows on the benches. I lean upon the parapet and gaze at the dark waters flowing swiftly by. No, they are ebbing. 'We are on our way to the sea,' they say. Lap, lap, lap against the wall. 'Come! Come!! Come!!!' they call. Another tram on the bridge, and as its wheels touch the divided rails, it echoes back, 'Come! Come!! Come!!!'

'Hold on, mate. Don't do that.' A firm hand is grasping my arm. Already one leg is over the parapet. A million miles away my voice says, 'Leave me alone, d—— you. This is my affair.' And then—a tug. I'm on my feet. A voice, hard but kindly, says, 'Come with me.'

Again, a coffee-stall. God, but that's hot. Thanks, brother. Who are you?

Clang! Clang!! CLANG!!!

I say, who are you brother?

Fact? Imagination? An actor's truth? Certainly the poverty was not imaginary. It is just that—at this stage, anyway—Drew was stripping a few shades too close to the buff. In April 1930 the nadir had not yet been reached.

(8)

By July, Dolores and Drew had left Devonshire Street and had moved together into lodgings above a tobacconist's, Winkoskie and White's, at 202 King's Road, Chelsea.

We have the odd fugitive glimpse of them at this period—"One day I met Drew walking with Dolores near Markham Square," writes a correspondent. "He was smoking a cigar and bemoaning the fact that the Six Bells had refused to serve him."

At 3.30 P.M. on July 14th, Drew, desperate for money, called at Scotland Yard and asked Berrett if he could have returned to him the small sum which had been found in the pocket of his blue trousers when they reappeared at St Albans. He was, he said, in a bad way, and in want of food. Berrett told him that it was still in the possession of the Reading police, and advised him to write to Chief Constable Burrows, which he did that same evening, mentioning in his letter, also, that he would like to know what compensation he might expect for his blue suit.

A day or two later he wrote to the *Daily Express*.

This letter was provoked by a series of articles on unsolved murders which had been appearing in the *Daily Express*, and by an item written by that paper's crime reporter on July 17th.

"One of the most noticeable effects of the findings of the Royal Commission on Police Powers and Procedures," wrote the *Express* crime man, "is that there is now a growing tendency on the part of the police to shirk vital decisions in murder cases, and to pass on the responsibility to the coroner and his jury. This is what was done in the Reading shop murder. Mr. T. A. Burrows does not go so far as to blame the royal commission for the police failure in this case, but he does say that the royal commission has made the work of the police more difficult. 'I am quite sure that witnesses are holding back information,' he said to me. 'The royal commission has had the effect of making it much harder to obtain statements. I know of one person in Reading who, I believe, is keeping something back, but I am powerless to do anything in the matter. I feel certain that, if everybody told me all they knew, we should be able to clear up the crime'."

Drew's letter was published on July 19th.

To the Editor of the *Daily Express*

SIR,

If there is a witness who can clear up this mystery of the Reading shop murder, why does he, or she, lurk in the background? Let those witnesses speak out and save a man from the hell which comes from suggestion and inference.

At the moment I have nothing more—in worldly possessions—than the clothes I wear. I have no money; I have no work, simply and solely because I am Philip Yale Drew, the actor who was a witness before the coroner in the Reading murder.

The suggestions made against me have been terrible. I am an American, and the newspapers in my own country have linked my name with the murder. One newspaper actually had a headline that I was 'Held for Murder,' and another that I had been thrown into prison.

Men and women, and even children, when I pass them in the streets of London, draw to one side and say: 'Oh! Drew, who did the Reading murder.'

It is intolerable. It is hell for me.

I thank the *Daily Express* for their articles on unsolved murders, for it is only by the influence of a great newspaper that I can be a free man again; free from suggestions only when the real murderer is known.

I still suffer for another's crime. My cloud has only half been lifted. I demand that every effort shall be made to clear, once and for all, my name beyond equivocation.

Ten months of hell—rubbing elbows with my fellow-men, in whose midst there still remain a few doubting Thomases.

For months I have waited—hoping against hope.

My work has been lost. My chances of a livelihood gone. I cannot find work in my profession. Often I sit alone in a tiny back room, wondering why all this hardship has been imposed on me.

I am hungry at times, without even a penny for the gas meter. Letters posted without stamps, clothes all pawned except what one stands up in—and stands in broken boots—this to try to keep the wolf from the door.

Greater artists than I, doubtless, have trod the rocky road, but after 200 plays I should be able to earn my keep and not have to depend on a few kind friends.

Why have I received no compensation for my mutilated blue suit? Why have the police not yet returned me the moneys in its pockets? Small as the sum may be, it would have saved me some humiliation.

I have written and asked for it. I have had no reply.

I pass along the streets and hear, 'There goes Drew.' Many stop, ask for a handshake, and wish me luck.

Who is it that committed this crime? Have they not already caused enough suffering, misery and hell?

Why is he silent? If there is a witness who can clear up this mystery, why does he, or she, lurk in the background? Are they fearful lest they should not receive protection? They need not be.

Why must my life, my career, my livelihood be sacrificed?

I learn that it has been suggested that my living in a house does no good for the reputation of that house.

It has been whispered, 'Yes, he got off, but I guess he did it.'

It ages one—unfits one for one's best work. It tears the courage to bits.

Why subject one to a public ordeal? Why not a private investigation?

I wonder how the murderer feels when he reads these lines and knows my mental anguish. I doubt if he cares. One who could commit so foul a deed surely has no conscience.

Meanwhile I wait and hope, even as Scotland Yard waits and hopes.

The crime reporter of the *Daily Express* fears that these hopes will never be realised. I am more optimistic, yet there are days when I see no clear road ahead, and when evening comes the longing to be in the theatre is not gratified.

I am shut out of that which is my rightful heritage—that which I have earned—but which is denied me.

Free, but still suspected. Well, the murderer is also free, is he not? But he is not suspected, is he?

True, one day he will have to face his God. Meanwhile I have to face my fellow-men.

PHILIP YALE DREW

Actually, following the receipt of Drew's letter to him on July 15th, Chief Constable Burrows had despatched the money—amounting to £1 16s. 0½d. in cash, and postage stamps to the value of eightpence—to Scotland Yard on July 16th, and on the morning of July 18th Sergeant Harris had called at 202 King's Road to hand it over to him. Drew was not, however, at home, so Harris left a message, and Drew called, by appointment, at the Yard at 4.15 that afternoon and received the money. He was also told that the question of compensation for his blue suit was to be considered by the members of the Reading Watch Committee at their next meeting. Drew was profusely grateful for the return of the money, and said that he did not expect to receive much in the way of compensation for his suit, as it had been well worn, and had he been in different circumstances he would not have asked for anything at all. He then told Harris that he had written to the *Daily Express*, mentioning in his letter that he had had neither his money returned to him nor any compensation for the loss of his suit. He said that he would telephone to the editor at once and request that these references be omitted, as "it wouldn't be cricket" to let them be printed now.

They were not, however, deleted, and when Harris read the letter in the paper he commented, "Drew was not living in a tiny back room, but was occupying at least two rooms with the notorious woman, Norine Lattimore, known as Dolores".

On July 19th, too, Drew and Dolores were involved in an accident. A taxi in which they were travelling along the upper reaches of the King's Road that night collided with another cab at the junction of Edith Grove. Dolores was taken in another taxi to St Stephen's Hospital, Fulham Road, where she received treatment for minor injuries to the head and face. She was then driven home with Drew.

The Reading Watch Committee met on July 22nd, and agreed to compensate Drew for the loss of his suit "to the amount of £2".

In the meantime, unaware of all these official activities, an organization calling itself The Reformers' Society—motto: "Fights for the Right, and to right Wrongs"—moved by Drew's doleful tale in the *Daily Express*, wrote from 14 Bryant Avenue, Thorpe Bay, Southend-on-Sea, as follows:

> George J. Warren.
>> Guardian of the Poor 1928–1930.
>> Land Tax Commissioner. Insurance Expert.
> To
>> Our Most Gracious Sovereign.
>> May it please Your Majesty to cause
>> Philip Yale Drew's case to receive consideration.
>
> 22nd July, 1930.

On the day that this request was received at Buckingham Palace —July 23rd—Drew was being sued at West London County Court, North End Road, West Kensington, for £6 15s. 1d., in respect of board and residence, by Mrs Edith Rosenty and her partner, Miss Eva Privett, trading as Meotti's Restaurant, at 177 King's Road, Chelsea. The original claim for £10 15s. 1d. was amended, Mrs Rosenty agreeing that Drew had paid £4 off the amount.

Drew admitted the debt, and asked by the Registrar, Mr George Shilton, how he could pay, replied: "I have nothing. I have had no work for six months. I have no work at the present moment and no furniture. I think as I have paid so well when I had money that it is a case where some favour should be shown to me."

The Registrar: "Well, what can you pay?"

Drew: "If I may say so, that is a hard question to answer. I have reason
to believe that I shall get an engagement very soon. I had a letter
this morning about a possible engagement."

Mrs Rosenty broke in: "He paid me a cheque which was returned by the bank, so one does not know what to believe. We have
tried to be kind to the man, but he seems able to go to the wineshop
and get drink, and if that is true he ought to be able to pay for his
board."

The Registrar: "I will make an order for the payment of £6 15s. 1d.
with nineteen shillings costs within one month."
Drew: "I shall do my best to pay in a month."

On July 24th the Home Office received the request of George
J. Warren, F.G.I., F.B.E.E., Honorary Secretary of the Reformers'
Society, forwarded by the Private Secretary's Office at the Palace,
and passed it on to the Commissioner of Police.

Sergeant Harris set off again for 202 King's Road on the morning
of July 28th, saw Drew there, and asked him if the Watch
Committee's offer of £2 compensation was acceptable to him.
He said that it was, and added that Dolores and he were moving
that day into another furnished flat, at 44 Cathcart Road, Fulham,
S.W.10.

A couple of days later, Harris was surprised to receive a letter
from Dolores. Ill-spelt and scrawled in pencil, it read as follows:

44 *Cathcart Road*,
Fulham.

July 30th, 1930
Dear Sargeant Harris
    I wonder if you would be kind enough to call and see me? I am,
as you know, not well enough to come to see you. If you would kindly
drop in to the above address I would arrange to see you alone with
my nurse.
                    Yours with kindest regards,

NORINE LATTIMORE
DOLORES

P.S. This is private please.

After conferring with Superintendent Nicholls and Inspector
Chapman (Berrett was away on annual leave), Harris decided to
call at Cathcart Road that afternoon, taking Sergeant Beard with
him as a witness. He had to go there in any case to give Drew his
£2 compensation, which had been received that morning from

Reading, and it was possible that Dolores might have something of importance to communicate.

When the two police officers arrived they found Dolores in bed, still suffering from the effects of the taxi accident. Drew was also present. When he momentarily left the room, Harris said to Dolores, "What do you want to see me about?"

"I can't tell you now," she whispered agitatedly. "*He's* here." And she pointed in the direction of Drew. "Can I write to you?"

"Certainly," said Harris. "Write down anything you wish to tell the police."

Drew then came back into the room, and nothing further transpired. But, as Harris and Beard were leaving, Dolores promised that she would write to Harris that evening. She did not, however, do so.

Both Harris and Beard came away with the impression that things were not running very smoothly between Dolores and Drew, but both also felt that it would be useless to call again to see her.

Drew's letter to the *Daily Express* still rankling, Harris reported: "Drew certainly looked somewhat shabby when seen by Chief Inspector Berrett and me on July 14th, but since then I have seen him in a new suit. When I first saw him on July 31st, he was in the act of paying 1/9d. for flowers from a street trader, while the rooms he occupied with Dolores at 44 Cathcart Road already contained a quantity of roses and carnations. His condition certainly did not give one the impression of dire necessity. He also gave me to understand that he is expecting to commence a theatrical engagement with Dolores in about three or four weeks time under the management of a Mr E. O'Brien, in a play called, *By Whose Hand?*, in which they are to tour the provinces."

It, too, was to prove a chimaera. Indeed, at West London County Court, where Drew found himself back again on November 10th answering a judgment summons in respect of £4 for rent still owing to Mrs Rosenty and Miss Privett, he said that he had not had any work since July, though he added the Micawberesque rider that something might turn up by the middle of next month. He had, he admitted, received £100 from sympathizers, but it had all been used up buying food and clothes. He did not mention drink.

Resignedly, the Registrar made an order for the payment of the amount by January.

From the previous July, Drew had (apart from ten days—September 29th to October 9th—spent at a rooming-house at 220 Stockwell Road, Brixton[1]) continued to live with Dolores at 44 Cathcart Road, but on November 28th he moved to 99 Edith Grove, Fulham. This, too, was a rooming-house. Whether or not he was accompanied there by Dolores is not clear, but in any event by this time their 'theatrical engagement' was practically over. Drew stayed at Edith Grove a mere fortnight, and by December 12th, when he departed, Dolores had faded from the picture.

Philip Yale Drew was alone once more.

(9)

Alone . . . but never for long out of mind, so far as the police were concerned.

Throughout the whole of 1930, intermittently, the investigation to demonstrate his guilt, or establish his innocence, was still going on. Still turning up no trumps.

June 23rd. A year and a day have gone by since Alfred Oliver was struck down. The *Daily Mail* states: "Detective Inspector Walter Walters, head of the Reading C.I.D., who is due to retire, has been permitted by the Watch Committee to extend his period of service. He is anxious to do so, so that he may continue his search for the Reading shop murderer. He has vowed that he will never rest until he has found the murderer and brought him to justice."

September 5th. Mrs Oliver received a letter, postmarked "Hackney, E.8 11.30 A.M. 4 Sep. 1930", and addressed:

> Missus Oliver
> Dobaconist
> Gross Street,
> Reading.

It read

Dear Madam
    the Murderer of your Husband is a tool Scootsman 5–10–6 foot ginger long Face and is a Stonemaison he has done a job at the time in

---

[1] In the voters' list for 1931 the names of Frederick A. W. Noone and Ada Noone appear among those of the occupants of 220 Stockwell Road. This Mr Noone may well be the taxi-driver who drove to Reading to see Drew, and he may have extended hospitality to him.

Reading he had got a Stoneyard with another Man in Dalston Fassett E.—Graham Road. B. Williams is his Name he has done or built a Bank at the time or the front of a Bank

A Workman

Mrs Oliver handed this letter to the Reading police. At their request Sergeant Harris made discreet inquiries. He found a firm of stonemasons, Rundle and Williams, in Fassett Road, Dalston, but soon satisfied himself that Mr Williams was not in any way connected with the crime at Reading.

October. Brought three letters from two correspondents, who promised much and provided—nothing. The first correspondent wrote—on October 9th and again on October 16th—mad, muddled letters, which Berrett read, filed and, sensibly, forgot. The second correspondent wrote an intricate, mysterious epistle, which whetted Berrett's appetite sufficiently for him to have the man interviewed. Unhappily, he turned out to be an inmate of the Chippenham Poor Law Institution.

And that, for 1930, was that.

(10)

April is the cruellest month . . . but for Philip Yale Drew, in 1930, it was unquestionably ousted by December. In April he had imagined life at its down-and-out ebb. In December he was to experience it.

Eight times in twenty days he was to shuttle uneasily between five different addresses. Four of them were hostels. None of them was home. A restless December. Out of 99 Edith Grove on December 12th and into a lodging-house at 27 Smith Street, Chelsea—for one night. Three nights at 2 Cremorne Road, Chelsea. Then, on December 16th, Rowton House, 221 Hammersmith Road; December 17th, Rowton House, King's Cross; December 18th, back to 27 Smith Street; December 19th, 20th, 21st, 22nd, and 23rd, a fourth doss-house—Bruce House, Kemble Street.

About noon on Saturday, December 20th, Drew called to see the news editor of a Sunday newspaper and asked him if he would be interested in an article about his experiences. Yes, he was told, and could he deliver the copy by five o'clock that afternoon. "Sure," said Drew . . . and trotted off to the general waiting-room at Charing Cross Station, where he sat down and wrote:

AMERICAN CONSUL AND MYSELF

Yesterday was Friday, December 19th, 1930. A cold rainy day. It is 3.30 in the afternoon. I am wet to the skin. No overcoat. One hears the squash-crunch-squash of my broken boots as I cross Oxford Circus. I find No. 18 Cavendish Square. I am admitted. I ask to see the American Consul. I ask for assistance, a passage home to America, where I have property, where for years I paid taxes. I inform him that I have no food, no roof, no bed and no money to procure same for the night. Can anything be done for me? No. The government has no funds for such purposes. Oh, yes, there is the American Relief at 37 The Strand. They might help. He will 'phone them that I will call at five o'clock. I was bowed out into the windswept, rain-blinding street. The door of No. 18 shuts behind me, enclosing the warmth of those comfortable quarters wherein is represented Uncle Sam.

Five o'clock finds me at the American Relief. I do not get beyond the door. Yes, they had received the 'phone message. Yes, if I had friends in America they would pay for a cable to ask if said friends would advance passage money and arrange for me. I had no such friends? Well, then, they would see what could be done about my working my passage home. That would take time. No, they could do nothing else except take my address. They did so. I have yet to hear from them.

The street again. It is colder now. The pavement is soon like ice. The fog is coming in. As I turn up my coat collar I think of an article I once wrote called, 'A Leaf From Life After Midnight.' No—I must not think of that. It is not good for me mentally to think of such things now. I met a man I had known long ago. He had eightpence. We go to a coffee-house, have a coffee each and split a ham roll. That's better. The street again . . . he to go God knows where. For myself? I'm not much interested. Well anyhow, the church will be a shelter.

The dawn is cold and grey. Covent Garden is busy at this early hour. Human beings are there. There is a chance of a stray apple, only a chance, but—yes—into the gutter have rolled two rather good turnips. A bit muddy, but that will wash off. I've liked raw turnips since I was a boy. The owner of the clasp-knife which I have borrowed watches me peel one. I eat. At last he says, 'Blimey, Drew! Are you that hungry?' I smile at him and reply, 'No, just sharpening my teeth.' He chuckles and throws another bag of onions on his van. 'How's it taste, mate?' 'Well, brother, it's better than some raw peas I had here one wet afternoon.' 'Sounds like you are a vegetarian.' 'Not by choice,' I reply. 'Feel like a cup of coffee?' he asked. 'I'd hate to think of missing it if one is going,' I said. It was good coffee.

It has been a long, nasty day. London is quiet Saturday afternoon.

There are matinées. Someone I know has just made a big hit. He used to 'support' me when I was starring. I have left a note with the stage-door keeper for him, asking him for assistance. I am calling for my reply at 5.15. The clock in the Charing Cross waiting room tells me it is very nearly that now. It's only five minutes' walk, so I shall soon know. Surely he will not let me down. If he does, the church is always open.

Tomorrow is Sunday, and perhaps the sun will shine.

PHILIP YALE DREW

Back he went triumphantly to the newspaper office, his deadline met, the finished article in his hand—and it was rejected.

"Too international," said the news editor. Not good for Anglo-American relations.

Just one more bitter disappointment.

Christmas Eve. At 2 Cremorne Road once more. And there he remained until December 29th, when he returned to 27 Smith Street, where he saw the old year out.

Christmas Day, 1930. In the small dog-eared diary which he kept, Philip Yale Drew wrote:

> Xmas Day. Alone in this garret room.
> Empty house. Inmates holiday-making.
> Cold, half snow and rain. Fog over
> the river. My feast? Coffee, a once-
> cooked bloater, dry bread.
> A Merry Xmas to Ye, Revellers.

Scene 2

THE LONG RESTING

(1)

THE term 'resting' is a theatrical euphemism for being unemployed. It most certainly does not imply any quality of repose. And for Philip Yale Drew, whose whole life had been dedicated—consecrated—to the theatre, this enforced exile from the footlights was purgatory. Purgatory rather than hell, because through even the darkest days, the deadliest nights, he never really abandoned hope of making a comeback. That was his tragedy—and his salvation. It was to stand him in good stead now, for during the first half of the year 1931 he was to be called upon to endure the bleakest period of his whole life.

From New Year's Day until January 17th, he was permitted a preliminary respite in a rooming-house at 75 Edith Grove, Fulham. But from January 18th onward it was back to the doss-houses—a couple of nights at 27 Smith Street, then to Bruce House, in Kemble Street, and Parker House, in Parker Street, both within a hand's clap of those same theatres above which, a dozen years before, Young Buffalo's name had been lit large in lights. And it was only when he was lucky enough to have the few pence wherewith to hire a doss-house cot that he could rely on even this shelter. Otherwise, it was a bench on the Embankment, or the fitful snatching of a derelict's huddled, uneasy slumber underneath the Arches, or in any out-of-the-way corner he could find.

He is a *Godot* figure, straight out of Beckett. Estragon-Vladimir, waiting for the messenger, the theatrical angel . . . but he has *not* forgotten . . . and he *does* know. This is purgatory and not hell, for purgatory allows movement, whereas hell is static.

During the day he moved about London like a wraith. Shrunken and seamed, he shuffled along the pavements, an outcast; in his fifties, an old, old man. Now, he knew hunger and, even worse for him, thirst. Old friends caught an occasional glimpse of him, but they passed by on the other side. He was dirty and unkempt. He smelt.

A man can lose himself in London—perhaps mercifully—and Philip Yale Drew was swallowed up in the city's great grey maw. It hid his shame. Its fogs and damps obliterated his dusty prints. Lost in its anonymous millions, he led a precarious Corvine existence, only just managing to cling on to life. That it was to take all of ten years finally to unseat him says much for 'Old Buffalo's' tenacious horsemanship—and even more for his good, solid American stamina.

We cannot know how he filled all the long and empty hours, or to what shifts and devices he resorted to keep warm and tolerably dry. Perhaps he dozed in public libraries, museums, and art galleries; sheltered in post-offices and large stores; almost certainly he found refuge, sanctuary, in churches, like St Martin's-in-the-Fields. He picked up dog-ends, begged a copper here, a sixpence there; made a tuppeny cup of tea in Lyons teashop or the A.B.C. last an hour or two in small sips.

We can only surmise.

And if the sun came out he would perhaps sit in the park, the Embankment Gardens, or the pocket-handkerchief of green in Leicester Square, sunk in nostalgic reverie.

How does a man kill time, that it may not kill him?

One thing is certain. He dreamt. Dreamt continually and doggedly of the day when, somehow, everything would come right. He would be back behind the footlights, the incomparable music of clapping hands ringing in his ears once more. And, solitary, he rehearses all the old triumphs, relives those long-ago days in Reading, when the cheering crowds struggled to touch the hem of his coat, and he addressed them, like a king, from a balcony. In procession remembered faces come . . . and fade. Frank and Marion Lindo, Fearnley-Whittingstall, that awesome coroner—What was his name? Martin? Yes, that was it. Mr Martin—Inspector Berrett, Sergeant Harris. And Dolores. Poor Dolores—like the rest of them, gone . . . all gone . . . as good as dead. Even that terrible inquest. Imagine remembering *that* with nostalgia! But at least one had mattered then. Counted for something. Now there is nothing. NOTHING.

The sun is going down. The wind turning chilly. The sun sets in the west. The West. America. Another world. Another hemisphere. On the other side of the earth. A dream less than half remembered. Would he ever go back? Ever see it again? Did he really want to? One should return in triumph, local boy made good—or not at all.

On and on his thoughts tread the wheel, turn the crank, resentments and regrets buzzing like angry bees in the upturned hive of his skull. Where did it all start to go wrong? That June day in Reading? Or long, long before that, when he first decided that he liked the taste of 'water that never freezes'—whisky? A shutter comes snapping down. The towel is up. With the alcoholic's confirmed irrelevance, his thoughts go smoothly flowing off into another channel. The tantalizing image of an amberish glass grows in the forefront of his mind and drowns out everything else. Perhaps someone will of their charity give him the price of a drink.

He gathers his rags about him and moves off into the shadows.

We lose sight of him.

He is gone.

(2)

Another quotation from that dog-eared diary of his.

"Tonight I sat in the big room of the hostel. A large number of these rough men were present—outcasts, derelicts, what not. What a day! What a night! Weather! With my chair tilted back, well in the shadows, away from the glare, I must have dozed. When I awakened I experienced a curious sensation as though something was happening that concerned me. It was. A general discussion was on. Opinions openly expressed regarding 'the actor chap and Reading'. It was a unique experience. Arguments for and against— very few for. It is seldom one hears, unreservedly, exactly just what is thought of one. Half-truths, half-knowledge, I sat and listened to. Illuminating? I could have screamed or laughed in turn. Rough chaps, these. Honest, no doubt, and strong both in their opinions and language. I had a great desire to join them, discuss, and put them straight in their reckoning. It would not have been fair. Rough, uncouth as they were, they would have been mortified."

Interview with Drew, reported in the *Sunday Post*, March 1st: "I received through the post a letter.[1] I opened it, thinking it might be

[1] Drew had an arrangement with the stage-door keeper at the Lyceum, who, for old times' sake, used to receive his letters for him.

an offer of work. It contained a piece of paper with one word written on it in red, 'MURDERER'—and underneath was a dangling noose of rope."

Philip Yale Drew stumbles on through the twilight . . . aimless. There is now but one fixed point in his life. Rain, hail, snow, frost, fog, or thin winter sunshine, he wends his way regularly to Bow Street Police Station, unfailingly to report as required at the Aliens Office. Trip upon trip, enormous distances walked. Limping feet. Broken boots. His battered figure came to be a familiar sight, dragging its way through Covent Garden Market, and always calling forth cheery greetings from the porters, who seem to have had a soft spot for him.

He was to be seen, too, from time to time, hanging about the various newspaper offices, hoping to sell an article. Sometimes he was successful. A diary entry records: "Ten shillings received for story. Such is the price of literature. Take heart ye pushers of pens!" Still, it meant another meal or two, another few nights' lodgings assured.

He wrote other things beside articles. Poems for instance, like this one, which was called "Disappointment".

> Your friends may disappoint you
>   And the world seem dull and grey,
> While your critics' voices hurt you
>   As you journey on your way.
>
> The thoughts you had of others
>   May recoil and strike you dumb,
> 'Cause you thought all men were brothers
> And you found that you'd but one.
>
> And that one was just the you-within,
>   Whom you thought that you had known,
> And discovered that he'd let you down
>   And to your real self can't atone.
>
> And in figuring up lost worldly things,
>   Fame—fortune—loot—or pelf,
> Find the greatest hurt the earthly brings
>   Is disappointment—in one's self.

Not great poetry. But in this, as in all the many poems he wrote throughout his life, he strives and strives. The ideas were boiling away all right under his Stetson. The steam of 'atmosphere' came curling out of his very ears. But his education was not equal to the task of disciplining that torrent of concepts and feelings into the ordered channels of verse. What he articulates is *poetic*—but not *poetry*. He is a mute, inglorious Milton, who can see, but cannot impart what he sees.

The self-disgust implicit—indeed, explicit—in "Disappointment" was surely his worst burden. For from self, and self only, there is no escape. No escape—but solace.

An unexpected facet of his character was that Drew believed himself to be psychic. He went in for automatic writing and his own brand of spiritualism. He was, in fact, a strongly religious man —in a rather unorthodox way. Poet, religious dreamer . . . an odd contemplative reverse side to the rip-roaring, man-of-action—who-thinks-with-his-trigger-finger image which he projected in his stage work. It is strange to think how, when the banks of lights had faded into darkness, the cowboy, the rumbustious extrovert of the public stage, was transformed into a kind of medium. Alone in the silence and privacy of his room, he would sit rapidly covering sheet after sheet with this curious automatic scribbling. Couched in the quaintest phraseology, the writings themselves, the messages, were unremarkable. They contained no tidings of great profundity, no evidence of deep cerebration or philosophical insight. It is the mere fact of their production, rather than their substance, that is remarkable. This was unexpected soil for the nurturing of such spiritual blossoms. It all adds to the enigma.

It is a well-known phenomenon that those who have suffered greatly, those who lie under sentence of disease or death, turn to the comforts and consolations of religion. When the Devil was sick, the Devil a saint would be: when the Devil was well, the devil a saint was he. But this mystical awareness, this deep running vein of religion, was no mere accretion of adversity. It had been with Philip Yale Drew all the days of his life. In the time of his prosperity he had, in the words of a friend who knew him well, "walked with God". And now, in the hour of his sorriest need, he felt that God walked with him. *This* was the solace. *This* was what turned his steps away from the beckoning river, deafened his ears to its treacherous promise of escape and seductive lappings of final peace, lifted his eyes to the stars that shine even above the gutter. For his dark night was not of the soul.

Listen closely. Go on, and on, and on, in this great cause. Study well that which is shown you. . . . What others say of this great truth, heed not if it agreeth not with thee of what thou know. Or better still mayhap 'twould better be to lead them to a kindlier light, that they might see the way as clear as thou, as onward spreads the light of thine own rays. And by so doing, will the courage grow of thine own self. I'll speak of this, and many times shall say, 'Look upward and observe the way, which we will show to thee when cross-roads come, and thou canst only half decide. Look upward to thy guide—to me'. . . . Impressions strong and true thou hadst, and yet cam'st times when far afield didst stray thy mind. Yet not so far but what didst see a beacon bright, far out ahead. Though what it did portend was half in mists enveiled of thy view, and yet I held thy course more true than some mariners who, with compass of neglect, their vessels on mighty rocks do strew. . . . And while 'tis true that many leagues are yet to be, and breakers loud shall roar, and looms the ragged coast close to thy lee, yet shall the channel deep, split clear mid-way, and a track shall keep thee ever on a safely way, and broiling seas but only half dismay. So watchful ever be, and keep a lookout ever watchful of the deep, and trust thou ever me. And know thou that when the voyage shall some day ended be, that he of baked sands and camels' lurch, in harbour safe will welcome thee, my charge. With anchor down and furlēd sails and landing near, I then to thee will more near seem, and will appear, and guide thee on, towards home, and . . . Him—

Lo! I am with you always.
Light.

That is an extract from a sheaf of what Drew labelled "Inspired Writings". It was written, 'automatically', on October 5th, 1920, nine years to the month before the inquest at Reading.

Now, the "ragged coast" was indeed gained, but the "harbour safe" seemed, in March 1931, a very distant prospect.

(3)

Drew's Doss-House Period ended on March 21st, when he returned once more to 220 Stockwell Road, and his Brixton Period began.

He remained at Stockwell Road for five months. Then, on June 18th, 1931, he moved into a room at 9 Burton Road, Brixton.

In an interview published in *Reynolds News* on October 25th, 1931, he spoke of his life during the two years that had gone by since his ordeal in Reading.

"Evil memories are lasting," he said. "In spite of my innocence and the length of time which has elapsed since the murder, the odium of those terrible days still dogs my life. It seems incredible, but it is perfectly true, that there are scores of thoughtless, inquisitive people who will not let me forget that awful nightmare. Wherever I go someone seems to recognize me, and it is quite a common experience to be asked such questions as: 'How does it feel to live under a cloud for two years?'—'Has it caused you great depression?'—'Have you ever contemplated suicide?'—'Why can't we come and see you act?'—'How do you account for it all?' Even where no words are spoken I am often looked at in a way that leaves no doubt in my mind as to what is meant to be conveyed. I have often paused, stood still, and calmly wondered just how long one could go on and on braving it all, right up against a blank wall, no light ahead, a helpless beating against the door that will not open. As far as the door—yes, but not through. Your art, your work, all you ever held dear and worked with—or for—wrenched from you. Your livelihood gone, endless longings and disappointments, hoping against hope, waiting, calling up smiles when the heart was aching, laughing and seemingly cheerful when you were almost breaking down, aimless wanderings until your limbs ached with fatigue. I know that at any time I can be recalled. I refuse to run away, or to even change my name. I owe a duty to myself to remain here, to live this thing down. I have no shame to hide."

In his diary, on December 15th, Drew wrote, for his eyes only: "Had to walk long way in rain. Soaked. Bad boots. Wet feet. (D— fool.) Bit of a throat. (Soon fix that.) B.[1] is in Reading. Hope he has good hunting. No food, no fire, no matches, no candle, no smokes, no money. Possible offer to go to Central Africa. Landlady wants her money. (I don't blame her.) Threatened with County Court for debt unless I pay part on account. A.M.—no favourable reply to those three S.O.S. wires—some people forget that I loaned them money. What is this game about? Work your body till it aches so you can give it food and drink and sheltered rest. Tomorrow is another day. I say that is fortunate, looking back on this one. I can welcome it. Adios."

An intriguing item was published by Bernard O'Donnell in the *Empire News* of December 27th.

---

[1] Bernard (O'Donnell).

Young Buffalo stops the traffic outside Irving's Lyceum

A backward glance to the high-noon of 1921

John Lancelot Martin: Reading Coroner

Drew and Dolores: Fated Lovers
Hyde Park, London. January 1930

"Two and a half years after the cruel murder of Alfred Oliver, new inquiries may result in a solution of this mystery which almost had been written down as one of the many unsolved murders of recent years. Information has come to hand which may yield the clue as to the identity of the murderer. I am able to give only a brief indication of the nature of this information, but it will show the lines on which further investigations are to be made. Some time in the spring of 1929, a man who possesses a house at a place just outside Reading, allowed an acquaintance of his who had fallen upon hard times to go down and stay at this house for some weeks. All that he asked in return was that the man should look after his dogs whilst there. The man referred to was a member of a little racing crowd who used to frequent a certain hotel in the West End of London, and the first intimation of his possible connection with the Reading murder came to me from a taxi driver who related how, one night when he had driven this particular crowd to the hotel I have mentioned, one of the party on alighting from his cab remarked to one of the others, 'Oh, yes, I know who did the Reading murder.' It was evident that some discussion had been going on regarding the crime. The taxi driver reported the fact to me, and I advised him to go to Scotland Yard, and tell them all that he had heard. This he did, and it is to be supposed that the matter was investigated. There for the time being the matter ended. A few days ago, however, there came to me other information which bore out the statement which the taxi driver made to the Yard, and it is this new information which may help to solve this baffling mystery. The man to whom the house was lent just outside Reading, is a well known frequenter of the hotel to which I have referred, and from the owner of the house I have learned that on the very week-end that Mr Oliver was done to death in his shop, he decided to run down to his house and see how his guest was faring. He did so without letting this man know that he was coming. On his arrival he discovered that his guest had fled the place, having first of all taken the dogs and sold them in a local market, and having also cashed a cheque in the name of the man who had befriended him. This man used to frequent race-courses, and it was not until recently when the man who lent him the house was introduced to Mr Drew, that he attached any significance to the man's disappearance from his house at the time of the murder. But when he saw Philip Drew he immediately remarked to his wife: 'Why he

is the living image of our friend ——', mentioning the absconding
man by name. This man had the same sort of hair, was the same
height, and almost identical in every way with Philip Drew, who, it
will be remembered, resembled the strange-looking man who was
seen in Cross Street, Reading, on the night of the crime—in spite
of the fact that a number of witnesses were called to show that
Drew could not have been there at the time stated. The facts mentioned above have been handed over to the authorities, and it is
hoped that the inquiries may lead to a final solution to the murder
of Mr Oliver. In the meantime Philip Yale Drew is busy rehearsing
for the London production of *The Tidal Wave*, a play which has
had a tremendous success in the States."

Alas! *The Tidal Wave* was not to wash Drew back into the
theatrical swim. He did not appear in it.

Neither did the new information supplied by Bernard O'Donnell
prove of any help to the police.

For them, too, 1931 had been a bad year.

(4)

"I have been trying to put the past behind me. For two years I
have been trying to come back. I had offers, but lack of funds
prevented me from being able to take them. Now I am trying to
make my come-back to the stage in London. It has been a hard
struggle. I have known what it was to go hungry and penniless. I
have known what it was to sleep in shelters and in the open. It has
been a bitter experience, but it has not been wasted upon me, and
when I saw how these derelicts managed to keep a stout heart in
the midst of adversity, I tried to grin myself. The cloud is lifting. I
am going back to my beloved stage work. Perhaps I can put the past
behind me now."

Thus, Philip Yale Drew talking to reporters in April 1932. He is
understandably elated. Caspar Middleton is to present a new and
"furiously funny" farce, *Are You Married?*, at the Grand Theatre,
Fulham, on April 25th, and he is to play the part of the President of
a South American republic. A mere fortnight . . . and at long last
he will be treading the boards again.

April 25th comes, and the curtain rises on Drew's triumphant
return. On April 30th it falls. But it was the comeback that never
came off. He had done well, but his performance brought none of

the so-devoutly-hoped-for offers of further work. He grits his teeth, notches up another heartbreak, and trudges gamely on through the seedy purlieus of Brixton.

On June 18th he quits Burton Road and moves into 2 Angell Road, just round the corner. Seven weeks there, and his Brixton Period ends.

He has spent seventeen months buried in this Victorian suburb. It has been for him a sort of limbo. He has occupied a room at three different addresses, but his precise location, the road he lived in, the number of the house, the position of his room, made little difference to the ordering of his days. He would get up at nine o'clock, shave with a frothy brush, put on his underpants (washed every two weeks) and his socks (washed once a week). Then, still, as of old, wearing his coat like a gesture, he would go out, no breakfast, to the corner shop, buy some cigarettes and a daily paper. Into the pub as soon as it opened. Steak and kidney pie at midday. In the afternoon, a bit of a walk round through streets he knew by heart. Into Brixton public library. A look at the magazines and newspapers in the reading-room, particularly the theatrical sections. Evening, back to the pub. Sometimes he would stand there withdrawn and brooding. Other times he would talk, reminiscing, and be a bit of a character, quite well liked by the working-class denizens of Brixton. A stodgy, cheap and filling supper. Then back, alone and early, to his room with a bottle. Bed. Such, with minor variations, would be the staple of his life, the lowest common denominator of what he did with himself at this period.

On August 6th, 1932, he wings northward to St John's Wood, and 15 Greville Place. Another rooming-house.

The year ends as it began, with Drew desperately anxious to feel the stage under his feet once more. He has an idea. Why not a revival of *The Shewing-up of Blanco Posnet*? He plots and plans and manoeuvres, and finally, on December 15th, manages to waylay George Bernard Shaw. They walked and talked. Drew was persuasive. G.B.S. was adamant. No. Sorry. Impossible. Couldn't be done. He was sailing next day in the *Empress of Britain* for his world tour. Would see him regarding it on his return in April.

Disappointment. But it is a disappointment that he is able to bear. For something had happened in August 1932 that was to change the entire shape of the future for Philip Yale Drew.

That 'harbour safe' had at last hove into sight.

Scene 3

THE LAST STAGE

(1)

RIFFLING through the pages of old programmes dating from the heyday of Young Buffalo's spectacular 1911 tour of Britain, one finds, listed among the cast of *King of the Wild West*, two names, Kitty Clover and Albert Magnus. Miss Clover is playing the part of Mrs Miles M'Carthy, fierce proprietress of Angel Gulch's Plaza Hotel. Mr Magnus, that of New York Harry.

You will search the theatrical record books in vain for reference to either of them. It was sheer chance that discovered, in an issue of the magazine *Pick-Me-Up*, dated February 6th, 1897, the following:

> *Sinbad the Sailor* at the Royal Surrey
> Theatre. . . .[1] There is some very
> nimble dancing by Kitty Clover, who is
> marvellously light on her fantastic toe.

It says little, but tells much. Confirms the evocation of the very name Kitty Clover—a skittish fragrance, an essence of old gas-lit theatres, an echo of tapping soubrette feet.

Kitty Clover and Albert Magnus! Resounding troupers' names—redolent of The Profession. Easy to imagine their owners in pantomime, doing the halls; all-rounders, with the occasional incursion from vaudeville into 'legit.' theatre when the opportunity offers. Never stars, never top or bottom of the bill, but twinkling away very efficiently in the middle distance as part of the supporting galaxy. Small names—big, generous-hearted people. An authentic part of the anonymous backbone of the theatre in its widest sense.

By 1932 Kitty's dancing years were over. A trim and dainty little creature of sixty, she still walked beautifully, and would often talk of her days with the flying ballet. Her mass of curly white hair and heavily powdered face gave her a stagey, almost doll-like appearance.

[1] Blackfriars Road, London, S.E.

Albert, rising seventy, was also small, though stocky. He always wore a toupee, dressed very smartly and, like Kitty, carried with him a distinct aura, a proud and omnipresent remembrance of having been a member of The Profession. He had, in fact, been not only an actor, but a musician also, his instruments the trombone and the violin. Now, his stage career behind him, he was doing a workaday bread-winning job as night-watchman at a City business premises, and would trot off each evening with his little attaché-case clasped in his—always—neatly-gloved hand.

This quaint, dapper and devoted little couple had lived since 1914 above a tiny pair of shops at 90 Upper Clapton Road, London, E.5. Their means were modest: their home, spick and span—and humble. Downstairs, behind the twin shops and approached by a long, narrow passageway between them, was a kitchen-living-room, with a back scullery leading off it. On the first floor, running across the top of the frontage of the shops, was the sitting-room, Kitty's pride and joy, its lolling chairs covered by her own hand with splendid jade material which she had painstakingly buttoned, its profusion of ornaments and knick-knacks carefully arranged so as to show to their best advantage, and lovingly dusted. At the back, on top of the scullery, was her roof-garden; very pretty, trailing with ivy, bright with primulas; a bijou jungle of variegated greenery. Her bedroom was also on the first floor, behind that show-piece lounge of hers and giving access through its window to the roof-garden. Albert slept upstairs in a kind of attic room. And that was the extent of the messuage. No bathroom. An outside lavatory.

Years before, Kitty's daughter by a previous marriage, Kate Isabella Stuart Stockwell, had lived with them. But she was married now, to Rex Rivington, and living in Kent, with a daughter of her own, Roxana. The old couple missed her, but there was really only room for two in that cramped little domain.

And yet . . . one day in August 1932, meeting their old friend Young Buffalo, seeing his shabbiness, realizing the lonely wretchedness of his plight, finding him a friend in need, they proved themselves friends in deed. They did what not a single one of his scores and scores of fairweather friends (all of them far better off than the Magnuses) ever considered doing. They invited him to stay with them.

Philip spent his first night under their roof on August 28th, 1932, and stayed there four weeks.

On September 27th, he returned to 15 Greville Place, but by
February 18th, 1933, he was back with the Magnuses. This second
visit lasted eight months, and it was while he was a guest at Upper
Clapton Road that he heard of the death of Frank Lindo. He died,
after a long illness, on Sunday, April 9th, and was buried in the
Jewish Cemetery at Golders Green.

From October 19th to December 5th, Philip was living again in
Greville Place, until, finally, he received, and accepted, Kitty and
Albert's invitation to come and make a permanent home with them.
He moved, lock, stock, and slender barrel, into 90 Upper Clapton
Road on December 6th, 1933.

The rescue by the Magnuses represented something far greater
than mere physical salvage; for Philip Yale Drew it was psychological salvation. It gave him something that he had not had for
more years than he cared to remember, a feeling of being wanted, a
sense of belonging.

Christmas 1933. Christmas at the Magnuses'. A Pickwickian
festival. There was turkey and Christmas pudding, and nuts and
mince-pies, and, of course, whisky. There was companionship, good-
fellowship, and affection. There was, for the first time for many
Christmases, laughter on his lips, and tears—of gratitude—in his
heart.

Not since he left Aunt Abbie's safe and cosy clapboard house
for the last time a dozen or so years before, had he known a real
home. Life had been a succession of lodging and rooming houses.
Other people's furniture. A roof and four hired walls. A place in
which to eat, drink, and sleep. That . . . and no more.

Now, after all those nowhere-bound journeyings, those non-
arrivals, he had found in this remote corner of East End London a
simulacrum of the lost sanctuary of his childhood.

Now, he had reached his 'harbour safe'.

Now, that long-ago promise of his spirit guide, 'Light', had
been fulfilled.

(2)

And what, during these past two years, of that remorseless
questing by the police of the killer of Alfred Oliver?

Inspector Walters, defeated, his vow unfulfilled, had retired.

Chief Inspector Berrett had left Scotland Yard on September

27th, 1931, exchanged his office for the rose garden that bowered his home at 74 Pentney Road, Balham.

Jack Harris was still in harness, but a whole new crop of fresh and more imminently important crimes were keeping him fully stretched. Against the immediate urgencies that made up his daily round, the Reading affair had inevitably receded, moribund, into history.

On January 19th, 1933, Mrs Oliver, widowed nearly four years but still hoping to avenge her husband's death, wrote to ex-Inspector Berrett:

> 98 *Hamilton Road,*
> *Reading.*
> Jan. 19th, '33

Dear Mr Berrett,

The recollection of your kindness of 3½ years ago is my excuse for troubling you now, and I hope that it will not tax your patience too greatly if I tell you of something that happened a few months ago, as I badly want your advice and opinion.

You remember Mrs. Taylor of Cross Street? She goes round the country in the summer helping a local caterer at Agricultural shows, and while at Eastbourne last August, a man who she knew very well having met him at various shows in his capacity as a weight guessing merchant, came up to her and said he had something to tell her.

She did not give him much encouragement but he was very insistent, and at last she drew on one side for him to say what he had to say.

He said, 'Here, Mrs. Taylor, you know that Cross Street Reading affair, well *Drew* did that.'

Mrs. Taylor gave a vague sort of answer, and then he asked her if she remembered Montague Fry[1] the actor who was a witness.

It seems Fry is 'down and out' and has joined a race course gang, goes round telling fortunes. To continue in this show man's own words, 'We got Fry drunk the other night, and he spilt it.'

Mrs. Taylor was serving in the bar and had not an opportunity for any more conversation with him, and I was away all August.

In September we started trying to find this show man to see if we could get out of him exactly what Fry had said. We did not want to have him scared by the police, so combed various fairs and shows, but could not find him.

At last we (Mrs. Taylor and I) went to Reading police station and told the chief detective all about it. They appeared to think it quite important, made a full report and sent it to Scotland Yard.

[1] Actually his name was Alfred George Fry.

Since then they might all be dead and buried for anything I know, I cannot get any news of any sort. Do you think it is of any use for me to go to the Yard and tell them personally all about it?

It is three months since we went, and I am terribly disappointed that I cannot get any news. I have not been near the police all this time to worry them, but you can imagine how glad I was when they encouraged me to think there might be something in all this, but now I have a feeling that they are not troubling.

Surely it has *something* to do with me.

I have been ill in a nursing home, and Mrs. Taylor stretched a point and let them think it was nothing but worry at not getting any satisfaction, but still blank silence! Do you think anything is being done to bring it home to the one who did it?

Do forgive me, I have written 3 times as much as I intended.

I hope you are well and enjoying your retirement, I read your book with great interest.[1]

With kindest regards and best wishes for 1933.

> I remain
> Yours very sincerely,
> ANNIE E. OLIVER

Berrett forwarded a copy of "poor Mrs Oliver's" letter to the Yard. He did not know whether or not the Reading police had in fact looked into the matter.

They had.

On October 14th, 1932, Chief Constable Burrows had written to Maidstone Borough Police respecting a man known as "Brummagem Jack", who was said to have visited the Kent County Show at Maidstone, July 11th–14th, 1932, with a weighing machine, and who it was thought might be able to assist in the tracing of Fry.

By October 26th, Burrows had received information that a man named Blake might know something about the elusive "Brummagem Jack". Burrows wrote to the Yard and asked if Blake could be found and interviewed.

Within days, a Mr G. Blake was traced to 21 Tunis Road, Shepherd's Bush. He was seen there by Sergeant J. Hodges and P.C. Rigg of the Metropolitan Force on November 1st. He admitted that he was the man in charge of one of the weighing-machines at the Kent County Show the previous July, and added that the man in charge of the other weighing-machine was a character whom he

[1] Berrett's memoirs, *When I Was at Scotland Yard*, had been published by Sampson Low on April 7th, 1932.

knew as "Brummy". He had never heard him referred to as "Brummagem Jack", and he did not know his correct name and address. Blake also mentioned that "a man named Lawrence, who gave unsatisfactory evidence at the Reading murder inquest" was the only person practising palmistry there. He thought that Lawrence was living somewhere in the Putney district.[1] He definitely did not know anyone named Fry.

These events of 1932 were virtually the last flickerings of police activity in what had proved a thoroughly unsatisfactory and frustrating investigation.

In June 1932, 'A Murder Echo' was reported in the *Star*—"Reading Town Council have refused a request from the Reading Borough Coroner, Mr J. L. Martin, for repayment of expenses in connection with the inquest in October 1929, on Alfred Oliver. The amounts claimed are 14 guineas for the writing of the depositions and 30s. travelling expenses."

(3)

The hunter and the hunted at rest—in Balham and in Clapton.

A *Star* reporter limns a pencil portrait of Jim Berrett. He found the 'relentless tracker of murderers' the perfect picture of the retired Englishman. A detective with a watering can. A sleuth among the slugs.

"With his shirt sleeves rolled up, his pipe between his teeth, and wearing a sun hat of truly Mexican proportions, he was standing in his front garden. At a distance he appeared to be doing nothing much but keeping one eye on the milkman, and the other (very casually) on me. But Mr Berrett is a tall man, and while he was lazily looking over his hedge he was busily watering it. No amount of murder has ever kept Mr Berrett out of his garden, but he is really able to give all his energies to it now. He has only a small suburban garden, but it is the perfect rose bower. The mere list of his varieties would suggest a Horticultural Society show. From the rose walk, which extends from the kitchen to the bottom fences, clusters of Dorothy Perkins buds hang like grapes, and there are American Pillars, climbing twelve or fourteen feet, and of a size which the ordinary amateur gardener only sees in his dreams. Some

[1] Mr John Lawrence, who gave evidence on the fourth day of the inquest, was at that time living at 59 Lower Richmond Road, Putney.

of the standards are so tall that, like the Inspector himself, they are visible from the top gardens in the road. People who see them from afar off call to inquire what they are, and when they see them they refuse to believe them. If ever the word 'tree' was merited in connection with roses it is here. These standards are not stems—they are trunks. When you ask him how it is done, Mr Berrett replies that it is just a matter of getting up early and not worrying. The real reason, of course, is that crime has no chance in his garden. The only time the weeds ever got going was when the Inspector was on a country job. But when he came back he rounded the whole six up and they came quietly. There was a visitor from the Yard early this year who produced a dandelion, which he said he found in the south-east bottom corner of the garden, but the Inspector was able to prove conclusively that this had been brought in by the visitor, and he obtained a conviction. Everybody is complaining about green-fly this summer, but there are no flies on Inspector Berrett's roses. Now and again, when detained late at the Yard, he used to come home and make a few midnight arrests of slugs, but the slugs simply do not call now. If they find they are anywhere in the neighbourhood they make a detour via No. 68, where the long arm of the law does not stretch."

Away to the north-east, Philip Yale Drew was still in the professional doldrums. Certainly, his personal situation was better than it had been for a very long time, although by no stretch of the imagination could it be said that everything in *his* garden was lovely. But the kindness of the Magnuses, plus that old irrepressible buoyancy of his, was keeping him afloat.

He bobbed up in the *Sunday Graphic* of September 23rd, 1934: "There is one thing that I wish now with all my heart. I wish that coroner's jury had not returned that verdict. I wish I had been committed to take my trial on a charge of murder. I know then that I should have been acquitted—that my innocence would have been proved beyond all doubt, and I should then have escaped the shadow cast over me ever since. But that shadow is going to lift. A well-known playwright has written a play for me—a play full of romance and drama set in the colourful atmosphere of the East. I am now endeavouring to get the play put on at a West End theatre, and when that time comes I know that the public who have ever been generous to me will rally round once more, and so banish the clouds. And—I shall not fail them."

The previous month Drew had heard of the death of Dolores. He was politely, conventionally, sorry, but it does not appear to have affected him deeply. Had he ever really loved her, ever considered marrying her? This is what, years afterwards, he told Kitty Magnus.

"Marriage? I've never been married, and am never likely to be. It's a closed book, old friend."

Kitty mentioned Dolores.

"Oh! That. What a pity, too. Poor publicity. It should never have been allowed to pass. Some mistakes can, may, I maintain, be termed glorious ones. This one did not belong in that category. I should have learned before from bitter experience that notoriety and publicity are as far apart as the poles. Marriage! Perhaps, in earlier days, in other lands! 'Twas a consummation devoutly to be wished, but would have proved equally as great a mistake. I lived, ate, drank, slept and existed on theatre, ever a tyrant and exacting mistress. No woman, much less a wife, would have put up with it. There is such a thing as jealousy, you know. Leave the marriage chapter out. It's taboo."

On October 22nd, 1934, the *Evening Standard* published an article on the Reading murder, "The Man Who Stroked Lamp-posts", by J. D. Beresford.[1] It was the fourth in a series generally titled, "Great Unsolved Crimes", and was headed by the facsimile of a letter written by Philip Yale Drew, to whom the article had evidently been submitted before publication.

19 October, 1934

The Editor.
The *Evening Standard*.

Dear Sir,

I have read the article written by Mr. J. D. Beresford in which he reconstructs the circumstances surrounding the killing of Mr. Oliver.

It is with considerable relief, and gratitude that I have read it, as it once and for all establishes, without any shadow of doubt, that the suspicions which were levelled against me at the time of the inquest have been finally removed.

I thank you for giving me the opportunity of reading the article before publication and am indeed grateful to you for affording the

[1] This article was subsequently reprinted in *Great Unsolved Crimes*, published by Hutchinson in 1935.

public an opportunity of realising and understanding that any suspicion
so far as I am concerned that may have been created at the time of the
inquest has, by this article, been entirely removed.

> Yours faithfully,
> PHILIP YALE DREW

Jubilant, emboldened by the article's clear-cut exonerations,
Drew promptly sat down and wrote two letters.
The first:

Franklin Roosevelt, Esq.
  The White House,
  Washington, D.C.,
    U.S.A.

Mr President, Sir,
  Midst all the stress of your activities, I yet dare claim your attention,
since as a loyal citizen I have suffered a great injustice.
  Not in the land of 'Uncle Sam', but here in the Islands of 'John
Bull' and the home of my ancestors. Yet here the Press has ever been
kind. Not so in the land of my birth.
  As a direct descendant of our Pilgrim Fathers I feel and resent it
deeply. I have on occasion found myself justified in suing the American
Press for libel.
  As regards the theatre, I have long been an International figure, but
for some four-odd years I have struggled under a cloud of suspicion. I
think the enclosed article by J. D. Beresford—London *Evening
Standard*—vindicates me.
  I quite understand that midst turmoil of millions every moment of
your valuable time is fully occupied, yet as one who admires your
great efforts and achievements, spare, I ask, an instant's thought and
if through your supreme influence via associated press, or, and broad-
casts assure the great American public, who in the past I have had the
honour of appearing before, the fact of the entire vindication of myself
against suspicions of a heinous crime.
  If you will accede to this, my wish, you will not only confer a great
favour upon me, but also bring joy to the hearts of two very dear old
ladies—the Misses Abbie & Susie Tilden in Marshfield Hills, Massachusetts, who brought me up.

> With every great respect,
> I am,
> PHILIP YALE DREW

The second:

The Chief.
  Radio City,
  New York City.

SIR,

With the enclosed by J. D. Beresford, London *Evening Standard*, may I claim your attention.

It was while I was under suspicion during the Autumn of 1929 that some saw fit to broadcast that which startled my good people—elderly people—in Marshfield Hills, Mass.

It had to do with me, an International theatrical figure, a star of two hemispheres. Now, perhaps, you will find it within the fairness as at the head of a great institution to graciously broadcast the fact of a vindication. This to in some small measure help to console a few of the true descendants, who still live in New England and whose blood has been instrumental in making the United States worth while.

With due regards and thanking you in anticipation.

I am,
PHILIP YALE DREW

And the following is the only reply he had:

Department of State,
Washington.

Mr Philip Yale Drew.

SIR,

The receipt is acknowledged, by reference from The White House, of your letter, with its enclosure, relating to your desire to have the American public assured of the fact of your "entire vindication" in connection with the death of Alfred Oliver on June 22, 1929, at Reading, England.

In reply you are advised that it would appear that a request such as that made by you should be directed to the judicial or other authorities of England who have intimate knowledge of the facts of the case as they were revealed at the time of the inquest, and later.

The newspaper clippings received with your letter are herewith returned.

Very truly yours,
For the Secretary of State,
Chief Division of
Foreign Service Administration

Philip was shattered. Surely, he had thought, surely they can't refuse me now. It was difficult, impossible, for him to realize that the greatest thing in his life was of the smallest interest to the world that was spinning busily about its own vast trivia beyond the fences of his private obsession.

There is one last penumbral glimpse of Philip in the year 1934. It is afforded by Andrew Melville, the son of Drew's old friend and manager. "I saw him one evening selling newspapers at Cambridge Circus, outside the bank just opposite the Palace Theatre. He had on a long, dark blue overcoat, done up at the neck. His hair was short, and he was looking dirty and very, very old."

Melville saw him again—for the last time—the following year. "It was by the pit door of the Prince's Theatre at the top of Shaftesbury Avenue. He was walking very slowly with a sort of down-and-out's shuffle towards Endell Street. He didn't recognize me, and I've always regretted that I didn't stop and talk to him."

On January 13th, 1935, the *Empire News* printed an open letter from Philip Yale Drew to Mrs Audrey Grace Jackson, who, at Weymouth that week, had been going through a coroner's 'inquisition' somewhat similar to his own.[1]

DEAR MRS JACKSON,

If ever the heart of one human being went out to another, mine went out to you during the past few days when you were enduring an ordeal which, thank God, few people are ever called upon to suffer.

It went out to you because I knew from bitter experience all the agony of suspense, all the anguish of mind at having to listen to the insinuations and suggestions which are being made concerning you.

I had suffered it myself, and when that inquest at Reading was over and the entire Press of the country were as one in denouncing the system of procedure in coroners' courts, I had hoped that that was the last time that any individual would ever be called upon to go through what I had gone through.

Had this been so, then I should at least have felt that my terrible experience had produced some good results, and that out of evil good had arisen.

[1] Mrs Audrey Grace Jackson was secretary-companion to Mr Jeffreys Charles Allen, an 86-year-old Somerset magistrate and sportsman, whose burned body was found in front of a fire at Mill House, Upwey, near Weymouth, on November 18th, 1934. At the resumed inquest on January 7th, 1935, Mrs Jackson was treated with great suspicion.

Like you, I had to sit day after day and listen to evidence that had been called with a view to proving that I had caused the death of an inoffensive and harmless old man. And I know only too well how, despite one's innocence, that ordeal creates a turmoil of misery and anguish in the mind.

I was an actor, and was used to appearing in the public eye before large audiences, so that the mere fact of appearing in a public court with the eyes of the morbidly curious upon me held no terrors.

It must have meant infinitely more to you, and as I read the report day after day I could visualise the effects which such an ordeal must have had upon a sensitive woman.

I know, too, what terrible effects such an experience may have on those who suffer it, both in their private lives and in their career.

It is a cruel and ghastly thing that anybody should needlessly have to go through all the torment through which you must have gone—a torment which even a triumphant verdict can never erase.

The aftermath can sometimes be as cruel as the experience itself. In my own case I have found that there are still wagging tongues and pointing fingers ever ready to revive the bitter memories of anguish suffered.

I only hope that in your case they will be shamed and stilled for ever, and that out of this great sorrow which was forced upon you there may come a greater happiness than you have ever known.

Drew is writing in the *Empire News* again on February 16th, 1936, on "My Trial By Inquest". It is the mixture as before. I dreamt . . . and awoke to a nightmare. He has really nothing to add. What *is* there to add?

It is about this time that Drew receives a telegram asking him urgently to meet a man well known to him. He does so. This man asks him to sign a paper whereby he is to receive 5 per cent of whatever accrues as a result of his introducing Drew to a certain Fleet Street firm. Drew signs it, a meeting is arranged, and takes place. The proposition is that Drew shall outline and write up ten episodic chapters of his life, bringing it up to date. His reward, he is told, can be estimated as anything up to a thousand pounds, and certainly not less than £600. Within twenty-four hours Drew had submitted a synopsis of the ten chapters. He is asked to call again for a further discussion. He arrives brimming with excitement and full of hope. It is now that the dirty part of the business rears its head. They wish more or less to dictate the writing of Chapter Ten. And what they want it to include would have made rare reading for certain-

minded people. It would have damned at least one person by its
implications, and yet side-stepped a libel action.

Drew was staggered, disappointed and angry. He asked them if
they were in his place, would they do it? The answer was a shame-
faced, "No". Would he, did they think, ever be able to look a real
man in the face again if he were to put pen to such an article?
Again, they were forced to answer, "No". Yet because of the fact
that there was money in it, because it was a good selling proposition,
they still wished to close the deal? "Yes." "Just what sort of men
are you?" roared Drew. "You who ask me to do this dirty thing?
This something for money, this which by your own admission you
would not contemplate if so it were that you found yourself in my
position. Do you then think that I have sunk so low? Do you consider yourselves superior to me in character? I fail to see it. Your
suggestion is as vile as my action would be if I acceded to your
proposition. Do you for one instant suppose that I have suffered all
these years for a principle, striving to live down unjust accusations,
only to throw it all away for a sum of tainted money, and so damn
my soul? If so, then you are sadly mistaken. I am surprised and
saddened to know that anyone dreamt that I was made of such stuff,
or for one moment hoped that I could be so cheaply bought. I
haven't the car fare home, gentlemen, but I can walk from here
with head erect. I wash my hands of the whole affair. Good morning." And, wearing his threadbare coat like a gesture, he swept out.

A blow. A decided blow. Never mind. There was still the theatre.
His comeback to arrange. All *would* yet be well.

Kitty Magnus writes: "I have known that during one afternoon
he has had no less than three verbal offers for different enterprises,
has been 'cast' for huge parts in plays and films, but always at the
last moment 'something happened'. How many times have I seen
him buoyed up in anticipation, only to suffer disappointment. I dare
not count. Blow after blow—days, weeks, months, years, this
hammering at the gates that would not open. One day, after an
exceptionally brilliant prospect loomed high upon the horizon,
when there seemed no possible obstacle could stand in the way,
everything suddenly collapsed like a house of cards. It staggered me.
He recounted it to me as one stunned. He seemed bewildered. And
then he sat there—staring, staring, staring. I knew that he had been
shaken to his very foundation, and I did not speak. At last he turned,
as though returning from a great distance, seemed to take up the

Kitty Magnus
Gentle mother-figure

Dolores
Passionate tragedienne,
by Epstein

A little late prosperity
Drew at the time of his
Gollancz libel action,
July 1937

Old Buffalo
The last photograph

threads of life again, and, apropos of nothing, quietly and normally remarked, 'What strange animals men are!' And once, when I had witnessed him take a lesser blow, he had said with that wry smile of his, 'It doesn't matter really. I am beyond the point where disappointment can hurt. Pray to God that you may be spared such a journey. The path is slippery, the foothold insecure, and then when the point is reached, perhaps just around the corner, who knows . . . ? Or perhaps the signpost reads, "Too Late".' "

On another occasion Drew worked for months to get a play placed. Through his efforts the money was found for its production, and a tour arranged. Then . . . at the last moment . . . 'something happened'. He was left out of the cast.

And so it went on—promises, promises. Drew most resolutely believed them all. Disappointment. The Don't-ring-us-we'll-ring-you brush-off. In the end, even he began to suspect that these monotonously recurrent collapses of bright prospects were something more than ill-fated coincidences; that these polite hedgings, these mealy-mouthed evasions, these tellings of half-truths and holdings out of half-promises added up to something that savoured of conspiracy. Then, desperate to know the true score, he went to one man, a man who was well up in most branches of the theatrical world, a man who listened with sympathy and understanding, and allowed Drew, figuratively, to back him against the wall. He agreed to "feel the pulse" of both stage and films for Drew. He kept his promise, and in due course told him flatly, precisely where he stood. It was the kindest thing that had had happened, and Drew was grateful. At last he knew.

He took the blow on the chin as usual, staggered but still standing. The one comment he allowed himself was, "It's such a waste. I wouldn't so much mind if only I could transfer what I know, ability I have developed after all these years of experience, two hundred-odd plays, if I could hand it all to some young man and say, 'Get on with it'. It's the waste that seems so great a pity."

And it was true.

As one critic wrote: "Philip Yale Drew is one of those superb actors who seem to have the faculty of being able to express more with mere finger-tips than their less fortunate brethren can portray by combining all the known arts of voice, gesture and emotion. For the want of a better name this is loosely referred to as personality, and happy is the artist on whom such a gift is lavished."

He gave so much while playing. He had enormous presence and vitality. He dominated a scene whenever he was on. And yet he never tried to steal that scene, although he certainly knew all the tricks that would have made it easy for him to do so, and there were few who could shoulder up with him. Undeniably, he provoked jealousy to an outstanding extent, but many—including several of his leading ladies—confessed that he was so good that he had spoilt them for working with another.

And J. Bannister Howard[1] wrote of him: "He is a fine actor and quite superior to the class of play in which he had to appear for many years. If I were still in management I should always be glad to engage him for heroic rôles. He was too rarely seen in a play worthy of his histrionic skill. He had something of the manner of the old powerful school and there was a magnetic quality about his acting."

But, unfortunately for Philip, Mr Bannister Howard was not still in management, and those who were were not glad to engage him for rôles of any kind.

Fleet Street and "the old Black Art we call the daily Press" seemed to exercise a curious fascination for Drew, and during the last ten years of his life he positively haunted that area.

Phyllis Davies, then on the *Daily Mail* and one of the street's star girl reporters, came to know him extremely well.

"I can't remember who it was who first introduced him to me," she told me, "but I know it was a reporter and it was in a pub. One of the first things Philip said to me was, 'What am I?' I said: 'I don't know what you mean. I don't understand your question.' And he said: 'Ah, there's the rub. I am an enigma wrapped in a mystery.' He seemed to take a shine to me. 'I like talking to you', he used to say, 'you're very compassionate.'

"As I got to know him better I sensed that he wanted to talk. I used to buy him drinks and give him packets of cigarettes and the odd meal. We would go to the Charing Cross Road and Covent Garden pubs. Sometimes to the Salisbury and the Mandrake Club in Soho. Once, he got very drunk and hinted that he had some great secret that he wanted to impart, and I wondered if he was going to tell me that he had done the Reading murder. He had not much tolerance for alcohol. Frankly, I didn't like him much. He

---

[1] *Fifty Years a Showman* (Hutchinson, 1938).

used to try to charm me, and he could be very entertaining. He was nicely spoken, obviously well bred, a splendid raconteur, and had a good sense of humour, but he behaved like a spoilt genius, put on an act—and I saw through it.

"You'd meet him wandering down Fleet Street in a crumpled Prince of Wales check suit, cigarette ash all down his front, very seamed face, dirty finger-nails, looking hopefully for reporters to have a drink with. Of course, he did cadge, but I don't think he hung around just to get free drinks. I think he was wanting to get the Press on his side; wanted us to believe him innocent. 'They tried everything short of hypnotism to make me appear guilty,' he told me once. He was completely obsessed about the Reading business, and we used to get fed up with it and say, 'For Christ's sake change the subject, Philip. You're a bloody bore.' And he'd say, 'Well, it's the one dramatic thing that's happened to me for years. I'm a good story. I'll always be a good story. Isn't that what you boys like—a good story?'

"In the end he became a nuisance. He would keep on ringing me up at the office and asking me to meet him. 'It's not just for drinks and cigarettes,' he'd say. 'I *like* talking to you. You're very compassionate.' Then one day I told him, 'Look here, I've got to work for my living. I'm busy. I don't want you bothering me like this all the time asking me to meet you.' He was puzzled, hurt. 'But you're my friend,' he said. My father was an actor-manager and Drew had once tried to get into his company. He seemed to think that that gave us a sort of common bond. 'No,' I told him, 'you're not my friend. We have got nothing in common.' He took that very badly.

"I remember one day we were walking down Regent Street together. We were just passing the Café Royal when out came Dolores. She and Philip fell on each other's necks and chatted away merrily. Then, after they had kissed goodbye, Philip walked off slightly ahead of me, out of earshot, and, with a venom in her voice that I shall never forget, Dolores spat out two words. 'The *bastard*,' she said.

"The last time I saw Drew I met him outside the London Pavilion at Piccadilly Circus, and we went for a drink in the basement bar at the Criterion. That must have been just before the last war."

In July 1937, Drew brought an action for libel against the publishers, Victor Gollancz, Ltd. It concerned a novel, *Death to the Rescue*, by Milward Kennedy, originally published in October 1931, and reissued in a cheap edition in 1934. One of the characters was named Garry Boon. Drew appeared to be gravely libelled in a great number of passages in the book in the person of Garry Boon, and immediately his attention was drawn to the book he instituted proceedings against the publisher, the author, and the printers, Camelot Press, Ltd.

The case was brought before Mr Justice Singleton in the King's Bench Division on July 29th, 1937. Mr J. P. Valetta appeared for the plaintiff; Mr G. O. Slade for Victor Gollancz, and Mr H. C. Leon[1] for Mr Kennedy and Camelot Press.

Mr Valetta announced that a settlement had been reached, and he asked that the record should be withdrawn on the terms endorsed on counsel's brief.

Drew was interviewed as he came out of court by Phyllis Davies. His shock of hair much greyer now than when, eight years before, he emerged from that other court at Reading, he told her over a drink in the Crypt Bar at the Law Courts: "I have been awarded substantial compensation, and handsome apologies were made to me. Wagging tongues and pointing fingers have made my life a misery. Since 1929 I have had one week's work, and I was so reduced some time ago that I slept on the Embankment. I have been the victim of poison-pen letter writers by the thousand. Always I have been buoyed up with the hope that one day—somewhere, somehow—the man who did that horrible crime will be found. I have tried time and again to find the man who murdered Oliver, following up clues among the letters that reached me after the inquest. One day the world will know how much an innocent man may be made to suffer when blind fortune crosses his path with that of a criminal."

And so, with his 'substantial compensation' in his pocket, Philip Yale Drew was enabled, briefly, to enjoy a little late prosperity.[2]

---

[1] Subsequently His Honour Judge Leon, and widely known under his literary *alter ego*, Henry Cecil.

[2] I have been unable to discover the amount of that 'substantial compensation', as the records are no longer in existence. It appears, however, that a request for settlement in terms of £300 and 50 guineas costs was refused, so we may take it that agreement was finally reached upon some sum rather less than this.

(4)

March 15th, 1938. Philip's fifty-eighth birthday. He has been living with the Magnuses for four years now, and his Clapton Period is moving towards its end. That end comes six months later. On September 5th, 1938, he leaves that haven at No. 90 Upper Clapton Road, and goes to what is to be the last address in the long itinerary of his maze-like odyssey—6 Maury Road, London, N.16, another rooming-house, the unaltering locus of his Stoke Newington Period. It is within easy walking distance of Clapton, and Philip is often there, seeing Kitty and Albert, with whom he is still on the best of terms.

A year drags by. Another birthday. And then, on September 3rd, 1939, war is declared. That Sunday morning he hears the ululating siren call. In the months that follow he becomes familiar with the whole new vocabulary of call-up, billeting, evacuation. He collects his gas-mask and his ration book. He grows accustomed to the new street furniture of A.R.P. shelters and pill-boxes, the strips of paper criss-crossing the windows, the boarded shop-fronts with their 'Business as Usual' placards, the great silvery sausages of balloons riding like captive zeppelins in the sky. He shuffles on through a sand-bagged and blacked-out London that has little reality for him. He is feeling ill. He has a persistent sore throat.

On May 7th, 1940, he is admitted to Lambeth Hospital, in Brook Drive, Kennington. The doctors have made their diagnosis. He has cancer of the larynx.

For two months he lies there, growing weaker and weaker.

His old adversary, Jim Berrett, precedes him into the shadows. He died of heart-failure at his home in Pentney Road, on May 24th. He left £1611.

Philip lingers on, that iron constitution of his making its last great stand.

And then, on Tuesday, July 2nd, 1940, aged sixty, he dies.

Those true and staunch friends, Kitty and Albert Magnus, perform a last sad service for him. They pay for his burial. Twelve pounds, ten shillings.

On Friday, July 5th, his body is taken to Chingford Mount Cemetery, Chingford, where, after a Church of England service conducted by the cemetery chaplain, the Reverend E. S. Gray, it is

laid to rest in a public grave. There are nine coffins below him—
there will be two more above him before that grave is finally closed.

Many years before, Philip Yale Drew had written his own
epitaph:

> *Here lies but remains of the frame of him I knew,*
> *Of letters forming words upon this fitting stone,*
> *Of my regards, no sculptor, however great, may hew,*
> *As would express my views, there is no language known*
> *Such thoughts as I shall always have of this mere man*
> *Are far too sacred to express in words 'tis true*
> *Against such an outward show I place a ban,*
> *That they may not be read by the curious such as you.*

You will search for it in vain among the monumental masonry of
Chingford.

In the Deaths Column of the *Stage* of July 18th, 1940, the following paid announcement appeared:

> Philip Yale Drew (Young Buffalo) passed away
> deeply mourned by his old friends Kitty Clover
> and Albert Magnus—90 Upper Clapton Road, E.5.

That was his only epitaph, for there was no 'fitting stone' upon
which to carve another.

Curtain-Call

CHORUS AND FINALE

ALFRED Oliver had been dead thirty-eight years, and Philip Yale Drew twenty-eight, when I began my reinvestigation into this case. But although the grass had grown tall on the graves of the two principal actors in the long-ago drama, many of the supporting cast were still alive, and I made it my business to see and talk with them.

Cumulatively, they were able to shed an oblique light on the mystery, and, weighing their testimonies, analysing and annealing, I was eventually to find myself in a position where it seemed possible to hazard an educated guess as to the likelihood of Philip Yale Drew's innocence or guilt.

I must emphasize that I began my researches with no preconceived notions, no prejudices, no axe to grind; no burning desire to inculpate Drew, no crusading zeal to exonerate or avenge his shade. Indeed, for many, many months I could not have given any convinced opinion as to whether he did or did not kill Alfred Oliver.

Drew's family and friends were, naturally, certain that he was innocent. But that I discounted. One piece of testimony was, however, to tip the scales heavily. It was that of William Arthur Fearnley-Whittingstall. I have the highest possible respect for his acuity. He acted for Drew. He was utterly and passionately convinced of Drew's entire innocence. Now, Fearnley-Whittingstall was no fool. As many learned to their cost, he was not a man whose eyes were susceptible to wool. They were sharp and unblinkered. If he expressed grave doubts, they merited grave recognizance. And as the work progressed, I came to share them.

In these last pages, then, I propose to throw aside the mantle of impartial judge and to enter the arena as counsel for the defence, arguing for a posthumous acquittal.

I am tempted to submit a plea of no case to answer, for, with respect, it does not seem to me that the prosecution was at any time in a position to offer anything that amounted to that sure proof of guilt which is required. All that we are given is conjecture, based upon no more solid a foundation than coincidence, speculation and hearsay. A spider's web, woven of strands of the flimsiest circumstantial gossamer, with the occasional firmer-seeming guide-line of congruence. A complex of conflict.

Let us consider first in what circumstances we are justified in holding a man to be guilty of a murder for which he denies responsibility, and which no person saw committed.

It is a matter of circumstantial evidence.

The learned author of *Wills on Circumstantial Evidence*[1] des-cribes it as that "evidence afforded not by the direct testimony of an eye-witness to the fact to be proved, but by the bearing upon that fact of other facts which are ... inconsistent with any result other than the truth of the principal fact".

There is a widespread misconception that circumstantial evidence is necessarily somewhat inferior in probative value to direct evi-dence: the one being the evidence of observation, whereas the other must by its nature be a matter of inference, and thus ultimately dependent upon opinion. It is, however, a fact that several classic miscarriages of justices resulted from the direct evidence of eye-witnesses, who, it subsequently transpired, had been relying upon faulty recollection, or who had been mistaken in the matter of identification. It is for this reason that many authorities hold that circumstantial evidence is the best evidence. Circumstantial evidence takes into account such factors as motive, means, opportunity, words or acts indicative of guilt or guilty intent, possession of incriminating material or guilty knowledge, evasions, falsehoods, the tampering with, or fabrication of, evidence, bogus alibis, flight, and scientific testimony.

What has been called the 'arithmetic of circumstantial evidence' is the presentation of a mounting progression of items of evidence which, although indirect, add up to a cumulative effect which seems to transcend coincidence, and may be more irresistible and less fallible than the direct sensory testimony of any single individual, whatever his probity. The resultant conviction is based upon the due exercise of logic, reason and common sense. The assaying of circumstantial evidence has been well described as "the application of common-sense under intellectually disciplined guidance".

[1] William Wills: *The Principles of Circumstantial Evidence.*

But there are intrinsical dangers. The strength of any chain of evidence is the strength of its weakest link, and there may be an unconscious tendency for the mind to supply the deficiencies, strengthen the link, so as to justify the conclusion which it wishes to reach. This applies to investigators as well as adjudicators.

Evidence of any kind—direct or indirect—signifies facts; facts learned in the legally prescribed manner. That is to say, juries are entitled to take cognizance only of material transmitted to them in court through their ears and eyes, not felt in their hearts or bowels. The yardstick of individual experience is, of course, inevitably applied both to the accused and to the witnesses, and also to the question of what is and what is not of probative value. That material —evidence—may not elicit the whole truth, but the judicial purpose and process is designed to exclude the false, and juries must make their findings 'according to the evidence'. All acceptable evidence must pass the filter of proof, proof being no more than excessive probability—but of such strength as to eliminate all reasonable doubt.

Justice means the upholding of reasonable doubt. But, remember, a jury is equally entitled to entertain reasonable doubt when asked to accept improbabilities. Intellectual conviction must precede legal conviction. Establish reasonable doubt, and you have secured your verdict.

It is my contention that in the case of Philip Yale Drew the sum of the evidence was made to appear greater than the sum of its parts. Taken individually, point by point, there is not one count of the indictment that could not have been torn to shreds by competent counsel. It is only in their aggregate that the dubious circumstances coalesce into a sinister shape. Each on its own, as I shall hope to demonstrate, falls. It could have indicated guilt, but, equally, it need not have done so. These are weak, ambiguous links; the benefit of their ambiguity *must* be accorded to the suspect.

The material evidence discovered at the scene of the crime was precisely nil. No weapon. No fingerprints. No personal belongings. The criminal left nothing behind to betray his identity. Neither was any money subsequently found that might have come from Mr Oliver's till.

In these circumstances, the search for the murderer could take only one form. It had to resolve itself into inquiries after anyone who might have been seen behaving suspiciously in the vicinity at the time.

That is how Philip Yale Drew was brought into it.

Witnesses came forward, though with testimony of varying value. They had noticed an odd figure cutting a crazy swathe through Cross Street. He was identified as Drew.

The witness William George Loxton testified that at about 1.30 P.M. a man came to the door of his shop and inquired if he had any calves' liver for sale.

He identified Drew as that man.

Between 2 P.M. and 2.40 P.M., the witness Sydney Eric Turnbull saw a man behaving peculiarly in Cross Street. He seemed to be under the influence of drink.

He said that the man resembled Drew.

The witness Thomas Harold Windle stated that at 4.40 P.M. he saw a man, evidently drunk and mumbling to himself, in Cross Street. He disappeared into the Welcome Café.

He identified Drew as that man.

George Thomas Nicholson said that at about 5.20 P.M. he saw a man in Cross Street. The man was drunk and appeared to be counting with his fingers on a lamp-post. He walked off in the direction of Friar Street at 5.30 P..M.

He did not identify Drew as that man.

Mrs Kathleen Earl saw, at 5.30 P.M., a man walking down the middle of the road in Cross Street. He was muttering to himself and behaving in an odd way. He walked off into Broad Street.

She identified Drew as that man.

Alfred John Wells said that at about 5.40 P.M. he met a man coming round the corner from Cross Street into Friar Street. He said that he recognized the man as one he had met at 7.30 A.M. that day in the Welcome Café, and added that he had also seen him in Cross Street two or three times during the course of the day.

He said the man definitely was not Drew.

William George Loxton further said that between 5.30 P.M. and 6.5 P.M. he saw in Cross Street again the same man who had asked him for calves' liver at 1.30 p.m. And that that man was Drew.

Mrs Alice James said that at 6.11 P.M. or 6.12 P.M. she saw a man standing in the doorway of Mr Oliver's shop. He was muttering to himself, appeared to be dazed, and was wiping blood off his face and nose.

She identified Drew as that man.

The witness Mrs Dorothy Gladys Irene Shepherd said that at

6.11 P.M. or 6.12 P.M. she saw a man run out of Mr Oliver's shop. He ran towards Friar Street, and then turned to the left.

She was unable to say whether or not it was Drew.

I will go no further at this stage than to put it to you that we are presented with grave disparities in the evidence of these eight witnesses.

The man in Cross Street has been described by two witnesses (Loxton and Wells) as having long, dark hair, and by another (Mrs James) as having iron-grey hair.

His age has been variously estimated as anything between thirty-five (Wells) and fifty-five (Turnbull). You may think that a twenty-year span represents an unusually wide difference in its range of assessment.

Five witnesses have said that the man was hatless, or that they observed no hat (Loxton, Mrs Earl, Wells, Mrs James, Mrs Shepherd). Three witnesses have said that he was wearing a trilby hat (Turnbull, who thinks it was grey; Windle; Nicholson, who thinks it was brown).

Four witnesses say that he had no coat, or that they did not observe any coat (Loxton, Mrs Earl, Mrs James, Mrs Shepherd). Four witnesses say that he had a mackintosh (Turnbull, Windle, Nicholson, Wells). And two of them further state that he was wearing this mackintosh over his shoulders like a cape (Turnbull, Windle).

Seven of the witnesses maintain that he was wearing a darkish, navy-blue or black suit. The other witness (Mrs Earl) did not notice what he was wearing. Mr Wells adds that he had on a pair of grey trousers.

Three witnesses observed that he wore brown shoes (Loxton, Turnbull, Wells).

Four witnesses positively identified Drew as the man they saw in Cross Street (Loxton, Windle, Mrs Earl, Mrs James). Two witnesses positively denied that Drew was the man (Nicholson, Wells). One witness would go no further than that Drew resembled that man (Turnbull). One witness was unable to say (Mrs Shepherd).

A case, you might think, of reasonable doubt.

As it happens, I do not think that one can—or need—deny that Drew was in and around Cross Street, both sober and in a fairly advanced state of intoxication, at various times on Saturday, June

22nd, 1929. But what, in the final analysis, does that fact amount to in the way of evidence of complicity in the murder? I say that it amounts to nothing. Scores of people, people who did not—as Drew most certainly did—go out of their way to register their presence, were, doubtless, in Cross Street, and in the vicinity of Cross Street, that day. It is surely not reasonable to suggest that mere proximity to the scene of a crime is *ipso facto* proof of involvement? And yet that, in the case of Philip Yale Drew, seems to be precisely what the police *did*, covertly, suggest.

We will admit that Drew was the natural, the tailor-made, suspect. He was his own worst enemy: the strongest prosecution witness. His conduct, his vacillations and evasions, damaged no one but himself. If these were the attitudes and avowals of a guilty man, they were crass stupidity. Remember, though, we are dealing with an eccentric man. A man who, by his own admission, is not as other men. He is a drunkard. He is besotted and bemused, vague and uncertain. He has a great deal to say, but nothing to tell. He cannot remember. He is, moreover, an alien creature. An actor. A theatrical.

I suggest that the police, albeit unconsciously, manipulated the facts to lock in with their interpretation, their genuine conviction of Drew's guilt. He did not fit the hole: they padded it to fit him.

The solitary *fact* they had against him was Mrs James' belief, her sworn statement, that, after a fleeting glimpse, she could, five weeks later, unequivocally identify Philip Yale Drew as the man she had seen in Oliver's doorway, the man who was wiping blood from his face.

It was not enough.

To be fair, shop crimes, like the murders of prostitutes, always present peculiar difficulty of solution; shops, like prostitutes' rooms, are public territory, easily accessible to any wandering despoiler.

Let us suppose that in the Reading shop murder the motive was the obvious, the normal, the expected one—robbery. And I believe it was. Was it a strong one for Drew? The evidence is that before the fact of the murder he did not stand in any particular need of money. He had two bank accounts, both in funds, and, in any event, if he needed money he could always obtain an advance from Mrs Lindo. And there is positive evidence that after the fact of the murder he showed no signs of sudden prosperity. On the contrary, Mrs Lindo testified that on the Sunday, the day following the commission of the crime, Drew actually had to borrow a small sum of money from her, as he said that he had temporarily run out.

What of the means? Had Drew—was Drew shown to have—the means of inflicting the types of wounds produced on Mr Oliver's head?

According to Dr Joyce, who carried out the post-mortem examination, those wounds were of a somewhat puzzling kind, in that while some presented indisputable characteristics of having resulted from the extremely violent use of a very heavy blunt instrument, others were clearly inflicted by a smaller, sharp-edged weapon. Dr Joyce postulated that it must have been either a single weapon with two edges, or else two separate instruments. He suggested a heavy coal-hammer or a spanner.

Publicly, the police suggested a jemmy. Privately, they thought that it might have been a stone ginger-beer bottle. The medical evidence for the use of such a weapon is non-existent, but the police had discovered that Drew was in the habit of purchasing stone bottles of ginger-beer, and, in the absence of any other possible weapon's having been traced to his possession, they decided in their own minds that, whatever the doctors said, that must in all probability have been "what he did it with".

Padding the hole to fit him.

A tyre-lever, a knuckle-duster, a crowbar, a packing-case opener, these were all alternative weapons suggested—and dismissed. The one weapon which nobody thought of was—a horseshoe.

When I met Drew's old friend, Andrew Melville, he made me a present of a horseshoe. He had found it buried away in a trunkful of Drew's possessions which Drew had deposited in his safekeeping. It had once been fitted to one of the hoofs of his performing horse, Rosy Dawn, and Drew had obviously kept it as a souvenir of his happier days. It is not a modern lightweight-alloy shoe, but an old-fashioned thick iron one. It is a heavy, blunt instrument, made even heavier by the fact that two thick wedges of rubber had been nailed to the heels to prevent Rosy Dawn from slipping as she came down the ramps on to the stage. It is also a sharp instrument, for the clip has a wicked point.

Drew was a theatrical. Theatrical people are notoriously superstitious—and sentimental, too. Drew was eccentric. It could be that he was sufficiently superstitious and sentimental to have kept Rosy Dawn's shoe—or shoes—for luck, and sufficiently eccentric to carry one of them around with him sometimes among the rat's nest of miscellanea that gather in a drunkard's overcoat pocket.

Suppose Drew *did* kill Alfred Oliver—not by premeditation but on the spur of the moment. Then it could be that here, nestling in his pocket, was the ready-made weapon, literally to hand. And, the split-second deed done, it would be an easy weapon to dispose of. Like Chesterton's postman, it would be too obvious to be seen. Even if those who were searching the streets and the fields, dragging the river, brought it to light, they would see it not as the murder weapon, but as . . . a horseshoe.

A better theory, I suggest, than the official stone ginger-beer bottle theory, but, like that theory, unsupported by a scintilla of evidence.

Now we come to opportunity. And here we are in the densest thicket of all, obscured moreover by clouds—a fog—of witnesses.

Bear with me now as I endeavour to disentangle the complexities of timing, for it is essential to grasp the significance of dissonances struck by variations of times stated by the witnesses.

There is, I think, no doubt that it was Philip Yale Drew who was seen by the butcher Loxton at his shop in Cross Street, at or about half-past one on Saturday, June 22nd.

I think that it *could* have been Drew who was seen in Cross Street by Mr Turnbull at some time between 2 P.M. and 2.40 P.M. But I am also of opinion that it *could* have been another man, who, as Turnbull himself expressed it, resembled Drew. This man, you will recall, was drunk and wearing a mackintosh and brown shoes. It is an important matter of fact that Drew did not possess either a raincoat or brown shoes.

Mrs Lindo said in evidence that between 2 P.M. and 2.30 P.M. that Saturday Drew was lunching with her and her husband at their lodgings, and that he then slept on the sofa in their sitting-room until she awoke him at about 4 P.M. She says that Drew then went to his own lodgings.

Mrs Goodall, Drew's landlady, put the time of Drew's arrival at his lodgings as between 3 P.M. and 3.30 P.M., and she stated that he went out again between 3.45 P.M. and 4 P.M., but, as we have seen, the clocks in her home were somewhat erratic in the matter of time-keeping.

And it was between 3.30 P.M. and 4 P.M. that the witness Mrs Winifred Greenwood saw Drew in Friar Street. He was, she said,

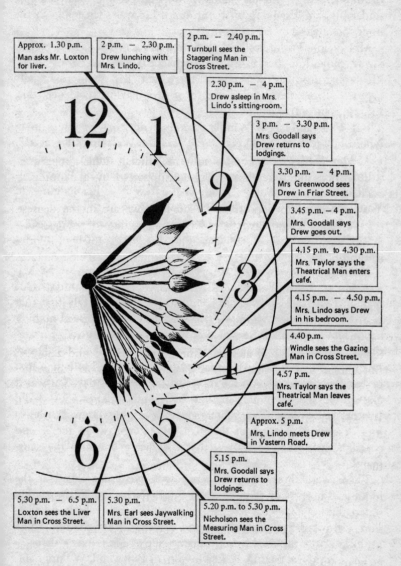

Approx. 1.30 p.m.

Man asks Mr. Loxton for liver.

2 p.m. — 2.30 p.m.

Drew lunching with Mrs. Lindo.

2 p.m. — 2.40 p.m.

Turnbull sees the Staggering Man in Cross Street.

2.30 p.m. — 4 p.m.

Drew asleep in Mrs. Lindo's sitting-room.

3 p.m. — 3.30 p.m.

Mrs. Goodall says Drew returns to lodgings.

3.30 p.m. — 4 p.m.

Mrs. Greenwood sees Drew in Friar Street.

3.45 p.m. — 4 p.m.

Mrs. Goodall says Drew goes out.

4.15 p.m. to 4.30 p.m.

Mrs. Taylor says the Theatrical Man enters café.

4.15 p.m. — 4.50 p.m.

Mrs. Lindo says Drew in his bedroom.

4.40 p.m.

Windle sees the Gazing Man in Cross Street.

4.57 p.m.

Mrs. Taylor says the Theatrical Man leaves café.

Approx. 5 p.m.

Mrs. Lindo meets Drew in Vastern Road.

5.15 p.m.

Mrs. Goodall says Drew returns to lodgings.

5.30 p.m. — 6.5 p.m.

Loxton sees the Liver Man in Cross Street.

5.30 p.m.

Mrs. Earl sees Jaywalking Man in Cross Street.

5.20 p.m. to 5.30 p.m.

Nicholson sees the Measuring Man in Cross Street.

Clock-face to show movements (1)

drunk, walking with his hands in his pockets and with his coat under his arm, dragging on the ground. He was then going in the direction of the Town Hall.

Mrs Nellie Taylor testified that between 4.15 P.M. and 4.30 P.M. Drew came into her café—the Welcome Café—in Cross Street. He was drunk. He had a meal there, and left at approximately 4.57 P.M. From the detailed nature of Mrs Taylor's evidence, this, I think, is incontrovertible.

But Thomas Harold Windle gave evidence that he saw a man, whom he identified as Drew, going *into* the Welcome Café at 4.40 P.M. This man was wearing a trilby hat and a raincoat, and was drunk. Was the man Drew? Or a man who resembled Drew?

At or about 5 P.M., Mrs Lindo met Drew near her lodgings in Vastern Road. He told her that he was going home to tea.

Mrs Goodall confirms that Drew returned to his lodgings, at 5.15 P.M., drunk, and remained there in her company until at least 6.10 P.M.

Meanwhile, however, between 5.20 P.M. and 6.5 P.M., Mr Nicholson, Mrs Earl, Mr Wells, and Mr Loxton are all seeing a mysterious man in Cross Street. Nicholson and Wells say positively that that man was not Drew. Mrs Earl, who seems to have observed nothing about him other than the fact that his face was "very red", nevertheless displays no hesitation in swearing that he was Drew. Loxton also asserts positively that it was Drew—the same man that he had seen at the door of his shop earlier that same day. But was it Drew? Or was it another man who resembled Drew? And did Loxton, one wonders, in subsequently describing Drew ascribe to him descriptive features of the man whom he saw on the *second* occasion, believing, of course, that they were one and the same man?

There were three other witnesses who were not called at the inquest. The first of these was Mr A. J. Rivers, of Tilehurst. He stated that at about 6.4 P.M. he saw a tall man of about six foot, slim, estimated age thirty-three, and dressed in a dark suit, come running across the road from the same side as Mr Oliver's shop.

The second was Mrs D. F. Lewington, of Pinewood, Wokingham. She said that between 6.5 P.M. and 6.8 P.M. she was knocked into by a man in Cross Street. The man, who answered Mrs James' description except for the fact that Mrs Lewington said he was fair-haired, appeared excited or half mad, and was talking to himself. He was not wearing a hat, and was rushing in the direction of Broad Street. When he collided with her it knocked her bag to the ground, and he said, "Clear out of the way".

The third witness was Mr David Edwards, a former detective sergeant in S Division of the Metropolitan Police. He said that he saw a man standing practically outside Mr Oliver's shop at 6.10 P.M. He thought that he recognized the man as a person named Blundell, whom he had arrested for larceny while serving at Barnet. A search at Crime Index, and through the charge books of all the police stations surrounding Barnet, failed, however, to disclose any man of that or similar name.

This is all very confusing. What it boils down to is this. If the evidence given by Mrs Lindo and Mrs Goodall is correct, then the man seen in Cross Street by Mr Nicholson, Mrs Earl, Mr Wells, Mr Loxton, Mr Rivers, Mrs Lewington and Mr Edwards *cannot* have been Philip Yale Drew.

One hesitates to invoke the fiction writer's stand-by of incredible coincidence, but it really does seem possible that there were two drunken men hovering about Cross Street that Saturday—Drew and another man, who may have borne at least a superficial resemblance to him. But that is not to suggest that either of them —or the man seen by Rivers and Edwards—was necessarily responsible for the attack on Mr Oliver.

There are two other witnesses, Mrs Winifred Greenwood and Mrs Elizabeth Crouch, whose evidence must be taken into account. Both testify that Drew was leaving his lodgings in King's Meadow Road at, according to Mrs Greenwood, around 6 P.M., and according to Mrs Crouch at between 6.10 P.M. and 6.12 P.M.

Mrs Florence Wheeler stated that between 6.10 P.M. and 6.15 P.M. she collided with a man whom she identified as Drew at the corner of Vastern Road and Blagrave Street, which would be the route that Drew would normally be expected to take from his lodgings in King's Meadow Road to the theatre.

And Mr Bertie Hathaway told how he saw Drew in Friar Street at about 6.15 P.M., and followed him to the Royal County Theatre, where he arrived at 6.14 P.M. or 6.15 p.m.

This approximate timing is confirmed by Mrs Lindo, who said in evidence that she first heard Drew moving about in his dressing-room at the theatre between 6.15 P.M. and 6.20 P.M.

If Mrs Greenwood, Mrs Crouch, Mrs Wheeler and Mr Hathaway

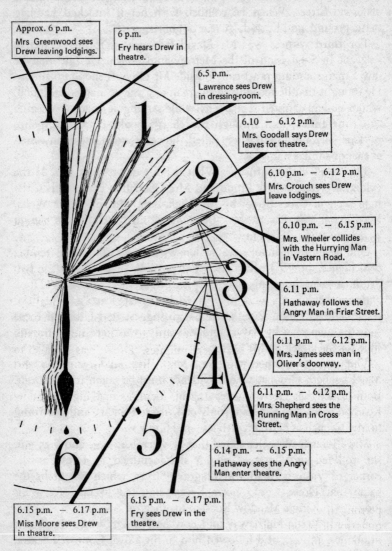

Approx. 6 p.m.
Mrs Greenwood sees Drew leaving lodgings.

6 p.m.
Fry hears Drew in theatre.

6.5 p.m.
Lawrence sees Drew in dressing-room.

6.10 — 6.12 p.m.
Mrs. Goodall says Drew leaves for theatre.

6.10 p.m. — 6.12 p.m.
Mrs. Crouch sees Drew leave lodgings.

6.10 p.m. — 6.15 p.m.
Mrs. Wheeler collides with the Hurrying Man in Vastern Road.

6.11 p.m.
Hathaway follows the Angry Man in Friar Street.

6.11 p.m. — 6.12 p.m.
Mrs. James sees man in Oliver's doorway.

6.11 p.m. — 6.12 p.m.
Mrs. Shepherd sees the Running Man in Cross Street.

6.14 p.m. — 6.15 p.m.
Hathaway sees the Angry Man enter theatre.

6.15 p.m. — 6.17 p.m.
Miss Moore sees Drew in theatre.

6.15 p.m. — 6.17 p.m.
Fry sees Drew in the theatre.

Clock-face to show movements (2)

are correct, it seems unlikely that the man seen by Mrs James in Oliver's doorway at 6.11 P.M. or 6.12 P.M., and by Mrs Shepherd (who, incidentally, in her first statement put the time at 6.8 P.M., and the man's age at twenty-five or twenty-six) running out of Oliver's shop and towards Friar Street, was Philip Yale Drew.

A case, you might think, of reasonable doubt.

We do not, I think, need to go through all the conflicting evidence regarding the time of Drew's arrival at the Royal County Theatre that evening. It is not necessary to accept Mr Lawrence's or Mr Fry's estimates, which place his arrival there between 5.30 P.M. and 6 P.M. I think that Mr Hathaway's estimate of 6.14 P.M. or 6.15 P.M., supported as it is by Miss Moore's and Mrs Lindo's testimonies, is the most reliable.

Neither is there anything to remark of Drew's behaviour during the course of that evening's performance of *The Monster*, except that it was unremarkable. That is to say, he did not display any signs of abnormality or emotional upset such as one might reasonably expect on the part of a man who, an hour or so before, had committed a singularly brutal murder.

There is the question of his delayed return to his lodgings. The fact that he left the theatre at 12.15 A.M. and took half an hour over a journey which, as he himself estimated, ought not normally to have occupied more than ten minutes. Drew was unable to provide any reason why it did take him half an hour that night. The coroner offered him the ready-made explanation that he had been very drunk. He emphatically rejected it. But I submit that he had in fact been drinking throughout the evening, and it may well be that when he got out into the fresh night air he decided to walk about a bit before going home to bed. Such action is certainly not incompatible with the known habits of inebriated men.

So far, I have said nothing about the fact that at no time were any traces of blood observed or discovered on Drew's clothing or person. In view of the ferocity of the attack on Mr Oliver, and the quantity of blood which had spurted about the shop, you may well think that his assailant would be likely to have been fairly extensively bloodstained, or at any rate not entirely innocent of some such traces. Drew's clothes were subsequently examined by forensic experts. They were put under the microscope. And yet not a single speck of blood was found anywhere on them.

A great deal of nonsense was talked about the suspicious circum-

stance of his having sent his overcoat, blue suit jacket, and
waistcoat—all of which, by the way, he had until that time continued quite openly to wear—to the cleaner's. But, remember, he
did not do this until five weeks after the murder, and that despite
the fact that he had had all of five weeks—five weeks in which, so
far as he knew, he was not so much as suspected of having the
remotest connection with the crime—in which to do so.

I think we may also safely dismiss the red herring of the calves'
liver. The suggestion was that if bloodstains had been found on
the lining of his pocket they could have been the result of his
having carried liver home in his pocket. But bloodstains were *not*
found in his pocket, so there was no need to postulate calves' liver,
or any other explanation.

There remains the curious affair of the missing blue trousers—
the trousers that disappeared at Reading and reappeared seven
weeks later at St Albans. This is certainly puzzling. If you believe
Drew guilty, the suggestion is that those trousers were somehow
marked with the indications of his guilt. Bloodstains, perhaps—
although, since the police had plainly stated that whoever murdered
Mr Oliver did not go behind the counter, one would have thought
that the assailant's trousers, shielded as they must have been by
the counter, would have been the least likely item of his clothing
to have been exposed to bloodstaining. But suppose the assailant's
trousers did somehow become bloodstained, and suppose for a
moment that Drew was that assailant, surely then his trousers
would remain as bloodstained in August as they had been in June?
Yet the simple fact is that when those trousers reappeared in
August, and were, naturally, minutely scrutinized by the police and
their experts, no blood or any other suspicious mark of any kind
was found upon them, nor was there any evidence whatsoever of
their having been washed or cleaned.

This, I submit, is a case in which the evidence of previous
character assumed considerable importance. An honest man, found
for the first time in dubious, suspicious circumstances, is entitled to
the bonus of presumption of innocence. It is the due dividend on a
lifetime's investment of good character. A known villain, discovered
in dubious, suspicious circumstances, must expect to pay the forfeit
of presumed guilt. It is the tax on the accruals of his previous
dishonesty. It may not be common justice—but it is common-sense.

What, then, do we know of Drew's character?

We know that from April 1920, when he returned to England, to October 1929, when he stood trial by coroner, he was going, slowly at first, but with accelerating speed, downhill due to drink.

We know, from the accumulated testimony of many friends, that he was in reality a much more complex person than might at first appear. He was, those friends and acquaintances affirm, very kind and charitable. He made a positive fetish of keeping his word, honouring a promise, even in cases where no written contract existed, and where it cost him the loss of much money to stick to a purely verbal bargain which he had impetuously struck. There was no malice in him. He was good-natured to a fault. When let down, as he so often was, he nurtured no resentment, he accepted it with a shrug and a certain wry humour. He was never one for 'getting his own back'. This very insouciance of his was perhaps responsible for much that caused him trouble in his life. In a sense, he never grew up; never became worldly-wise, sophisticated. He loved—and believed implicitly in—melodrama, the fairy-tales he acted on the stage. He had a pathetically naïve belief in the happy ending, the triumph of right over might, good over evil. He was a big boy scout, doing his daily good deed. He found out too late that life wasn't like that . . . and even then he couldn't believe it. "A big baby", that was how his friends described him, and not one of them considered it even remotely possible that he could ever be guilty of murder. He was not, they said, a violent man.

There is a saying that "men run truer to form than racehorses". The basic pattern of that form is, no doubt, moulded fairly early in life; the years merely add crockets and demolish finials. I have taken as wide a sweep as possible, personally interviewing, or, if that was impossible, corresponding with, those who knew him—his family, his friends, his acquaintances; the police and legal personalities who found themselves professionally involved with him; those witnesses who came fleetingly into contact with him about the time of his ordeal; even the doctor who dissected his body.

When, in 1968, I began the research for this book, Drew's only surviving close relative was his brother Harry, a musician, former orchestra-leader, retired violin-teacher. He was then aged ninety, and living in Waterville, Maine. I corresponded with him, but beyond affirming his belief in Philip's innocence, he had not much to add to the story. He died in November 1969.

Philip's other brother, Frank, had died in 1966, aged ninety.

He had lived all his life in Marshfield Hills, where he earned his living, first as a grocer, and then as a horticulturist. His daughter, Mrs Dorothy Drew Damon, who still lives in Marshfield Hills, told me: "My Uncle Philip was gay and popular, generous and likeable, and I shall always remember how his tenderness for his old aunts—Abbie and Susie—continued through the years and across an ocean. There was never any indication of violence or animosity in his make-up or character, and no one who knew him questioned his innocence of that terrible crime."

Drew's second cousin, Miss Eleanor Magoon, also still living in Marshfield Hills, told me: "My father knew Philip well, and he said that he never could have killed anyone. *We* all know that Philip had nothing to do with the murder of Mr Oliver, because it was just not in his nature to be violent—ever."

Philip's dearly-loved Aunt Abbie died in 1937. She never really got over the shock of his involvement in the Reading affair, and her relatives believe that its shadow hastened her end. His Aunt Susie outlived him by three years, dying in 1943. Both aunts carried their implicit faith in their nephew's innocence to the grave with them.

You may think that the opinions of family and relatives are likely to carry too favourable a bias to count as evidence, but I believe that it is essential that they should be quoted, for it was my purpose to find out *all* that I could about him. I did not want to end up with a dancing skeleton, but with a fully rounded man, and it is my view that any fragments which come from the place where he was born and shaped, the place which he loved, and to which his heart must have returned time and time again during the days of his long-drawn-out agony, must be heeded.

The last person to bear witness to Drew's early character is Mr Robert P. Oakman. He knew him as a young man in Marshfield Hills. He toured with him in America in 1908 as a fellow-actor and came over to England with him in *King of the Wild West* in 1910. Writing to me from Middleboro, Massachusetts, in 1968, Mr Oakman said: "I am 78 now, and I am about the only living friend of Phil's over here. Phil was one of the best natured men in the world, and I never saw him mad. Everyone took a liking to him. I can never bring myself to believe that he was anything but innocent of that crime. After he had made one or two trips over to England and back here, he began not to come back home at all.

He said he loved England and was going to stay there. He liked the way you folks took him, and was kind of bitter when he was here and in New York, because he reckoned he didn't get ahead fast enough with his career this side of the pond. Then Aunt Abbie was the only one to hear much from him. I'm glad I was never over there with him to watch him go down hill. I just will say that drink got him and turned him crazy like. You know, as the saying goes, Phil came over in the *Mayflower*, via Peregrine White, and that kind of stock never has gone around murdering people."

Among the papers left to Mrs Dorothy Drew Damon by her father, Guy Frank Drew, was a manuscript entitled, "Injustice: My Twenty-odd Years' Impressions of Philip Yale Drew—'Young Buffalo'." Its author, "K.I.S.M., A Student of Psychology", was Kitty Magnus.

In it, she tells how she first met Drew in the summer of 1911, and was engaged by him to play a small part in the tour of *King of the Wild West*.

"I had been out of a job for some considerable time and was preparing myself for an embarrassing few moments in asking for a sub before I had earned it. I took my courage in both hands and approached him. All humiliation left me as I met his genial smile and generous offer of any sum I required. A kindly shake of the hand wishing me success in my forthcoming performance and, as he strode down the passage to his dressing-room he turned, as if an afterthought had suddenly struck him, and called to me telling me to come to him again if I wanted any more. The weeks rolled happily by, and before I realized it the summer vacation was on us, and Drew was off to spend a well-earned rest at his home in far-away Marshfield Hills. I had precious little in the bank for a six weeks' vacation, and Young Buffalo seemed to sense this, for, on wishing me good-bye, he said, 'Now see here, ole feller (I might add that he was in the habit of calling his horse, dog, or boy, 'Feller'), though I'm going three thousand miles across the herring pond, if during my absence some unfriendly elephant steps on and flattens your bank account, remember the cables were laid to be used. Give me a tinkle across the pond and we'll attend to that and put it right, sure.' Needless to say the Cable Company accepted my mite—and the desired amount arrived in due course."

A telling little vignette of Philip Yale Drew in the days of his power and pride.

And now . . . another vignette, equally telling. The time: eighteen years later. November 1929.

"And then comes the time when I am in London, and I go to the theatre where Drew is playing. I waited in his dressing-room. He rushed in after the second act, stood stock-still as he saw me, then, with a glad cry which I can never forget, rushed to me and eagerly welcomed me. The genuineness, the deep tone of sincerity, moved me. It sounded a new note. A few moments before, I had listened to the laughter and the applause that his work had produced. Now, just me. He was so glad to see me, and I marvelled. 'I've only a few minutes', he said. 'I'm on all the time. I open each act. But know before you go that you are talking to the unhappiest and most depressed man on earth. I had thought that sunshine lay ahead, that the clouds had rolled away. I feel that this is not so. This popularity is but fleeting, a flash in the pan. It is said that two hundred thousand pounds could not have bought my recent publicity. They used the wrong word. It was notoriety, old friend. And that is destroying, even as each hour is destroying, that something which I thought I had—friendship, in vast numbers, because I was what I was. It is not so. I see the finger-post ahead. A time —and then they, when the limelight wanes, will desert me, as rats flee from a sinking ship. Nemesis? No, I think not, for knowingly I have not angered that God. But it is written that my path ahead is an unsightly thing. There's the bell, I must go. But first, know that I need your friendship. I have always needed it, and now more than ever. God knows if it may not be all that is left to me. I feel that this is so. I shall come to you.' And he was gone, swallowed up in the atmosphere of make-believe land. I was staggered. All the way home, and after, his words rang in my ears."

And come to her he did. More than once, he allowed her full access to all his papers so that she could write that memoir, which was never to see the light of print.

My friend, I have indeed delved deeply into your papers, from which I have gleaned much of your heart, and even your thoughts. More, perhaps, than you dream.

Drew took blow after blow. As he often said, there must have been a lot of Irish blood in his Scottish ancestry, for, 'Sure, and I never know when I'm licked.' But he has also told me that at times it has seemed almost impossible for him to realize that all this had happened, and was happening, to him. He said that it was a strange sensation to be in the world and not of it, as it were; detached, standing aside, and seeing it roll by; years pass; people pass; surroundings change; and still the hurt remaining. Drew's hidden pools of will and fortitude seemed inexhaustible. And, amazingly, he was never soured. One day he burst in on me with all the rush and eagerness of a harbinger of good news. 'An engagement?' I asked. 'No, nothing so commonplace,' he said. 'Something really worth while. Listen, a man stopped me today and said, "I want to shake hands with you, Drew, you saved my life." I shook hands and apologised for not remembering him or the incident, but said that he was welcome whatever it was, and that I hoped he'd enjoyed it, living I meant. "No, no, you don't understand," he replied. "It's this way. I thought that I had all the worry in the world. It was too much for me. Couldn't stand it. I was about to end it all. Then I read about you, and saw you. My whole outlook changed. I said to myself, compared to this man's, my trouble is but a flea-bite. If he can weather such a storm, surely I can tackle my little bit. Well I did. I've won through, and I'm all right— thanks to you." "Fine work," I replied, "and I hope you have good hunting in the future." And he went on his way.' 'What was his name? Where does he live?' I asked. 'Didn't say, old friend, and somehow I feel that I don't want to know. Strange! Perhaps it is that he just represents one of the many. It's a thought, and if true, then all I have been through is after all of some use ... well, worth it.' "

The Kitty Magnus manuscript is not only a spirited defence of Drew, it is a document which has filled in many gaps for me, and contributed valuable light and shade to the portrait of Drew's personality.

Another friend of many years' standing is Andrew Melville, the son of the well-known actor-manager of the same name, who, it will be remembered, took Drew under his wing in 1920. I paid several visits to Mr Melville at his home at Chalvington, in Sussex, and we had long discussions about Drew.

"I was only a boy when I first knew Buff, and he was my boyhood idol. He was a marvellous companion for a lad, full of exciting things to do and always good tempered and kind. His aunt used to send him American papers and he would always give me the comics out of them. But there was, too, a sort of mysterious side to him which, even as a child, I recognized. I remember one night I had to share the same bed with him, and he was talking away all night in a foreign language to, I think, an invisible Indian. My father told me afterwards that Buff believed in spiritualism, and had an Indian guide. He was incredibly tough—never wore an overcoat, whatever the weather—and when we were on tour, at New Brighton, I believe, he cracked his elbow at a local roller-skating rink. We all thought that his injury would put him out of the show, but not a bit of it. That same night, his arm in a sling, he came thundering on to the stage at full tilt, firing his six-shooter with his one good hand and making his horse rear as usual. For a time, Buff stayed with us at our home—Melrose, 1 Fitzroy Park, Highgate—but my mother found him a troublesome house guest. For one thing he was frightfully untidy, and it was also a terrible business trying to get him to take a bath. He would sit, fully dressed, in the bathroom making splashing noises with the water. In the end my father used to go in and give him a good scrubbing himself. Later, Buff lived for two or three months in a sort of beach hut which we had at Hove, near Portslade, and he seemed quite happy camping out there. At that time he had got hold of a motor-bike, and he used to go roaring about on it all done up in a leather suit, goggles and the rest. I remember being in the side-car one day when he ran into a pedestrian on the front at Hove. There was a frightful uproar, but luckily no one was seriously hurt."

Mr Melville, too, found it impossible to think that Drew had committed the murder—"He was just a big, cuddly teddy-bear of a man, and a very sweet person". But, unlike Kitty Magnus, he had seen Drew violent.

"One night—he was drunk, of course—he went for his dresser over some trifling thing that he had done or omitted to do, and nearly throttled him. The man had to be taken away for treatment. Buff was terribly upset about it afterwards."

As we have already seen, Frank and Marion Lindo were among the most vociferous of Drew's defenders, repeatedly and vehemently airing their absolute faith in his innocence. There is, however, a suggestion that, although they stood by him at the time of his ordeal, afterwards, when the limelight had faded, they treated him rather shabbily. I may say that, reading between the lines of Kitty Magnus' memoir, this does seem to come through. There is another and more sinister suggestion that the Lindos privately considered Drew guilty, and decided to sever their connection with him as soon as they decently could. Whatever the truth of the matter, they certainly do appear to have dropped him like a red-hot brick after December 1929. To be fair, though, the Lindos did suffer at Drew's hands.

Of course he meant them no harm, but lack of intent does not really compensate for damage done. They found him difficult, a severe trial because of his continual drinking, and I suspect that the time came when they had simply had enough and, probably under duress from their daughter, Olga's, powerful and not always pleasant personality, they agreed to have done with him.

Marion Louise Lindo spent her last years at 62 Sydney Street, Chelsea, and died aged seventy, on January 9th, 1947. Olga Lindo continued to live there until her death, aged sixty-nine, on May 7th, 1968. When I approached her she absolutely refused to discuss Drew and his relationship with her parents. The late Henry Oscar told me that it was generally believed in theatrical circles—and what notorious chatterboxes they are—that Drew and Marion Lindo were having an affair, and although others have said the same, I have my doubts about this. Even so, it seems possible that it was the recollection of this old gossip that put the bridle on Miss Lindo's tongue. A thing does not need to be true to be painful.

Apart from the Lindos, Drew's staunchest supporter in the hour of his trouble was the crime reporter of the *Empire News*, Bernard O'Donnell.

O'Donnell had in fact known Drew long before the Reading affair, and held him in high regard. He was completely certain that he had no hand in the killing of Alfred Oliver—an opinion not to be lightly dismissed, for O'Donnell was a very shrewd and widely experienced crime man. And long after the furore had died down, O'Donnell was still seeing Drew socially and doing anything that he could to put a little much-needed money in his way.

Bernard O'Donnell died, aged eighty-three, on February 7th, 1969, but in January 1968 I spent a long day as his guest at his home in Margate, going over the entire ground with him.

He was strong for Drew as ever.

"Philip was one of the most genial and likeable souls I ever met in the course of my journalistic career," he told me, "and it has always been a source of great satisfaction to me that I was able to produce that eleventh-hour witness, the butcher, Mr Wells, whose evidence helped to save him. Of course Buff didn't do it. He wouldn't have hurt a fly. But the police had it in for him, you know. I admit the evidence against him *seemed* strong, but it was all coincidence, miracles of coincidence which make truth stranger than fiction. He liked calves' liver. He sent his clothes to the cleaner's. Those were the two fundamental reasons for suspicion being directed against him. As a matter of fact I had known Drew for years. I first met him back in 1921 when he was starring as Young Buffalo in *The Savage and the Woman* at the Lyceum. I had written a story about him then, and met him on a number of occasions since that time. And, knowing him, it was inconceivable to me that this rugged, gentle actor, almost child-like in his simplicity, could possibly be guilty of such a wanton and vicious crime. Anyway, I went to see him. It was in August 1929, when he was appearing at St Albans. 'Well, you old scamp,' I greeted him, 'what do you mean by having your clothes cleaned?' His eyes crinkled into a grin. 'You know how it is, Bernard,' he drawled in that unmistakable cowboy accent of his. 'The grease-paint oozes from the pores of your skin and gets all round the collar of your jacket making it all mucky, and you just have to get it cleaned some time.' We talked things over. I was not the newspaperman then—just a friend. He told me all that had happened between him and the police, and how they had asked him if he was in the habit of buying calves' liver in the towns he visited. And he had told them that he was. Philip also told me that two people, Mr Loxton and Mrs James, had identified him as the man in Cross Street and as the man in Mr Oliver's doorway. Realizing the unhappy position he was in, I suggested that he ought to let me publish a story under his name in my paper, telling the public all that had taken place so far. He thought it was a good idea, and on September 8th, 1929, the *Empire News* carried it as an exclusive. It was the frank and detailed statement of a man with nothing to hide. I was with Philip all through the long ordeal of his trial by coroner. I stayed at the same hotel as he did, and every day accompanied him to and from the court through the cheering crowds. At the end of the first day, having seen the way the evidence was going, I said to him over dinner, 'I think you ought to be legally represented, old man.' He looked up, startled. 'What on earth for, Bernard? I haven't done anything,' he said. 'I know you haven't,' I replied, 'but the police think you have and they are going all out to prove it.' And so, on his behalf, I engaged a solicitor, Mr Ratcliffe, of Reading. A few weeks before I had watched a young barrister named Fearnley-Whittingstall cross-examining expert witnesses in the Sidney-Duff poisoning case at Croydon, and I had been greatly impressed by the way he had handled them. I asked Mr Ratcliffe to retain Mr

Fearnley-Whittingstall for Philip, and that is how he came into the case. My newspaper agreed to bear all the costs. Thank God, Philip was never sent for trial, for if there is one thing that I know, it is that that man was as innocent of the murder of poor Alfred Oliver as a new-born babe."

Another journalist, John C. Cannell, was equally convinced of Drew's innocence—"I hold strongly to the view that the murder was committed by some tramp who had come to the Reading district for Race Week".

Cannell stayed at the Great Western during the inquest and met Drew many times.

He wrote: "Philip Yale Drew is an excellent actor and a kindly man. In the dark phase through which he passed, I was in contact with him from day to day, smoked with him, talked with him, and almost shared his thoughts. When Drew described himself during the inquest as a strange man, he showed not only candour, but accurate self-judgment. He is strange because he is a whimsical man who loves primroses, the hardships of ranch life, the Psalms, very long cigars, church bells, horses that jump well, and old-fashioned songs. He's a dreamer, is Drew. You could have told that he was a dreamer if you had talked to him as I did for three hours in his bedroom during an adjournment in the inquest. There were just the two of us, and we talked of most things. Drew has the face of a poet, the body of a cowboy and the heart of a lad. There is a peculiar pale blueishness about his eyes, and as he walked to and fro in the tiny bedroom his eyes became bluer as the light from the window fell upon them. I shall always remember Drew by his eyes. He did not rest for a moment during our long talk. This man has a strangely impressive personality, I thought, as I sat on his bed and watched him with his square figure, fine head, and thick grey hair. Cigar-ends piled up on the ash tray as our talk went on. He is a good talker, and his mind moves swiftly, for he shot back answers to my questions like a man who is, mentally, extremely efficient. But his nerves were disordered. His hand shook as he held out a lighted match for my cigarette. He often smiled, but he never laughed. Mr Lindo had told me that he was sleeping badly. Like all good actors, he has touches of the theatrical in voice and gesture. A casual observer would think that Drew, in his private conversation, was acting a part. A closer observer would find out that Drew was indeed acting a part, but the part of Philip Yale Drew.

There is something definitely boyish about Drew at times. He revealed it more and more as our talk continued. I soon came to understand why he had aroused the mother instinct of Mrs Lindo. An expression of boyish helplessness came over his face at moments and then died away. He does not ask for pity; he arouses and attracts it. Drew wept a little as I was with him in that little room overlooking the railway station at Reading, where the crowds were ceaselessly going to and fro. No hard-bitten American this, but just a 'big baby', as he was called at the inquest, and, as I met him, as innocent. Then we parted, he to return to the ordeal of the witness-box and I to think about this sensitive, emotional man into whose life a dark shadow had floated. When I saw him again the verdict had come, and he was as excited and happy as a child on Christmas morning. He walked quickly about the hotel, stumbling over mats and colliding with people. A long cigar was in his mouth. As I wished him good-bye that far-away look came into his eyes again, and I asked, 'What are you thinking about now, Drew?' 'Oh,' he said, 'I am just thinking of the cloud that lifted.' He turned away quickly."

By sheer chance, I was fortunate enough to discover two people who remembered Drew during his Clapton Period—Mr Sidney Spring and Mrs Minnie Green.

Mr Spring is a dentist who rented one of the shops at 90 Upper Clapton Road from Mr Magnus as his surgery. He knew Philip and the Magnuses well, and recalled how they would sometimes go for a drink at the Crooked Billet in Upper Clapton Road. It was bombed in 1941, the same night as No. 90 was destroyed, and he remembered seeing Albert and Kitty crawling out of a grating from beneath the ruins of their home. "Drew was a picturesque figure", he told me. "Very pleasant to talk to, and I couldn't imagine his hurting anybody."

Mrs Minnie Green now lives in Limpsfield, in Surrey, but she used to work as a secretary at the Crooked Billet Garage in Upper Clapton Road, and remembers Drew's coming to live with the Magnuses. She told me: "In 1933 Kitty just announced, 'Philip Yale Drew is coming to live with us. He has nowhere to go.' I often wondered where he slept, because they only had a tiny place and there didn't seem to be room for him. Philip was always well-dressed and clean. Kitty told me she had had to fit him up with a whole set of new clothes. He was rather flamboyant and 'swagger'. He had a pleasant, cultured voice, and looked and sounded like a gentleman. He seemed happy with the Magnuses, and used to sit in their little kitchen-living-room with them chatting, but not bombastically, and he would always be wearing his jacket—you'd never see him in his shirt-sleeves. I think he used to go to the public library at Hackney, or the one in the post office at the corner of Northwold Road, and also to one in a little bookshop near-by. I had a big black and white collie called Michael. He was one of those dogs that lift their lip and 'smile' at people they like. He would always smile and wag his tail at Philip. He really loved him. Philip used to take him out for walks, and he would hold a conversation with Michael as they went along the road, pointing things out to him. Once, when Michael was very ill and I was worried, Philip said, 'Leave him with me, my dear'. I did, and he brought him back to me fit and well later the same day. I remember on one occasion hearing him ring up the Hackney Empire, trying, unsuccessfully, to get some complimentary tickets on the strength of old acquaintance with the players. 'This is Philip Yale Drew here . . .' he said. It was very pathetic. The last time I ever saw him was one day when I met him coming down Walsingham Road. He told me that he was on his way to see Kitty, and when I expressed surprise he said, 'Oh, I'm in Maury Road now.' I thought privately that there must have been some friction between the Magnuses over him. I'd always thought that Kitty was in love with him. It was Philip, Philip, Philip, all the time. But he was a charming man, and I often used to look at him and wonder if he did that murder. I don't think he did."

Mrs Green told me that after the Magnuses were bombed out they lived for four years at Stansted, in Essex, and then moved in with Kitty's widowed daughter, Mrs Rex Rivington, at 119 Whitstable Road, Canterbury. Kitty died there, aged seventy-three, on January 4th, 1946, of heart failure and cerebral haemorrhage. Albert died, aged eighty-six, three years later, on February 28th, 1949. He was then living at 81 The Greenway, Hendon, where he had spent his last years looked after by an old family friend, Mrs Fleming.

So far in my investigations I had not encountered a single person who had anything but good to say of Philip Yale Drew, nor anyone who thought him guilty of murder. Now, however, I needed to see the police, and here, perhaps understandably, I was to find the suspicion index considerably higher.

In 1969 I interviewed John Maurice Harris, that same Sergeant Harris who, with Jim Berrett, had toiled so long and fruitlessly on the case.

At eighty-one, ex-Divisional Detective Inspector Harris was still an immense, rumbling giant of a man, unbowed, clear of mind and eye. So far as Drew was concerned, his blunt and instant reaction was, "That's the beggar who did it". And he told me, "Berrett and Burrows were convinced that he did it, too".

Harris frankly did not like Drew. "He was a drunken sot, though I'll admit he had charm. I'd say he was a gentleman. He had a soft, pleasant speaking voice, not much of an American accent. He looked clean enough to me, but he was very untidy as to his clothing. He was a very highly strung sort of a man, and cried very easily. To me, his whole demeanour was that of a guilty man. He made a great show of willingness to help, but when you pinned him down on any point he wriggled and evaded it."

I asked Harris what it was that Dolores had wanted to tell him. "She said that Drew had admitted to her that he had done the murder. They had had a quarrel, and Drew, while drunk, tried to throttle her. He said to her, 'I've done one murder, and I'll do another', meaning that he would kill her. Then he flung himself out of the house and left her. Dolores was terrified. She was crying. Scared stiff. Asking for police protection. She said she was prepared to go into the witness-box and testify, but we decided that she wouldn't make a suitable or credible witness."

Harris also said that the foreman of the coroner's jury had told him that nine of the jury were in favour of committing Drew for trial, but two members stuck out. "They were scared by the mob demonstration. You see, for the last couple of days the inquest was transferred from the police court to the Town Hall, and the jury's retiring room there looked out on to the street where a milling crowd of several thousand were demonstrating for Drew. So the change of venue helped towards the verdict. The other nine jurors, fed up and wanting to get back to their jobs as soon as possible, gave in and agreed."

I put it to Mr Harris that there was no real motive for the murder so far as Drew was concerned, and he completely agreed. "If he did it—and I'm sure he did—he did it in a drunken frenzy," he said. "I think that Drew knew that he had done it, and was bitterly sorry, deeply distressed about it. In one sense, he wasn't a murderer, even though he did kill Oliver. I wouldn't have wanted him topped. I would regard it as more of a case of very, very bad manslaughter —if there had been such a thing. But he ought to have been put away."

In other words, guilty—but a suitable case for diminished responsibility.

I would comment on one point. I do not think that we should attach too much significance to Drew's alleged outburst to Dolores —"I've done one murder . . ." I suggest that in his drunken fury he was not making a statement of fact, but airing resentment at what he regarded as an unjust accusation. What he was conveying was irony, saying in effect, "They say I've done one murder. They believe, you all believe, I did it. All right, now I'll really do one." But, of course, he did not.

Ex-Detective Chief Superintendent Percy Richard Ellington— in 1929, Detective Sergeant—of the Nottingham Force, was equally emphatic regarding Drew's guilt.

When I met him in 1969, he told me: "I neither liked nor disliked Drew. I didn't know him socially. But he lived in a seedy sort of world—boarding-houses and kippers—in reality, and in a tough, violent, imaginary world on the stage. I reckon that when fuddled by drink, and in awkward circumstances, he translated that stage world into real life. I don't have the slightest doubt that he was guilty. I think that he clobbered the tobacconist because he caught him with his hand in the till. I think the crime was committed with a stone ginger-beer bottle, which he then put in his jacket pocket and afterwards threw over Caversham Bridge. Drew was pretty well an alcoholic, you know, and he always used to carry a bottle of ginger-beer in his pocket to the theatre, so that he could drink it before going on to the stage, and the gas in it would sober him up. I am certain that if the interrogation had been left to Superintendent Doubleday and me we would have got an admission out of him. We believed in the gentle approach, and Drew wasn't afraid of us. Berrett and Harris were big, intimidating men, with an aggressive technique. They applied psychological pressure and that rather frightened Drew. As a matter of fact, I felt that Drew was on the verge of confessing, when someone knocked on the door, and Drew, pulling himself together, said, 'Bloody well find out.' I was sure he was guilty at the time, and I haven't thought about it much since—but I am still sure that he was guilty all right."

Mr John Lancelot Martin was appointed Reading Coroner in 1912. When I saw him fifty-six years later, he was still Reading Borough Coroner. And, at eighty-nine, a most remarkable man, for he was able, off the cuff, to recall not only the names and details of witnesses, but even the dates upon which they appeared before him, at an inquest which had taken place all of forty years before. His attitude to Drew at that time was, as we have seen, scarcely sympathetic, so that it was particularly interesting to me to try to discover what, if any, changes his opinion might have undergone in the intervening years.

"Yale Drew was a very strange-looking man," he told me. "The sort of man once seen you would not forget, and I was impressed by Mrs James' and Mr Loxton's evidence as to identification. I was also influenced by the fact that on the night of the murder Drew was the last to leave the theatre, and that instead of going directly home to his lodgings he had gone in the direction of the tow-path of the Thames, perhaps to dispose of the murder weapon in the river."

Then he made a startling admission to me.

"The murderer did not have to be Yale Drew. There were a number of very queer characters who came into Reading during Ascot week, but the police thought Drew guilty, and they had no other suspect in view."

William Arthur Fearnley-Whittingstall died prematurely in 1959, but I was able to see his widow, Mrs Nancy Fearnley-Whittingstall, and, through her, learn what her husband's feelings had been in the matter.

"I never remember William Arthur getting himself so worked up over a case as he did over the Reading murder. He was far more anxious over it than he was over the Croydon poisoning case. Why? Because he was so sure that Drew was innocent and so anxious to see that he was not sent for trial. 'He's just a poor old drunk who's got himself tangled up in a web of coincidences and circumstantial evidence,' he told me, 'and the cards are stacked against him.' My husband never thought that the police had in any sense rigged the case against Drew, or been unfair to him. He said that they, and the coroner, genuinely thought that they had got the right man. But William Arthur was equally genuinely sure that they had not. I remember his coming home when it was all over and saying, 'I knew all along that he was innocent, but he was very lucky not to be committed'. But when a friend remarked to William Arthur that

Drew had been lucky, he got very angry. 'Lucky?' he snapped. 'What do you mean? He hadn't done anything.' And long afterwards he said to me, 'If he'd been a murderer he'd have done it again, especially when he was drinking and needing money. But he never did.' "

By a strange accident of timing it was on the precise anniversary of the day upon which, thirty-nine years before, she had found the mortally injured Mr Oliver, that I interviewed Mrs Nellie Taylor, proprietress of the Welcome Café.

This is what she had to tell me of Drew: "He first came into my café on the Wednesday (June 19th). That time he went into the back room. He came in again on the Saturday. This time he sat in the front room among all the barrow boys. He was drunk, waving his arms around and reciting Shakespeare. I went over and took his order myself. I remember it to this day, because it was the first time I'd ever been given an order like that. He asked for, 'Two rashers and three fried eggs, turned'. When he'd eaten his meal and I'd taken his money, he said, 'My dear, would you help me on with my coat?' I said, 'I most certainly won't. I'm far too busy. If I helped all my customers on with their coats I'd never get time to finish my work.' He didn't seem to mind. He just said, 'All right, my dear', and he put it on himself. He was very well spoken; a well-educated and gentlemanly sort of man. He had an air about him, you knew he was somebody out of the ordinary, you couldn't mistake him. I must say I find it hard to imagine his battering Mr Oliver like that, and I don't think he did. One thing I do think is that *if* Drew did it, he didn't do it for robbery. I think he might have gone to Mr Petty's, the newsagent's next-door, to collect that special stage paper he had ordered. Well, Petty's closed on Saturday afternoons, and Drew, drunk, may have been annoyed to find the shop closed and gone into Oliver's and started cursing and swearing about it. And if he did, Mr Oliver would have been quite likely to have got annoyed, too—he didn't like bad language—and to have ordered Drew out of his shop. There might have been an argument, and then blows. And I think that somebody might have come into the shop afterwards and taken the money. Of course there were all sorts of rumours in Reading. They said Oliver's shop was used as a betting shop. That was nonsense. I happen to know that Mr Oliver was strongly opposed to any form of gambling. They said that Nancy—that's what I always called Mrs Oliver—

was carrying on with someone else. But that was all rubbish. Absolute rubbish. Mrs Oliver died in May 1966. She was 89 then, and to the end she was never really sure in her own mind who killed her husband. At the time of the murder, Inspector Wally Walters, the head of the Reading C.I.D., was away on holiday. Later on he told me, 'If I'd been here I'd have caught the murderer.' And later still he said, 'One day I'll tell you the real truth about that murder. You'll be amazed.' But he died in 1941—and he never did tell me."

I saw, too, Mr Alfred John Wells, Bernard O'Donnell's eleventh-hour witness. Aged eighty-one, he was still working in a butcher's shop in Reading, and still convinced that Drew, whom he described as "a very nice sort of man", was innocent.

"Drew was not the only drunken man in Cross Street that day," he said. "And that other man, the man whom I had seen in the Welcome Café at half-past seven in the morning, was also hanging about there on and off all day—though he was perfectly sober. He was carrying a light-grey, washed-out-looking mac. Sometimes he had the mac on, sometimes off. Sometimes he had a hat on. Sometimes he had his hat off. He bore no resemblance to Drew whatsoever, and I am quite sure in my own mind that this man was the murderer."

Mr Wells was insistent that it was at about 6 P.M., and not 5.40 P.M. as stated in evidence, that he last saw the Welcome Stranger in Cross Street—"I remember I was late on my way back from tea to the shop. I'd been to have my tea at a house in The Forbury. I used to go to tea at half-past five, and was due back at the shop at six. Well, it would be a minute or two *after* six as I came round the corner from Friar Street into Cross Street, and I passed the stranger as I came round by the Gas House. He was hurrying, and he was on the same side as Oliver's shop, in the act of crossing the road diagonally in the direction of the station, so I only saw him from his right profile. But it was the Welcome Stranger all right."

In considering the events of June 22nd, 1929, one question which inevitably tantalizes is what are we to make of the curious conduct of the boy, Jefferies? It seems inconceivable that any lad of twenty-one could, on discovering a seriously injured and bleeding man, simply walk out of that shop and leave that helpless man there—for all he knew, to die. Why did he do it?

Forty years later, I was able to put that question to George Charles Jefferies himself. The boy was now a 61-year-old man.

"I was just an illiterate lad then," he told me. "I didn't know then what I know now. I didn't know what to do. I was frightened. I didn't want to be involved. And I don't want to be involved now. It's over. Dead and gone. I don't know why you want to rake these things up. I have forgotten all about it."

I put it to you that we have by now established a great many weak links in the chain of circumstantial evidence against Philip Yale Drew. I suggest that the sum of the various matters of conflict is equivalent to that reasonable doubt which I set out to establish.

You may think that although the jury were not perhaps entirely sure, not without certain misgivings, on the evidence put before them they could not bring in any verdict other than that which they did.

I may say that they were upheld in their action by two Directors of Public Prosecutions.

Sir Archibald Bodkin said, after perusing the depositions in the case—sent to him in November 1929 by Sir Trevor Bigham—that if Drew had been committed for trial, he would, in his opinion, have been acquitted.

And in April 1930, Bodkin's successor, Edward Hale Tindal Atkinson, confirmed his view.

But if it was not Drew, you may ask, then who?

Strictly, that is not a proper question. It is no part of our obligation to provide an alternative suspect. The defence of Drew does not involve the onus of counter-accusation.

I have heard it categorically stated in several quarters in Reading that Mr Oliver was killed by a man, another shopkeeper, with whom Mrs Oliver was conducting a secret liaison. That may, I think, be dismissed as the sort of irresponsible rumour that is so often, and so wrongly, noised abroad in cases of this kind. A canard, hardly pure but certainly simple.

Was the murderer a member of a race-gang? Some rough who sought to remedy his day's losses on the race-track by helping himself to Mr Oliver's day's takings in his shop? A distinct possibility. Bernard O'Donnell believed so—"That was my opinion then, and that is my opinion now", he told me. "What is more, it is the view that was held and worked upon by the police for five weeks—until Philip Yale Drew entered the picture. It has always seemed to me that the anonymous letter from Leeds received by Mrs Lindo confirmed my belief."

But was it, in fact, a murder of premeditation at all? Did Alfred Oliver perhaps catch someone with his hand in the till? And did that someone strike him down in sheer panic? If so, what weapon did he employ? Nothing that could have been used as a weapon was missing from the shop. That circumstance would seem to argue that whoever did the deed must have brought the weapon with him. And that, in turn, argues that there was premeditation, felonious intent. It need not, however, have been a racing man. It could have been any stray criminal, any wandering, chance-seeking predator.

Again, it may be that in correlating the murder with the robbery we are making a false assumption. It is possible that someone—Drew, the prosecution would suggest—had a heated disagreement with Mr Oliver. High words were exchanged. That someone, perhaps drunk, perhaps merely of violent character, attacked Oliver physically, struck him down, left him lying senseless and bleeding on the floor of his shop, and fled. And then some other person came into the shop and, taking advantage of the situation into which he had fortuitously stumbled, helped himself to the money. A neat enough hypothesis, but we are still left with the problem of the weapon.

The novelist J. D. Beresford, in that article of his which so delighted Drew, formulates the theory of 'The Very Queer Customer.' He writes: "Alfred Oliver was murdered by a criminal lunatic, a man of about forty years of age, wearing a dark suit, with brown shoes trodden over at the heels (Mr Wells' testimony), who was in the habit of mumbling to himself, and had an extraordinarily queer habit of stroking things, his face, his hair, the back of a motor, or even a lamp-post. Also, he had a marked north country accent. What happened in my opinion, was that the unfortunate Mr Oliver was knocked out by the first blow, and that the succeeding twelve blows would have been delivered only by a homicidal maniac. I would suggest further that the murderer had paid a previous visit to the shop some forty minutes or so before the crime was committed. In the confused statements made by Mr Oliver he says, 'There was a man came; I thought he was from the Gas office,' and afterwards that he last saw an attaché case on the table *before tea* when he 'got some change for a man. I think he was from the Gas office.' And how did this very queer customer of mine escape justice? Well, putting aside the fact that the police were on a false trail, I should say that he was precisely the sort of man who would get away.

He was probably unaware, for one thing, that he had anything to conceal. He had, in fact, the 'innocence' of the insane. What became of him afterwards we can only guess. He may have been knocked down and killed by a car, or have been sentenced for another crime—or he may have been the man that Arthur Rouse took for a ride.'

There is one more circumstance which, while considering the possibilities of alternative suspects, it is my duty to place on record.

On September 16th, 1932, a Mr Charles J. Maberly, of 7 The Granthams, Lambourn, Berkshire, wrote to Scotland Yard:

> The news of the tragedy was brought to Lambourn by a drayman in the Simonds brewery employ, some hours before the details were published in the papers, if I remember aright. I had halted just opposite him and the group of men with whom he was conversing. I did not nose in, but distinctly heard one of the group say, "Have they got the party who did it?" And the drayman replied, "I dunno about that, but I have no doubt it was — He's the biggest blackguard in the whole town, a rotten thief up to any mischief, and would do his grandmother in for a packet o' fags." In the face of that it seemed somewhat remarkable that — hardly figured in the case.

I know the identity of the person to whom Mr Maberly was referring, as indeed did Sergeant Harris and Inspector Berrett, but the matter was never officially pursued, and the law of libel prevents me from disclosing that person's name.

We come now to the crucial question of Drew's alcoholism and its bearing upon the possibility of his guilt.

If it was Drew's hand that struck down Alfred Oliver, then the genesis of that act of murder was surely to be found in drink. I am certain that the sober, right-minded Drew was not capable of murder. If Drew was the killer—and again I reiterate that I do not think that he was, although as he himself said, "Everything is possible"—then it was a drunken and diseased creature of grievously impaired responsibility who committed the guilty act.

We will make no bones about it, Drew was a drunkard. And to that extent he was undoubtedly a victim of his circumstances. That is not offered as a vindication or an excusal, but as a statement of fact. Taking a drink with the customers after the show was almost a contractual obligation, for, during the early years of the century, it was an understood thing in the world of the lesser theatres and music-halls that the performers should come down to the bar after curtain-fall, and there mingle with the audience, thus encouraging them to spend money in the theatre bar. Indeed, it was so that they could cope financially with this additional burden that actors and actresses were paid such relatively high salaries. The fulfilment of this unwritten law led many theatricals to drink far more than was good for them and, in a great many cases, was the cause of their early death. Charlie Chaplin's father, for instance, died of drink at the age of thirty-seven as a direct consequence of honouring this pernicious obligation, and hundreds of others endured the living death of chronic alcoholism.

Doubtless, this convention of the time played its part in giving —or at least confirming—that taste for drink which was to prove Drew's ultimate downfall.

It is customary when a man drinks to excess to seek to discover some reason, some psychiatric flaw, which will elucidate his self-destructive motivation. Is he unhappy, psychologically insecure, uncertain of himself, endeavouring to drown out some residually unpleasant memory? These are the sort of questions that the psychiatrist asks.

In Drew's case no easy answer presents itself. He was not the product of an unhappy childhood. He was not a failure—very much the reverse. He had not been unlucky in love. His addictive alcoholism is a puzzlement. Perhaps he was easily bored. Perhaps he was basically shy and needed the boost of alcoholic self-confidence, particularly in the recurrent challenge-situations presented by his mode of livelihood. Perhaps he just liked the sensation of being drunk. It may have been as simple as that. But whatever the trigger mechanism, the effect was the same. A progressive alcoholic erosion and deterioration of the personality, a loosening of the grip on reality, a lessening of efficiency, violent toxically induced mood-swings, phases of amnesia, periods of irresponsibility.

Alcohol is an irritant, and it made Drew irritable, even violent on occasion. We know that he attacked his dresser, and, if she is to be believed, Dolores, when drunk. He has been described as "arrogant and bullying" in drink, full of braggadocio, inflated and querulously intolerant. But never before, or after, the Reading affair was he known to carry violence, or threat of violence, to the horrendous extremity of murder. There is an enormous gulf between the hot-blooded flare-up of drunken pugnacity and the cold-blooded battering of an old man to savage death. Can one think that Drew once, and once only, crossed that gulf?

It is possible; everything is possible; but is it likely? In any event, it is a question that must be put, and how we decide to answer it must be taken into the reckoning.

The drunkard is continually exposed to the malice of the sober. He outrages them, arouses their contempt, their scorn, and this, through sheer repetition, eventually penetrates even the haze of his alcoholism. And when it does, it brews a pathological hatred, a corrosive resentment made all the more bitter because the alcoholic hates *himself*. The consequent baffled ambivalence of his reaction frequently expresses itself in violence. Frustrations boil up and boil over in a display of aggression that is directed, often through others, at himself. Did Drew, after years of slights accepted, insults swallowed, mockeries ignored, suddenly reach boiling-point that June evening in 1929, and vent all of his accumulated vengeance on the shattered head of Alfred Oliver? Did his unconscious thus ritually cleanse itself—and, the deed done, the Freudian censor of his id block the channel of remembrance? We are in strange territory when we essay the mapping of the vagaries of a poisoned mind, and remember, Philip Yale Drew had been slowly poisoning his body for nearly thirty years.

There are, too, certain purely physiological factors which must be considered in this context. They are concerned with the effect of blood-sugar level on the brain-waves and behaviour.

Dr William Sargant has shown that although a man may have completely normal brain-waves while well fed, when fasting, and with a consequent low blood-sugar content, he may exhibit abnormal brain-waves, possibly indicating a state of mental irresponsibility over which he would have no control, and which could express itself in a release of impulsive violence.

Beer contains sugar, and a significant intake will therefore significantly raise the blood-sugar level. But three or four hours later this will sink to a very low level. In this condition of hypoglycaemia, brain-waves—and conduct—may become grossly abnormal.

Since we know that Drew ate a substantial meal in the Welcome Café between 4.15 P.M. and 4.57 P.M.—that is, approximately one hour before the attack on Mr Oliver— it does not appear likely that his blood-sugar level would be reduced.

However, in 1967, Drs N. H. Moynihan and J. G. Benjafield published the results of an investigation which they had carried out into the blood-sugars of alcoholics, and they postulated the existence in some individuals of a constitutional aberration in carbohydrate metabolism, with susceptibility to hypoglycaemia. This, they thought, might be an underlying cause of the excessive alcohol intake of certain alcoholics. "More recent work has demonstrated," they add, "the existence of hypothalamic centres sensitive to changes in the blood sugar. It is possible that hypoglycaemia of alcoholic origin is linked up with an action of these cells."

Vincent Marks and V. E. Medd, in the *British Journal of Psychiatry* (1964), point out that for hypoglycaemia to appear clinically a combination of factors is necessary, and that these may include prolonged under-nutrition, hypovitaminosis, and possibly magnesium deficiency.

Drew, we know, ate irregularly and "did not bother" much about food. Over a sustained period, this could amount to technical chronic malnutrition.

Moynihan and Benjafield conclude that there is ample evidence that alcohol *lowers* the blood-sugar in certain alcoholics, either through the hypothalamic centre or by an interference in some other way, as yet undefined, with carbohydrate metabolism.

It is possible that Drew was of this constitutionally idiosyncratic category of alcoholic, in whom both cause and effect of alcoholism is physiological.

Last, I call Philip Yale Drew himself.

Long after the trial by coroner was over, Andrew Melville's Aunt Minnie—Mrs Minnie Pigeon, his father's sister, an actress who used the stage-name of Minnie Waller—who had always been an especially close friend of Philip's, and who was a forthright and blunt-spoken old lady, asked him point-blank, "Tell me, Buff, *did* you do it?"

Easy, the ordeal behind him, the dismissal made, to answer, "Of course not".

But what does he say?

He says something that surely expresses the puzzled anguish of a drink-fuddled, the self-torturing honesty of an innocent, man.

He says, "I wish to God I knew."

That, then, is my case.

I put the likelihood of Drew's innocence no higher than probability, but I put that probability very high.

But you are the jury. I have placed all the evidence before you. It is for you now to consider that evidence and reach your verdict.

Curtain-Fall

EXEUNT OMNES

PLOT F. 13. Grave No. C/R. 36528. Chingford Mount Cemetery. Three coffins down lies Philip Yale Drew.

The weeds are kind: they hide an old tragedy. The man whose green pall they weave has come a long way to this last resting-place far beyond the footlights.

Three thousand miles away, ninety years ago, he first saw the light of day, opened blue infant eyes to the rolling seaboard hills of Marshfield, Massachusetts. He rode the sage and brushwood range, and trod the boards of a hundred lost and vanished stages in two hemispheres. He knew Hollywood at the high-noon of its days of silent promise. He stood firmly top-of-the-bill at Irving's old Lyceum.

But now the Stetson and spurs are finally hung up; the boots and saddle empty. Young Buffalo would surely have rested better at Boot Hill or Arizona than in this petrified white forest of suburban monumental masonry. Not a bucking bronco in sight ... only the endless stream of 'horseless carriages' heading for the London bonanza.

Alfred Oliver had died in a swift and bloody moment on a June evening eleven years before. That was his tragedy—sudden death.

Philip Yale Drew had been eleven years in the dying. That was his tragedy—a drawn-out death in life.

In a sense, Oliver had had the better part of the bargain.

If Drew *was* his murderer, his punishment had been full and terrible. If he was *not*, then fate had dealt him as cruel and unjust a blow as any innocent man has ever been called upon to endure. And there is no third verdict possible. Either he was a murderer— or a martyr.

It is an old, old story now. Oliver and Drew are both "beyond the need of weeping, beyond the reach of hands". They lie, forty miles apart, beneath the same wide arc of sky. Perhaps somewhere, in another narrow earthen bed, there lies another man. A man who destroyed them both.

I rather think so.

" LIQUOR UP OLD BOY,

NOTE

No adequate work of research can be successfully concluded without the aid of those most admirable institutions, the public libraries. I should like to pay sincere tribute to the following librarians and their staffs, who so willingly tackled, and sorted out for me, the various problems with which I burdened them: Mr G. I. John, A.L.A., A.R.P.S., Librarian, Aberdare; Mr W. E. Critchley, F.L.A., City Librarian, Aberdeen; Mr Alun R. Edwards, M.A., F.L.A., County Librarian, Aberystwyth; Mr W. E. French, F.L.A., Borough Librarian, Aldershot; Mr S. J. Butcher, F.L.A., Borough Librarian, Barnet; Mr W. W. Yeates, F.L.A., Director, Public Library, Museum and Art Gallery, Blackburn; Mr P. Dunderdale, F.L.A., Chief Librarian, Blackpool; Mr J. S. Reeves, Reference Librarian, Bognor Regis; Mr Thomas Ashworth, F.L.A., Chief Librarian, Bolton; Mr H. E. Radford, F.L.A., Borough Librarian, Bournemouth; Mr H. Bilton, F.L.A., City Librarian, Bradford; Mr G. Llewellyn, F.L.A., County Librarian, Brecon; Mr Angus Dunn, F.L.A., L.G.S.M., Borough Librarian, Bridgwater; Mr John N. Allen, B.A., F.L.A., Chief Librarian, Brighton; Mr Richard Caul, M.C., F.L.A., Borough Librarian, Burnley; Mr William R. Maidment, F.L.A., Borough Librarian, Camden; Mr F. Higenbottam, B.A., F.L.A., City Librarian, Canterbury; Mr J. E. Thomas, F.L.A., City Librarian, Cardiff; Mr Kenneth Smith, F.L.A., City Librarian, Carlisle; Mr H. Turner Evans, F.L.A., County Librarian, Carmarthen; Mr C. Edwards, F.L.A., Librarian for Chelsea; Mrs Y. M. Fennell, B.Sc. (Econ.), A.L.A., Reference Librarian, Chester; Mr H. K. Gordon Bearman, F.L.A., County Librarian, Chichester; Mr Alexander Wilson, F.L.A., Director, Coventry Library; Mr A. O. Meakin, F.L.A., Chief Librarian, Croydon; The Librarian, Douglas, Isle of Man; Mr John Hoyle, F.L.A., Director, Dudley Library; Mr D. M. Torbet, F.L.A., City Librarian, Dundee; Mr J. K. Sharp, F.L.A., Librarian, Dunfermline; The Durham City Divisional Librarian; Mr C. S. Minto, City Librarian and Curator, Edinburgh; Mr T. S. Cardy, F.L.A., Borough Librarian, Gateshead; Mr E. H. Trevitt, J.P., F.L.A., Borough Librarian, Grimsby; Mr C. J. Long, F.L.A., Borough Librarian, Hackney; Mr L. F. Hasker, F.L.A., Borough Librarian, Hammersmith; Mr G. A. Dickman, A.L.A., County Librarian, Haverfordwest, Pembroke; Mr D. J. Bryant, F.L.A., Chief Librarian, Hull; Mr C. A. Elliott, F.L.A., Chief Librarian, Islington; The Librarian, London Borough of Lambeth Reference Library; Mr A. B. Craven, City Librarian, Leeds; Mr Roy D. Rates, F.L.A., Borough Librarian, Lewisham; Mr Alfred Joyce, F.L.A., Borough Librarian, Maidstone; Mr N. H. Parker, F.L.A., Librarian, Malvern; Miss Elizabeth Leach, Librarian, Arts Library, Manchester; Mr T. R. Whitney, Chief Librarian, Merthyr Tydfil; Mr L. Edwards, A.L.A., Librarian, Neath; Mr Richard Blundell, F.L.A., Borough Librarian, North Shields; The

Chief Librarian, Nottingham; Mr J. W. Carter, F.L.A., Director, Central Public Library, Oldham; Mr Ralph Malbon, F.L.A., City Librarian, Portsmouth; Miss Jane A. Dowton, M.A., F.L.A., Borough Librarian, Preston; Mr Jon Elliott, A.L.A., Borough Librarian, Rawtenstall; Mr Stanley H. Horrocks, F.L.A., Borough Librarian, Reading; Mr G. E. Thornber, A.L.A., Director, Public Libraries and Arts Services, Rochdale; Miss Muriel Wilson, F.L.A., City Librarian, St Albans; Mr H. C. Caistor, F.L.A., Chief Librarian, St Helens, Lancashire; Mr Mervyn Edwards, M.A., F.L.A., Director, Scarborough Library; Mr John Bebbington, F.L.A., City Librarian, Sheffield; Mr K. D. Miller, D.P.A., F.L.A., City Librarian, Stoke-on-Trent; Miss Valerie A. G. Allen, Branch Librarian, Tenby; Mr John R. Pike, F.L.A., Borough Librarian, Torquay; Mr A. W. Ball, B.A., F.L.A., Borough Librarian, Watford; Mr Richard B. Ludgate, A.L.A., Borough Librarian, West Bromwich; Mr K. C. Harrison, M.B.E., F.L.A., City Librarian, Westminster; Mr N. E. Willis, F.L.A., Director of Libraries and Arts, Wigan; Miss E. A. Humphreys, Reference Department, Wolverhampton Library.

If libraries are essential, then newspapers and magazines are vital. They play a supremely important role in furnishing the raw and contemporary material for the historical documentary, such as this sets out to be. May I, therefore, gratefully acknowledge my profound indebtedness to the proprietors, editors, and ground force of journalists of the following publications: The *Daily Chronicle*, the *Daily Express*, the *Daily Herald*, the *Daily Mail*, the *Daily News*, the *Daily Sketch*, the *Daily Telegraph*, *The Times*, the *Evening News*, the *Evening Standard*, the *Star*, the *Empire News*, *Reynolds News*, the *Sunday Graphic*, the *Sunday Post*, the *Berkshire Chronicle*, the *Hackney Gazette*, the *Kent Messenger*, the *Kentish Observer & Canterbury Times*, the *Liverpool Echo*, the *Nottingham Evening Post*, the *Nottingham Journal*, the *Oldham Standard*, the *Pittsburg Leader*, the *Reading Evening Post*, the *Reading Mercury*, the *Stratford Express*, the *West Wales Weekly Observer*, the *Whitstable Times*, *John Bull*, *Pearson's Weekly*, the *Era*, *Pick-Me-Up*, the *Stage*, the *British Journal of Psychiatry*, and the *Law Journal*.

RICHARD WHITTINGTON-EGAN

Index

FOR THE BEST IN PAPERBACKS, LOOK FOR THE 🐧

In every corner of the world, on every subject under the sun, Penguin represents quality and variety – the very best in publishing today.

For complete information about books available from Penguin – including Pelicans, Puffins, Peregrines and Penguin Classics – and how to order them, write to us at the appropriate address below. Please note that for copyright reasons the selection of books varies from country to country.

In the United Kingdom: Please write to *Dept E.P., Penguin Books Ltd, Harmondsworth, Middlesex, UB7 0DA*

If you have any difficulty in obtaining a title, please send your order with the correct money, plus ten per cent for postage and packaging, to *PO Box No 11, West Drayton, Middlesex*

In the United States: Please write to *Dept BA, Penguin, 299 Murray Hill Parkway, East Rutherford, New Jersey 07073*

In Canada: Please write to *Penguin Books Canada Ltd, 2801 John Street, Markham, Ontario L3R 1B4*

In Australia: Please write to the *Marketing Department, Penguin Books Australia Ltd, P.O. Box 257, Ringwood, Victoria 3134*

In New Zealand: Please write to the *Marketing Department, Penguin Books (NZ) Ltd, Private Bag, Takapuna, Auckland 9*

In India: Please write to *Penguin Overseas Ltd, 706 Eros Apartments, 56 Nehru Place, New Delhi, 110019*

In Holland: Please write to *Penguin Books Nederland B.V., Postbus 195, NL–1380AD Weesp, Netherlands*

In Germany: Please write to *Penguin Books Ltd, Friedrichstrasse 10–12, D–6000 Frankfurt Main 1, Federal Republic of Germany*

In Spain: Please write to *Longman Penguin España, Calle San Nicolas 15, E–28013 Madrid, Spain*

In France: Please write to *Penguin Books Ltd, 39 Rue de Montmorency, F-75003, Paris, France*

In Japan: Please write to *Longman Penguin Japan Co Ltd, Yamaguchi Building, 2–12–9 Kanda Jimbocho, Chiyoda-Ku, Tokyo 101, Japan*

FOR THE BEST IN PAPERBACKS, LOOK FOR THE 🄟

PENGUIN BESTSELLERS

Is That It?   Bob Geldof with Paul Vallely

The autobiography of one of today's most controversial figures. 'He has become a folk hero whom politicians cannot afford to ignore. And he has shown that simple moral outrage can be a force for good' – *Daily Telegraph*. 'It's terrific . . . everyone over thirteen should read it' – *Standard*

Niccolò Rising   Dorothy Dunnett

The first of a new series of historical novels by the author of the world-famous *Lymond* series. Adventure, high romance and the dangerous glitter of fifteenth-century Europe abound in this magnificent story of the House of Charetty and the disarming, mysterious genius who exploits all its members.

The World, the Flesh and the Devil   Reay Tannahill

'A bewitching blend of history and passion. A MUST' – *Daily Mail*. A superb novel in a great tradition. 'Excellent' – *The Times*

Perfume: The Story of a Murderer   Patrick Süskind

It was after his first murder that Grenouille knew he was a genius. He was to become the greatest perfumer of all time, for he possessed the power to distil the very essence of love itself. 'Witty, stylish and ferociously absorbing . . . menace conveyed with all the power of the writer's elegant unease' – *Observer*

The Old Devils   Kingsley Amis

Winner of the 1986 Booker Prize
'Vintage Kingsley Amis, 50 per cent pure alcohol with splashes of sad savagery' – *The Times*. The highly comic novel about Alun Weaver and his wife's return to their Celtic roots. 'Crackling with marvellous Taff comedy . . . . this is probably Mr Amis's best book since *Lucky Jim*' – *Guardian*

Cat Chaser   Elmore Leonard

'*Cat Chaser* really moves' – *The New York Times Book Review* 'Elmore Leonard gets so much mileage out of his plot that just when you think one is cruising to a stop, it picks up speed for a few more twists and turns' – *Washington Post*

The Mosquito Coast   Paul Theroux

Detesting twentieth century America, Allie Fox takes his family to live in the Honduran jungle. 'Imagine the Swiss Family Robinson gone mad, and you will have some idea of what is in store . . . Theroux's best novel yet' – *Sunday Times*

Skallagrigg   William Horwood

This new book from the author of *Duncton Wood* unites Arthur, a little boy abandoned many years ago in a grim hospital in northern England, with Esther, a radiantly intelligent young girl who is suffering from cerebral palsy, and with Daniel, an American computer-games genius. 'Some of the passages would wring tears of recognition, not pity' – Yvonne Nolan in the *Observer*

The Second Rumpole Omnibus   John Mortimer

'Rumpole is worthy to join the great gallery of English oddballs ranging from Pickwick to Sherlock Holmes, Jeeves and Bertie Wooster' – *Sunday Times* 'Rumpole has been an inspired stroke of good fortune for us all' – Lynda Lee-Potter in the *Daily Mail*

The Lion's Cage   John Clive

As the Allies advance across Europe, the likes of Joe Porter are making a killing of another kind. His destiny becomes woven with that of Lissette, whose passionate love for a German officer spells peril for Porter and herself – and the battle for survival begins.

Deep Water   Patricia Highsmith

Her chilling portrait of a psychopath, from the first faint outline to the full horrors of schizophrenia. 'If you read crime stories at all, or perhaps especially if you don't, you should read *Deep Water*' – Julian Symons in the *Sunday Times*

Farewell, My Lovely   Raymond Chandler

Moose Malloy was a big man but not more than six feet five inches tall and not wider than a beer truck. He looked about as inconspicuous as a tarantula on a slice of angel food. Marlowe's greatest case. Chandler's greatest book.

God Save the Child   Robert B. Parker

When young Kevin Bartlett disappears, everyone assumes he's run away . . . until the comic strip ransom note arrives . . . 'In classic wisecracking and handfighting tradition, Spenser sorts out the case and wins the love of a fine-boned Jewish Lady . . . who even shares his taste for iced red wine' – Francis Goff in the *Sunday Telegraph*

The Daughter of Time   Josephine Tey

Josephine Tey again delves into history to reconstruct a crime. This time it is a crime committed in the tumultuous fifteenth century. 'Most people will find *The Daughter of Time* as interesting and enjoyable a book as they will meet in a month of Sundays' – Marghanita Laski in the *Observer*

The Michael Innes Omnibus

Three tensely exhilarating novels. 'A master – he constructs a plot that twists and turns like an electric eel: it gives you shock upon shock and you cannot let go' – *The Times Literary Supplement*

Killer's Choice   Ed McBain

Who killed Annie Boone? Employer, lover, ex-husband, girlfriend? This is a tense, terrifying and tautly written novel from the author of *The Mugger*, *The Pusher*, *Lady Killer* and a dozen other first class thrillers.

FOR THE BEST IN PAPERBACKS, LOOK FOR THE 🐧

PENGUIN CLASSIC CRIME

The Big Knockover and Other Stories Dashiell Hammett

With these sharp, spare, laconic stories, Hammett invented a new folk hero – the private eye. 'Dashiell Hammett gave murder back to the kind of people that commit it for reasons, not just to provide a corpse; and with the means at hand, not with handwrought duelling pistols, curare, and tropical fish' – Raymond Chandler

Death of a Ghost Margery Allingham

A picture painted by a dead artist leads to murder . . . and Albert Campion has to face his dearest enemy. With the skill we have come to expect from one of the great crime writers of all time, Margery Allingham weaves an enthralling web of murder, intrigue and suspense.

Fen Country Edmund Crispin

Dandelions and hearing aids, a bloodstained cat, a Leonardo drawing, a corpse with an alibi, a truly poisonous letter . . . these are just some of the unusual clues that Oxford don/detective Gervase Fen is confronted with in this sparkling collection of short mystery stories by one of the great masters of detective fiction. 'The mystery fan's ideal bedside book' – *Kirkus Reviews*

The Wisdom of Father Brown G. K. Chesterton

Twelve delightful stories featuring the world's most beloved amateur sleuth. Here Father Brown's adventures take him from London to Cornwall, from Italy to France. He becomes involved with bandits, treason, murder, curses, and an American crime-detection machine.

Five Roundabouts to Heaven John Bingham

At the heart of this novel is a conflict of human relationships ending in death. Centred around crime, the book is remarkable for its humanity, irony and insight into the motives and weaknesses of men and women, as well as for a tensely exciting plot with a surprise ending. One of the characters, considering reasons for killing, wonders whether the steps of his argument are *Five Roundabouts to Heaven*. Or do they lead to Hell? . . .'

PENGUIN TRUE CRIME

Titles published and forthcoming:

Who Killed Hanratty? Paul Foot

An investigation into the notorious A6 murder.

Norman Birkett H. Montgomery Hyde

The biography of one of Britain's most humane and respected judges.

The Complete Jack the Ripper Donald Rumbelow

An investigation into the identity of the most elusive murderer of all time

The Riddle of Birdhurst Rise R. Whittington-Egan

The Croydon Poisoning Mystery of 1928–9.

Suddenly at the Priory John Williams

Who poisoned the Victorian barrister Charles Bravo?

Stinie: Murder on the Common Andrew Rose

The truth behind the Clapham Common murder.

The Poisoned Life of Mrs Maybrick Bernard Ryan

Mr Maybrick died of arsenic poisoning – how?

The Gatton Mystery J. and D. Gibney

The great unsolved Australian triple murder.

Earth to Earth John Cornwell

Who killed the Luxtons in their remote mid-Devon farmhouse?

The Ordeal of Philip Yale Drew R. Whittington-Egan

A real life murder melodrama in three acts.